CORVAIR OWNERS HANDBOOK of Maintenance & Repair

Includes
Turbocharged Spyder and 4 X 1 Engines
Covers All Models

Originally published by:
FLOYD CLYMER PUBLICATIONS
This 2016 edition published by:
www.VelocePress.com

ANNOUNCEMENT

The Chevrolet Corvair has attained a unique position in the American automobile market. It was introduced as a compact family sedan but was quickly seized upon by knowledgable drivers who appreciated its sporting character and, at this point, it is being sold as a sort of genteel sports car. Regardless of the use or the attitude of the buyer, the Corvair has a great amount of personality and is certainly one of the most enjoyable cars in the world to drive. I have owned several Corvairs and have driven them many thousands of miles cross-country and around town with complete satisfaction.

Like any piece of machinery, they require maintenance, and correct maintenance is the key to their long life and excellent performance. For this reason we have been especially happy with the CORVAIR OWNERS HANDBOOK which is now in its second edition. The reader will find that it is quite complete in those areas where he may want to maintain or repair. Certain portions, such as the Powerglide are best left to the Chevrolet trained mechanic and we advise that the owner seek out his friendly dealer for service on such components.

In this edition, the basic car, as introduced in 1960, is covered in the first section of the book. Inasmuch as many parts have been unchanged and service procedures remain the same, this portion can be used as a guide to all models. The 164 cubic engine, introduced in 1964, and altered suspension of the 1965 models, plus any other 1965 differences are covered in the section beginning on page 269.

We hope that this handbook will enable you to have more pleasure from your Corvair, to operate it more economically and realize a greater return at trade-in time.

Floyd Clymer

CONTENTS

Subject	Page
Identification	4
General Information	5
Lubrication	8
Suspension	30
Wheels & Tires	33
Brakes	40
Engine	59
Power Train	72
Service Operations	83
Engine Disassembly	106
Engine Component Repairs	119
Engine Assembly	138
Clutch	160
Rear Axle	166
Manual Transmissions	170
Automatic Transmission	181
Engine Tune Up	185
Electrical System	218
Windshield Wiper	227
Wiring Diagrams	228
Fuel System	241
Exhaust System	259
1962-1963 Monza Spyder	261
1965 SECTION	**269**
Special Tools	351
Wiring Diagrams	355
Specifications	365

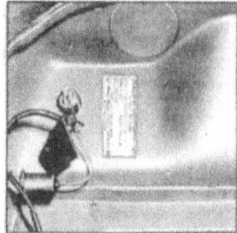 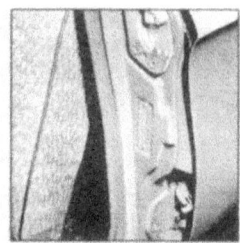 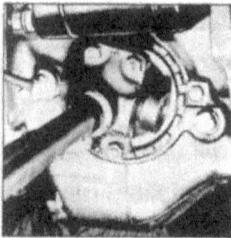

Fig. 1-2—Body identification tag located on left rear wheel house inner panel, inside engine compartment.

Fig. 1-3—Serial number tag located on left front lock pillar.

Fig. 1-4—Differential number stamped lower left side of casting.

Fig. 1-5—Engine number stamped on top of engine block, immediately forward of generator-oil filter adapter.

Fig. 1-6—Generator information on tag affixed to generator outer case.

Fig. 1-7—Starter serial number and production date stamped into outer case, toward rear.

Fig. 1-11—Serial number tag.

Model Year [1]	Body Style [2]	Assembly Plant [3]	Unit Number
0	0569	W	100025

[1] Last number of model year (1960).
[2] See Model Identification in this section.
[3] K—Kansas City, O—Oakland, W—Willow Run.
[4] Unit numbering will start at 100,001 at all plants. Fig. 1-11 shows tag for twenty-fifth car built at Willow Run.

4

GENERAL INFORMATION

ENGINE NUMBER

The engine number (location shown, fig. 5) contains manufacturing plant, month and day of manufacture, and transmission type. A typical engine number, and transmission type. A typical engine number would be T0430-Z, which would breakdown thus:

    T—Manufacturing Plant (Tonawanda)
    04—Month of Manufacture (April)
    30—Day of Manufacture (Thirtieth)
    Z—Transmission Type (Z—Powerglide, Y—Manual)

Vehicle Serial Number

A typical vehicle serial number tag (fig. 1-11) yields vehicle type, model year, assembly plant and production unit number when broken down as shown in the following chart. See figure 1-3 for tag location on vehicle.

SELECTION OF GASOLINE AND ENGINE OIL

Gasoline

The Corvair is designed to deliver peak performance on what is designated as Regular Fuel in the continental U. S. and Canada. It must be noted, however, that regular gasoline may vary in octane between manufacturers, or from one section of the country to another for the same manufacturer. If unfavorable performance is encountered because of either or both of these factors, dealer adjustment of ignition timing will restore the vehicle to normal operation.

The Monza model with Powerglide and all Corvairs equipped with the Super Turbo-Air engine are designed to operate most efficiently on Premium gasoline.

For operation of vehicle in foreign countries where only fuels of octane ratings lower than U. S. standards are usually available, the customer should be referred to:

    Chevrolet Motor Division
    General Motors Corporation
    Technical Service Department
    Detroit 2, Michigan

This department will give detailed information as to the availability of fuels in a given area and any service or adjustment which may be necessary to adapt the vehicle to the fuels available.

Engine Oil

American Petroleum Institute designations MS or DG. These letters refer to service application and DO NOT indicate viscosity.

Oil Viscosity

Oil viscosity is designated by the Society of Automotive Engineers and is indicated by number (i.e., SAE 10 W, SAE 20W, SAE 30). The higher the number the heavier bodied and slower flowing the oil.

For winted operation, the lighter bodied oils are used to ease starting and to offset the affect of cold weather on oil circulation, while the higher operating temperatures of summer require the use of heavier oils.

The following table will assist in the selection of the proper viscosity oil at various seasons of the year.

Lowest Anticipated Temperature	Recommended SAE Viscosity Oils
32° F	SAE 30
—10° F	SAE 10W
Below —10° F	SAE 5W-20

After the first 1,000 miles of driving, if average daytime temperature is below 60° during the break-in period, the original heavy duty break-in oil should be drained from the engine and the crankcase refilled with oil as shown in the accompanying table.

If average daytime temperature is above 60°F. during the break-in period, change initial break-in oil to SAE 30 oil after the first 500 miles of operation.

Every 4000 miles thereafter, under normal operating conditions, drain and refill the crankcase in the same manner. Adverse driving conditions; such as extreme dust conditions or short trip winter driving (less than 1,000 miles per month) makes it advisable to change oil every month. Similar dusty or short trips in the summer make it advisable to change oil every two months.

Check the oil level on the dipstick frequently. The level should be somewhere between the "add oil" and "full" marks on the dipstick. Do not overfill. The oil filter element should be changed after the first 5000 miles of driving and every 4000 miles thereafter, more often under adverse driving conditions.

PUSHING CAR TO START

NOTE: Towing car to start is not recommended due to the possibility of the disabled car accelerating into tow car.

AUTOMATIC TRANSMISSION — Turn ignition to "ON" pull choke knob ⅓ of the way out, and place transimission selector lever in Neutral ("N" on indicator) until car reaches 25 mph; then move selector to low ("L" on indicator).

When engine starts, move selector to drive ("D" on indicator). MANUAL TRANSMISSION — With gear shift lever in third, pull choke knob ⅓ of the way out, depress clutch pedal and turn ignition to "ON." When car speed reaches 15 mph, slowly release clutch pedal.

EMERGENCY TOWING

If a vehicle equipped with Powerglide becomes disabled and

requires towing or pushing, speed must not exceed 30 mph.

Both manual and Powerglide transmissions should be towed in Neutral only, with parking brakes fully released.

When towing a vehicle on its front wheels, the steering wheel should be secured to maintain a straight forward position.

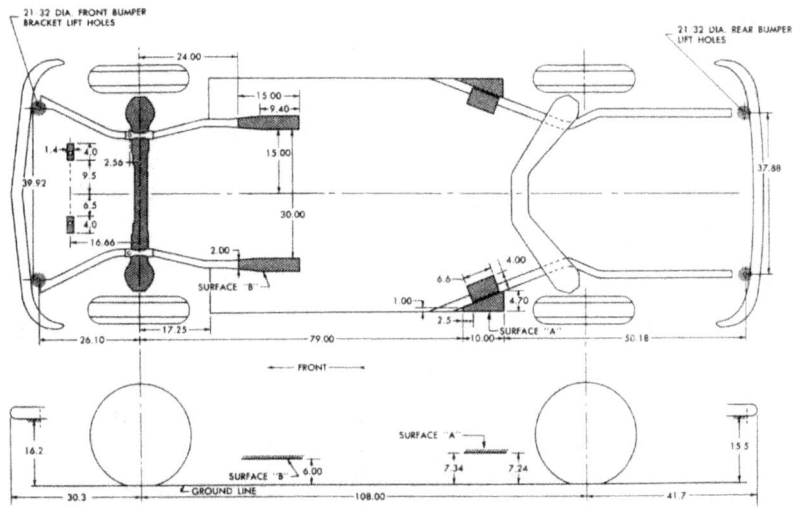

Fig. 1-18—Corvair lifting point diagram.

STANDARD TORQUE TABLE

(Steel Bolts)

The following table lists bolt torque specifications for applications involving steel bolts and parts only. **DO NOT** use this table when torquing aluminum bolts or when torquing steel bolts which are threaded into, or bearing on, aluminum parts.

The specifications in this chart are provided for use in cases where specific torque specifications are not given.

Bolt Grade*	Comm. Low-Carb.	GM-280 SAE-5	GM-290 SAE-7	GM-300 SAE-8
Head Marking	None	⬡	⬡	⬡
Bolt Size	**In.-Lbs.**			
#4-40	8			
#6-32	12			
#8-32	20			
#10-24	25			
#10-33	30			
#12-24	35			
	Ft.-Lbs.	**Ft.-Lbs.**	**Ft.-Lbs.**	**Ft.-Lbs.**
¼-20	4	7	9	11
¼-28	5	9	11	13
5⁄16-18	9	15	19	23
5⁄16-24	10	17	21	26
3⁄8-16	15	27	35	42
3⁄8-24	18	33	42	50
7⁄16-14	25	45	60	70
7⁄16-20	30	55	70	80
½-13	40	75	90	105
½-20	45	85	105	120
9⁄16-12	60	110	135	150
9⁄16-18	65	120	150	165
5⁄8-11	80	140	170	200
5⁄8-18	90	155	200	230
¾-10	125	240	300	350
¾-16	140	275	350	400
7⁄8-9	175	375	500	575
7⁄8-14	200	400	550	625
1-8	250	575	750	850
1-12	275	630	825	950

*The physical properties of a bolt primarily determine its assignment to a Bolt Grade, thus explaining the considerable difference in recommended installation torques for bolts of the same size, but of different grade. Bolts of lower grade than those used as original equipment, should therefore, never be used as replacement.

GENERAL LUBRICATION

The selection of the proper lubricant and its correct application at regular intervals does much to increase the life and operation of all moving parts of the vehicle.

Lubricants and lubrication requirements are outlined in the following paragraphs and the points of lubrication are indicated on the lubrication diagram. The diagram is coded to show recommended lubricant and mileage intervals.

ENGINE

CRANKCASE OIL

When checking or adding oil in crankcase, be careful to avoid dripping or spilling oil onto engine shrouding. This may result in objectionable fumes entering the passenger compartment.

Crankcase Capacity

Refill	4 qt.
Dry	5½ qt.
For Oil Filter add	½ qt.

Lubrication — First 500 to 100 Miles

The engine crankcase of all new vehicles is filled with a special, heavy duty oil. This oil will assure the proper "break-in" of the engine components. Use this oil only during the first 1000 miles if temperatures are below 60°F, or 500 miles if temperatures are above 60°F. Check frequently and maintain the proper level. If it is necessary to add oil, use one of the oils described under "SAE Viscosity Oils." At the end of the first 500 to 1000 miles, drain the original oil when hot and refill with an oil of the Viscosity Number and Type indicated below.

Lubrication — After 500 to 1000 Miles

After the first 500 to 1000 miles the crankcase oil should be selected to give the best performance under the climatic and driving conditions in the territory in which the vehicle is driven.

During warm or hot weather, an oil which will provide adequate lubrication under high operating temperatures is required.

During the colder months of the year, an oil which will permit easy starting at the lowest atmospheric temperature likely to be encountered, should be used.

Unless the crankcase oil is selected on the basis of viscosity or fluidity at the anticipated temperature, difficulty in starting will be experienced at each sudden drop in temperature.

SAE Viscosity Oils

SAE Viscosity Numbers indicate only the viscosity or body of the oil, that, whether an oil is a light or a heavy body oil, and do not consider or include other properties or quality factors.

The lower SAE Viscosity Numbers, such as SAE 5W and SAE

10W which represents the light body oils, are recommended for use during cold weather to provide easy starting and instant lubrication. The higher SAE viscosity Numbers such as SAE 30 and SAE 20, which represents heavier body oils, are recommended for use during warm or hot weather to provide improved oil economy and adequate lubrication under high operating temperatures.

Oils are available which are designed to combine the easy starting characteristics of the lower SAE Viscosity Number with the warm weather operating characteristics of the higher SAE Viscosity Number. These are termed "multi-viscosity" oils; SAE 5W-20, SAE 10W-30, SAE 20W-40, etc.

The following chart will serve as a guide for the selection of the correct SAE Viscosity Number for use under different atmospheric temperature ranges, and suggests the appropriate SAE Viscosity Number when a multi-viscosity oil is used.

If the lowest anticipated temperature during the interval in which the oil will remain in the crankcase is:	The following SAE viscosity oils are recommended:	Multi-Viscosity oils recommended:
32° F	SAE 30	SAE 10W—30
—10° F	SAE 10	SAE 10W—30
Below —10° F	SAE 5W	SAE 5W—20

CAUTION: *Operation with SAE 10W above 60° F is not recommended.*

Types of Oils

In service, crankcase oils may form sludge and varnish and under some conditions, corrosive acids unless protected against oxidation. To minimize the formation of these harmful products and to supply the type of oil best suited for various operating conditions, the oil industry markets several types of crankcase oils. These types have been defined by the American Petroleum Institute as follows:

"Service ML" (Comparable to former Regular Types)—Generally suitable for use in internal combustion engines operating under light and favorable service conditions.

"Service MM" (Comparable to former Premium Type) — Oil having the characteristics necessary to make it generally suitable for use in internal combustion engines operating under moderate to severe service conditions which present problems of sludge, varnish or bearing corrosion control when crankcase oil temperatures are high.

"Service MS" and "Service DG" (Comparable to former Heavy-Duty Types) — Oils having the characteristics to make them generally suitable for use in internal combustion engines operating under unfavorable or severe types of service conditions.

For maximum engine protection under all driving conditions, oils designated "For Service MS" or "For Service DG" are recommended.

Maintaining Oil level

The oil gauge rod is marked "Full" and 'Add Oil.' These notations have broad arrows pointing to the level lines. The oil level should be maintained between the two lines, neither going above the "Full" line nor under the "Add Oil line.

Check the oil level frequently and add oil when necessary.

NOTE: It is advisable, when taking a long trip, to recheck the oil level after the first 100 miles of the trip. This is a precautionary measure, due to the possibility of crankcase dilution which would give a false initial oil level reading. The diluents which are usually the result of incomplete engine warm-up (traveling short distances) are driven out of the crankcase with high speed driving or sustained normal engine operating temperatures.

When to Change Crankcase Oil

Favorable Conditions

Oils have been greatly improved, driving conditions have changed and improvements in engines, such as the crankcase ventilating system, have greatly lengthened the life of good lubri-

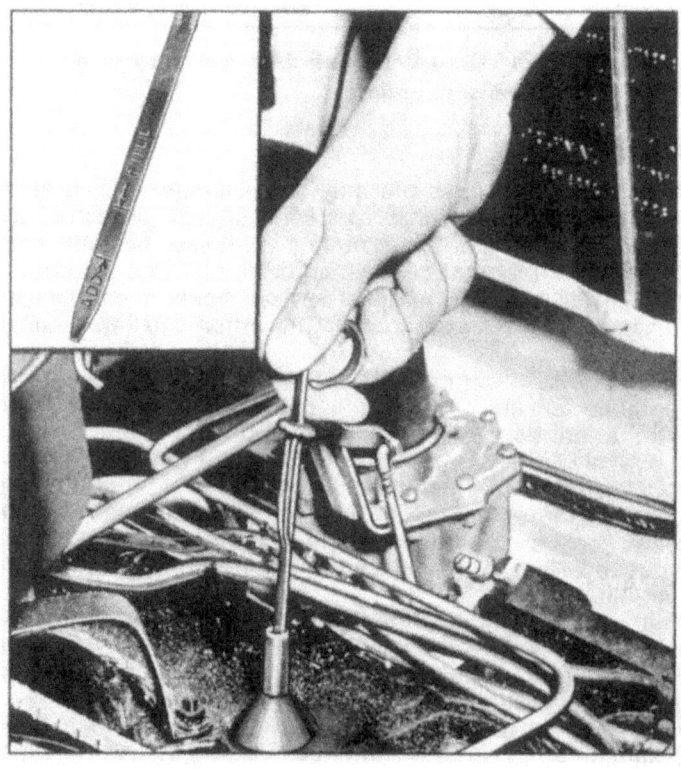

cating oils. However, to insure continuation of best performance, low maintenance cost and long engine life, it is necessary to change the crankcase oil whenever it becomes contaminated with harmful foreign materials. Under favorable driving conditions draining the crankcase and refilling with fresh oil every 4000 miles is recommended.

It is always advisable to drain the crankcase only after the engine has become thoroughly warmed up or reached normal operating temperature. The benefit of draining is, to a large extent, lost if the crankcase is drained when the engine is cold, as some of the suspended foreign material will cling to the sides of the oil pan and will not drain out readily with the cold, slower moving oil.

Under the driving conditions described in the following paragraphs, it may become necessary to drain the crankcase oil more frequently.

Dust Area Operation

Driving over dusty roads or through dust storms introduces abrasive material into the engine. Carburetor air cleaners decrease the amount of dust that may enter the crankcase. The frequency of draining depends on severity of dust conditions and no definite draining periods can be recommended, but should be more frequent than under favorable driving conditions.

Low Temperature Operation

Short runs in cold weather, such as city driving and excessive idling, do not permit thorough warming up of the engine and water, fuel and acid may accumulate in the crankcase. Water in the crankcase may freeze and interfere with proper oil circulation. These factors also promote corrosion and sludge formation and may cause clogging of oil screens and passages. Under favorable driving conditions this water is removed by the rapid warm-up inherent in this type of engine. However, if crankcase diluents accumulate, they should be removed by draining the crankcase as frequently as may be required.

Crankcase Dilution

Probably the most serious phase of engine oil deterioration is that the of crankcase dilution which is the thinning of the oil by fuel vapor leaking by pistons and rings and mixing with the oil and by condensation of water on the cylinder walls and crankcase.

Leakage of fuel, or fuel vapors, into the oil pan occurs mostly during the "warming up" period when the fuel is not thoroughly vaporized and burned. Water vapor enters the crankcase through normal engine ventilation and through exhaust gas blow-by. When the engine is not completely warmed up, these vapors condense, combine with the condensed fuel and exhaust gases and form acid compounds in the crankcase.

As long as the gases and internal walls of the crankcase are hot enough to keep water vapors from condensing, no harm will result. However, when the engine is run in low temperatures moisture will collect and unite with the gases formed by combustion resulting in an acid formation. The acid thus formed is likely to cause serious etch or pitting which will manifest itselw in excessively rapid wear on pistons pins, crankshaft bearings and other moving parts of the engine, oftentimes causing the owner to blame the car manufacturer or the lubricating oil when in reality the trouble may be traced back to the character of fuel used, or a condition of the engine such as excessive blowby or improper carburetor adjustment.

Automatic Control Devices to Minimize Crankcase Dilution

The engine is equipped with automatic devices which aid greatly in minimizing the danger of crankcase dilution.

The thermostatic control, mounted in the left engine shroud, controls the cooling air throttle valve ring which governs the air flow through the engine shrouds, thus minimizing the length of time required to reach efficient operating temperature, reducing the time that engine temperatures are conductive to vapor condensation.

A road draft tube on the rear of the engine ventilates the crankcase and removes condensation and vapors that tend to accumulate.

An automatic choke reduces the danger of raw or unvaporized fuel entering the combustion chamber and leaking into the oil reservoir.

Crankcase Lubrication

Crankcase oil change intervals for 1962 models will be as follows:

Prevailing Daytime Temperature	Initial Oil Change Interval	Regular Oil Change Interval
Above 32°F.	First 4000 mi.* or first 60 days, whichever occurs first.	Every 4000 miles or every 60 days, whichever occurs first.
Below 32°F. or during adverse operating conditions.	First 4000 miles or first 30 days, whichever occurs first.	Every 4000 miles or every 30 days, whichever occurs first.

*If the prevailing daytime temperature is above 60°F. change to SAE-30 or SAE-10W-30 oil after the first 500 miles of driving.

OIL FILTER

A full flow oil filter filters all of the oil delivered by the oil pump; for this reason the interval of cartridge change is very important. The oil filter cartridge should be replaced after the first 5000 miles and every 4000 miles thereafter.

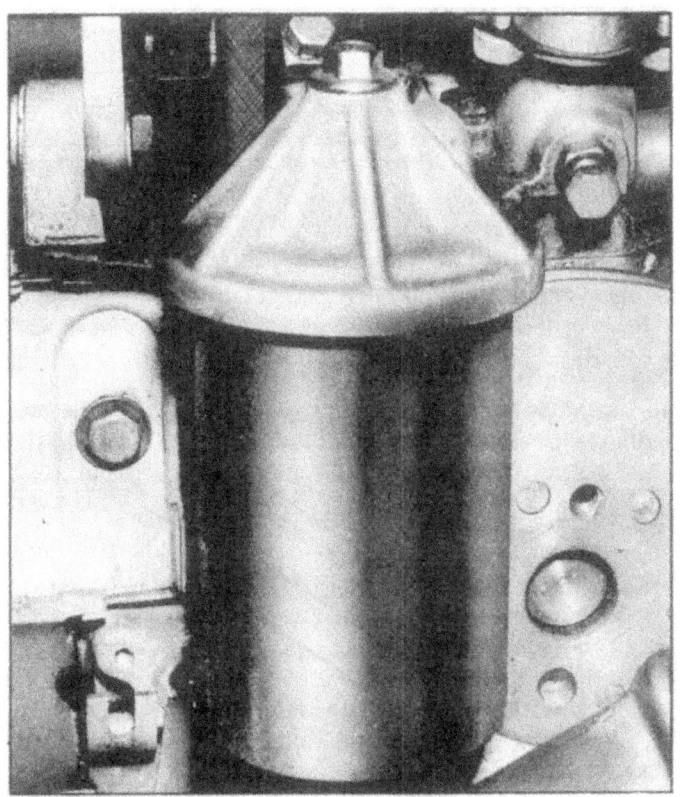

Changing of Oil FILTER CARTRIDGE

Unscrew cartridge container center bolt to remove filter cartridge.

Before installing new cartridge clean out cartridge container and place new gasket in position in oil filter body casting. Clean up any oil spilled as this oil, if in contact with blower belt, will cause blower belt to slip and effect generator operation and cooling efficiency.

NOTE: Be certain to remove old seal from oil filter. If not removed, new seal will block oil passage in filter and not allow filtering of dirty oil.

Oil filter center bolt should be tightened to 9-15 ft. lbs. torque.

Replacement recommendations for the oil filter cartridge have been changed as follows for 1962:

Replace the filter cartridge after the first 4000 miles of driving and every 4000 miles thereafter, or every six months, whichever occurs first.

The oil filter center bolt should be tightened to 20-25 ft. lbs. torque. On air conditioned vehicles both the center bolt and the bolt attaching the cartridge to the adapter should be torqued to 20-25 ft. lbs.

FRONT SUSPENSION AND STEERING LINKAGE

For chassis lubrication, consult the lubrication chart. It shows the points to be lubricated and how often the lubricant should be applied. There are four fittings on the steering linkage and four on the front suspension.

The term "chassis lubricant" as used in this manual, decribes a semi-fluid lubricant designed for application by commercial pressure gun equipment. It is composed of mineral oil (300 to 500 seconds Saybolt Universal viscosity at 100°F) combined with approximately 8% soap, or soaps which are insoluble in water.

CLUTCH CONTROL CROSS SHAFT

The cross shaft should be lubricated through the fitting every 1000 miles with chassis lube also coat both ends of shaft.

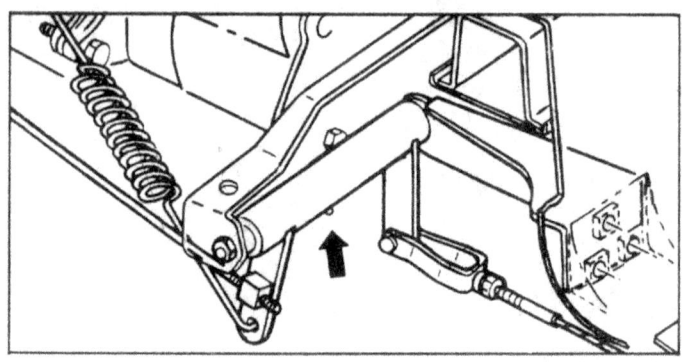

Clutch Control Cross Shaft

STEERING GEAR

The steering gear is filled at the factory with a special all-season gear lubricant. Seasonal change of this lubricant is unnecessary and the housing should not be drained. Whenever required, additions should be made using a lubricant which, at low temperatures, is fluid and will not "channel" or cause "hard steering" and which will provide satisfactory lubrication under extreme summer conditions. Steering gear lubricant are marketed by many oil companies.

To check the steering gear, it will be necessary to reach up under the front bumper to gain access to the filler plug.

GENERATOR

Every 1000 miles the oiler on each end of the generator should be filled to the top of the cap with a light engine oil.

NOTE: Over oiling at the front oiler may result in damage to the generator.

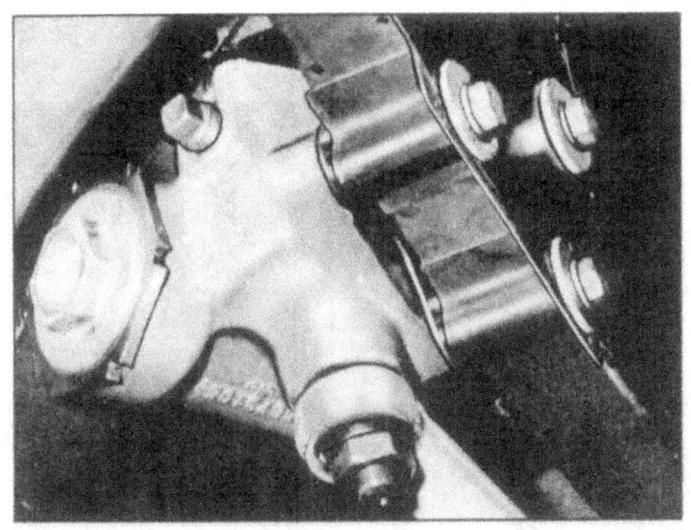

Steering Gear Filler Plug

Generator Lubrication

DISTRIBUTOR

A hinge cap oiler (1960-61 models) on the side of the distributor housing should be filled with light engine oil every 1000 miles.

Distributor cap should be removed every 5000 miles. Apply a small amount of Delco-Remy cam and ball bearing lubricant or other suitable high melting point non-bleeding grease on distributor cam surface.

Add a few drops of light engine oil to the breaker lever pivot.

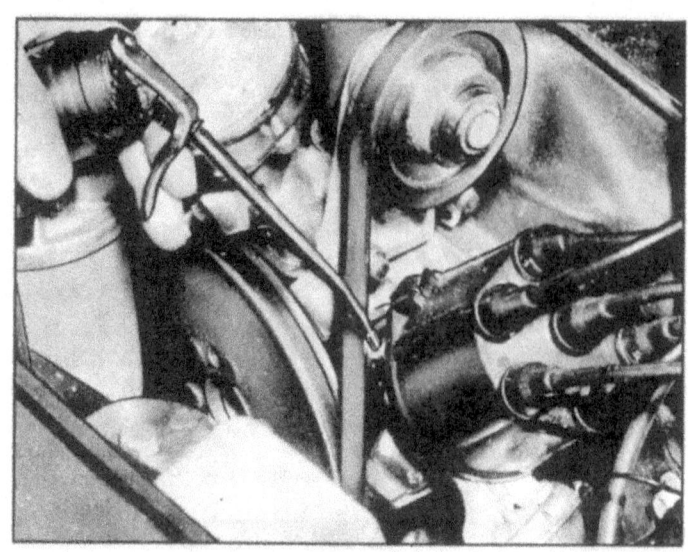

Distributor Lubrication—Hinge Cap Oiler

Distributor Lubrication—Breaker Cam

AIR CLEANERS

The air cleaner elements should be removed and cleaned every 2000 miles. Immerse element in kerosene to clean, squeeze dry, re-immerse in light engine oil (SAE 10W-30), squeeze to remove most of the oil and reinstall.

FRONT WHEEL BEARINGS

It is necessary to remove the wheel and hub assembly to lubricate the bearings every 10,000 miles. The bearing assemblies should be cleaned before repacking with lubricant. Do not pack the hub between the inner and outer bearing assemblies or the hub caps, as this excessive lubrication results in the lubricant working out into the brake drums and linings.

Front wheels of all passenger car models are equipped with roller bearings and should be packed with a high melting point water resistant front wheel bearing lubricant.

> **CAUTION: Do not mix wheel bearing lubricants. Be certain to thoroughly clean bearings and hubs of all old lubricant before repacking.**

The proper adjustment of front wheel bearings is one of the important servce operations that has a definite bearing on safety. A car with improperly adjusted front wheel bearings lacks steering stability, has a tendency to wander or shimmy and may have increased tire wear. The adjustment of these bearings is very critical. The procedure is covered under Front Wheel Bearing Adjustment.

UNIVERSAL JOINTS

The universal joints are lubricated and sealed at the factory. It is recommended that they be disassembled, cleaned and lubricated every 25,000 miles with a high-melting point, wheel bearing type lubricant.

TRANSMISSION — AXLE — ASSEMBLY

STANDARD TRANSMISSION ASSEMBLIES

Recommended Lubricants

Since both units are connected by internal passages, SAE 80 "Multi-Purpose" gear lubricant must be used.

> **CAUTION: Straight Mineral Oil gear lubricants or any "lead soap, active sulphur" lubricants must not be used.**

G.M. No. 3772661 SAE 80 is recommended for year around use.

Lubricant Additions

The lubricant level in these units should be checked periodically (every 1000 miles).

To check "trans-axle" unit, check first at the axle, if low, also check the transmission.

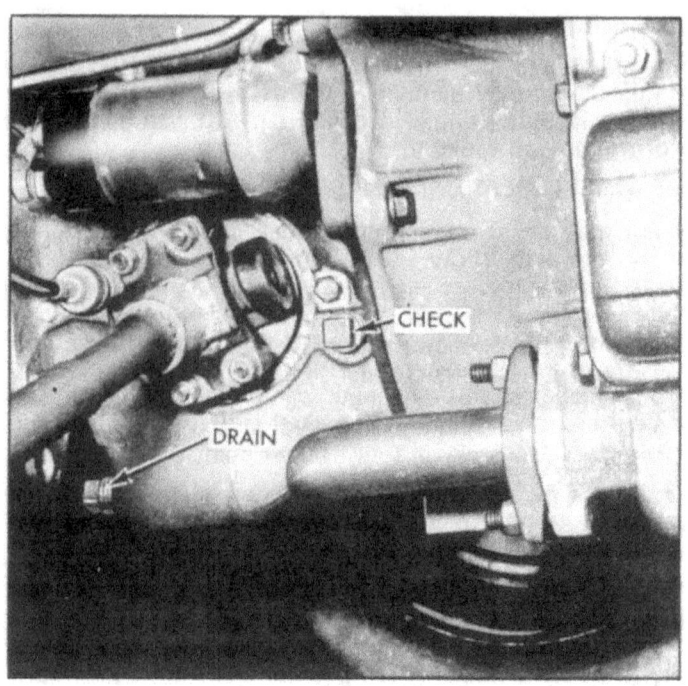

Checking Axle Lubricant

When checking lubricant level, both units should be at operating temperature. With unit at operating temperature the lubricant should be level with bottom of the filler plug hole. If the lubricant level is checked with the unit cold the lubricant level should be ½ inch below the filler plug hole.

Lubricant Changes or Refill

Drain out the original lubricant at the end of the first 1000 miles and every 10,000 miles thereafter. When both units have been emptied for one reason or another, lubricant must be added to each unit. After refill (5 pints total), check level at both units.

Rear Axle and Transmission

It is no longer necessary to drain the axle (automatic transmission models) or the axle and transmission (manual transmission models) after the first 1000 miles of driving. However, the manual transmission and axle and the axle only in automatic transmission equipped models should be drained at 10,000 mile intervals and refilled with SAE-80 Multi-purpose Gear Lubricant.

"Multi-Purpose" Gear Lubricants

Gear lubricants that will satisfactorily lubricate hypoid rear axles have been developed and are commonly referred to as "Multi-Purpose" gear lubricants.

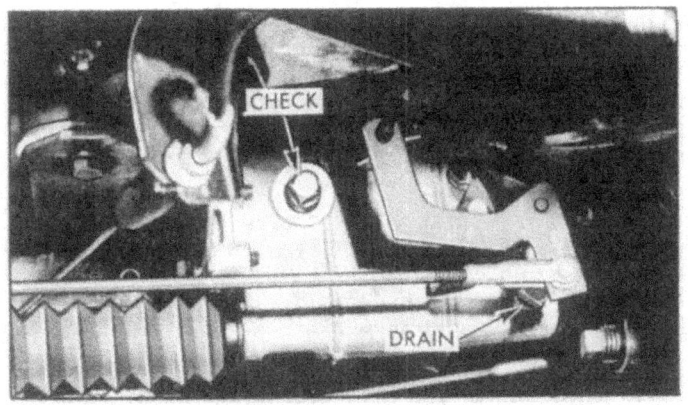

Checking Transmission Lubricant

"Multi-Purpose" gear lubricants must be manufactured under carefully controlled conditions and the lubricant manufacturer must be responsible for the satisfactory performance of his product. His reputation is the best indication of quality.

Positraction Rear Axle

Lubricants and drain periods for the Positraction Rear Axle are the same as given above for the standard rear axle.

AUTOMATIC TRANSMISSION ASSEMBLIES

Recommended Lubricants

When this vehicle is equipped with an automatic transmission,

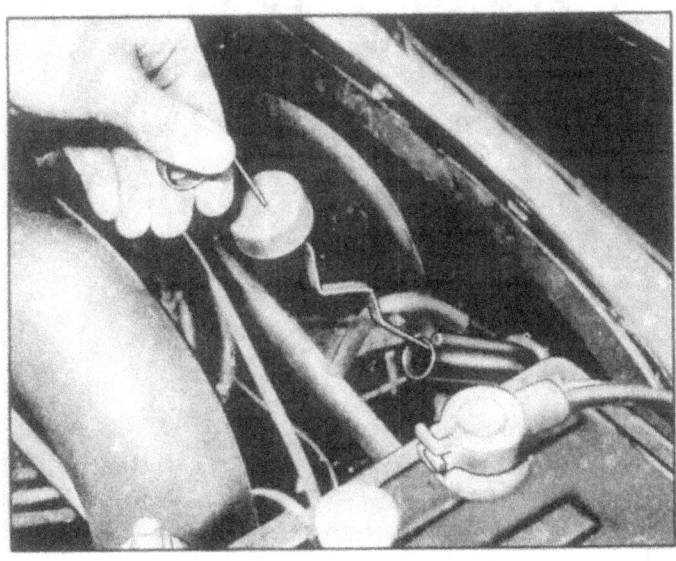

Checking Automatic Transmission Lubricant Level

the units are handled on an individual basis (similar to standard passenger car, because they are not inter-connected) as far as lubrication is concerned. The lubricant used in the rear axle is the same as mentioned above, and the recommendations still apply to this unit, but for the automatic transmission, the special transmission oil must be used (type "A" bearing the mark AQ-ATF).

Lubrican Additions

Check oil level every 1000 miles, with engine idling, parking brake set, transmission warm and control lever in Neutral (N) position. Add only Automatic Transmission Fluid Type "A," bearing the mark AQ-ATF when level reaches "add" mark on oil level rod (one pint low). Do not allow dirt to enter filler tube.

NOTE: If the above type fluid bearing the mark (AQ-ATF—number—A) is not available, it is permissible to use automatic transmission fluid Type "A" with an AQ-ATF mark.

Lubricant Changes or Refill

It is not necessary to drain this unit initially, seasonally or peridically. However, the rear axle portion should be handled as outlined under "Standard Transmission Assemblies." On an overhaul of automatic transmission unit, and if converter has not drained out, a refill will take 6 pints; on a "dry" transmission, 13-14 pints are needed.

Battery Terminal Washer Lubrication

BATTERY

The battery positive terminal has a felt washer between top of case and cable connections to minimize corrosive action of battery acid. This felt washer should be saturated with engine oil every 1000 miles.

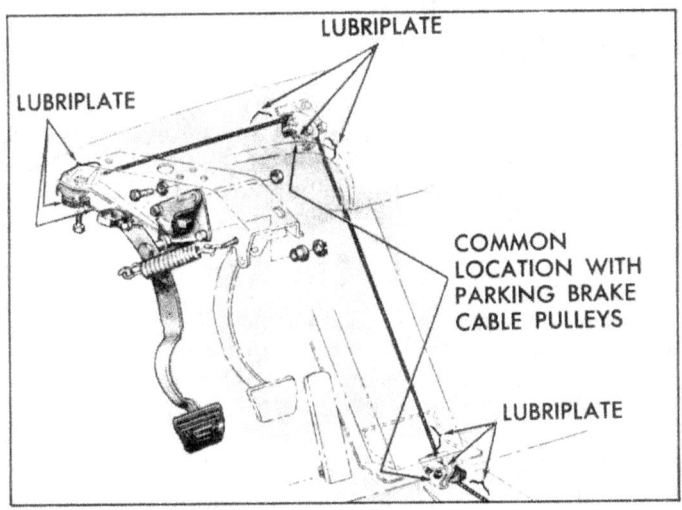

Pulley Lubrication—Clutch Cable

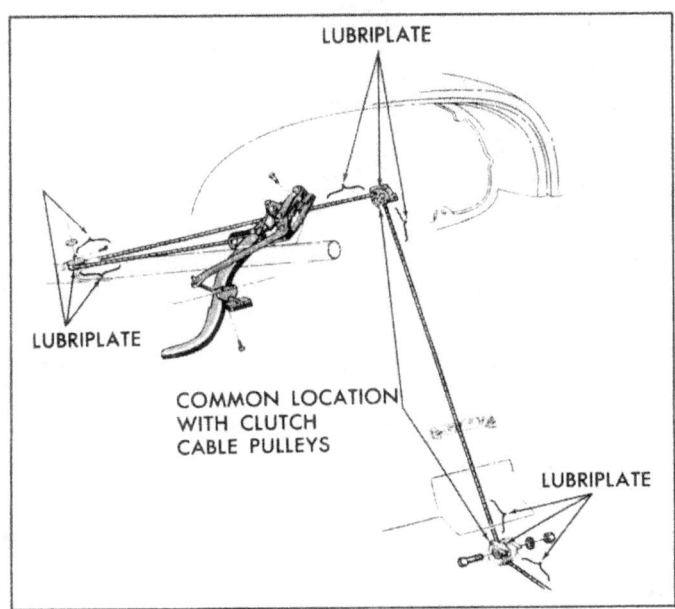

Pulley Lubrication—Parking Brake Cable

HYDRAULIC BRAKE CYLINDER

FLUID LEVEL

Every 1000 miles, the fluid level in the brake main cylinder should be checked. The level of the fluid should be even with the cast boss on inside of cylinder casting. If low, add only G. M. Hydraulic Brake Fluid Super No. 11.

PARKING BRAKE AND CLUTCH CABLE

PULLEYS AND CABLES

The six pulley bearing areas and the cables at the pulleys should be lubricated with Lubriplate at 10,000 miles intervals. Four of these pulleys utilize two common shafts, while the remaining two are on separate shafts.

BODY LUBRICATION

Many of the annoying squeaks and noises that occur in closed bodies are due to neglecting a very important maintenance service which all bodies should receive regularly.

The movable mechanical parts of the body are lubricated at the factory for easy operation and to eliminate squeaks caused by frictional contact. This lubrication should be maintained and replenished at periodic intervals.

Most body lubrication points do not carry heavy loads like the chassis, and for this reason many of the points do not require as heavy nor as frequent lubrication as the chassis points. But because of the more frequent use of some parts such as door locks and door lock strikers, it is important that these readily accessible parts be lubricated at least twice a year. Other body parts should be lubricated whenever access to the parts is available.

For body lubrication, a specific kind of lubricant, the one best suited for individual points, should be used. Knowing what to use and where to use it, together with a little care and cleanliness will bring many returns in the satisfaction and pleasure of driving a car properly serviced. Wipe off all lubrication points before applying new lubricant. Remove all excess lubricant where necessary to prevent staining of trim or clothing.

THE FOLLOWING PARTS SHOULD BE LUBRICATED TWICE EACH YEAR

Front and Rear Door Lower Hinge Assembly

Wipe off dirt and apply a light coat of Lubriplate or equivalent to areas indicated by arrows in Figure 2-14. Wipe off excess lubricant. Lubrication of front and rear door hinges is typical of lubrication of lower hinges.

Door Lock Striker

Wipe off dirt and apply a light coat of stick-type lubricant to top surface of lock bolt teeth at areas indicated by "1."

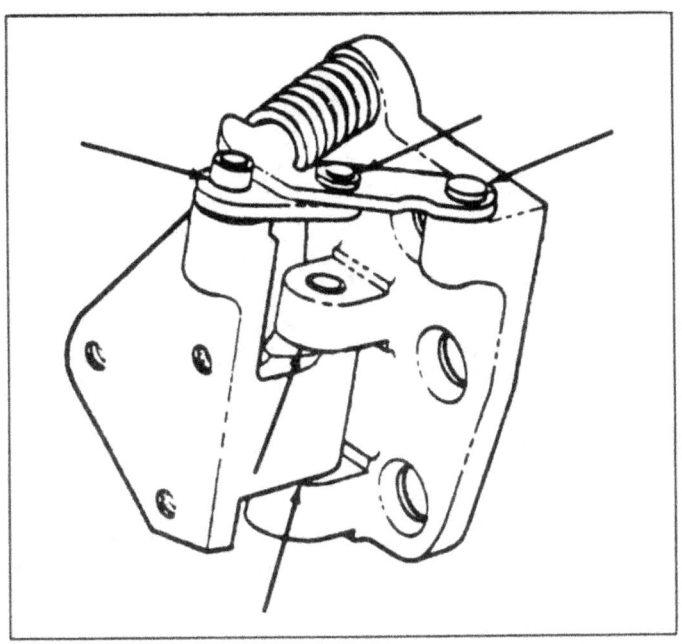

Fig. 2-14—Front and Rear Lower Hinge Assembly

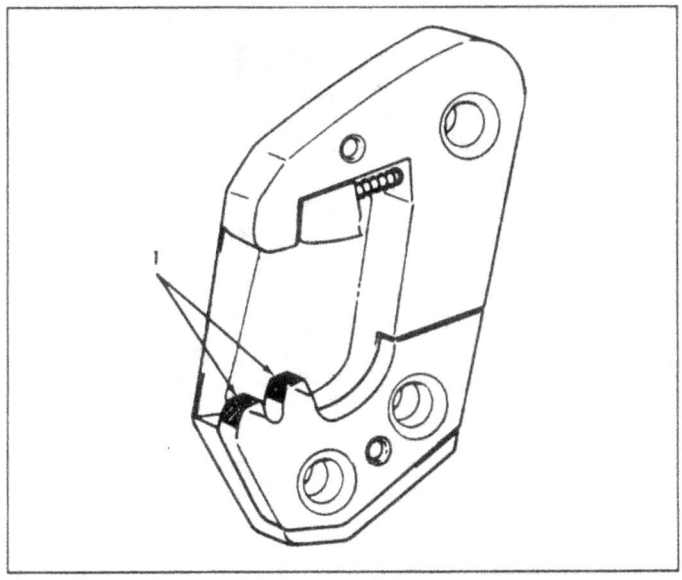

Door Lock Striker

Instrument Panel Compartment Door Hinge

Wipe off dirt and apply a sparing amount of dripless oil to the hinge and hinge stop friction points. Operate door and wipe off all excess lubricant.

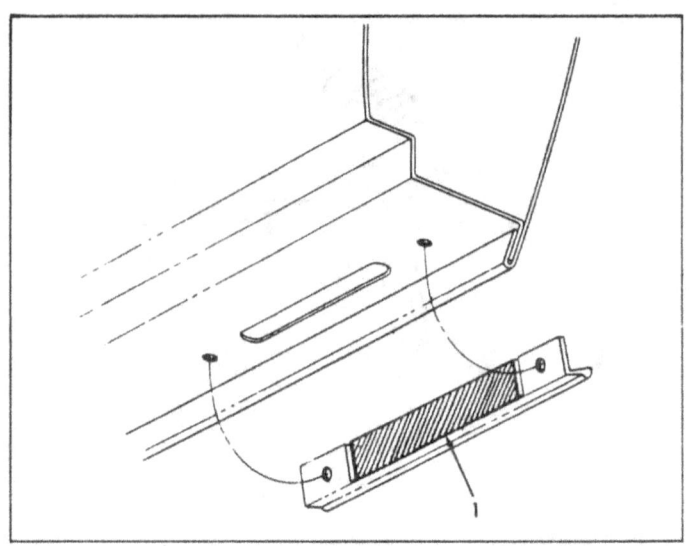

Door Bottom Drain Hole Sealing Strip

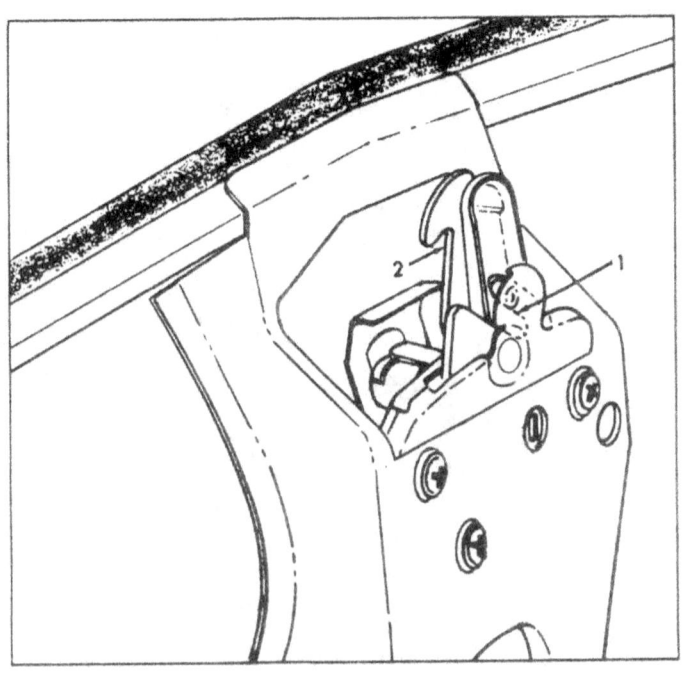

Front Compartment Lid Lock

Door Bottom Drain Hole Sealing Strip

Apply a sparing amount of silicone rubber lubricant to surface of sealing strip at area indicated by "1." This operation is performed to prevent lip of sealing strip from adhering to inner panel and plugging drain hole in bottom of door.

Front Compartment Lid Lock

Wipe off dirt and apply Lubriplate or equivalent along area of slot in lock bolt as indicated by "1" and in notch of latch as indicated by "2." Wipe off excess lubricant. Lubrication of the engine compartment latch is similar to the lubrication of the front compartment lid lock latch.

Door Jamb Switch

Wipe off dirt and apply a thin coat of Lubricate or equivalent to end surface of switch plunger. Wipe off excess lubricant.

Gas Tank Filler Door Hinge

Wipe off dirt and apply a few drops of dripless oil to all hinge bearing points.

Front Compartment Lid Hinges and Torque Rods

Wipe off dirt and apply a molybdenum disulfide lubricant to front compartment hinge friction points at hinge pin area and to tab on movable portion of hinge which engages outboard end of torque rod. Wipe off dirt and apply Lubriplate or equivalent to torque rod bearing points at lower inboard edge of retainer, as indicated at "2." Wipe off excess lubricant from torque rod bearing point.

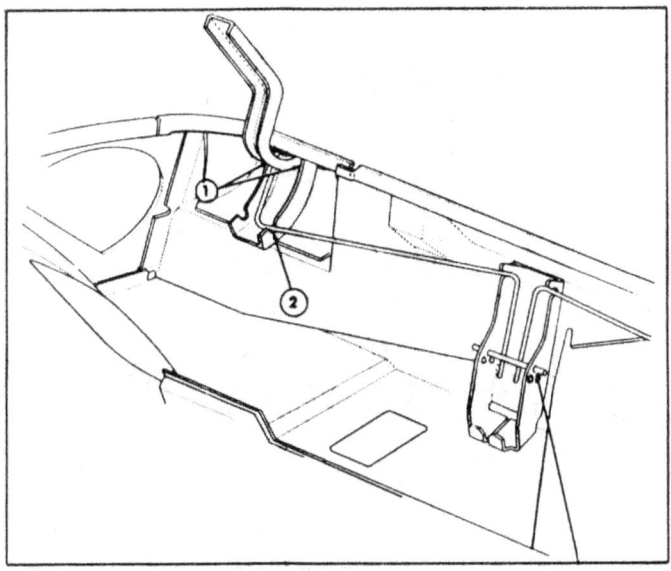

Front Compartment Lid Hinges and Torque Rods

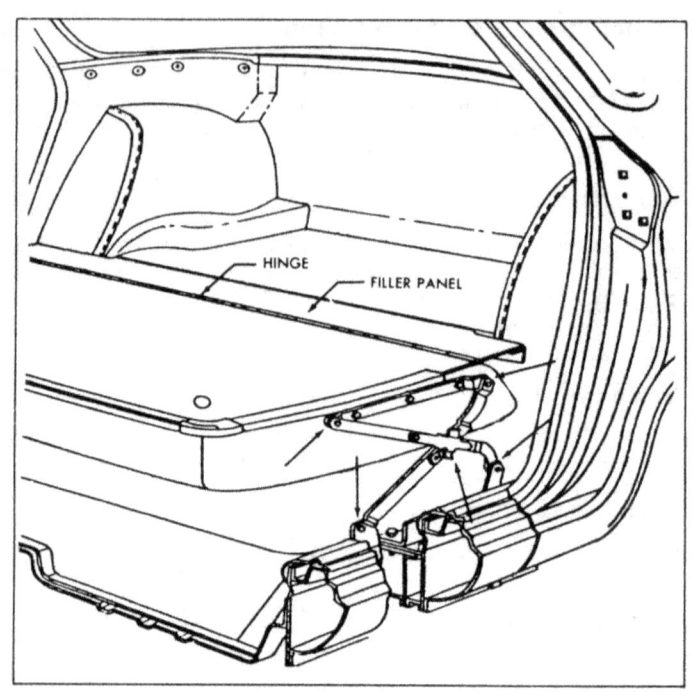

Rear Folding Seat Back Support Link Assembly

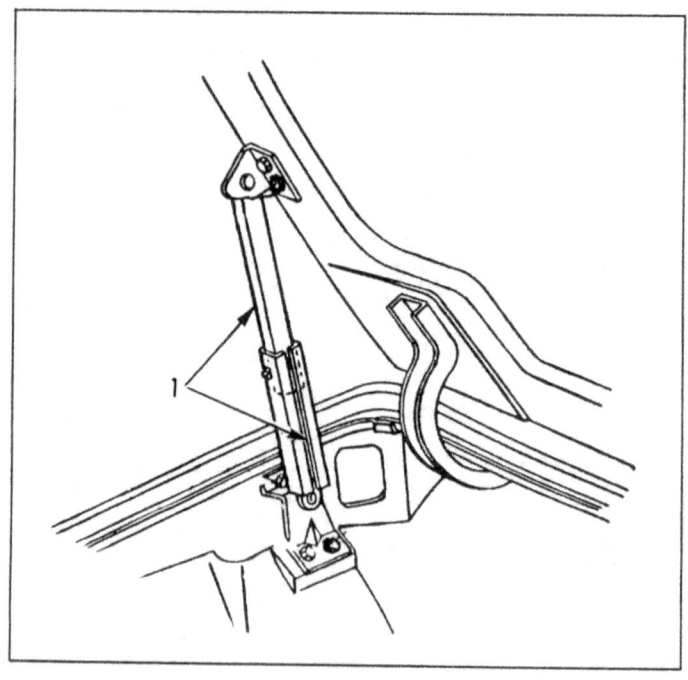

Engine Compartment Lid Support

Rear Folding Seat Back Support Link Assembly

Wipe off dirt and apply a few drops of dripless oil to link assembly bearing points indicated by arrows. Operate seat and remove all excess lubricant.

Rear Folding Seat Back Filler Panel Hinge

Wipe off dirt and apply a few drops of dripless oil to friction areas of hinge. Wipe off excess lubricant.

Door Weatherstrip

Carefully apply a sparing amount of silicone rubber lubricant to surface of door weatherstrip.

Engine Compartment Lid Support

Wipe off dirt and apply a coat of Lubriplate of equivalent to channel portions of lid support as indicated by "1."

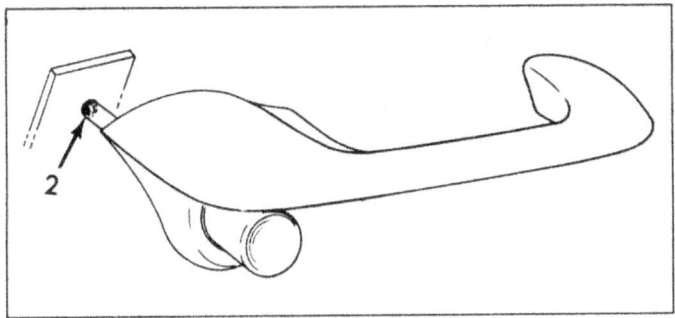

Door Outside Handle

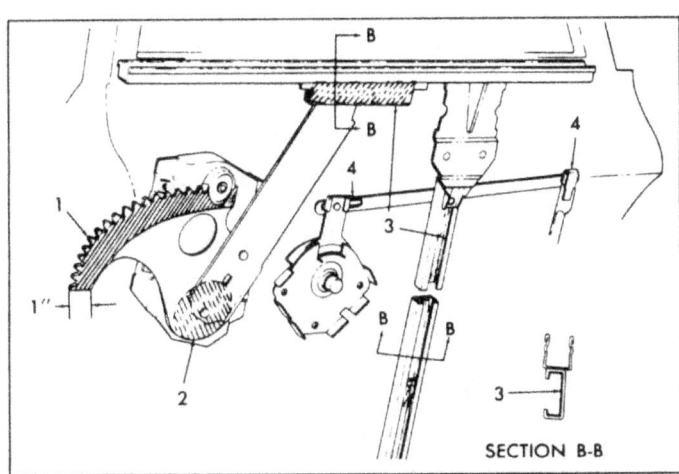

Door window Regulator

LUBRICATE WHEN ACCESS TO PARTS IS AVAILABLE
Door Outside Handle

Apply a light coat of Lubriplate or equivalent to end surface of lock cylinder shaft contacting bell crank as indicated by "2."

Door Window Regulator and Cams

Apply a coat of Lubriplate or equivalent to area of regulator sector indicated by "1," to bearing surface of regulator arm as indicated at "2," and to sliding surface of guide channels and cam as indicated by "3". Lubrication of rear door parts is typical of lubrication required on front door parts.

Door Lock Parts

Lubricate moving parts of door lock with Lubriplate or equivalent.

Door Locking Mechanism

Apply Lubriplate or equivalent to pivot points at ends of all connecting linkage as indicated by "4." Lubrication of rear door locking mechanism is typical of lubrication required on front door locking mechanism.

Rear Engine Compartment Lid Hinges

Apply Lubriplate or equivalent to hinge friction points at hinge pin area.

NOTES

SUSPENSION

All models utilize the S.L.A. (Short-Long arm) type front suspension with spherical joints connecting the control arms and steering knuckles (fig. 3-1). "Brake dive" and acceleration torque is controlled by strut rods running from the outer ends of the lower control arms to brackets that trail back from the front cross member. "Cornering-sway" is controlled by rubber bushed control arms.

The rear suspension is independently sprung with individual control arms. The rear axles operate through universal joints mounted on each side of the axle case.

ADJUSTMENT OF FRONT WHEEL BEARINGS

The proper adjustment of the front wheel bearings is one of the important service operations that has a definite bearing on safety. A vehicle with improperly adjusted front wheel bearings lacks steering stability, has a tendency to wander or shimmy and causes excessive tire wear. In an effort to provide for more accurate adjustments, the spindles are drilled both vertically and horizontally and the adjusting nuts are slotted on all six sides.

1. Raise and secure front of vehicle. Remove hub cap and dust cap. Remove cotter pin from end of spindle.
2. Tighten adjusting nut to 100 in. lbs. while rotating wheel.
3. Back off adjusting nut 1 flat (1/6 turn of nut).

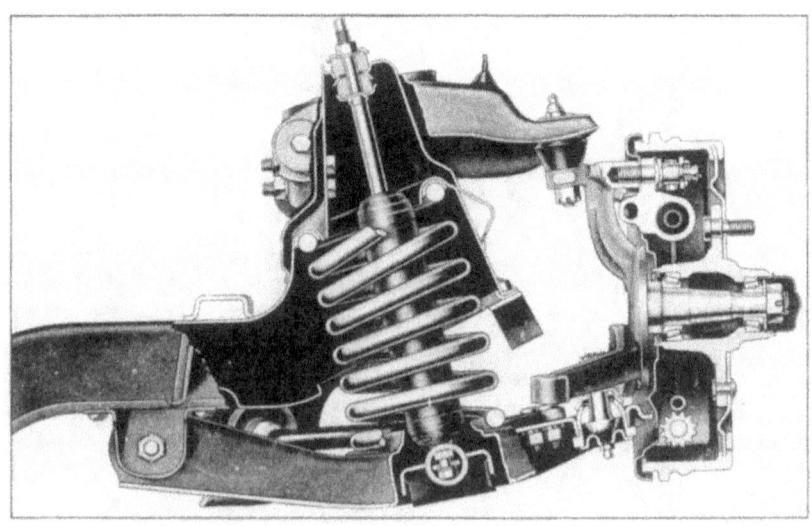

Front Suspension Cross Section

4. Insert cotter pin if slot in nut and hole in end of spindle align. If not, back off nut an additional ½ flat (1/12 turn of nut) or less and insert cotter pin.
5. Spin the wheel to make certain that it rolls freely. Properly lock the cotter pin by spreading the end and bending it around.

   NOTE: These tapered roller wheel bearings should have zero preload and from .000" to .004" end play when properly adjusted.
6. Install dust and hub caps.
7. Repeat operation (if necessary) on opposite side.
8. Lower vehicle to floor.

Front Wheel Bearings — 1962

1. Jack up front end of vehicle. Remove hub cap and dust cap. Remove cotter pin from end of spindle.
2. Tighten spindle nut to 15 ft. lbs. (or 180 in. lbs.) torque while rotating wheel.
3. Back off adjusting nut one flat and insert cotter pin.
4. If slot and cotter pin hole do not align, back off adjusting nut an additional ½ flat or less as required to insert cotter pin.
5. Spin the wheel to make sure that it rolls freely. Properly lock the cotter pin by spreading the end and bending it around.

   NOTE: These tapered roller wheel bearings should have zero preload and .000" to .007" end movement when properly adjusted.

   Install the dust cap and hub cap or wheel disc.
6. Remove jack.

FRONT SHOCK ABSORBERS

Removal

1. Properly support vehicle with hoist and / or jack stands so that front suspension 'hangs free" and so that clearance is sufficient on front lower control arms to allow removal of shock absorber.
2. Hold shock absorber upper stem on flat section and remove upper attaching nut, cup washer and grommet.
3. Remove the two shock absorber lower attaching bolts and lockwashers.
4. Withdraw shock absorber and remove cup washer and grommet from upper end of shock absorber shaft.

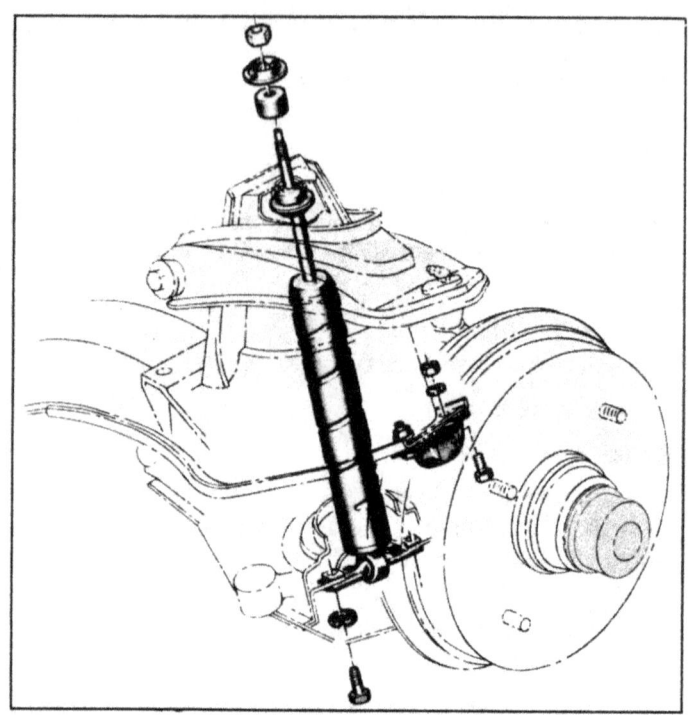

Front Shock Absorber Installation

Installation

1. Install cup washer and new grommet on shaft. Pull out shock absorber shaft to extend it to its full length.
2. Install shock absorber up through lower control arm and through coil spring. Be certain shaft protrudes out of small hole in top of spring tower.
3. Install both lower attaching lockwashers and bolts.
4. Holding upper flat, install upper retaining nut.
5. Lower vehicle to floor, or remove jackstands.

Lower

The lower control arm spherical joint should be replaced whenever wear is indicated in the upper joint inspection.

WHEELS AND TIRES

All models carry disc type wheels with tubeless type tires. The wheels are connected to the front wheel hubs and rear axle shaft flanges by four studs and nuts each.

The tires used on 1960-61 models are 6.50 x 13-4 ply.

The spare tire is mounted in the front compartment. A scissors type jack stowed under the tire, and a combination rachet type jack wrench, wheel nut wrench and hub cap remover are supplied with all models.

All 1962 models carry disc type wheels and 4-ply rating tubeless tires available in blackwall and thinline whitewall. Tire sizes are 6.50 x 13-4 PR except Station Wagons which have 7.00 x 13-4 PR. Front and rear wheels pilot on redesigned and strengthened hub pilot diameters instead of wheel stud diameters as used in past models.

TESTING TIRE PRESSURES

The correct tire pressure is:

Front — 15 pounds cold
Rear — 26 pounds cold

Frequent checking is essential with low pressure tires as variations of only a few pounds make an appreciable difference in riding qualities, handling ease and tire wear. It should also be general practice to check tire pressures each time a car is brought in for service, not only as a convenience to the owner, but also to reduce the possibility of owner complaint of riding, steering or tire wear due solely to improper tire inflation. Checking inflation pressure should be a part of every lubrication job. **If too high a pressure is used in the front, a complaint of oversteer may develop.**

Starting Pressure—Front—15 pounds
—Rear —26 pounds

Hot Pressure—Front—18 pounds
—Rear —30 pounds

The pressures do not increase more than 4-5 pounds when heated under hard driving. Do not "bleed" tires to reduce this higher pressure.

When checking tires, servicemen should be careful to reinstall valve stem caps. These caps provide an essential function in keeping dirt out of the valve thus reducing the possibility of slow leaks through the valve.

CHANGING ROAD WHEELS

To change the road wheels using the jack that comes with the car, observe the following procedure:

1. Set hand brake and block front wheels if rear wheel is being changed.

2. Remove hub cap or wheel disc and break wheel mounting nuts loose.

   NOTE: If large size balance weights have been used to balance the wheel and tire assembly, their removal is necessary to be able to remove the accessory trim Ring. Reinstall weights in same locations.

3. Place the jack directly under the side edge of body, approximately 10" toward center of vehicle from forward edge of rear fender opening or 4" back of front seam of sill and raise car until wheel clears ground.

4. Remove wheel mounting nuts and remove wheel from hub or drum.

5. To replace road wheel, reverse the above instructions. Proper torque on nuts is 45-65 ft. lbs.

INTERCHANGING TIRES

Normal tire wear is uneven between the front and rear wheels because of the difference in the functions of the front and rear tires. To minimize tire wear and tire noise, it is recommended that tires be interchanged both as to front or rear use and as to change of direction at intervals of from 4,000 to 5,000 miles.

In addition, utilizing the spare tire in rotation with the other four tires gives 20% more total car mileage before replacement tires must be purchased.

The recommended plan for interchanging tires is based on the following steps.

Move the left front wheel to right rear, right rear to right front, right front to left rear, left rear to spare and spare to left front.

In detail, the plan provides the changes as shown each time the tires are interchanged.

If the spare tire is not used, criss-cross the tires to obtain balanced tire wear (left front to right rear, etc.).

NOTE: Be certain to readjust tire pressures after rotating or criss-crossing.

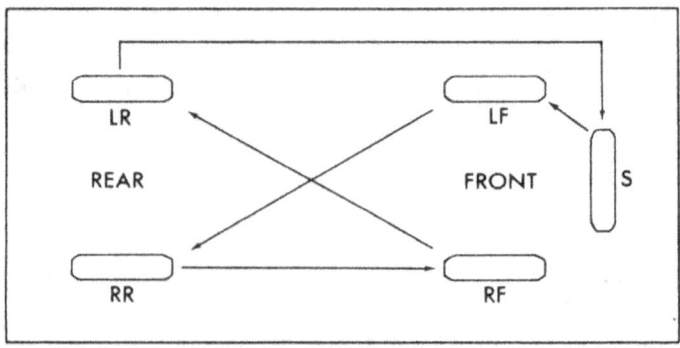

Tire Rotation Plan

CLEANING WHITEWALL TIRES

A great deal or ordinary road dirt which collects on white sidewall tires may be sponged off with clear water or a mild soap solution.

Chevrolet Whitewall Tire Cleaner, however, is a quicker and more effective cleaner for removing dirt and stains from whitewall tires and in many cases it will remove stains and discoloration that the simpler method of soap and water will not remove.

Under no circumstances should gasoline, kerosene or any cleaning fluid containing a solvent derived from oil be used to clean whitewall tires. Oil in any form is detrimental to rubber and a cleaner with an oil base will discolor or injure whitewall tires.

SERVICE OPERATIONS

CORECTION OF IRREGULAR TIRE WEAR

Heel and Toe Wear

This is a saw-toothed effect where one end of each tread block is worn more than the other.

The end that wears is the one that first grips the road when the brakes are applied.

Heel and toe wear is less noticeable on rear tires than on front tires, because the propelling action of the rear wheels creates a force which tends to wear the opposite end of the tread blocks. The two forces, propelling and braking, make for more even wear of the rear tires, whereas only the braking forces act on the front wheels, and the saw-tooth effect is more noticeable.

A certain amount of heel and toe wear is normal. Excessive wear is usually due to high speed driving and excessive use of brakes. The best remedy is to interchange tires regularly.

Side Wear

This may be caused by incorrect wheel camber, under-inflation, high cambered roads or by taking corners at too high a rate of speed.

The first two causes are the most common. Camber wear can be readily identified because it occurs only on one side of the treads, whereas underinflation causes wear on both sides. Camber wear requires correction of the camber first and then interchanging tires.

There is, of course, no correction for high cambered roads. Cornering wear is discussed further on.

Misalignment Wear

This is wear due to excessive toe-in or toe-out, front or rear. In either case, tires will revolve with a side motion and scrape the tread rubber off. If misalignment is severe, the rubber will be scraped off of both tires (or all four tires if front and rear toe is not correct); if slight, only one will be affected.

The scraping action against the face of the tire causes a small feather edge of rubber to appear on one side of the tread and this feather edge is certain indication of misalignment. The remedy is readjusting toe-in within specifications, or rechecking the entire front end alignment or rear toe setting if necessary.

Uneven Wear

Uneven or spotty wear is due to such irregularities as unequal caster or camber, bent front or rear suspension parts, out-of-balance wheels, brake drums out-of-round, brakes out-of-adjustment or other mechanical conditions. The remedy in each case consists of locating the mechanical defect and correcting it.

Cornering Wear

Since the introduction of independently sprung front and rear wheels, improvements in spring suspension have enabled drivers to negotiate curves at higher rates of speed with the same feeling of security that they had with the older cars at lower speeds. Consequently, curves are being taken at higher speeds with the result that a type of tire wear called 'Cornering Wear," frequently appears.

When a car makes an extremely fast turn, the weight is shifted from an even loading on all four wheels to an abnormal load on the tires on the outside of the curve and a very light load on the inside tires, due to centrifugal force. This unequal loading may have two unfavorable results.

First, the rear tire on the inside of the curve may be relieved of so much load that it is no longer geared to the road and it slips, grinding off the tread on the inside half of the tire at an excessive rate. This type of tire shows much the same appearance of tread wear as tire wear caused by negative camber.

Second, the transfer of weight may also over-load the outside tires so much that they are laterally distorted resulting in excessive wear on the outside half of the tire, producing a type of wear like that caused by excessive positive camber.

Cornering wear can be most easily distinguished from abnormal camber wear by the rounding of the outside shoulder or edge of the tire and by the roughening of the tread surface which denotes abrasion.

Cornering wear often produces a fin or raised portion along the inside edge of each row in the tread pattern. In some cases this fin is almost as pronounced as a toe-in fin, and in others, it tapers into a row of tread blocks to such an extent that the tire has a definite step wear appearance.

TROUBLES AND REMEDIES

Symptoms and Probable Cause	Probable Remedy

Hard Steering

a. Lack of lubrication.
b. Improper wheel alignment.
c. Sagging front or rear spring.
d. Bent wheel or spindle.
e. Broken wheel bearings.
f. Tight spherical joints.
g. Underinflated tires.
h. Improper steering gear adjustment.
i. Tie rod ends out of alignment.

a. Lubricate according to instructions.
b. Front end alignment correction.
c. Replace springs as required.
d. Straighten or replace wheel or replace spindle.
e. Replace necessary bearings.
f. If not corrected by lubrication, replace joints.
g. Inflate tires to recommended pressure.
h. Adjust steering gear.
i. Align tie rod ends with ball studs.

Front Wheel Shimmy

a. Underinflated tires.
b. Broken or loose wheel bearings.
c. Worn spherical joints.
d. Improper caster.
e. Unbalanced wheels.
f. Steering gear loose.
g. Tie rod ball loose.
h. Loose wheel lugs.
i. Bent wheel.
j. Improper alignment.
k. Wheel out-of-balance.

a. Inflate tires to recommended pressure.
b. Replace or adjust wheel bearings.
c. Replace joints.
d. Adjust caster.
e. Balance wheel and tire assemblies.
f. Adjust steering gear.
g. Replace tie rod end.
h. Tighten lugs.
i. Replace or tighten wheel.
j. Front end alignment as per specifications.
k. Balance wheel.

Excessive or Uneven Tire Wear

a. Wheels out of balance.
b. High speed cornering.
c. Improper air pressures.
d. Not rotating tires as recommended.
e. Improper acting brakes.
f. Improper alignment.
g. Rapid stopping.

a. Balance wheels.
b. Instruct driver.
c. Inflate tires to recommended pressure.
d. Rotate tires according to instructions.
e. Correct brakes as required.
f. Align front end as per specifications.
g. Apply brakes slowly on approaching stop.

Vehicle Too Flexible

a. Faulty shock absorber.

a. Disconnect shock absorber and test action (there should be considerable and steady resistance in each direction when held in upright position), replace if necessary.

Hard Riding

a. Shock absorber broken or seized.
b. Excessive tire pressure.

a. Disconnect shock absorber and test action, replace if necessary.
b. Check tire pressure, maintain 13 pounds front and 26 pounds rear (cold).

Road Wander

a. Underinflated tires.
b. Lack of lubrication.
c. Tight steering gear.

a. Inflate tires to recommended pressure.
b. Lubricate chassis and steering gear.
c. Adjust steering gear.

d. Improper toe-in.
e. Improper caster and camber.
f. Worn tie rod ends.
g. Loose relay rod.

Noise in Front or Rear Wheels

a. Loose wheel lugs.
b. Broken or loose brake shoe return springs.
c. Broken or rough wheel bearings.
d. Scored drums.
e. Lack of lubrication (wheel bearings).

Wheel Tramp

a. Wheel assembly out of balance.
b. Blister or bump on tire.
c. Improper shock absorber action.

Shock Absorber Noisy

a. Faulty shock absorber.
b. Improper grommet installation or loose retaining nuts.

Shock Absorber Leaks Fluid

a. Faulty shock absorber.

---

d. Adjust toe-in.
e. Adjust caster and camber.
f. Replace tie rod ends.
g. Adjust relay rod joint.

a. Tighten wheel lugs.
b. Replace return springs.
c. Replace bearings according to instructions.
d. Replace brake lining and machine drums.
e. Lubricate as per instructions.

a. Clean wheel and balance assembly.
b. Replace or repair tire.
c. Replace shock absorber.

a. Disconnect shock absorber and test action, replace if necessary.
b. Inspect and correct as necessary.

a. Replace shock absorber.

BRAKES

The brakes used on both front and rear of all models are the Duo-Servo single anchor type which utilize the momentum of the vehicle to assist in the brake application. This self-energizing or self-actuating force is applied to both brake shoes at each wheel in both forward or reverse motion. The brake shoe facings are bonded to the shoes and have a total area of 120 square inches. The cast iron brake drums have a contact area of 9" in diameter by 1¾" in width. Wheel cylinders are the double piston type permitting even distribution of pressure to each brake shoe. To keep out dust and moisture, both ends of each wheel cylinder are sealed with a rubber boot. The wheel cylinders have no adjustments.

The main cylinder consists of a piston which receives mechanical pressure from the brake pedal and transmits it through the brake lines as hydraulic pressure to the wheel cylinders. The filler cap is accessible from inside the trunk compartment.

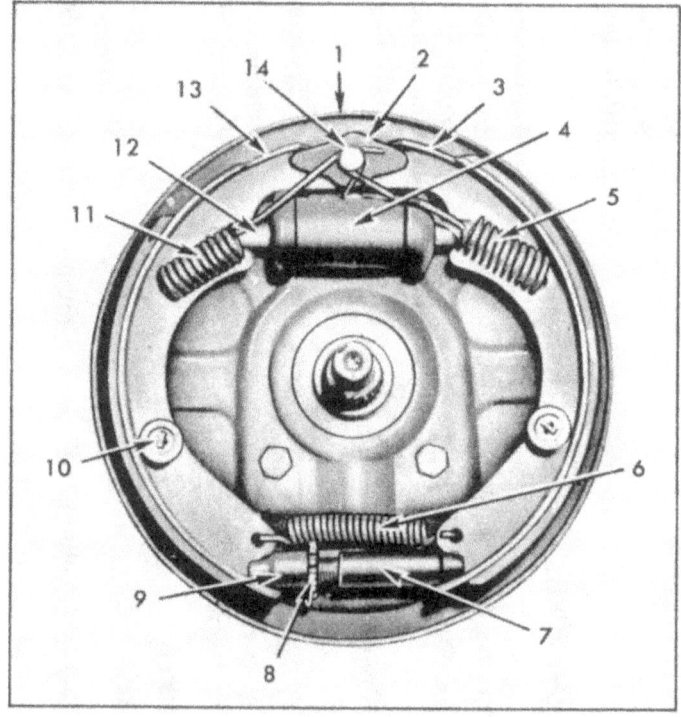

Duo-Servo Brakes

1. Flange Plate
2. Shoe Guide Plate
3. Secondary Shoe
4. Wheel Cylinder
5. Secondary Shoe Return Spring
6. Adjusting Screw Spring
7. Adjusting Screw Nut
8. Adjusting Screw
9. Adjusting Screw Socket
10. Shoe Hold Down Assembly
11. Primary Shoe Return Spring
12. Wheel Cylinder Push Rod
13. Primary Shoe
14. Anchor Pin

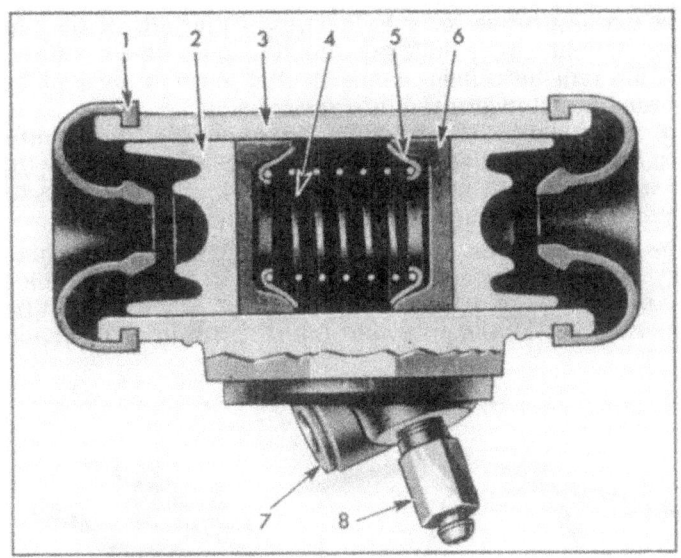

Wheel Cylinder

1. Push Rod Boot
2. Piston
3. Housing
4. Spring
5. Piston Cup Expander
6. Piston Cup
7. Fluid Inlet
8. Bleeder Valve

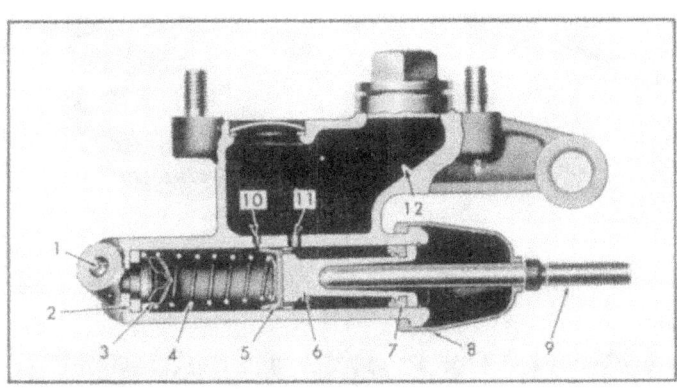

Main Cylinder

1. Outlet
2. Valve Seat
3. Valve
4. Spring
5. Primary Cup
6. Piston
7. Secondary Cup
8. Push Rod Boot
9. Push Rod
10. Compensating Port
11. Fluid Inlet
12. Fluid Level Rib

The parking brake lever is located to the left of the steering column. A cable type linkage, directed over three pulleys and routed through the tunnel, connects this lever to an equalizer at the under body forward of the transmission.

Force applied at the parking brake lever is transmitted to both right and left rear brakes by means of a single actuating cable which passes through the equalizer and is connected at each end to an actuating lever within the brake assembly.

The parking brake lever is of the single stroke rachet type and incorporates a trigger release which is located in the lever grip. For correct adjustment procedure of service and parking brakes consult **Maintenance and Adjustments** in this section.

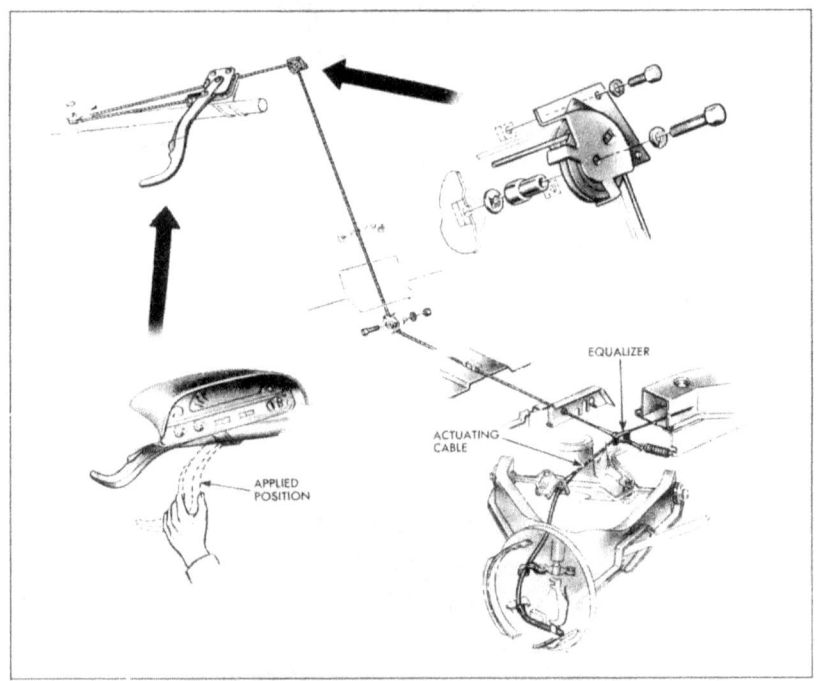

Parking Brake System

MAINTENANCE AND ADJUSTMENTS

In any service operation it is extremely important that absolute cleanliness be observed. Any foreign matter in the hydraulic system will tend to clog the lines, ruin the rubber cups of the main and wheel cylinders and cause inefficient operation or even failure of the braking system. Dirt or grease on a brake lining may cause that brake to grab first on brake application and fade out on heavy brake application.

HYDRAULIC BRAKE FLUID

Only G. M. Hydraulic Brake Fluid Super No. 11 should be

used when servicing brakes. This brake fluid is satisfactory for any climate and has all the qualities necessary for satisfactory operation, such as a high boiling point to prevent vapor lock and the ability to remain fluid at low temperatures.

In the event that improper fluid has entered the system, it will be necessary to:

1. Drain the entire system.
2. Thoroughly flush the system with clean alcohol, 188 proof, or a hydraulic system cleaning fluid, such as "Declene."
3. Replace all rubber parts of the system including brake hoses.
4. Refill the system with G. M. Hydraulic Brake Fluid Super No. 11.

BLEEDING HYDRAULIC SYSTEM

The hydraulic brake system must be bled whenever any line has been disconnected or air has in some way entered the system. The system must be absolutely free of air at all times. Bleeding should be done on the longest line first and the proper sequence to follow is left rear, right rear, right front and left front. Bleeding of brake line may be accomplished by one of two methods: Either pressure or manual.

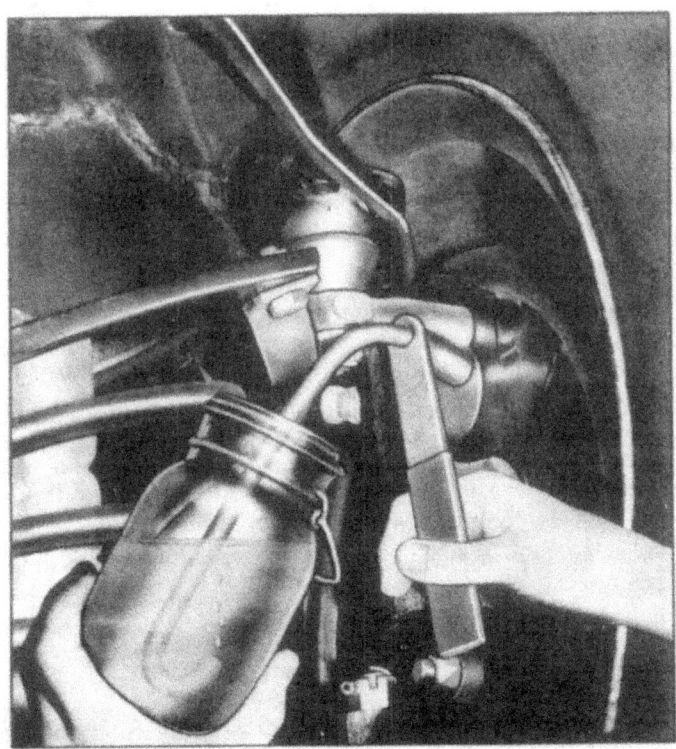

Bleeding Brakes

NOTE: Fill main cylinder reservoir only up to rib which is cast into reservoir wall.

Pressure Bleeding

1. Clean all dirt from top of main cylinder and remove filler plug.
2. Connect hose from bleeder tank to main cylinder filler opening and open valve.
   NOTE: Make sure fluid in pressure bleeder is up to operating level and that the equipment is able to exert at least 30 to 50 lbs. hydraulic pressure on the brake system.
3. Remove bleeder valve dust cover. Position one end of hose on bleeder valve, placing other end of hose in a transparent container holding sufficient fluid to cover end of hose.
4. Open bleeder valve by turning ¾ of a turn in a counter-clockwise direction and observe flow of fluid at end of bleeder hose.
5. Close bleeder valve tightly as soon as bubbles stop and fluid flows in a solid stream.
6. Remove bleeder hose.
7. Repeat operations 2 thru 6 at each wheel.

Manual Bleeding

1. Clean all dirt from top of main cylinder and remove filler plug.
2. Fill main cylinder reservoir.
3. Remove bleeder valve dust cover, position one end of hose on bleeder valve, placing other end of hose in a transparent container holding sufficient fluid to cover end of hose.
4. Open bleeder valve by turning ¾ of a turn in a counter-clockwise direction. Depress foot pedal. When pedal reaches floor close bleeder valve. Return pedal to brake released postion with valve closed. Repeat this operation until air bubbles no longer appear in discharging fluid.
5. Close bleeder valve tightly as soon as fluid flows in a solid stream.
6. Remove bleeder hose.
6. Repeat operations 2 thru 6 at each wheel.

NOTE: Fill main cylinder reservoir only up to rib which is cast into reservoir wall.

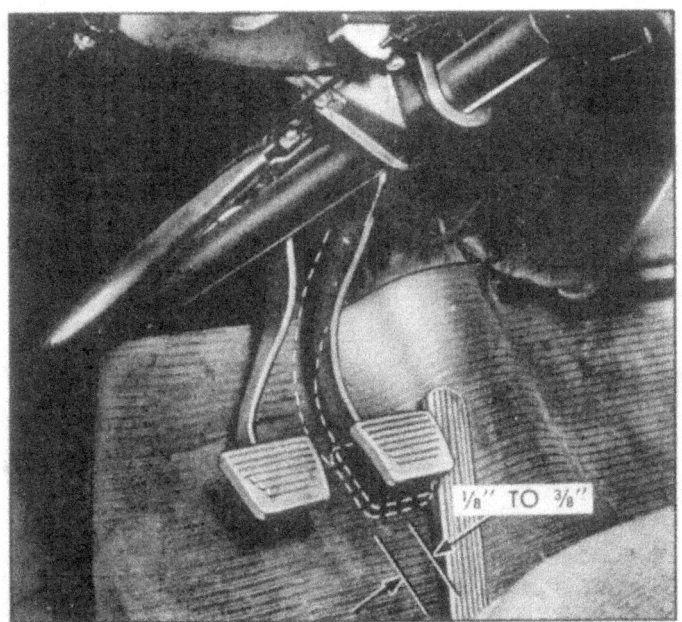

Brake Pedal Free Movement

PUSH ROD TO MAIN CYLINDER CLEARANCE

Early Models

The brake pedal has a definite stop which is permanent and not adjustable. This stop consists of a rubber bumper at the release end of pedal travel. Before adjusting push rod to main cylinder clearance, make sure pedal returns to the fully released postion freely and that the pedal retracting spring has not lost its tension, then proceed as follows:

1. Loosen check nut on the swivel.
2. Turn push rod in proper direction to secure correct adjustment. Movement of pedal pad before the push rod end contacts the main cylinder piston must be $\frac{1}{8}$" to $\frac{3}{8}$" (fig. 5-6).
3. Tighten check nut against swivel.

LATER MODELS

Later models are equipped with a nonadjustable pushrod which is set at proper clearance at factory.

HYDRAULIC BRAKE LINES

Hydraulic Brake Hose

The flexible hoses which carry the hydraulic pressure from the steel lines to the wheel cylinders are carefully designed and constructed to withstand all conditions of stress and twist which they encounter during normal vehicles usage.

The hoses require no service other than periodic inspection for damage from road hazards or other like sources. Should damage occure and replacement become necessary, the following procedure is to be followed.

Removal

1. Separate hose from steel line by turning double flare connector out of hose fitting.
2. Remove "U" shaped retainer from hose fitting and withdraw hose from support bracket.
3. Turn hose fitting out of wheel cylinder inlet.

Replacement

1. Install new copper gasket on cylinder end of hose (male end).
2. Moisten threads with brake fluid and install hose in wheel cylinder inlet.
3. With weight of car on wheel and suspension in normal position (front wheels straight ahead) pass female end of hose through support bracket, allowing hose to seek its own position. Insert hex of hose fitting into the 12 point hole in support bracket in position which induces least twist to hose.

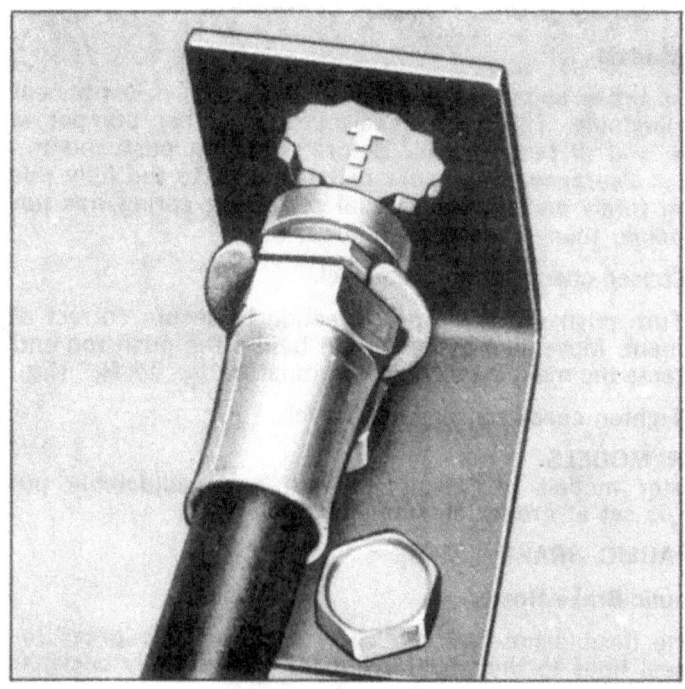

Brake Line Support Bracket

NOTE: Do not twist hose unduly during this operation as its natural curvature is absolutely necessary to maintain proper hose-to-suspension clearance through full movement of the suspension and steering parts.

4. Install "U" shaped retainer to secure hose in support bracket.

5. Inspect by removing weight completly from wheel; if working at front wheels turn steering geometry from lock to lock while observing hose position. Be sure that hose does not touch other parts at any time during suspension or geometry travel. If contact does occur remove hose retainer and rotate the female hose end in the support bracket one or two points in appropriate direction, replace retainer, and re-inspect as outlined in this paragraph.

6. Place steel tube connector in hose fitting and tighten securely.

7. Bleed all brakes as outlined in this section.

HYDRAULIC BRAKE ADJUSTMENT

Hydraulic brake adjustment is confined to a single operation on each brake assembly. A spring snap cover plate is pried from the back of the flange plate, exposing a hole through which a tool

Adjusting Brakes

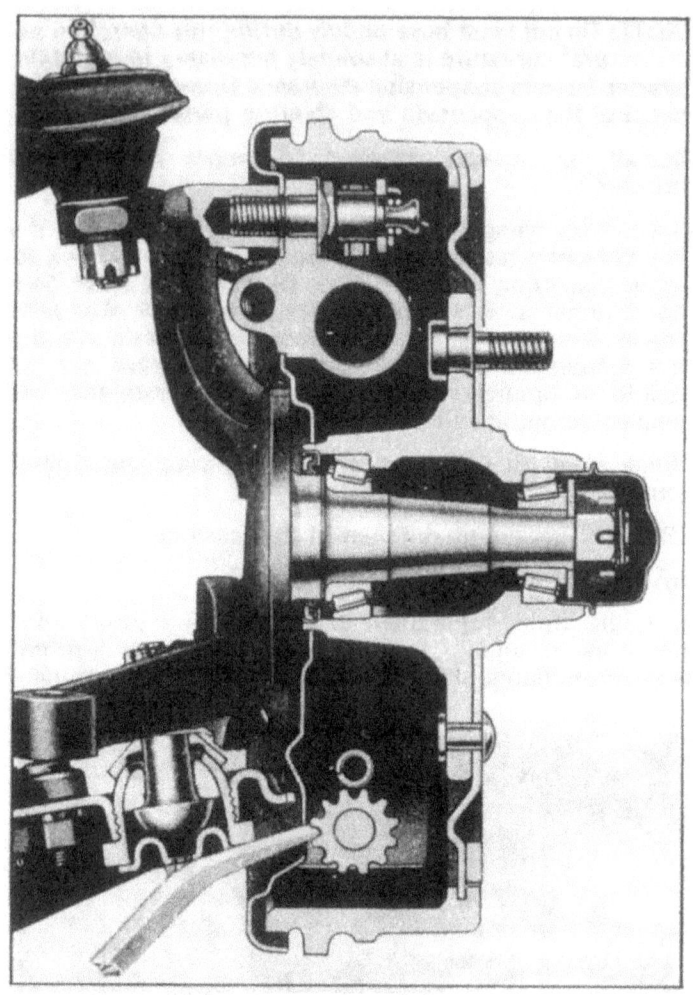

Turning Adjusting Screw Spur Wheel

is inserted to engage the spur wheel and thus turn the single adjusting screw.

Adjustment (Front or Rear)

1. Jack all wheels clear of floor.
2. On rear brakes loosen the check nut at the parking brake cable equalizer to remove tension from brake cable.

   NOTE: If cable has been adjusted too short, the rear brake shoes will be forced away from the anchor pins in brake release position, making correct shoe adjustment impossible.

3. Remove adjusting hole cover from brake flange plate. Ex-

pand brake shoes by turning adjusting screw until a heavy uniform drag is felt on the brake drum.

NOTE: Moving the outer end of tool upwards expands the shoes.

4. Turn adjusting screw back (to retract brake shoes) 12 notches on front brakes and 15 notches on rear. This will provide adequate running clearance between shoes and drums.
5. Repeat operations 3 and 4 at each wheel and replace hole covers.
6. After the hydraulic brakes are adjusted, adjust the parking brakes as outlined under "Parking Brake Adjustment."

Metallic Brake Shoe Linings

As brake shoes with this type lining require specially finished brake drums (honed to a 20 micro-inch finish), metallic facings are not recommended for service replacement on vehicles with standard brake drums that have not been honed to specified finish.

All service operations remain the same as the standard brakes, except for the adjustment and seating of the linings to the drums after replacement. New linings may be used with the old drums as is, provided surface smoothness of drum is as specified.

NOTE: Parts used to fabricate brake assemblies with metallic lining are of special heat resistant material; therefore, it is extremely important that parts designed for this usage be used, if replacement is required.

After the brakes have been adjusted to 12 notches loose on front wheels and 15 notches loose on rear wheels, the following recommended "lining seating" procedure should be accomplished:

1. Make six to eight stops from 30 mph with moderate pedal pressure to aid in seating and to modulate any tendency to dive.
2. Make six to eight complete stops from maximum legal highway speed at approximately one mile intervals, to fully seat the linings.
3. Readjust brakes as required.

PARKING BRAKE

The service brake must be properly adjusted first as a base for the parking brake adjustment.

Adjustment

1. Jack up both rear wheels.
2. Pull parking brake lever up 4 notches from fully released position.

3. Loosen the forward check nut on the equalizer and tighten the rear one until a heavy drag is felt when rear wheels are rotated.

4. Tighten check nuts securely.

5. Fully release parking brake and rotate rear wheels; no drag should be present.

Inspection

If complete release of the parking brake is not obtained when release handle is pulled, or if application effort is high, check parking brake lever assembly for free operation. If operation is sticky or a bind is experienced, correct as follows:

1. Clean and lubricate brake cables and pulleys.

    NOTE: These pulleys must be lubricated, every 10,000 miles.

2. Inspect brake lever assembly for straightness and alignment (replace if necessary).

3. Clean and lubricate parking brake lever assembly, which must operate freely.

4. Check condition and installation of return spring.

SERVICE OPERATIONS
FORWARD PARKING BRAKE CABLE

Removal

NOTE: Remove positive cable from battery to eliminate possibility of creating short circuits under dash.

1. Release parking brake.

2. Remove equalizer check nuts and separate cable stud from equalizer.

3. Remove underbody tunnel cover.

4. Remove toe pan tunnel cover.

5. Remove cable pulley from upper toe board bracket.

    NOTE: On cars equipped with manual clutch, clutch cable must be disconnected to relieve tension on pulley.

6. Remove cable ball from hand lever clevis and withdraw cable from car.

Installation

1. Thread cable through all pulley brackets, guides, and rear tunnel wall.

2. Lubricate cable ball and position in hand lever clevis.

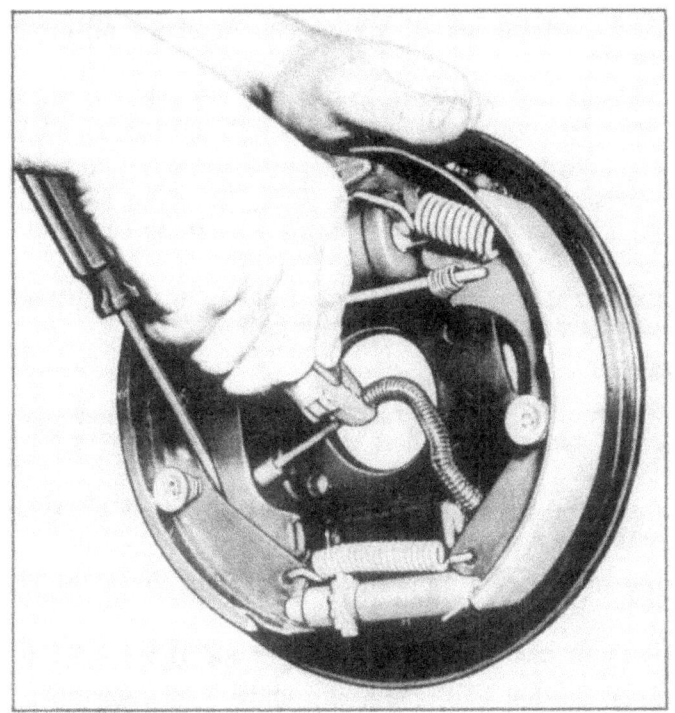

Removing Parking Brake Cable (Axle Removed for Clarity)

3. Lubricate and reinstall pulley, carefully positioning cable(s) in pulley grooves. Connect clutch cable, if so equipped.
4. Place one check nut on cable stud and insert into equalizer, then place second nut on stud.
5. Replace toe pan tunnel cover and underbody tunnel cover.

    NOTE: Attach toe pan cover with original length screws only; longer screws may puncture fuel tank.
6. Replace positive battery cable.
7. Continue as outlined under **Parking Brake—Adjustment.**

REAR PARKING BRAKE CABLE ASSEMBLY
Removal

1. Release parking brake.
2. Remove return spring.
3. Remove rear equalizer check nut and separate forward cable stud from equalizer.
4. Extract "U" clips from support brackets which are bolted to control arm pivot bars.

5. Snap conduit out of spring clip at shock absorber lower mount.
6. Remove rear wheels, brake drums and axle bearing retainer bolts and pull axle flange away from brake assembly.
7. Pry actuating lever from behind secondary brake shoe with screwdriver, then separate cable tip from actuating lever by compressing retoning spring and lifting cable tip up and out of "U" shaped junction in lever.
8. Compress expended conduit locking fingers at the flange plate entry hole and withdraw cable.

Installation

1. Pass end of cable and conduit up through flange plate entry hole, making sure that conduit locking fingers all expand fully.
2. Compress retaining spring and position cable in "U" shaped actuating lever junction.
3. Replace bearing retainer, retainer bolts, universal joint "U" bolts, brake drum and wheel.
5. Pass die cast conduit tip through support bracket and secure
4. Snap conduit into spring clip under shock absorber.
   with "U" clip.
6. Position rubber boot over conduit tip, carefully indexing bead of boot in groove provided in tip casting.
7. Place equalizer on cable and insert forward cable stud. Install check nut and return spring.

NOTE: To perform its intended function, equalizer must be free to slide on rear cable. Lubricate with chassis grease on assembly and every 5000 miles thereafter.

8. Proceed as outlined under **Parking Brake—Adjustment.**

BRAKE SHOES

In all cases of brake complaints denoting actual brake lining or shoe failure, the brake drum should be removed. Before disassembly of the shoes from the flange plate, all linings should be inspected for wear, improper alignment causing uneven wear, and oil and grease on the linings. If any of these conditions exist, it will be necessary to replace the shoes. If, in checking the linings it is noted that they have the appearance of being glazed, this is a normal condition with the hard type lining used. Do not use a wire brush or an abrasive on the lining to destroy this glazed surface as it is essential for proper operation. When brake lining replacement is necessary, all shoes and linings should be replaced. In no case should a single lining and shoe be replaced. However, in exceptional cases, it may be satisfactory to replace the shoes and linings on both front or both rear wheels.

Removal

1. Raise vehicle and place on stand jacks.
2. Loosen check nut at parking brake cable equalizer sufficiently to remove all tension from brake cable.
3. Remove rear brake drums and front hub and drum assemblies.

   NOTE: Front brake drums are non-demountable and are removed with front wheel hubs. Rear brake drums may be removed by removing rear wheel retaining nuts.

4. Unhook brake shoe pull back springs from anchor pin.

   NOTE: Since boots are recessed in grooves on wheel cylinders to prevent pistons from leaving cylinders, it is not necessary to install wheel cylinder clamps when brake shoes are removed. Brake pedal, however, must not be depressed while drums are removed.

5. Remove brake shoe hold down pins and springs.
6. Spread shoes to clear wheel cylinder connecting links and remove shoes from backing plate. Push out adjusting hole covers.

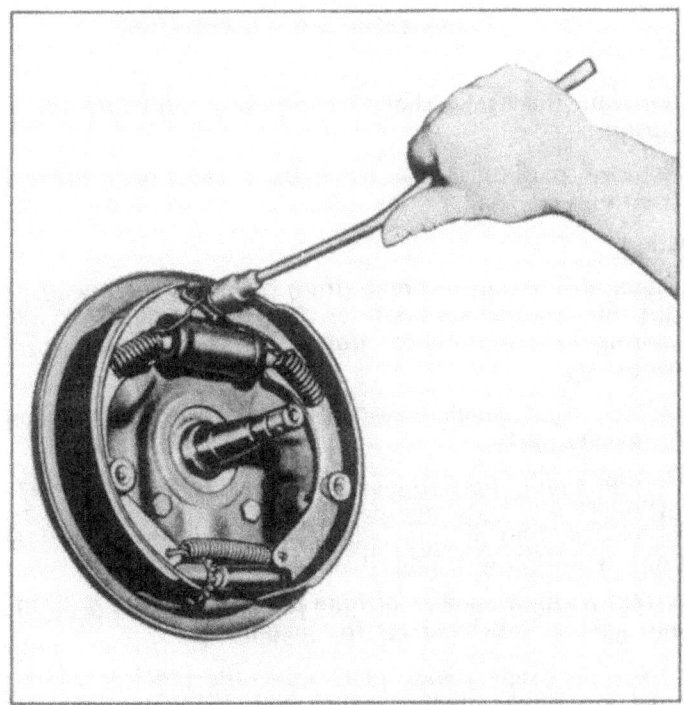

Removing Brake Shoe Return Spring

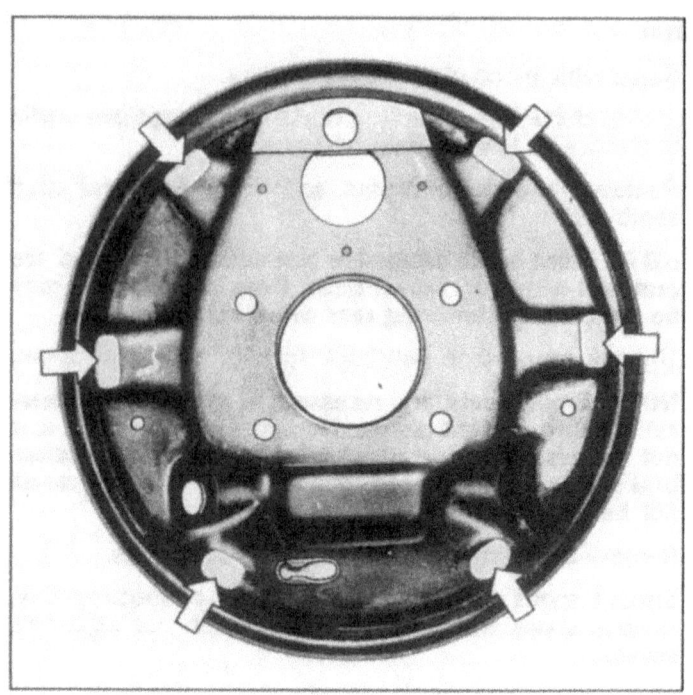

Shoe Contact Surfaces on Flange Plate

7. Separate the brake shoes by removing adjusting screw and spring.
8. Remove parking brake lever from secondary brake shoe (rear only).

Inspection

1. Clean all dirt out of brake drum using care to avoid getting dirt into front wheel bearings. Inspect drums for roughness, scoring or out-of-round. Replace or recondition drums as necessary.
2. Inspect front wheel bearings and oil seal and replace any necessary parts.
3. Carefully pull lower edges of wheel cylinder boots away from cylinders and note whether interior is wet with brake fluid. Excessive fluid at this point indicates leakage past piston cups requiring overhaul of wheel cylinder.

   NOTE: A slight amount of fluid is nearly always present and acts as lubricant for the piston.
4. Check all brake flange plate attaching bolts to make sure they are tight. Clean all rust and dirt from shoe contact faces on flange plate, using fine emery cloth.

Installation

1. Inspect new linings and make sure there are no nicks, burrs or bonding material on shoe edge where contact is made with brake flange plate.

   NOTE: Keep hands clean while handling brake shoes. Do not permit oil or grease to come in contact with linings.

2. If working on rear brakes, lubricate parking brake cable.

3. On rear brakes only, lubricate fulcrum end of parking brake lever and the pin with Bendix or Delco brake lube or Lubriplate, then attach lever to secondary shoe with pivot pin, wave washer, and tru-arc retainer ring. Make sure that lever moves freely.

4. Lubricate threads and socket end of adjusting screw with Bendix or Delco brake lube or Lubriplate.

5. Connect brake shoes together with adjusting screw spring, then place adjusting screw, socket and nut in position. **CAUTION: The socket and adjusting screw must be adjacent to the primary shoe (front) on the left side and adjacent to the secondary shoe (rear) on the right side.**

6. Attach brake shoes to brake flange plate with the hold down pin-spring-washer assemblies; at the same time engage shoes with wheel cylinder connecting links. The primary shoe (short lining) goes forward.

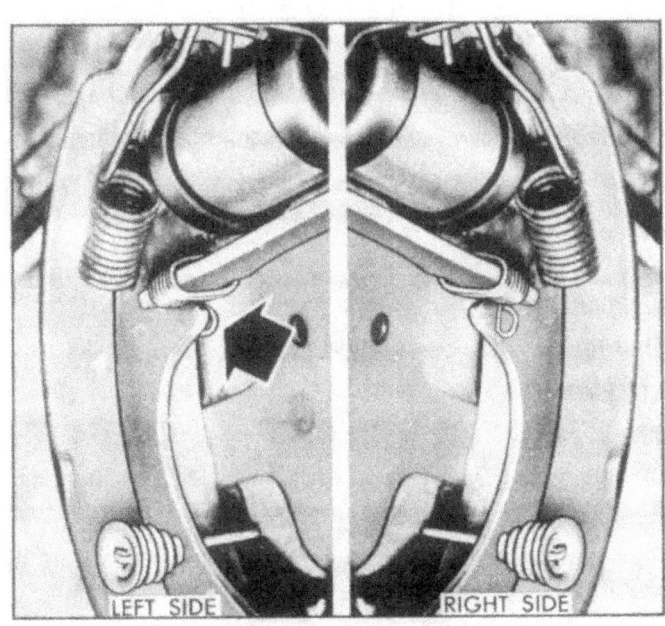

Parking Brake Strut Anti-Rattle Spring

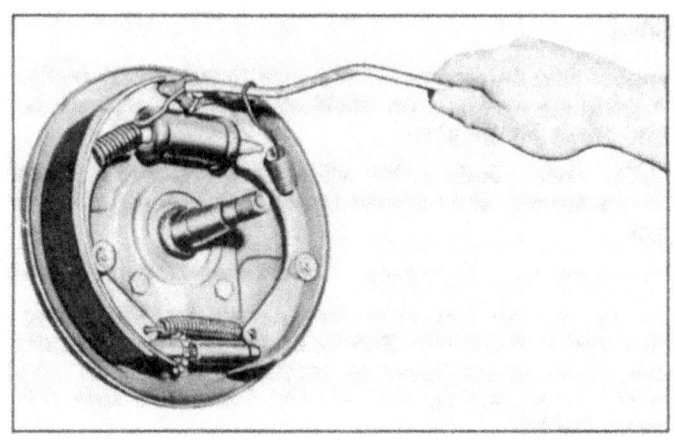

Installing Brake Shoe Return Spring

7. On rear brakes, connect parking brake lever to secondary shoe and install strut between lever and primary shoe as installation is made. The small extended loop on the strut anti-rattle spring is installed as illustrated.

8. Install guide plate over anchor pin. Install springs on shoes and position spring hooks over anchor pin. Springs should be replaced if they appear distorted or if strength is doubtful.

9. Pry shoes away from backing plate and lubricate shoe contact surfaces with a thin coating of Bendix or Delco brake lube or Lubriplate. On rear wheels, sparingly apply this same lubricant where brake cable contacts flange plate.

    CAUTION: Be careful to keep lubricant off facings.

10. Install brake drums. Whenever working on front brakes, lubricate and adjust wheel bearings. Install front and rear wheel tire assemblies.

11. Adjust all brakes and brake cables as outlined under 'Maintenance and Adjustments."

12. Thoroughly test operation of brakes.

MAIN CYLINDER

Removal

1. Disconnect hydraulic lines from outlet end of cylinder.

2. Remove pedal return spring.

3. Remove the three retaining nuts and lockwashers holding main cylinder to dash wall.

4. Removel cylinder-pedal assembly from car.

NOTE: Considerable caution will be required at this point to prevent staining the car interior with brake fluid. Protect floor mat, seats, etc., with suitable cover. It is further suggested that the lines removed from the main cylinder be capped if the wheel cylinders are to be disturbed.

Disassembly

1. Remove push rod assembly from boot end of main cylinder.
2. Remove boot from end of main cylinder.
3. Remove piston stop snap ring, secondary cup and piston from main cylinder.
4. Remove the primary cup, spring, valve assembly and valve seat.
5. Remove filler plug from top of main cylinder.

Inspection

1. Wash all parts in clean alcohol. Make sure that compensating port in main cylinder body and bleeder holes in piston are clean and open.

    NOTE: Before washing parts, hands must be clean. Do not wash hands in gasoline or fuel oil before cleaning parts. Use soap and water to clean hands.

2. Inspect cylinder bore to make sure it is smooth.

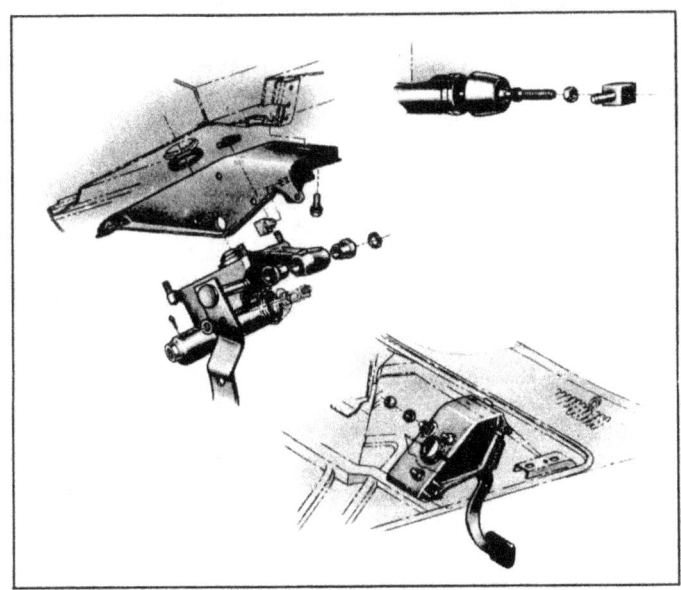

Main Cylinder Assembly Removal

3. Inspect primary and secondary cups, valve and valve seat for damage or swelling. Swelling of rubber parts is due to the use of improper brake fluid or washings parts in gasoline or kerosene.

   NOTE: The primary cup has a brass support ring vulcanized in its base to prevent it from imbedding in the bleeder holes during braking action.

4. Check piston fit in cylinder bore. The clearance between piston and wall of the cylinder should be from .001"-.005".

TROUBLES AND REMEDIES
BRAKE SYSTEM

Symptom and Probable Cause	Probable Remedy
Pedal Spongy	
a. Air in brake lines.	a. Bleed brakes.
All Brakes Drag	
a. Mineral oil in system.	a. Flush entire brake system and replace all rubber parts.
b. Improper push rod-to-main cylinder piston clearance.	b. Adjust clearance.
c. Compensating port in main cylinder restricted.	c. Overhaul main cylinder.
One Brake Drags	
a. Loose or damaged wheel bearings.	a. Adjust or replace wheel bearings.
b. Weak, broken or unhooked brake shoe return spring.	b. Replace retractor spring.
c. Insufficient running clearance between brake shoes and drum.	c. Correctly adjust brakes.
d. Incorrect parking brake adjustment.	d. Readjust parking brake at equalizer.
e. Damaged or frozen parking brake cable.	e. Free-up or replace brake cable assy.
Excessive Pedal Travel	
a. Normal lining wear or improper shoe adjustment.	a. Adjust brakes.
b. Fluid low in main cylinder.	b. Fill main cylinder as outlined under "Main Cylinder-Installation."
Brake Pedal Applies Brake but Pedal Gradually Goes to Floor Board	
a. External leaks.	a. Check main cylinder, lines and wheel cylinder for leaks and make necessary repairs.
b. Main cylinder leaks past primary cup.	b. Overhaul main cylinder.
Brakes Uneven	
a. Grease on linings.	a. Clean brake mechanism; replace lining and correct cause of grease getting on lining.
b. Tires improperly inflated.	b. Inflate tires to correct pressure.
c. Front suspension faulty.	c. thoroughly check and adjust all front suspension components.
Excessive Pedal Pressure Required, Poor Brakes	
a. Grease, mud or water on linings.	a. Remove drums—clean and dry linings or replace.
b. Full area of linings not contacting drums.	b. Free up shoe linkage, sand linings or replace shoes.
c. Scored brake drums.	c. Turn drums and install new linings.
Brake Pedal Hop or Chatter	
a. Brake drums warped.	a. Replace drums.

ENGINE

The 1960 Turbo-Air horizontal-opposed air cooled six cylinder engine has a compression ration of 8.0:1 and a displacement of 140 cubic inches, with a 3⅜" bore and a 2.60" stroke. The 1961 (and later) engine is enlarged to 145 cubic inches via a 3 7/16" bore. 2.60" stroke.

The cast aluminum alloy crankcase is vertically divided into two halves which are held together by bolts at the parting line. Each crankcase half has three pilot openings for individual cast iron cylinders which are positioned to the opening by means of four long studs at each cylinder. These studs pass freely through the cylinder head and serve to secure the cylinders and head to the crankcase.

The two opposing and identical cast aluminum cylinder heads incorporate cooling fins and integral intake manifolds and contain wedge-shaped combustion chambers and valves for each cylinder. The valves are actuated by push rods through stamped rocker arms similar to convential Chevrolet V-8 engines. Steel alloy valve seat inserts are provided for durability.

Engine Top View Cross-Section

Engine Cross-Section Across Crankshaft

Starting mid 1961 and carried over to 1962, Monza 9-1 compression ratio engines use a cylinder head with a revised combustion chamber consisting of filled in roof surfaces around the valves and spark plug holes.

Steel tubes are used to house the push rods in the open area between the crankcase and cylinder heads adjacent to the cylinders. These tubes serve to protect the exposed push rods as well as drain back oil from the cylinder heads to a relatively shallow oil pan bolted to the bottom of the crankcase.

The alloy cast iron camshaft, which actuates the push rods through hydraulic lifters, is nested between the two halves of the crankcase below the crankshaft. This camshaft deviates from a convential camshaft design in that each of three exhaust valve lobes are twice the width of the intake valve lobes and actuate a pair of exhaust valve lifters. The camshaft journals ride directly on the machined base metal of the crankcase. Thrust of the camshaft is taken by a thrust washer, located between the camshaft gear and front bearing.

A forged steel crankshaft is housed above the camshaft between the split halves of the crankcase. The crankshaft has six throws arranged in pairs, each crankpin being removed 180°

from the other member of its pair. Pairs are located 60° apart. No separate main bearing caps are required since the four steel-backed babbit bearings are supported entirely by the crankcase halves. The crankshaft drives the camshaft through a composite gear and drive hub. The front crankshaft seal is installed to the cast aluminum clutch housing (or flywheel housing) which mounts to the front of crankcase assembly.

Pistons are the convential flat head aluminum alloy type with cast in steel struts. Each piston is coated with a light tin plate and utilizes two compression rings and a two piece oil control ring. The piston pin is a press fit in the connecting rod. All connecting rod bearings are steel-backed babbitt inserts.

The cast aluminum engine rear housing mounts to the rear of the crankcase over four free fitting long studs. This housing contains the oil pump, crankshaft seal and primary oil passages. It provides a mounting for the distributor and the generator adapter to which the fuel pump, oil fill pipe, generator, oil filter and idler pulley are mounted.

A rectangular aluminum crankcase cover mounts to the top of the crankcase and forms a base for the centrifugal blower.

Engine Mounting

The engine-transmission-axle is mounted as a unit to the chassis on a three-point mounting system at the rear of the vehicle. The two shear-type front mounts secure the transmission to the rear crossmember, while the single shear type mount centered at the rear of the engine secures the engine to the body. The engine is sealed in its compartment against entrance of road dust and dirt from below.

Cylinder Numbering and Firing Order

The front of the engine in the installed position is the flywheel end. Engine rotation, as viewed from the rear of the vehicle, is counterclockwise. Cylinders are numbered from the rear of the engine. The right rear cylinder is No. 1 and the left rear cylinder is No. 2. Thus reading in order from the rear, the right bank is numbered 1, 3 and 5 and the left bank 2, 4 and 6.

The cylinder firing order is 1-4-5-2-3-6.

Lubrication System

Oil in the oil pan sump is drawn through the sump pick-up tube and screen assembly and forced through the lubrication system by a spur gear pressure type pump, which is driven by the end of the distributor shaft. A spring loaded pressure regulator located in the engine rear housing, regulates the maximum pressure of the lubrication system to 35 psi.

All the oil discharged by the oil pump enters a passage (16) formed by cast hollows in the rear of the crankcase and adjacent front face of the engine rear housing. The oil then travels up to the top of the crankcase (10) where it enters a full flow oil filter (7) (disposable cartridge type). The oil filter incorporates a 10 psi filter by-pass valve (9), which by-passes the filter cartridge, if the filter becomes plugged.

Leaving the oil filter, oil passes through an air-cooled oil cooler (22). The oil cooler also incorporates a 10 psi by-pass valve (4). Oil leaving the oil cooler enters another gallery (17) formed by the crankcase and rear housing, and then passes on to the main oil galleries.

The main oil galleries which are parallel passages running longitudinally through the crankcase, intersect the valve lifter openings and act as valve lifter oil galleries as well as main oil galleries. The four main bearings and four camshaft bearings are supplied with oil at full system pressure through holes drilled in the crankcase. With rear bearings designated as No. 1 the right bank main oil gallery flows to No. 1 and 3 main bearings and No. 1, 3 and 4 camshaft bearings. The left bank main oil gallery flows to No. 2 and 4 main bearings and No. 2 camshaft bearing.

Oil is carried from the main oil gallery through lubricating holes in the main bearings and crankshaft journals, then through the crankshaft to the connecting rod journals and bearings. Overspray from the connecting rod bearings lubricates the cylinder bores and pistons.

Front main bearing oil also lubricates the timing gears, which are enclosed by the front end of the crankcase and the rear side of the flywheel housing. Lubrication for the timing gears is accomplished by overspray oil from the front main bearing and camshaft bearing.

The main oil galleries supply oil directly to the hydraulic valve lifters, which in turn supply the hollow push rods. A lubri-

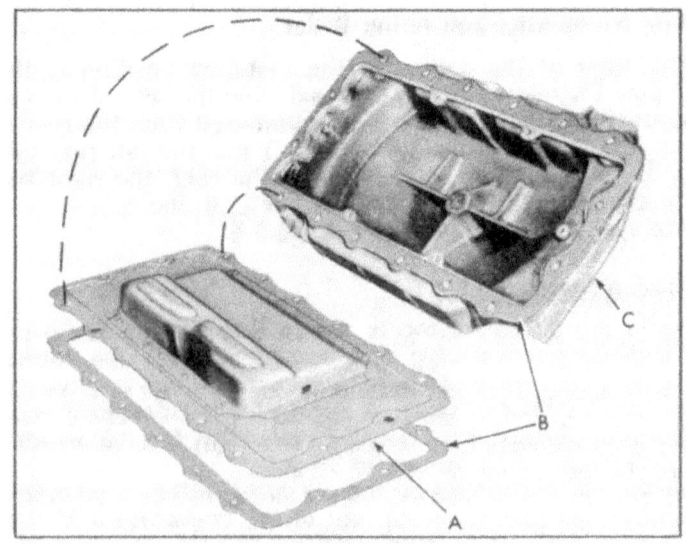

Crankcase Cover and Vent Assembly

A. Crankcase Vent
B. Gaskets
C. Crankcase Cover

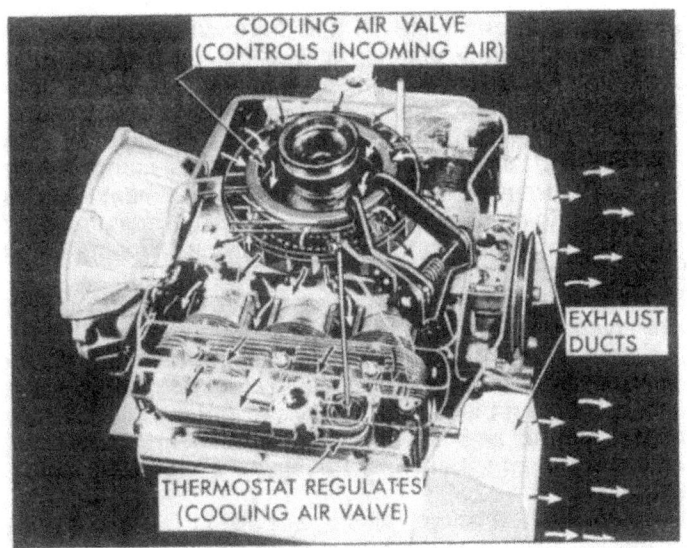

Engine Cooling System

cating hole in the upper side of each push rod allows oil to spray out the side of the push rod into the valve spring and valve stem area. The tappet rotates and in turn rotates the push rod which sprays the valve chamber. The through hole of the push rod indexes once during every revolution with the hole in the rocker arm, sending oil upwards to the rocker arm ball, which in turn carries oil to the rocker arms, rocker arm studs, and valve stems.

The fill pipe fits into the oil filter and generator adapter. Oil being added to the system drains between the rear housing and the crankcase into the oil pan. The oil level gauge fits into its tube at the right rear side of the engine.

Crankcase Venting

A vent tube is provided which passes out of the crankcase cover on top of the engine, then out on the right hand side and downward. The oil separator or crankcase vent, is basically a louvered plate with a separating chamber spot welded to the upper side. It is assembled between gaskets and mounted between the crankcase cover and crankcase.

Cooling System

The engine is entirely shrouded with sheet metal pieces attached directly to the engine to form a plenum chamber.

A centrifugal blower, mounted to the top of the crankcase cover, spins on a vertical shaft to deliver cooling air outward and downward over the cylinders and cylinder heads. The air then enters a duct under each bank from where it travels rearward to be exhausted at openings at the rear of the engine.

The rate of engine cooling is regulated by a bellows type thermostat mounted in the lower part of each engine lower shroud and exhaust duct. The exhaust duct damper doors in the exhaust duct are controlled by the thermostat to start opening at 195°F. and are fully opened at 210° F. In normal operation, exhaust duct damper door angles will vary between full open and closed to maintain engine temperatures in operating range.

The cooling air thermostat (with expanded convolutions) is filled with Butyl Alcohol under vacuum, thus compressing the bellows. In the event of a failed thermostat, atmospheric pressure is equalized and the bellows returns to its normal position(expanded), automatically bringing the damper cooling air doors to full open position.

The engine front shrouds have openings for heater installation and are covered when heater is not installed.

The blower, which runs on a sealed, permanently lubricated ball bearing, is belt driven by a pulley mounted at the extreme rear end of the crankshaft. A generator drive pulley at the left rear of the engine and an idler pulley at the right rear provide a means of changing belt direction from a vertical plane at the blower pulley.

An oil cooler, through which a portion of the cooling air passes before discharge, is mounted above the air exhaust duct near the left rear corner of the engine.

MAINTENANCE AND ADJUSTMENTS

VALVE LASH ADJUSTMENT — (ENGINE RUNNING)

> NOTE: To catch excess oil, cut a discared valve cover to 1/3 its normal size, which can be used as a trough.

1. Remove valve cover and install oil trough at the bottom of the cylinder head to catch any oil that may run out.

2. With the engine normalized and running at idle, back up valve rocker arm nut (one at a time) until the valve rocker starts to clatter against the valve, then turn the valve rocker nut down until the clatter of the valve rocker arm is **just** stopped.

3. Turn off the engine and turn down each valve rocker arm nut exactly ¾ of a turn.

   NOTE: On Super Turbo-Air engines turn nut exactly 1¼ turn.

   This will set the plunger of the hydraulic lifter in the center of its operating travel.

   NOTE: Adjustment procedure is the same for both cylinder heads.

4. Install valve rocker covers with new cover gaskets. Torque valve rocker covers 30 to 50 inch pounds.

Valve Lash Adjustment — Engine Running — 1962

1. After the engine has been normalized, remove valve cover and install a reworked valve cover (cut the top out of a used

valve cover) and gasket on cylinder heads to prevent oil from running out.

2. With the engine running at idle, back off valve rocker arm nut until the valve rocker arm starts to clatter.

3. Turn nut down ¼ additional turn and pause 10 seconds until engine runs smoothly. Repeat additional ¼ turns, pausing 10 seconds each time, until nut has been turned down 1 full turn from the zero lash position.

   NOTE: This 1 turn pre-load adjustment must be done slowly to allow the lifter to adjust itself to prevent the possibility of interference, between the inlet valve head and top of piston, which might result in internal damage and/or bent push rods. Noisy lifters should be replaced.

5. Repeat Steps 2, 3 and 4 to adjust the rest of the valves.

6. Remove reworked cover and install valve cover, using new gasket.

HYDRAULIC VALVE LIFTERS

Hydraulic valve lifters very seldom require attention. The lifters are extremely simple in design, readjustments are not necessary, and servicing of the lifters require only that care and cleanliness be exercised in the handling of parts.

The easiest method for locating a noisy valve lifter is by use of a piece of garden hose approximately four feet in length. Place one end of the hose near the end of each intake and exhaust valve with the other end of the hose to the ear.

In this manner, the sound is localized making it easy to determine which lifter is at fault.

Another method is to place a finger on the face of the valve spring retainer. If the lifter is not functioning properly, a distinct shock will be felt when the valve returns to its seat.

The general types of valve lifter noises are as follows:

1. **Hard Rapping Noise**—Usually caused by the plunger becoming tight in the bore of the lifter body to such an extent that the return spring can no longer push the plunger back up to working position. Probable causes are:

   a. Excessive varnish or carbon deposit causing abnormal stickiness.

   b. Galling or "pick-up" between plunger and bore of lifter body, usually caused by an abrasive piece of dirt or metal wedging between plunger and lifter body.

2. **Moderate Rapping Noise** — Probable causes are:

   a. Excessive high leakdown rate.

   b. Leaky check valve seat.

c. Improper lash adjustment.

3. **General Noise Throughout the Valve Train** — This will, in almost all cases, be a definite indication of insufficient oil supply, or improper lash adjustment.

4. **Intermittent Clicking** — Probable causes are:

   a. A microscopic piece of dirt momentarily caught between ball seat and check valve ball.

   b. In rare cases, the ball itself may be out-of-round or have a flat spot.

   c. Improper Lash adjustment.

In most cases where noise exists in one or more lifters, all lifter units should be removed, cleaned in a solvent, reassembled, and reinstalled in the engine. If dirt, varnish, carbon, etc. is shown to exist in one unit, it more than likely exists in all the units, thus it would only be a matter of time before all lifters caused trouble.

In instances where parts are damaged, particularly the plunger or lifter body, the complete lifter unit should be replaced. However, in rare or emergency cases an Arkansas hard stone may be used to remove metal scatches or humps; and if after correcting the plunger will operate freely in the lifter body, the parts may be thoroughly cleaned and the unit assembled and installed.

A few precautions to follow when servicing the valve lifter are:

1. Plungers are not interchangeable, they are a selective fit at the factory. Should a plunger or lifter body become damaged, it is necessary to replace the whole unit.

2. The plunger must be free in the lifter body. A simple test for this is to be sure the plunger will drop of its own weight in the body.

3. There must be no excessive leakdown and there must be no ball check valve leakage.

ENGINE CLEANLINESS

Engine cleanliness is very important, oil leaks or contaminants within the engine shrouding in the engine compartment may result in objectionable fumes within the passenger compartment.

Sources of all such leaks should be promptly corrected and the area thoroughly cleaned.

Areas of suspicion would be push rod oil drain tubes at their seals, oil cooler seals and oil cooler adapter gasket, oil filter gaskets, oil filter and generator adapter gasket, valve rocker cover gaskets, engine top cover gaskets, crankcase ventilator tube seal and gasket, cylinder head gaskets, engine cylinder gaskets, engine rear housing gasket, ignition timer distributor gasket, and exhaust manifold sleeve gaskets.

Oil or grease should not be left on engine or engine shrouding after service operations, as this condition tends to accum-

Oil Cooler Access Hole Cover

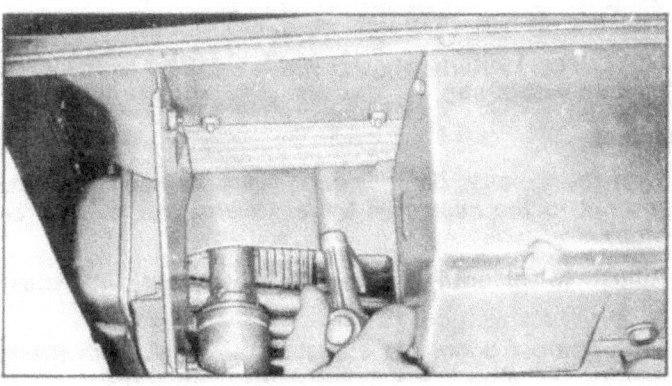

Removing Foreign Matter from Oil Cooler

ulate foreign material deposits causing objectionable fumes that could be forced into the passenger compartment.

Since the cylinder and cylinder head fins are cooled directly by the air forced over them by the blower, it is important that they be kept clean and free of foreign matter.

The cooling fins can be cleaned with the use of an air gun, after removing the engine lower shrouds.

Every 5000 miles — Remove oil cooler access cover and brush or blow out accumulated dirt.

NOTE: Material usually found in the oil cooler consists primarily of twigs, straw, chaff, and leaves.

Cleaning Oil Cooler

1. Remove oil cooler access hole cover and brush foreign particles away from oil cooler fins.

2. With the oil cooler access hole cover removed, insert an air

hose gun under oil cooler and blow up through oil cooler fin.
NOTE: Hold exhaust door open with a block of wood.

3. Replace oil cooler access hole cover.

COOLING SYSTEM EXHAUST DUCT DAMPER

In the event of a failed thermostat bellows, the exhaust damper door will remain in the open position allowing a maximum air flow over the engine to prevent overheating. Recirculating slots are located in each exhaust duct for circulating warm air into the engine compartment.

When installing a new thermostat, it is necessary to adjust the exhaust duct damper door opening to provide the correct air flow. This adjustment should be made with the exhaust duct assembly installed on the engine.

NOTE: The thermostat rod is attached to the thermostat bellows by threads. The thermostat is fastened securely to the thermostat mounting bracket with a nut. The damper door actuating rod is provided with flats to attach a wrench when tightening rod to thermostat.

NOTE: The 1960 thermostat rod is retained to the thermostat bellows with a clip

Adjustment

1. With the exhaust damper door full open, pull the actuating rod out to the maximum travel (thermostat against bracket stop).
2. Adjust swivel until it enters damper door and retain with clip.
3. Both damper doors are adjusted the same, with thermostat against the stop bracket, measure from the flat of damper door edge to the exhaust duct upper edge. This opening should measure approximately 2 11/32".

NOTE: Thermostat can be installed by attaching it to actuating rod and bracket, then insert the thermostat, bracket and actuating rod through the exhaust duct damper door opening.

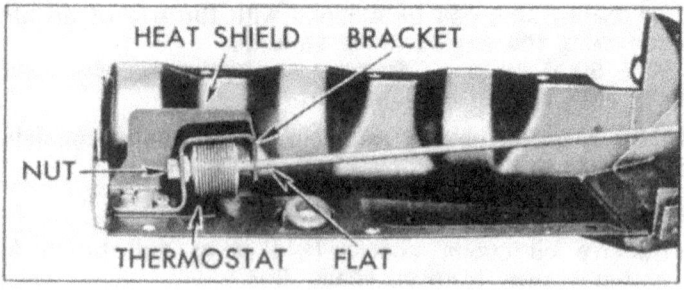

Cooling Air Exhaust Door Thermostat

Adjustment

1. With the swivel inserted into the hinge lever, pull up on the thermostat rod until the bellows is stopped within its mounting bracket.
2. Measure the opening of the cooling air valve as shown and adjust swivel to produce a 1½ inch opening. This measurement is to be made below the center line of the air horn.

   NOTE: Do not pull upon edge of cooling air throttle valve while making this adjustment, pull on thermostat rod only.

   NOTE: If the thermostat rod is pulled up after the thermostat touches the stop the thermostat rod can be removed from the retaining clip.

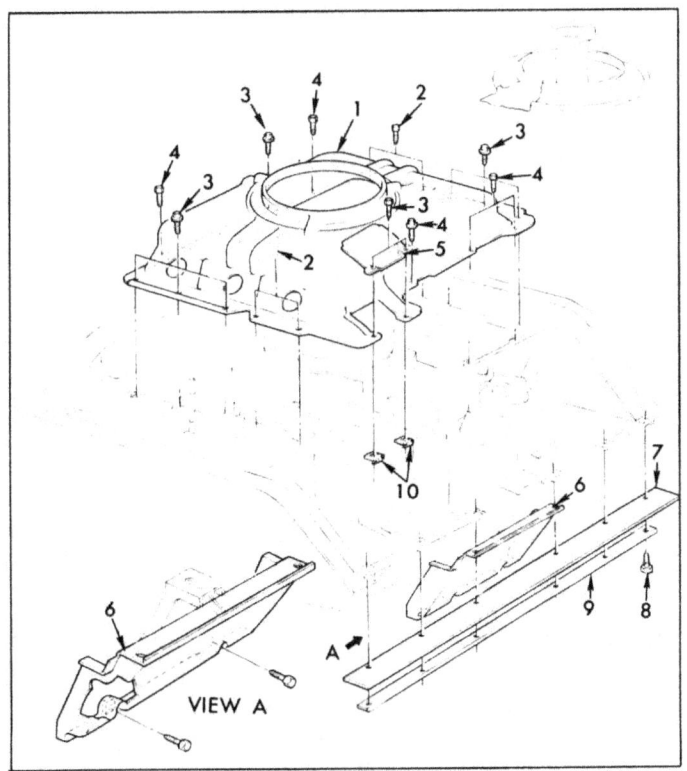

Engine Upper Shroud Assembly, Rear Shield and Center Shroud

1. Upper Shroud Assembly
2. Bolt
3. Bolt
4. Screw
5. Oil Cooler Access Hole Cover
6. Rear Shield
7. Seal
8. Screw
9. Seal Retainer
10. U-Nuts

ENGINE 6A-10

ENGINE SERVICE REFERENCE GUIDE

Some service operations can be done either in or out of the vehicle. Items in the left column printed in boldface letters, indicate service operations that require removal of the power train from vehicle. The most practical method should be followed, depending on the conditions involved.

REMOVE THESE PARTS FOR EASY ACCESS WHEN SERVICING THESE PARTS → / Item to be Replaced or Serviced	Drain Crankcase	Rear Grille	Rear Center Shield	Rear Mount	Remove Engine	See Engine Disassembly	Air Cleaner	Accelerator Linkage	Air Horn Support	Carburetor Cross Shaft	Wire Harness	Fuel Lines	Carburetor	Vacuum Balance Tube	Blower Belt	Thermostat	Upper Shroud	Spark Plugs	Blower and Pulley	Crankcase Cover	Coil Right Bank Only	Side Shield Left	Side Shield Right	Lower Shroud Left	Lower Shroud Right	Valve Cover	Rocker Arms	Rocker Studs	Push Rods	Push Rod Guides	Push Rod Tubes	Exhaust Manifold	Cylinder Head	Cylinder	Fuel Pump	Generator	Oil Filter	Oil Filter & Gen. Adpt.	Crankshaft Pulley	Skid Plate	Oil Pan	Oil Cooler	Exhaust Duct Left	Exhaust Duct Right	Rear Shroud Left	Rear Shroud Right	Front Shroud Left	Front Shroud Right	Front Shield	Oil Cooler Adapter	See Comment Procedure
Bearings	•					•																																												
Crankshaft	•				•	•																																												
Connecting Rod					•	•																																												
Blower Bearing			•																																															
Camshaft	•				•	•																																												
Carburetor							•	•	•	•																																								
Connecting Rod							•	•	•	•	•	•	•																																					
Crankshaft	•				•	•	•	•	•	•	•	•	•																																					
Crankshaft Pulley																			•																				•											
Crankcase Cover & Vent.		•	•		•		•	•	•	•	•	•	•	•	•	•	•	•	•	•																														
Cylinder (Left Bank)							•	•	•	•	•	•	•									•		•		•	•	•	•	•	•	•	•	•																
Cylinder (Right Bank)		•	•		•		•	•	•	•	•	•	•										•		•	•	•	•	•	•	•	•	•	•																
Cylinder Head (Left Bank)										•		•										•		•		•	•	•	•	•	•	•	•																	
Cylinder Head (Right Bank)		•	•		•					•		•									•		•		•		•	•	•	•	•	•	•																	
Exhaust Manifold			•																													•																		
Flywheel Housing					•																																													
Front Mounts					•																																													
Fuel Pump Eccentric																																																		
Fuel Pump Push Rod																																				•														
Gaskets																																																		
Cylinder Head (Left)																																																		
Cylinder Head (Right)																																																		
Crankcase Cover & Vent.																																																		
Exhaust Manifold																																																		
Flywheel Housing		•	•	•																																														
Rear Housing		•	•	•																																														
Oil Filter & Gen. Adapter		•	•	•																																														
Oil Cooler Adapter		•	•	•																																														
Oil Pump Cover																																																		
Oil Fan																																																		
Valve Rocker Cover																																																		•

REMOVE THESE PARTS FOR EASY ACCESS WHEN SERVICING THESE PARTS																																																		
Gears																																																		
Camshaft Drive	•	•	•		•	•																																												
Crankshaft	•	•	•		•	•																																												
Distributor Drive	•	•	•		•	•																																												
Oil Cooler																																										•									
Piston	•	•	•	•			•	•	•	•	•	•	•	•	•	•	•	•	•	•	•	•	•	•	•	•	•	•	•	•	•	•	•	•																	
Piston Rings	•	•	•	•			•	•		•	•	•	•	•				•			•		•		•	•	•	•	•	•	•	•	•	•																	•
Push Rods	•																									•	•		•																						
Rear Housing	•	•	•		•	•																																												
Seals																																																		
Flywheel Housing	•	•	•		•	•																																												
Rear Housing	•	•	•		•	•																																												
Push Rod Drain Tube	•																									•	•	•	•	•	•																				
Rocker Arm Ball Stud																										•	•	•																							
Spark Plugs											•							•																																	
Sending Unit																																																		
Oil Pressure																									•																										
Oil Temperature	•																								•																										
Suction Screen and Tube	•																																								•										
Thermostat and Cooling Air Valve							•	•	•	•														•																											
Valve Rocker Arms																										•	•																								
Valve Rocker Studs																										•	•	•																							
Valve Lifter																										•	•	•	•	•	•																				
Engine Sheet Metal																																																		
Engine Front Shield												•		•																																			•		
Engine Upper Assembly							•	•	•	•	•	•	•	•	•	•	•																																		
Engine Side Shield (Left)																						•																													
Engine Side Shield (Right)																					•		•																												
Engine Rear Shroud (Left)																																										•	•		•						
Engine Rear Shroud (Right)																																												•		•					
Engine Lower Shroud																								•	•																										
Engine Front Shroud (Left)																								•								•															•				
Engine Front Shroud (Right)																									•							•																•			
Cooling Exhaust Duct (Left)																																											•								
Cooling Exhaust Duct (Right)																					•																							•							

CHART KEY: Column on left indicates item to be serviced. Column on the top indicates item to be removed in sequence to perform service operation listed in the left column.

EXAMPLE: To Service Exhaust Manifold.
- Remove Lower Shroud
- Remove Exhaust Manifold

POWER TRAIN

The 'Corvair" power train consists of a horizontally-opposed, air-cooled six-cylinder engine integrated with a Transaxle to form a compact unit.

The standard driveline is a manual shift three speed transmission coupled with a 3.27:1 rear axle. Optional transmissions include a four-speed transmission and an automatic transmission. 3.55:1 ratio rear axle is available with any of the transmissions, 3.89 with either manual.

As illustrated, the transmission is separated from the engine by the differential carrier (rear axle). In relation to their installed positions, the transmission is toward the front of the vehicle and the engine is at the rear.

Tracing the power flow engine torque is transmitted to the transmission by means of a shaft from the clutch which runs axially through the pinion shaft. The torque is then multiplied in the transmission or passed on in the same ratio to the rear axle pinion which is splined to the transmission shaft. From this point, the power flow is conventional as the pinion drives a ring gear bolted to a differential which drives the axle shafts through its side gears.

An essentially alike power flow results with the optional automatic transmission version, the major exceptions being that a torque converter is mounted at the clutch location and two shafts run from the converter to the Powerglide unit. Considering the turbine shaft as functionally comparable to the clutch shaft except that it is hollow, the second shaft is necessary to drive the front pump of the automatic transmission.

Schematic Driveline Diagram

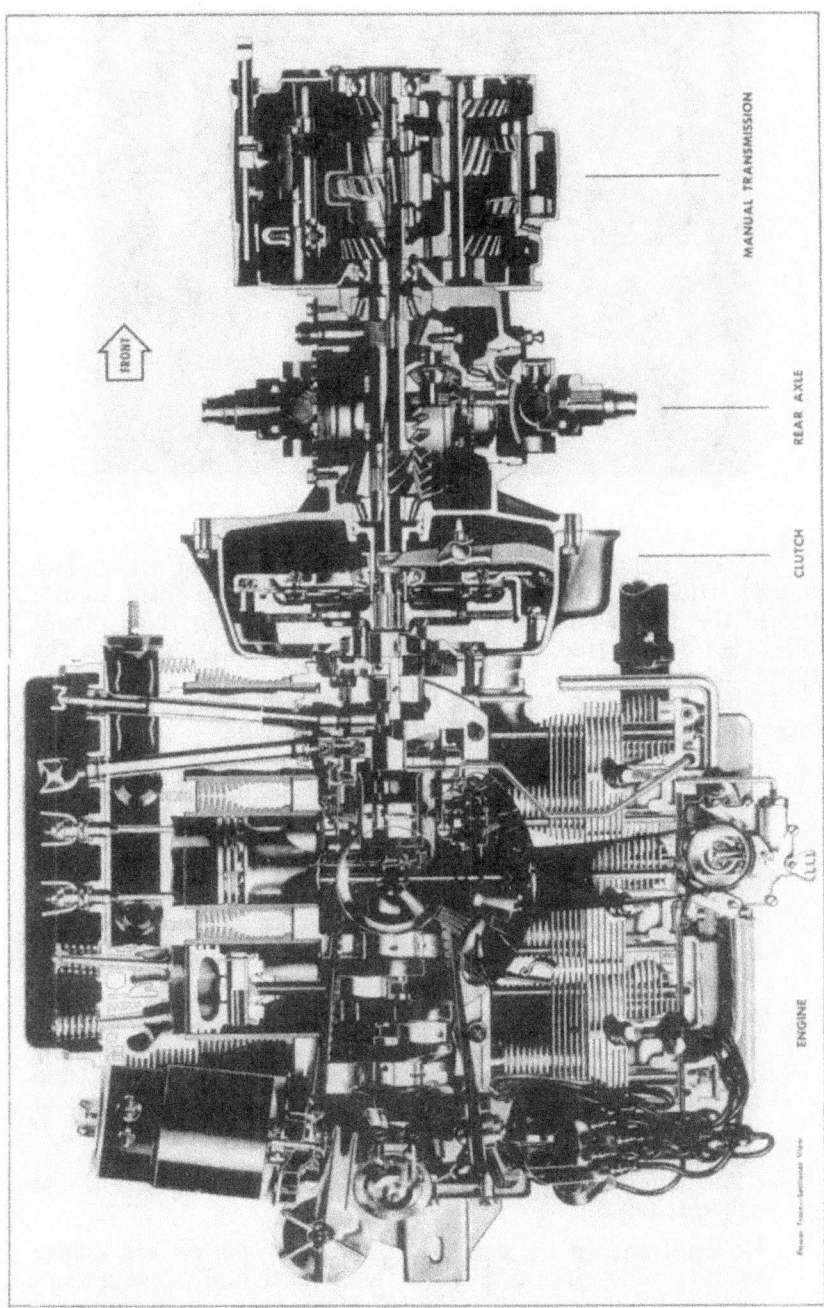

Engine Installation

A three point mounting is used with the power train. Two mounts attached to the transmission support the front of the unit at the rear suspension cross-member and the third mount is located at the rear center of the engine and attaches to the integrated bodyframe.

Listed below are some of the major precautions to be observed when removing or installing a power train.

1. Do not support the complete power train except at the engine pan rail. Under no circumstances should it be supported on the pan itself. Jacking Fixture J-7894 has been designed to properly support and lock the power train in a balanced position.

2. No jacking fixture (or floor support) should be used unless it is capable of supporting the weight of the power train approximately 460 pounds).

3. No jacking fixture of questionable stability should be used. The base must be sufficiently wide and the jack adequately braced to prevent tipping or collapsing with the power train raised to the maximum lift position of the jack. Rough or uneven floors will complicate this problem. The center of gravity or balance point of the complete power train is located approximately .200" behind the front face of the cylinder block.

4. No jack should be used that does not permit the power train to be lowered gradually. This is essential to avoid damage to components when "tight" clearances are encountered during removal.

REMOVAL OF POWER TRAIN

Related Component Locations

1. Main Fuel Line
2. Heater Fuel Line
3. Starter Motor
4. Carburetor Cross Shaft Control Rod
5. Rear Idler Lever Control Rod
6. Engine Skid Plate
7. Skid Plate Bolt

Standard Transmission—Power Train Installation

1. Speedometer Cable
2. Front Engine Mount
3. Shift Coupling (Transmission)
4. Emergency Brake Tension Spring
5. Clutch Cable Clevis
6. Clutch Control Cable Cross-Shaft
7. Clutch Fork Pull Rod
8. Clutch Fork Return Spring
9. Engine Side Seal Retainers

1. On coupe and sedan models (1961-62) remove spare tire; on station wagon models, remove engine access cover.
2. Remove carburetor air cleaners.
3. Disconnect return air hose for air heater if car is so equipped.
4. Remove engine-to-body front seal retainer.
5. Disconnect return spring and throttle rod from left carburetor at the carburetor cross-shaft.
6. Disconnect tunnel choke cable at its attachment to the choke bridle by loosening the screws securing the cable sheath clamp and cable clamp. (1960-61 models).

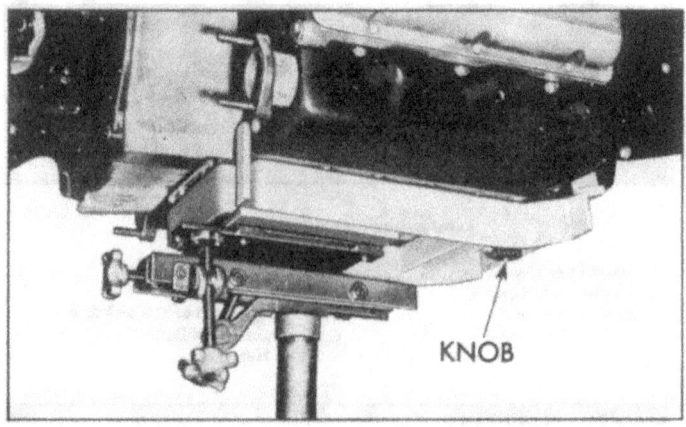

Engine Lift Fixture J-7894 Installed

Power Train Removed—Automatic Transmission Shown

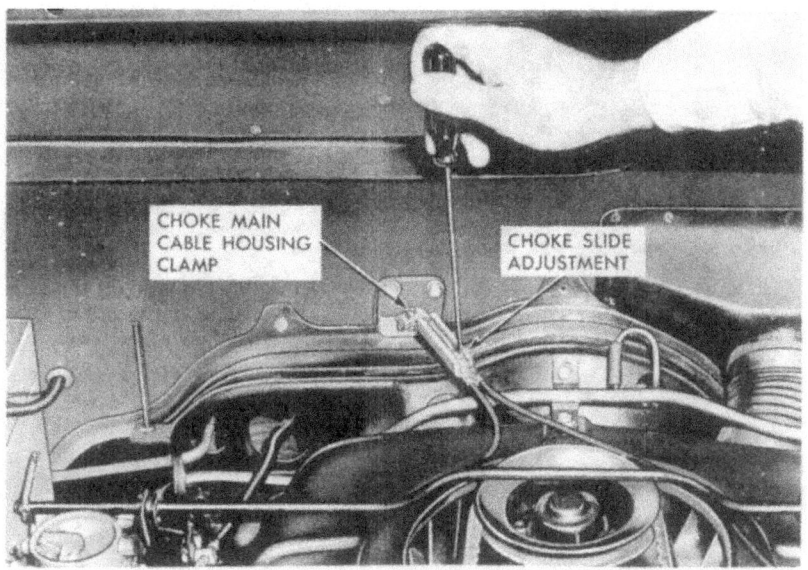

7. Make the following electrical disconnections:
   a. Disconnect battery cable from battery positive terminal.
   1962
   Disconnect the battery cable from the battery positive terminal and the wire from the battery positive terminal to the regulator BATT terminal at the regulator.

   b. At generator, disconnect ground strap and blue and brown leads to voltage regulator.

   c. Disconnect yellow and purple ignition leads at the starting motor harness connector in the engine compartment.

   d. Disconnect the left and right engine-to-body ground straps (not shown).

   e. Disconnect yellow lead from ignition coil and disconnect leads to temperature and oil presure switches.

8. Raise vehicle on hoist, then complete electrical disconnections by removing the battery cable and yellow and violet ignition leads from the starter solenoid.

9. Remove engine rear grille and skid plate, then remove retainers from rear and side engine seals.

10. Disconnect parking brake return spring from engine front mount crossmember.

11. Pull choke cable forward until it clears the engine front mount.

12. Disconnect accelerator control rods at the transmission idler lever. Push the lever-to-carburetor rod up into the engine compartment.

13. Disconnect fuel line by loosening clamps securing fuel line

1. Accelerator Rod   2. Oil Filler   3. Oil Level Gauge   4. Engine Rear Mount   5. Engine Radio Ground

hose connection and plug lines to prevent leakage. Disconnect speedometer cable at the differential carrier.

14. If vehicle is equipped with an air heater, disconnect flexible hoses at the engine.
15. If vehicle is equipped with gasoline heater, disconnect heater fuel line.
16. Pull U-joints from differential carrier by removing axle shafts.
17. The following procedures apply only to vehicles equipped with manual three or four speed transmission.
    a. Disconnect shift tube coupling at transmission shifter shaft by removing cotter pin and removing pin securing cou-

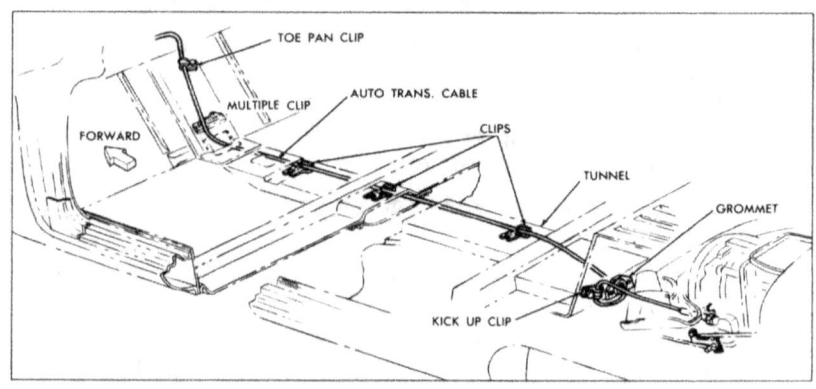

Shift Control Cable Routing

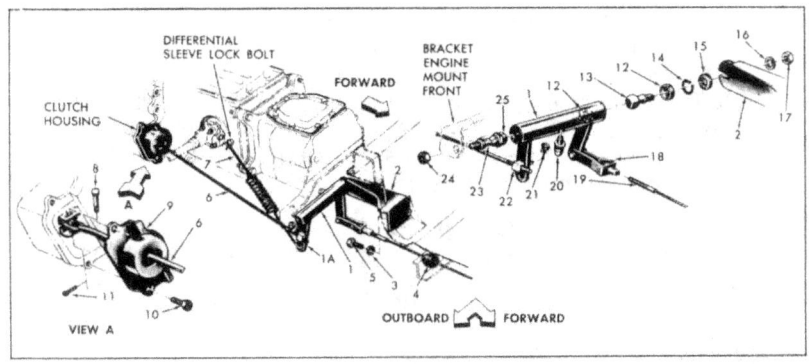

Clutch Linkage Exploded

1. Clutch Lever Control Cable Cross-Shaft
2. Shaft Mounting Bracket
3. Lockwasher
4. Cable Seal
5. Bolt
6. Clutch Fork Pull Rod
7. Return Spring
8. Clevis Pin
9. Dust Seal Assembly
10. Bolt
11. Cotter Pin
12. Ball Stud Seat
13. Ball Stud
14. Retainer Spring
15. Flat Washer
16. Lockwasher
17. Nut
18. Clevis Assembly
19. Control Cable
20. Lube Fitting
21. Cotter Key
22. Swivel
23. Ball Stud
24. Lock Nut
25. Items to be Lubricated before assembly with Lubriplate

pling to transmission shifter shaft. Then loosen coupling clamp nut and push shift tube coupling into tube until it is clear of the engine front mount.

b. Disconnect clutch return spring, then disconnect clutch pull rod from outer lever.

c. Remove nut securing clutch cross shaft to engine front mount and loosen stud nut at inboard end, then push inboard end from slot in mount and remove cross shaft. Unfasten clutch cable sheath clamp at engine front mount and drop clutch cable and cross shaft clear of power train.

d. If equipped, remove back-up light switch from four speed transmission housing. Provide a container for oil as switch is below normal transmission oil level.

18. If vehicle is equipped with automatic transmission, the following steps are necessary.

   a. Disconnect the transmission shift cable by removing the screw securing cable to transmission case and removing grommet plate in rear of control tunnel. Remove cable from transmission by rotating throttle valve (TV) lever its full limit counterclockwise and then withdraw cable from case.

   b. Place a receptacle for transmission oil beneath transmission, then remove transmission filler tube.

19. Position a hydraulic transmission jack stand under the engine assembly.

20. Remove cotter pins and two castellated nuts from front engine mount (at transmission) and one cotter pin and castellated nut from the engine rear mount.
    NOTE: If front engine mounting bracket and shims are remove from the transmission, the same amount of shims removed must be replaced. Rear "toe-in" will be affected if shims are altered.

21. Lower the power train gradually and watch for possible interference at rear mount and left rear lower control arm.

22. Remove exhaust pipe and muffler assembly.

INSTALLATION OF POWER TRAIN

Be sure all harness wires, fuel lines, and levers are out of the way prior to installation of the power train to prevent damage.

1. Position hydraulic jack stand with power train to prevent damage.

2. Raise power train until front and rear engine mounting brackets are in place on mounts, then install nuts. Torque front mounts to 60-80 ft. lbs. and rear mounts 50-60 ft. lbs. Install cotter pins at both mountings.

    NOTE: If engine front mounting bracket and shims are removed from the transmissions, the same amount of shims removed must be replaced. Rear "toe-in" will be affected if shims are altered.

3. On vehicles equipped with an automatic transmission, perform the following operations:

    a. Install filler tube in transmission oil pan, then fill transmission.

    b. Lubricate new "O" ring seal and insert into bore in transmission case.

    c. Rotate the TV lever its full limit counterclockwise and insert ball end of shift cable into transmission case. Secure cable to case with cap screw, then install cable grommet plate in tunnel rear cover. If cable is properly installed, hole in TV lever will be approximately $3/8$" below transmission pan rail. Install cable clip in kick-up area.

4. On manual transmission equipped vehicles, perform the following operations:

    a. Connect shift tube coupling to transmission shifter shaft by installing clevis pin and securing with flat washer and cotter pin. Pull shift coupling boot so it fully covers transmission shifter shaft seal.

    b. Shift three speed transmissions into first or four speed transmissions into fourth, then with an assistant holding the gear shift lever in the gear position, tighten clamp nut.

    c. Insert outboard ball stud end of clutch cross shaft through engine front mount, then rotate inboard stud end into cross shaft bracket. Secure cross shaft in bracket and transmission front mount by tightening stud nuts at each end.

    d. Attach clutch return spring to lower hole in outboard lever and to stud on differential carrier, then pull clutch rod full forward until swivel aligns with upper hole in outer lever. Back off swivel two complete turns, then insert swivel into upper hole in lever and secure with clips.

    e. On four speed transmissions equipped with back-up lights, install back-up light switch. Fill transmission and differential carrier to level of filler plug holes with SAE 80 Multi-purpose Gear Lubricant.

5. Install axle shafts in differential carrier.

6. On gasoline heater equipped vehicles, connect heater fuel line.

7. On vehicles equipped with air heater, connect flexible air delivery hoses to the left and right sides of the engine.

8. Connect engine fuel line to line from tank with hose and secure with two clamps. Connect speedometer cable to speedometer driven gear in the differential carrier.

9. Connect accelerator control rods to transmission idler lever.

10. Push choke cable through its grommet up into the engine compartment.

11. Connect parking brake return spring to engine front mount and parking brake cable bridle. Install engine rear and side seal retainers, then install skid plate and engine rear grille.

12. Connect battery cable to starter solenoid terminal "B" and install the violet and yellow leads from the starting motor harness to the solenoid terminals marked "R" and 'S', respectively.

13. Lower vehicle to floor, then make the following electrical connections.

    a. Connect yellow lead to ignition coil and connect leads to temperature and oil presure switches.

    b. Connect left and right engine-to-body ground straps (not shown).

    c. Connect yellow and purple ignition leads by inserting them into the connector of the starting motor harness.

    d. Connect ground strap to generator, then connect brown lead from voltage regulator to rear terminal of generator and dark blue to forward terminal of generator.

    e. Connect battery cable to battery positive terminal.

14. Connect tunnel choke cable to choke bridle by first tightening cable clamp and then securing cable sheath clamp.
15. Connect throttle rod to left carburetor (fig. 6-4) and connect throttle return spring. If position of swivel on throttle rod has been disturbed, it will be necessary to check carburetor synchronization.
16. Install engine-to-body front seal retainer.
17. If vehicle is equipped with air heater, connect return air hose to passenger compartment duct and to duct in engine top shroud.
18. Install carburetor air cleaners.
19. On coupe and sedan models, install spare tire; on station wagon models, install engine access cover. Start engine and check for oil leaks. Also check for proper operation of throttle linkage, shift linkage, and clutch linkage.

SERVICE OPERATIONS

On all service operations where threads enter aluminum, use anti-seize compound, such as Permatex No. 404 or its equivalent.

NOTE: Whenever working inside of engine compartment, insert a pin or bolt through safety locking holes in compartment lid support. This will prevent accidental unlocking of the support.

ENGINE SHEET METAL COMPONENTS

Adequate engine cooling greatly depends on proper alignment of engine sheet metal components.

Handle sheet metal components carefully to prevent bending or distortion.

Upper Shroud Assembly

Removal

1. Remove air cleaner assemblies and supports.

2. Disconnect fuel lines at fuel pump and carburetors. Disconnect accelerator and throttle linkage, choke cable assembly and heater hose at upper shroud. Remove blower belt.

3. Remove carburetor cross-shaft and disconnect vacuum balance tube from carburetor mounting flange and upper shroud assembly. Remove both carburetors.

4. Remove wire harness from each spark plug.

5. Remove all fuel lines and oil level gauge.

6. Remove generator bracket bolts at engine upper shroud and swivel generator bracket out of the way.

7. Remove all engine upper shroud assembly retaining screws and remove upper shroud.

   NOTE: Tip engine upper shroud asembly away from the oil filter and generator adapter.

Installation

1. Install engine upper shroud, tipping while lowering over blower assembly.

   NOTE: When tightening engine upper shroud retaining screws, turn blower to assure adequate clearance of blower to engine shroud.

2. Install all engine upper shroud screws and torque 30 to 40 in. lbs. Install generator bracket bolts and tighten.

3. Install carburetors and connect fuel lines and vacuum balance tube. If removed, install and connect heater hose at upper shroud.

4. Install carburetor cross-shaft, throttle linkage and choke

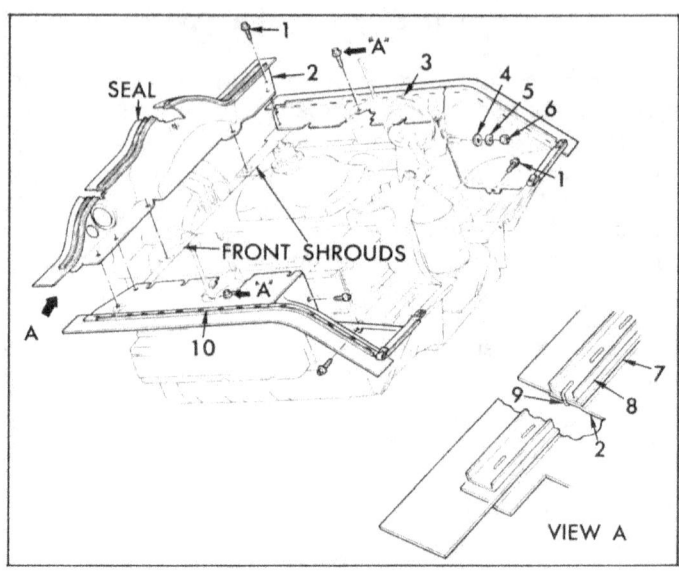

Front and Side Shields

1. Screw
2. Front Shield Assembly
3. Right Side Shield Assembly
4. Washer
5. Lockwasher
6. Nut
7. Seal
8. Seal Retainer
9. Wire Staple
10. Left Side Shield Assembly

    cable assembly. Install supports and air cleaners. Adjust accelerator and throttle linkage.

5. Install wire harness and oil level gauge. Install blower belt and adjust.

Upper Shroud Assembly — 1962

Removal

1. Remove air cleaners assemblies and supports.
2. Disconnect fuel lines at carburetors and at fuel pump "tee" fitting. Disconnect spark advance hose at right carburetor.
3. Disconnect accelerator rod at cross-shaft, disconnect choke control rod at choke lever and remove upper choke control rod.
4. Disconnect and remove carburetors and cross-shaft as an assembly. Remove blower belt.
5. Remove wire from each spark plug and remove vacuum balance tube.
6. Remove generator outboard bracket bolts at upper shroud and front bolt on pulley and swivel generator rearward.

7. Disconnect heater hose (if so equipped) at engine compartment wall.
8. Remove remaining upper shroud retaining screws and lift out shroud with heater hose attached.

   NOTE: Raise front of shroud first and rotate clockwise to clear oil filter and generator adapter.

Installation

1. Install upper shroud in same manner of removal.
   NOTE: When tightening retaining screws, turn the blower to assure adequate clearance of blower to shroud.
2. Install upper shroud screws and torque 30 to 40 in. lbs. and install generator bracket and tighten generator as outlined to prevent breaking generator mounting.
3. Connect heater hose if so equipped, install vacuum balance tube and screw to the warm air tube.
4. Install spark plug wires and blower belt.
5. Install carburetors and cross-shaft as an assembly. Connect choke control rod and accelerator rod.
6. Connect spark advance hose at right carburetor and install fuel lines to carburetors.
7. Install air cleaner bracket and air cleaners.
8. Check carburetor synchronization.

Front Shield

Removal

1. Remove air cleaners and air cleaner supports. Remove vacuum balance tube. Remove vacuum balance tube strap retaining bolts and six screws from engine front shield.
2. Remove accelerator rod and fuel lines entering front shield.
3. Disconnect choke cable assembly and heater hose connection to upper shroud.
4. Remove engine front shield.

Installation

1. Install engine front shield, while guiding front seal edges into front shield seal retainer.
2. Install six retaining screws and two in the support strap.
3. Install accelerator rod, fuel lines and throttle rod through engine front shield.
4. Replace vacuum balance tube. Install air cleaner supports and air cleaner assemblies.

Front Shield — 1962

Removal

1. Disconnect battery ground strap at battery.
2. Remove air cleaners and air cleaner supports.
3. Remove vacuum balance tube and heater hose if so equipped.
4. Remove front seal retainer and disconnect accelerator rod at cross-shaft.
5. Remove front shield retaining screws and move shield rearward to gain access to starter solenoid connections and fuel line connection.
6. Disconnect fuel line from tank at fuel pump.
7. Disconnect fuel line hose connection at rear line and remove fuel line rearward through shield. Remove grommet from shield.
8. Disconnect battery cable at solenoid and the other two wires at quick-disconnect in engine compartment. Slide wires through grommet opening in shield.
9. Remove shield over accelerator rod and dust boot.

Installation

Reverse the Removal procedure to install.

Side Shield Assembly

(Left Side)

Removal

1. Remove air cleaners and left hand support. Loosen retaining screws at engine upper shroud, attaching engine side

Removal and Installation of Engine Side Shield

shield to the cylinder head. Remove screw from under carburetor and remove screws attaching side shield to the lower shroud and exhaust duct assembly.

2. Remove oil cooler screws attached to engine side shield assembly. Disconnect radio ground.
3. Remove screws attached at engine rear shield seal.
4. Remove engine side seal retainer and remove engine side shield assembly, by sliding out from under the upper shroud assembly.

Installation

1. Slide engine side shield assembly under the engine upper shroud and into place.
2. Install attaching screws in engine side shield to rear shield.
3. Install screw under carburetor. Install screws attaching engine side shield to the cylinder head. Install radio ground.
4. Install retaining screws to lower shroud exhaust duct assembly and engine side shield seal retainer.
5. Tighten all screws at engine upper shroud, attaching side shield to cylinder head.
6. Install air cleaner support and air cleaner assemblies. (1961-62).

SIDE SHIELD ASSEMBLY
(RIGHT SIDE)

Removal

1. Remove spare wheel and tire. (If present) Remove coil and coil mounting bracket. Remove muffler support and muffler shield.
2. Remove engine side shield seal retainer.
3. Remove air cleaners and right hand support. (1961-62) Remove screw under carburetor at side shield right side.
4. Loosen retaining screws at engine upper shroud, attaching engine side shield to the cylinder head. Disconnect radio ground.
5. Remove screws attaching side shield to the lower shroud exhaust duct assembly and rear shield.
6. Remove engine side shield assembly by sliding out from under the upper shroud assembly.

Installation

1. Slide engine side shield into place, under engine upper shroud. Install screw under carburetor.

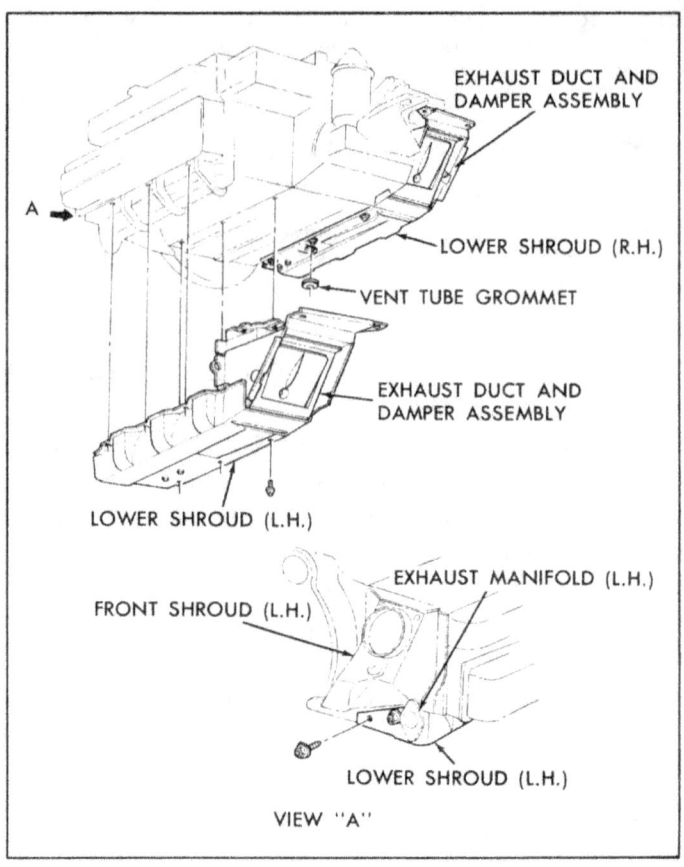

Engine Lower Shroud and Exhaust Duct

2. Install all attaching screws at lower shroud exhaust duct assembly and rear shield seal.
3. Install coil bracket and coil. Install exhaust muffler baffle and support.
4. Tighten all retaining screws at upper shroud, attaching side shield to cylinder head.
5. Install support and air cleaner assemblies. (1961-62)

Lower Shroud and Exhaust Duct

Removal and Installation

1. Remove attaching screws from lower shroud and exhaust duct entering cylinder head. Remove screws attaching lower shroud and exhaust duct to front shroud and side shield assembly. Loosen side shield at rear so lower shroud and exhaust duct can be pivoted outward.

2. Remove screws at rear center shield, retainer and rear seal retainer.
3. On left lower shroud and exhaust duct, remove screws at oil cooler; and on right lower shroud and exhaust duct, remove coil and bracket and muffler support bracket.
4. Remove engine lower shroud and exhaust ducts.
5. Install engine lower shroud and exhaust duct in position. On the right side lower shroud, align shroud so that the crankcase vent tube centers in hole on the lower shroud.
6. Align matching holes with an awl or other pointed tool. Install all retaining screws in shroud.

NOTE: Do not leave out any screws attaching shroud components to the engine. This will cause unnecessary rattles.

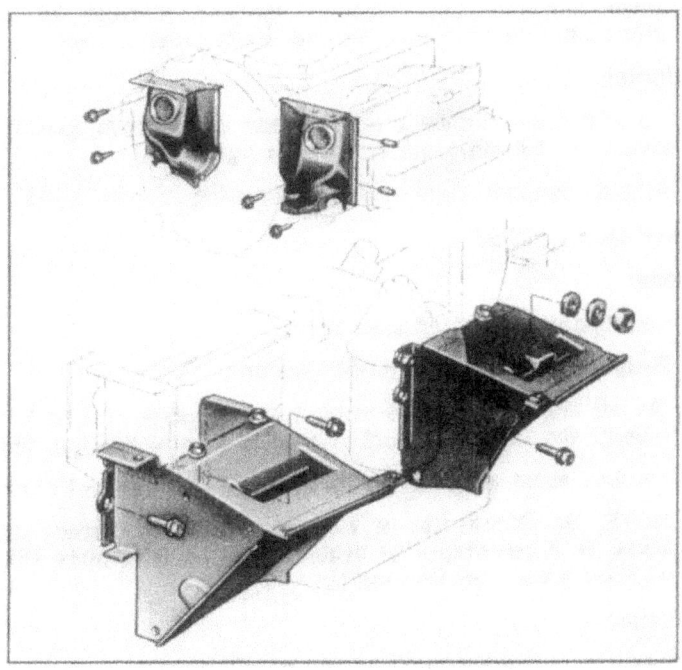

Engine Front Shrouds and Exhaust Ducts

7. Install coil and bracket on right side and screws attaching oil cooler to lower left shroud assembly.

NOTE: Replace gasket seal between exhaust manifold and lower shroud, if damaged.

Lower Shroud

An interim change in 1961 and 1962- the lower shroud is a separate piece from the exhaust duct and damper assembly. The exhaust duct damper thermostat is in the same location and is adjusted in the same manner. The lower shroud, however, may be removed without the duct and damper assembly to service the oil pressure and engine temperature sending units and the choke stove unit on the 1962 engines.

The procedure is as follows for both right and left sides.

Removal

1. Loosen thermostat screws.
2. Remove sheet metal screws to duct assembly.
3. Remove eight shroud-to-head and crankcase cap screws.
4. Lower the duct and move it rearward enough to release thermostat tension and remove thermostat screws.

Installation

1. Reverse the removal procedure for installation, guiding the road draft tube through opening in right side.
2. Adjust exhaust duct damper opening as in 1961.

Exhaust Duct — 1962

Removal

1. Remove lower shroud assembly.
2. Remove engine rear seal and retainer.
3. On the left duct remove screws at oil cooler and rear center shield. On the right duct remove coil and muffler bracket.
4. Remove remaining screws to duct and remove duct assembly.

NOTE: On Greenbrier or Lakewood Station Wagons or Vans, it is necessary to drain the oil and remove the oil filler tube to remove duct.

Installation

1. Reverse removal procedure for installation.
2. Check adjustment of duct damper.

Front Shrouds

Removal and Installation

1. Remove engine lower shroud assemblies and exhaust mani-

folds.

2. Remove screws retaining front shrouds to the cylinder head.

   NOTE: If heater equipped, disconnect heater attaching hoses.

3. Remove engine front shrouds.
4. Install front shrouds into place, and install retaining screws attaching shroud to crankcase and cylinder head.
5. Install exhaust manifolds using new gaskets, and engine lower shroud assemblies with retaining screws.

Front Shroud — 1962

Removal

1. Remove lower shroud.
2. Remove exhaust manifold.
3. Remove three screws from front shield in upper compartment.
4. On right side remove two bolts holding exhaust muffler shield.
5. Remove heater duct hoses if direct air heater equipped.
6. Remove remaining bolts and remove front shroud assembly. (On left side one bolt is inside heater duct opening.)

Installation

1. Reverse removal procedure to install.
2. Check adjustment on exhaust duct damper.

Rear Shroud

(Left Side)

Removal

1. Remove oil cooler retaining bolts and screws.
2. Remove oil cooler seals.
3. Remove screws retaining lower shroud and exhaust duct assembly to the engine rear shroud, and remove lower shroud assembly.
4. Remove all screws retaining engine, rear shroud to cylinder head and shrouds.
5. Remove engine rear shroud.

Installation

1. Install engine rear shroud to place on crankcase cast lips.
2. Install attaching screws to cylinder head. Install lower shroud

and exhaust assembly.

3. Install new oil cooler seals (two) in place on oil cooler adapter.

4. Install oil cooler retaining bolt and torque 8 to 12 ft. lbs. and install screws attaching oil cooler at lower shroud exhaust duct assembly.

5. Install remaining screws retaining engine rear shroud.

6. Start engine and check for oil leaks around engine oil cooler.

**Rear Shroud
(Right Side)**

Removal

1. Remove muffler shield and muffler support from engine right side cylinder head.

2. Remove retaining screws from rear shroud. Disconnect oil temperature and oil pressure sending unit wires.

3. Remove spare tire and wheel assembly.

4. Remove bolt and nut securing coil and coil bracket to cylinder head. Remove screws retaining engine upper shroud to engine rear shroud at cylinder head.

5. Remove lower shroud exhaust duct assembly.

6. Remove engine rear shroud.

Installation

1. Install shroud in place and install all retaining screws.

2. Install coil and coil bracket retaining bolt and nut at stud (6).

3. Install muffler support and muffler shield to cylinder head and engine rear shroud.

4. Connect engine oil temperatures and oil pressure sending unit connections.

5. Install lower shroud and exhaust duct.

6. Install spare tire and wheel asembly.

1960 EXHAUST DUCT ASSEMBLY

Removal

1. On left side exhaust duct, remove attaching screws from oil cooler and engine rear shield seal. On right side exhaust duct, remove choke manifold heated air intake pipe.

2. Remove attaching screws from engine rear center shield and engine skid plate. Remove screws from engine lower shroud and engine side shield at exhaust ducts.

3. Remove exhaust duct.

OIL COOLER

Removal

1. Remove all screws retaining oil cooler to engine shrouds, shields and cylinder head.
2. Remove oil cooler access hole cover and remove long oil cooler mounting bolt (3/8-16) x 3" long) with flat washer and remove oil cooler. Remove and discard worn seals from oil cooler adapter.
3. Invert oil cooler and allow oil to drain from cooler. Clean radiation fins of oil cooler with an air hose before and after cleaning in solvent.

Installation

1. Install new oil cooler seals in place on oil cooler adapter.
2. Install oil cooler with long retainer bolt and flat washer and torque 8 to 12 ft. lbs.
3. Install all screws and bolts to engine shrouds, shields and cylinder head.
4. Start engine and check for oil leaks around oil cooler at oil cooler seal location.

OIL PAN

Removal and Installation

1. Drain crankcase oil and remove all bolts retaining oil pan to crankcase. Remove oil pan and discard oil pan gasket.
2. Clean oil pan rails on crankcase and oil pan, using cleaning solvent. Install a new oil pan gasket, using a little petrolatum to adhere gasket to crankcase while installing oil pan.
3. Install oil pan, bolts and torque bolts 40 to 60 in. lbs.
4. Fill engine with 4 quarts of oil (wet engine).

CRANKCASE VENT TUBE AND GASKET

Removal and Installation

1. Remove engine upper shroud assembly.
2. Remove blower pulley.
3. Remove crankcase vent tube retaining bolt and clamp.
4. Remove crankcase vent tube and discard gasket.
5. Install a new cork gasket over crankcase vent tube end, and insert into crankcase cover.
6. Install crankcase vent tube retainer clamp with bolt and tighten securely.
7. Install blower pulley and engine upper shroud assembly.

Engine Compartment—Cylinder Head
Removal and Installation

CYLINDER HEAD AND COMPONENT PARTS
CYLINDER HEAD (Left Bank)
Removal

1. Drain crankcase oil.

2. Disconnect battery cables and ground connection to the generator. Disconnect radio ground strap.

3. Remove air cleaner, accelerator return spring and left air cleaner support. (1961-62)

4. Disconnect accelerator rod from carburetor. Remove crossshaft retainer at shaft support.

5. Remove two (1960) or three (1961-62) attaching screws from left side carburetor cross-shaft support and disconnect from carburetor.

6. Disconnect fuel line and choke cable (1961) at carburetor. Remove carburetor attaching stud nuts from carburetor, and remove left carburetor. Remove outboard carburetor stud (long stud) from carburetor mounting pad.

7. Remove vacuum balance tube from carburetor mounting flange. Remove generator bracket mounting bolts and swivel generator bracket, up away from the engine upper shroud.

8. Remove wires and spark plugs from cylinder head. Remove spark plug gaskets and discard.
9. Loosen all engine side shield retaining screws and remove screw from engine side shield under carburetor in engine compartment attached to cylinder head. Remove engine side shield.
10. Remove oil cooler access hole cover and remove oil cooler (this allows engine rear shroud freedom of movement during cylinder head removal).
11. Raise vehicle on a hoist.
12. Remove both engine side seal retainers and engine rear seal retainers.
13. Remove the engine rear center shield and seal assembly.
14. Remove lower engine shroud and exhaust duct retaining screws and bolts and remove engine lower shroud and exhaust duct. Remove exhaust pipe to manifold nuts.
15. Open french locks on the exhaust manifold and remove holding clamp nuts. Remove exhaust manifold and discard gaskets.

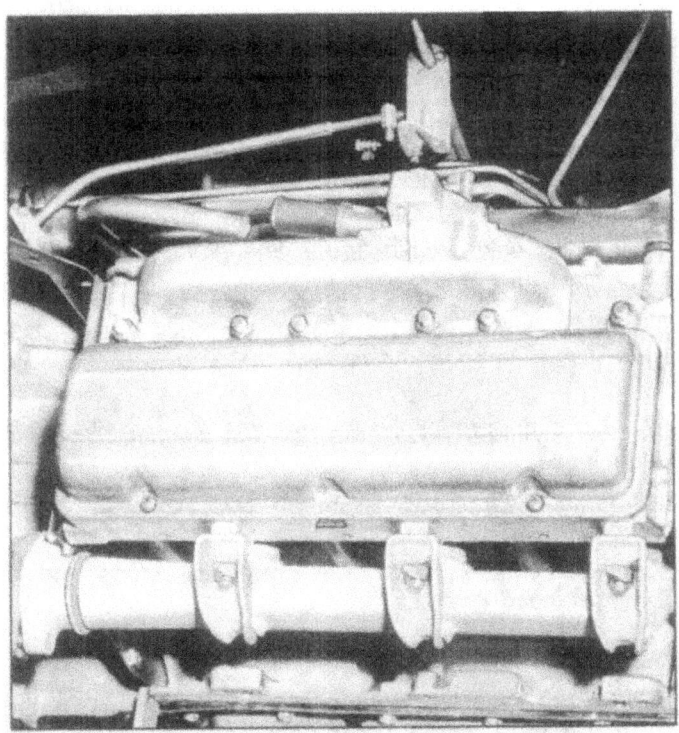

Engine Assembly—Showing Access to Cylinder Head

Removal and Installation of Valve Rocker Arms, Balls and Nuts

16. Remove engine rear mounting cotter pin, nut and washer from rear mounting bracket bolt.
17. Remove four valve rocker arm cover screws and remove valve rocker cover, while holding a pan below, to catch oil draining from cylinder head.
18. Remove rocker arm nuts, balls and rocker arms. Remove push rods, valve rocker studs and push rod guides.
19. Remove "O" rings from cylinder head.
20. Remove "O" rings from bottom of push rod drain tubes, with a pair of hooked tweezers, then remove from cylinder head.
21. Remove cylinder head nuts and flat washers, retaining cylinder head.
22. Carefully lower engine assembly approximately 3" to clear cylinder head carburetor flange.
23. Remove cylinder head from crankcase studs and discard cylinder head gaskets.

Cylinder Heads — 1962

Cylinder head service procedure change from 1961 only because the automatic choke control rod passes through the head to reach the thermostat and must be removed before the head can be removed.

Installation

1. Install new cylinder head gaskets in cylinder head. Guide cylinder head over crankcase studs. Install new lubricated 'O" rings (use engine oil) in cylinder head at valve rocker stud hole location.

2. Install push rod drain tubes, using new "O" rings.

   NOTE: Push rod drain tubes must be installed before push rod guides. The "O" ring on bottom of oil drain tube next to the crankcase must be put on after oil drain tube is inserted through the cylinder head, otherwise, "O" ring may shear when pushed through cylinder head.

3. Install push rod guides (chamfered side up) under valve rocker studs. Install valve rocker studs using anti-seize compound. Install cylinder head flat washers and nuts on studs protruding through the cylinder head.

4. Torque cylinder head in sequence.

5. Install push rod guides (early production engines) and torque attaching bolts 60 to 80 in. lbs.

   Insert push rods with .050" side oil hole (end of push rod with a blue band) up to the cylinder head and the other end of push rod seated in the valve lifter seat.

6. Install valve rocker arms, balls and nuts. Lash the valves.

7. Install the valve rocker cover with a new gasket and torque cover screws 30 to 50 in. lbs.

Removal and Installation of Valve Rocker Studs

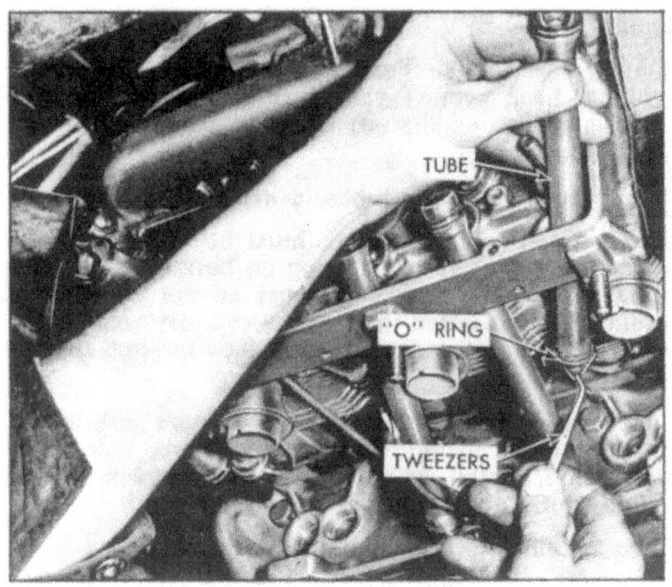

Removing Push Rod Oil Drain Tubes

Cylinder Head Removed (Showing Access to Cylinders and Pistons)

8. Install the oil cooler with new seals and torque mounting bolt 8 to 12 ft. lbs.
9. Install engine side shield assembly. Raise engine assembly and install the rear mounting nut, washer and torque nut 50 to 60 ft. lbs. Install cotter pin.
10. Install left, right and center shield seals. Install exhaust manifold with new gaskets and tighten.

11. Install engine lower shroud and exhaust duct. Install engine skid bolt and torque 20 to 30 ft. lbs. Hook up exhaust pipe to exhaust manifold.

    Lower vehicle to ground level and continue the following operations:

12. Tighten all upper shroud screws. Install spark plugs with new copper gaskets. Attach wiring harness to spark plugs. Install carburetor and carburetor fuel line. Install carburetor cross-shaft and retainer.

13. Install generator bracket bolts, using anti-seize compound, and tighten "Electrical System."

14. Install vacuum balance tube and carburetor linkage. Adjust throttle and accelerator linkage.

15. Install left air cleaner support, heater connection at upper shroud and air cleaner assembly.

CYLINDER HEAD (Right Bank)

Removal and Installation of the right bank cylinder head, is essentially the same as the left, except the soil, oil pressure and cylinder head temperature sending units must be disconnected. (Also the choke heat pipe and choke fresh air pipe from the exhaust manifold on 1960 models.)

VALVE ROCKER ARMS, BALLS AND NUTS

Removal and Installation

1. Remove valve rocker cover and gasket.
2. Remove valve rocker arm nuts, balls and rocker arms.
3. Replace rocker arms, balls and nuts and lash valves.
4. Install valve cover and gasket. Torque valve cover screws 30 to 50 in. lbs.

VALVE SPRINGS

Removal and Installation

Drain engine crankcase oil.

1. Remove valve cover and gasket.
2. Remove valve rocker nut, ball and valve rocker arm.
3. Remove spark plug from cylinder requiring valve spring replacement and use compressed air to retain valves in the closed position.
4. Install a valve rocker nut on valve rocker stud, compress valve spring far enough to remove valve locks. Remove valve spring cap and valve spring.
5. Install valve spring on valve spring seat shim with cap. Compress valve spring and install valve locks.

6. Install valve rocker arm, ball and nut. Lash valves and install valve cover and gasket. Install engine oil 4 quarts full.
7. Start engine and check for leaks.

PUSH RODS

Removal and Installation

1. Remove valve cover and gasket. Loosen valve rocker arms, balls and nuts from cylinder requiring push rod replacement.
2. Install push rod with .050" side oil hole up into cylinder head (blue band marked end).
3. Lash valves.

HYDRAULIC LIFTERS

Removal and Installation

1. Drain crankcase oil.
2. Remove valve rocker cover and gasket.
3. Remove engine lower shroud (and exhaust duct on 1961-62 models.)
4. Remove valve rocker arms, balls, valve rocker studs, push rod guides, push rod and push rod drain tubes from cylinder, that valve lifter is to be removed.
5. Remove lifter with a strong magnet or:
    a. Remove snap ring retaining the push rod seat and remove the push rod seat. Remove valve lifter with a pair of pliers inserted in the valve lifter snap ring groove.
    b. If valve lifters are coated with varnish and are hard to remove, the oil pan should be removed and the lifter body squirted with solvent to remove all varnish on the lifter body.
6. Install valve lifters well lubricated with engine oil.
7. Install push rod drain tubes with new "O" rings, and set push rods in place on lifter seat with side oil hole up next to valve rocker arms.
8. Install push rod guides, valve rocker studs and torque studs.
9. Install valve rockers, arms, balls, and nuts.
10. Install valve rocker cover and gasket.
11. Add engine oil.

OIL PUMP PRESSURE REGULATOR

Removal and Installation

1. Drain crankcase oil.

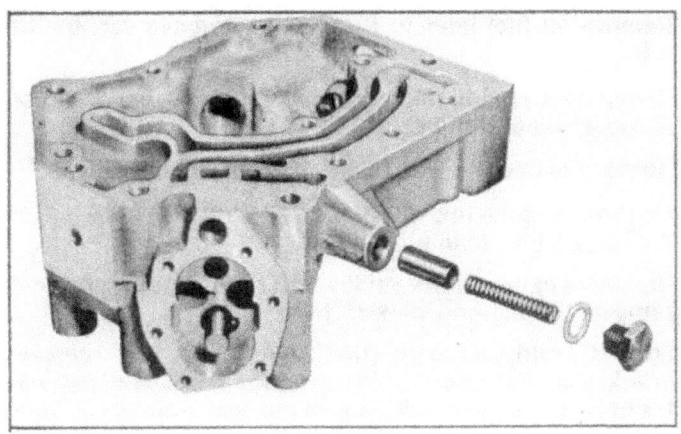

Oil Pump, Pressure Regulator Exploded

2. Remove left side lower shroud and exhaust duct retaining screws and remove engine lower shroud and exhaust duct. (On 1960 models, remove **right** side.)

3. Remove presure regulator plug, nylon gasket, spring and valve.

4. Install valve, spring, nylon gasket and plug.

5. Install lower shroud and exhaust duct retaining screws. Add engine crankcase oil.
NOTE: Remove plug on top of oil filter and generator adapter, and install an oil pressure gauge to check oil pressure. Oil pressure regulator should regulate at 35 psi oil pressure.

6. Start engine and check for oil leaks.

CONNECTING ROD BEARINGS
Removal

1. Disconnect battery ground cable. Remove air cleaner assemblies and air cleaner support.

2. Remove carburetor linkage and choke cable assemblies.

3. Disconnect fuel lines to carburetor. Disconnect and remove carburetor cross-shaft. Remove left bank carburetor.

4. If direct air heater equipped, disconnect heater hose at upper shroud.

5. Disconnect spark plug wires from spark plugs.

6. Release idler pulley tension on blower pulley belt and remove from engine assembly.

7. Remove all fuel lines to fuel pump. Remove vacuum balance tube.
8. Remove all engine upper shroud retaining bolts and screws. Remove generator brace.
9. Remove screws on each side of front engine shield.
10. Remove engine upper shroud, tipping front lip up so that it clears front engine shield.
11. Remove engine blower pulley and blower, retaining bolts and remove blower and blower pulley.
12. Loosen crankcase vent tube clamp bolt and remove from crankcase. Remove crankcase cover bolts and flat washers. Remove crankcase cover, gaskets and crankcase vent.
13. Position connecting rod by using a remote starter switch to crank engine. Remove connecting rod nuts, cap and bearing insert.
14. Install a piece of 5/16" plastic hose on each connecting rod stud, to protect crankshaft juornals.
15. Remove spark plug from cylinder requiring new rod bearing. Position connecting rod and remove rod cap and bearing insert from connecting rod.

Installation

1. Refer to "Connecting Rod Bearing Clearance" for connecting rod bearing installation and specifications. Torque connecting rod nuts 20 to 26 ft. lbs.

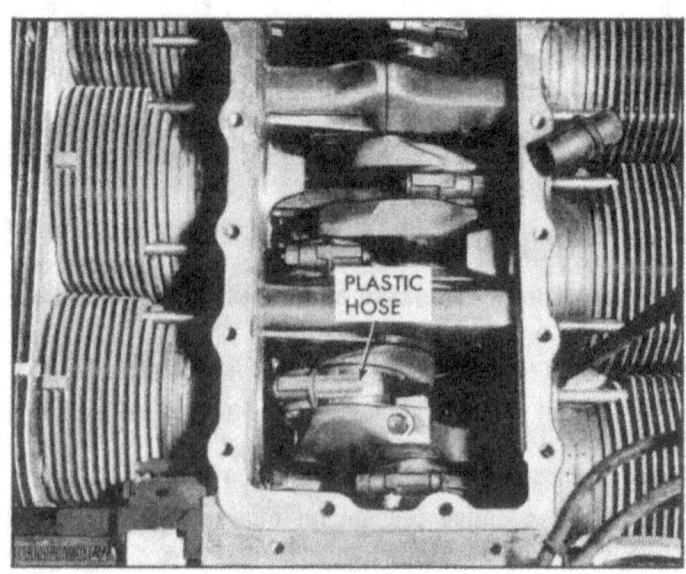

Connecting Rod Bearing Installation—No. 2 Shown

2. Clean gasket surface of crankcase, crankcase vent and crankcase cover with solvent.

NOTE: Do not use a scraper on gasket surfaces because it may scratch or nick the crankcase gasket surface.

3. Install crankcase gasket, crankcase vent and gasket and crankcase cover. Install crankcase ventilator, vent tube and gasket. Install crankcase cover flat washers and bolts using anti-seize compound on all threads. Torque bolts 7 to 13 ft. lbs.
4. Install blower and blower pulley.
5. Install spark plugs using new gaskets and torque 20 to 25 ft. lbs.
6. Install engine upper shroud and connect heater hoses. Install cooling air throttle valve assembly.
7. Install all retaining bolts in engine upper shroud.

NOTE: Rotate blower while tightening upper shroud bolts. Check for interference at blower to upper shroud.

8. Torque generator bolts in sequence.
9. Install pulley belt and adjust.
10. Install carburetor, vacuum balance tube and carburetor linkage. Install air cleaner support and air cleaner assembly.
11. Install wire harness and hook up to each spark plug.
12. Install carburetor cross-shaft and retainer.
13. Install carburetor choke assembly. Adjust carburetor throttle linkage as outlined under "Carburetor Synchronization."
14. Add engine oil, start engine and check for leaks. Tune-up engine assembly.

CRANKSHAFT PULLEY AND ENGINE REAR HOUSING SEAL

On some vehicles the engine rear housing seal is installed with the flange on the inside. If flange is on the inside of rear housing, engine will have to be removed from the vehicle and the rear housing removed. If flange is on the outside proceed with procedure below.

Removal

1. Disconnect battery cable to engine. Drain crankcase oil.
2. Remove all side shield seal retainers.
3. Remove engine rear center shield.
4. Remove engine rear body grille and engine rear mount.
5. Remove clutch return spring and disconnect clutch control cable. Disconnect clutch pull rod.

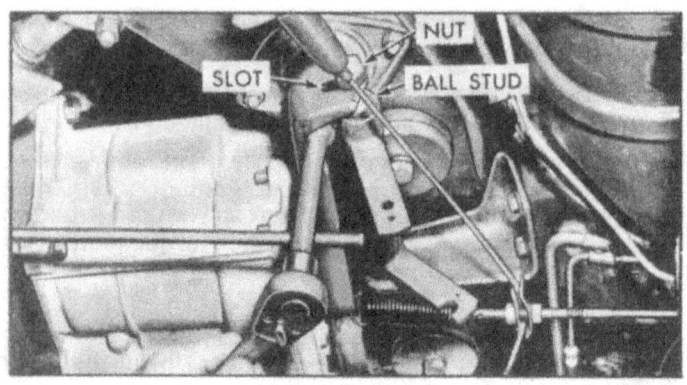

Lowering Front Engine Mount

Removing Crankshaft Pulley—Engine Installed

6. Loosen outboard stud nut and slide, part way, out of the engine front mounting bracket slot. Remove shift rod coupling.

7. Remove cotter pins and loosen front mounting nuts and lower engine until nuts are flush with the front engine mount studs.

   NOTE: Do not remove front mounting nuts.

8. Lower engine assembly far enough to remove engine rear mounting bracket.

9. Remove the oil filter and pulley belt.

   NOTE: Install bolts in pulley hub a depth of ¼" only, Otherwise the bolts will injure the rear housing seal.

10. Remove crankshaft pulley. Remove engine rear housing seal, by prying on the outer edge of the seal with a couple of

screw drivers. Remove and discard seal.

Installation

NOTE: The sealing lips of the rear housing seal are coated with high melting cup grease for the life of the seal (350°F.).

1. Install seal over crankshaft and tap in place with a wooden drift.
2. Install crankshaft pulley, flat washer and bolt, using crankshaft pulley bolt as a jack screw, tighten until crankshaft pulley is in place. Back bolt off ½ turn and then tighten bolt 60 to 80 ft. lbs. torque.
3. Install oil filter and torque bolt 9 to 15 ft. lbs.
4. Install engine rear mounting bracket, washers and nuts. Torque nuts 20 to 30 ft. lbs.
5. Raise engine and install rear engine mount. Torque rear engine mount 50 to 60 ft. lbs. and install retainer cotter pin.
6. Tighten front engine mount nuts 60 to 80 ft. lbs. torque, and install cotter pins. Slide outboard ball stud into place, and continue clutch linkage adjustment.

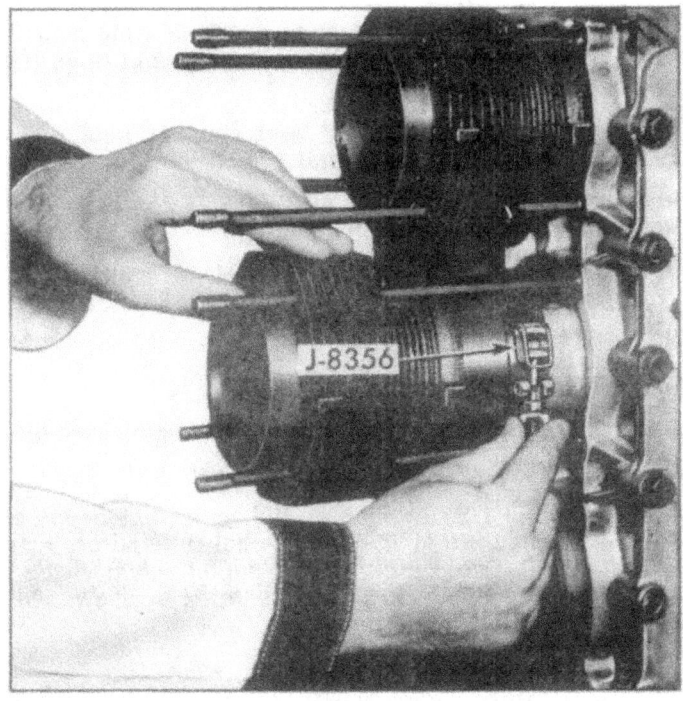

Compressing Piston Rings

7. Install rear body grille, rear center shield and seal assembly. Remove engine Tool J-7894 and install engine skid plate bolt. Torque bolt 20 to 30 ft. lbs.

8. Install side shield seal retainers and seals. Roll front shield seal into place at engine front shield.

9. Install battery cable to engine.

10. Add engine oil, start engine and check for leaks.

PISTON RING REPLACEMENT

Keep in mind that cylinders and pistons are serviced as a unit and the operation outlined below, is only for one or more pistons in one bank, requiring ring replacement. The operation below is not intended for complete engine piston and piston ring overhaul.

1. Drain crankcase oil and remove cylinder head.

2. Remove piston rings and install new rings. Position oil control ring gap towards the top of the engine and compression rings with the gap 45° from the oil ring gap location.

   NOTE: When installing compression rings, make sure the face with the bevel is assembled away from the top of the piston and the ring face markings are to the top of piston.

4. Lubricate piston rings with engine oil and slide over piston rings. Tighten just enough to compress piston rings (Do not overtighten) into the piston.

5. Install a new cylinder gasket over cylinder pilot and slide cylinder over piston and piston rings.

6. Install cylinder head using new gaskets for each cylinder. Refer to "Cylinder Head Installation."

7. Add engine oil, start engine and check for leaks.

ENGINE DISASSEMBLY

1. Remove transmission from "Power Train."

2. Remove the differential carrier from the engine assembly.

3. Remove clutch assembly if so equipped from engine.

4. A difference of 1 5/8" between the center line of the crankshaft and engine rear mounting bracket requires a special lifting adapter as shown. This adapter when made from angle iron (3" x 3" x ¼") and mounted as shown will provide a center line lifting point.

5. Remove air cleaner assemblies.

6. Disconnect throttle linkage and remove carburetor cross-shaft.

7. Release tension on blower belt, at idler pulley and remove blower belt from engine.

Fuel Pump

8. Disconnect fuel lines at carburetors and fuel pump. Loosen locknut at holding screw and remove fuel pump, push rod return spring from oil filter and generator adapter.
9. Disconnect generator at generator brace, oil filter and generator adapter and remove generator.
10. Disconnect vacuum balance tube at engine carburetor mounting pads. Remove vacuum balance tube. Remove engine front shield.

Flywheel

11. With lifting adapter bolted to the rear engine mounting bracket as shown, attach a chain and shackle to lifting adapter and at the flywheel housing lifting eye. Remove

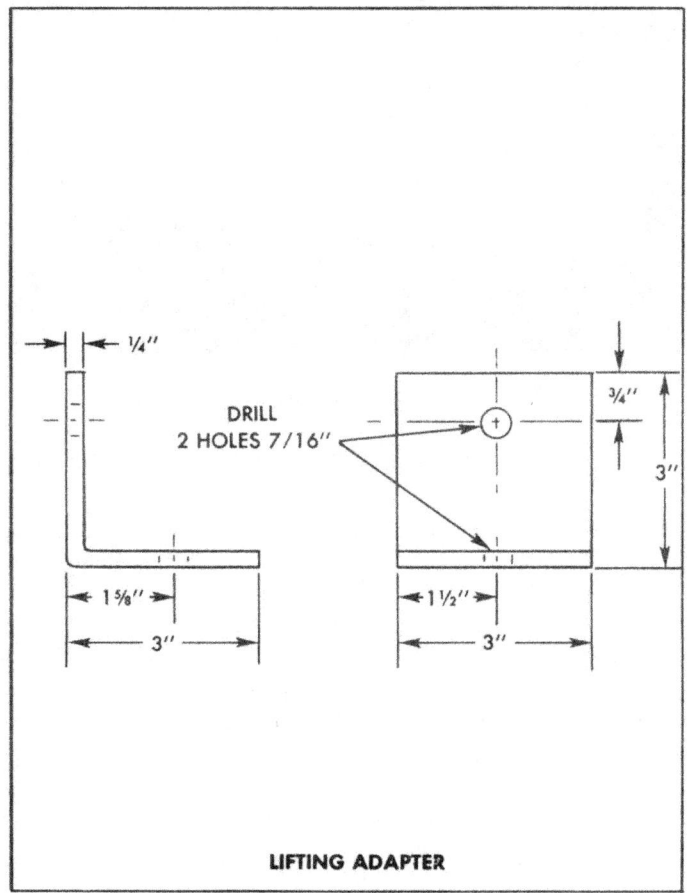

LIFTING ADAPTER

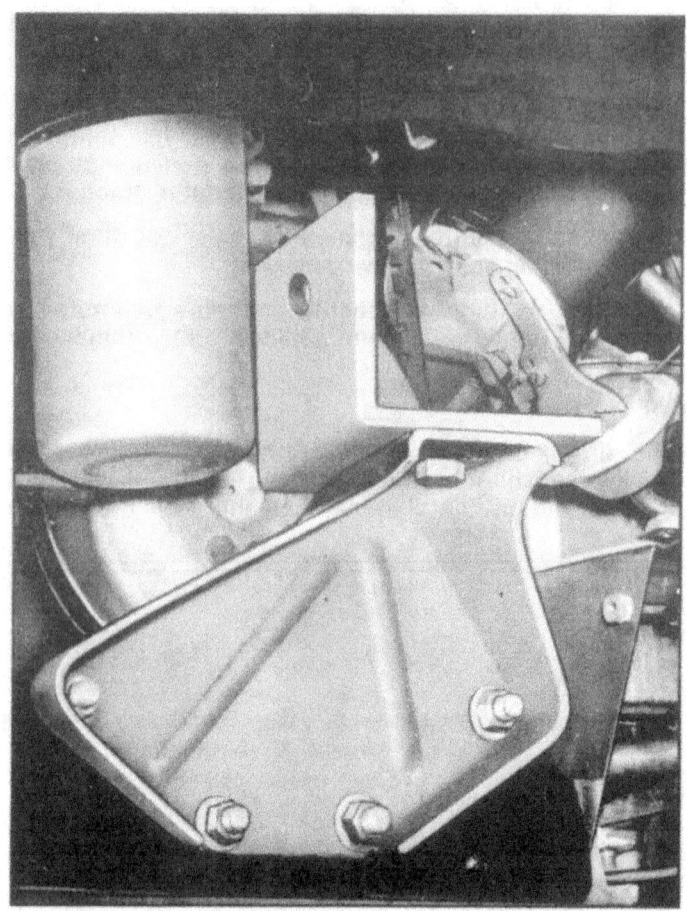

Engine Lifting Adapter

flywheel or flex plate retaining bolts and remove flywheel or flex plate.

12. Lift engine with chain sling off of lifting jack. Install engine assembly onto engine stand by mounting flywheel housing to adapter. Drain crankcase oil.

13. Remove both carburetors. Disconnect and remove cooling air throttle valve. Remove fuel lines and oil level gauge.

14. Disconnect and remove wire harness at spark plugs and distributor. Remove distributor and cap assembly.

15. Remove coil and generator brace from cylinder head. Remove engine upper shroud and left and right side shields. Remove all spark plugs and gaskets.

16. Remove oil filter and generator adapter retaining bolts and

Removing Fuel Pump

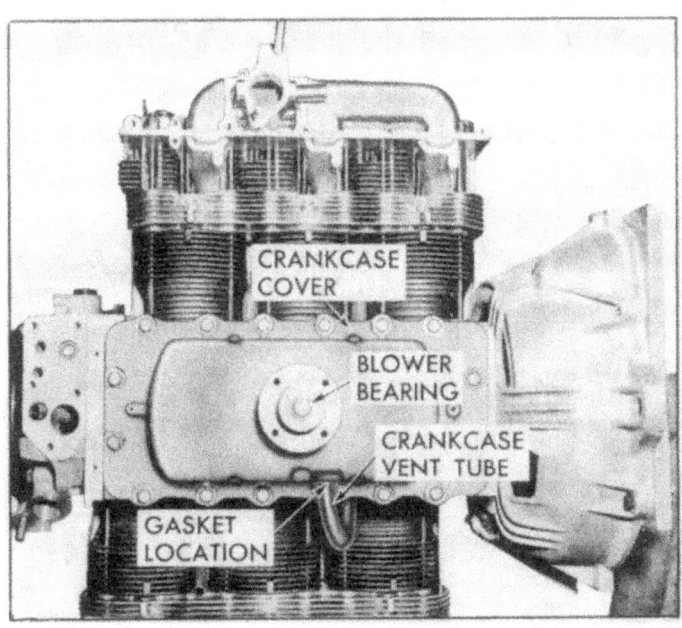

Crankcase Cover, Vent Tube and Blower Bearing Assembly

washers and remove oil filter and generator adapter. Discard adapter gasket.

17. Remove the blower pulley and blower assembly from the crankcase cover. Remove the crankchase vent tube and gasket.

18. Remove the crankcase cover, blower bearing assembly crank-

Exhaust Manifold Installed

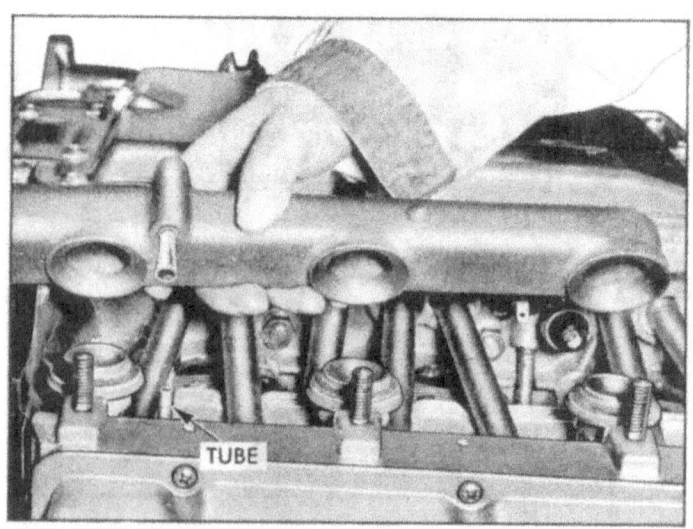

Exhaust Manifold Gasket and Choke Heat Tube Location

Cylinder Head Assembly—Valve Cover Removed

case cover gasket, vent assembly and the vent to crankcase gasket. Discard gaskets.

19. Remove engine rear and lower shrouds and exhaust ducts. Remove muffler bracket and shield.

Oil Pan

20. Invert engine on work stand and remove oil pan retaining bolts and remove oil pan and discard gasket.

Exhaust Manifold

21. Bend french lock tabs back and remove nuts. Remove exhaust manifold holding clamps.
22. Remove exhaust manifolds and discard gaskets.

    NOTE: Exhaust manifold to exhaust port sleeves are a press fit and should be removed with a soft hammer. If exhaust sleeves are removed, they should be replaced with the next largest diameter exhaust sleeve.

23. Remove engine front shrouds.
24. Remove engine rear mounting bracket and engine skid plate at engine rear housing.

Cylinder Head

25. Remove valve rocker cover and discard gasket. Remove valve rocker arm nuts, balls and rocker arms.
26. Remove push rods and identify, so they can be reinstalled in their original locations.
    NOTE: The side .050" oil hole in each push rod must be installed up, and next to the valve rocker arms. If by error a push rod is installed with the side oil hole

down, lubrication to that particular valve rocker arm and ball would be cut-off.

27. Remove retaining bolts and remove push rod guide plates (early production). Remove valve rocker studs, flat chamfered washer (early production) and push guides on (present productions), and discard "O" rings.

NOTE: Valve rocker stud "O" rings must be replaced with new "O" rings.

28. Remove nuts and flat washers (attached to long studs) from cylinder head.

29. Remove bottom "O" ring from push rod oil drain tubes and remove push rod oil drain tubes.

30. Remove cylinder head assemblies and discard cylinder head gaskets.

NOTE: Cast Iron Cylinders will need a holding fixture when crankshaft is turned for engine disassembly, which can be readily made. Six ½" O.D. steel tubes 4 ¼" long to be used on long cylinder studs, one on each cylinder. Six ½" O.D. steel tubes 3½" long will also be needed for each short stud.

31. Install one long 4½" x ½" tube on one long stud and one short 3½" x ½" tube on each short stud on each cylinder.

Push Rods Installed

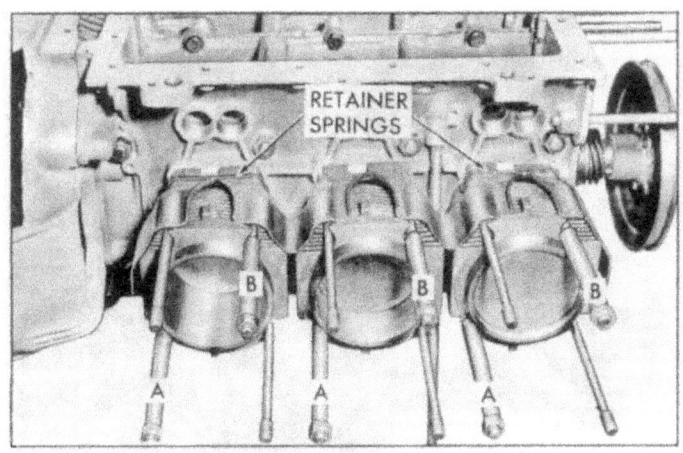

Cylinder Holding Tube Fixture

Hydraulic Lifters

32. Remove hydraulic lifters from lifter bores with a strong magnet or wire hook and identify so they can be replaced in their proper places after cleaning.

Piston and Connecting Rod Assemblies

33. Invert engine on stand so crankcase cover rail is up. Install two 3/8"-16" bolts in crankshaft pulley.

    NOTE: Install bolts in pulley hub a depth of ¼" ONLY, otherwise bolts will injure rear housing oil seal.

    NOTE: Crankshaft can also be turned with a wrench on the pulley attaching bolt.

34. Using a bar between the bolts on crankshaft pulley, turn crankshaft, positioning connecting rod so connecting rod cap and bearing can be removed.

    NOTE: Mark cylinder numbers on each connecting rod and piston to identify for reassembly, if they are not marked.

    NOTE: Cylinders are numbered from the rear of engine: right side 1, 3 and 5. — left side 2, 4 and 6.

35. Remove cylinder holding fixture (long and short tube) from one cylinder at a time.

Cylinder Air Baffle

36. To remove spring retainers on cylinder air baffle, refer to figure and remove air baffle.

37. Remove each cylinder with piston and connecting rod assembly as a unit.

Turning Crankshaft, using Crankshaft Pulley

Removal and Installation of Cylinder, Piston and Rod

Piston and Cylinder Bore

38. Piston assembly can be removed from cylinder, by pushing piston through cylinder with the end of a hammer handle.

    NOTE: Ridge and/or deposits from the upper end of cylinder can be removed after piston is removed from cylinder. A cylinder mounted ridge reamer is available at local jobbers.

39. Remove ridge and/or deposits from cylinder bore while holding cylinder with studs or bolts mounted on a wooden board.

Crankshaft Pulley

40. Remove crankshaft pulley retaining bolt and flat washer. Remove crankshaft pulley. Remove rear engine housing bolts and washers and remove engine rear housing. Discard the gasket.

41. Disconnect flywheel housing and crankcase assembly from engine stand and place on a couple of short lengths of 2" x 4" wood (to protect oil pump screen and pick up tube).

Camshaft and Crankshaft

42. Remove flywheel housing and gasket.

    On 1960, remove front oil slinger snap ring and remove front oil slinger.

    NOTE: Be careful not to scratch or score crank sealing surface.

    NOTE: Chamfer side on I.D. is installed away from oil slinger.

Removing Crankshaft Pulley

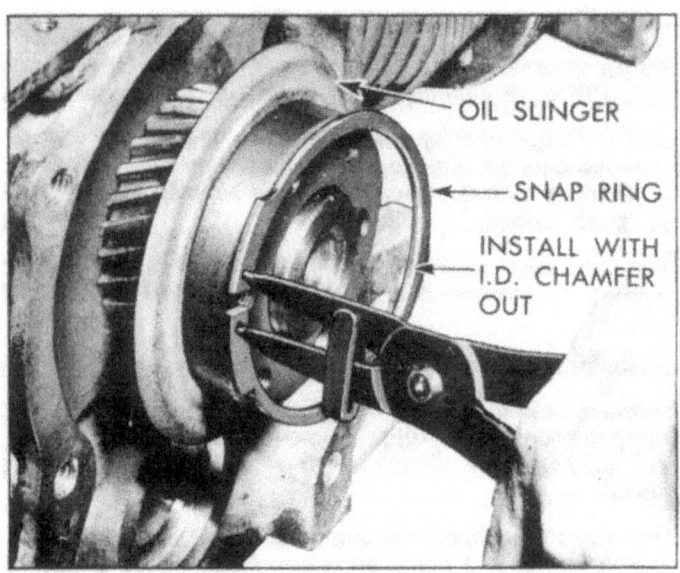

Removing Front Oil Slinger

43. Loosen crankcase bolts (located on side of crankcase), 8 long and 1 short bolt. Engines provide just one small bolt for mounting, the oil pump suction pipe clamp. (Place crankcase on a block of wood at an angle of about 15° so crankshaft and camshaft will not fall out when crankcase half is removed.)
44. Remove left crankcase half.
45. Remove camshaft by turning while lifting.

NOTE: Handle camshaft carefully, to avoid injury to camshaft bearing surfaces in crankcase.

47. Place assembly in an arbor press to remove camshaft gear.
48. Remove crankshaft, lifting straight out to avoid injury to rear crankshaft bearing.

NOTE: Crankshaft end thrust is taken at the rear bearing and crankshaft rear journal flange surfaces.

49. Remove oilslinger (1960) and distributor drive gear. Remove spacer and fuel pump eccentric.

NOTE: Be sure tool is on distributor gear solidly, so gear will not be damaged during removal operation.

50. Remove crankshaft gear.
51. Install crankshaft on a hydraulic press. Remove gear from crankshaft using a small piece of round steel to press crankshaft out of crankshaft gear.

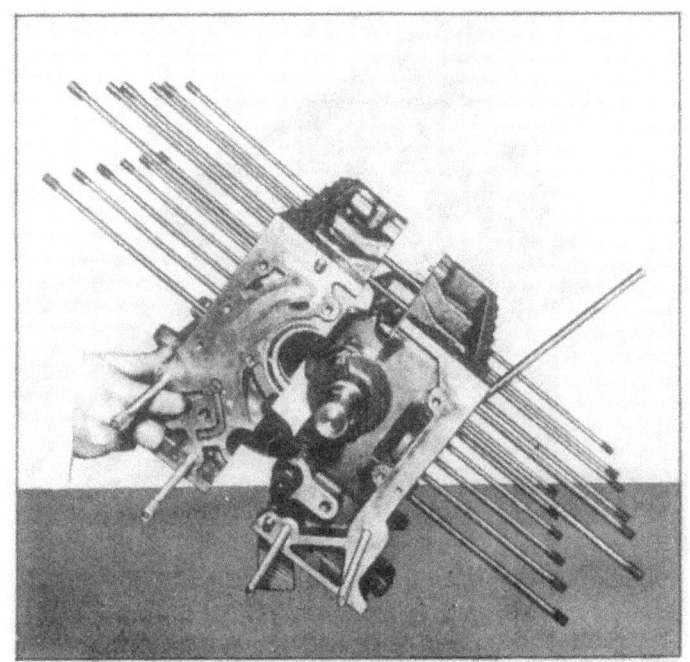

Removal and Installation of Crankcase Sections

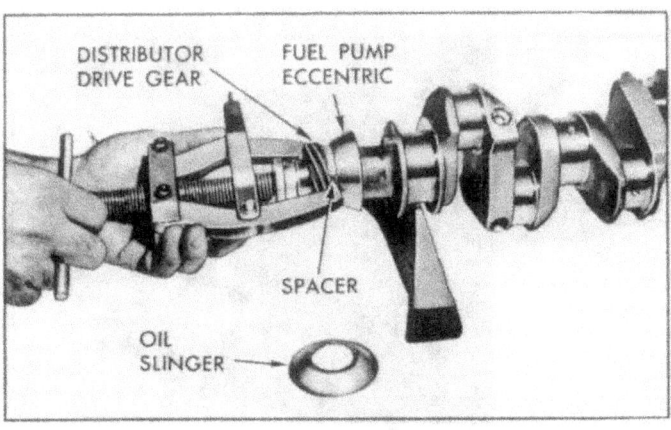

Removing Distributor Drive Gear

Main Bearings

52. Remove main bearing inserts from each half of crankshaft by rotating bearing insert with fingers, tank end first. Identify each bearing insert and place on a board or suitable storage area.

   NOTE: The engine rear housing incorporates the oil pump, pressure regulator and oil cooler by-pass valve.

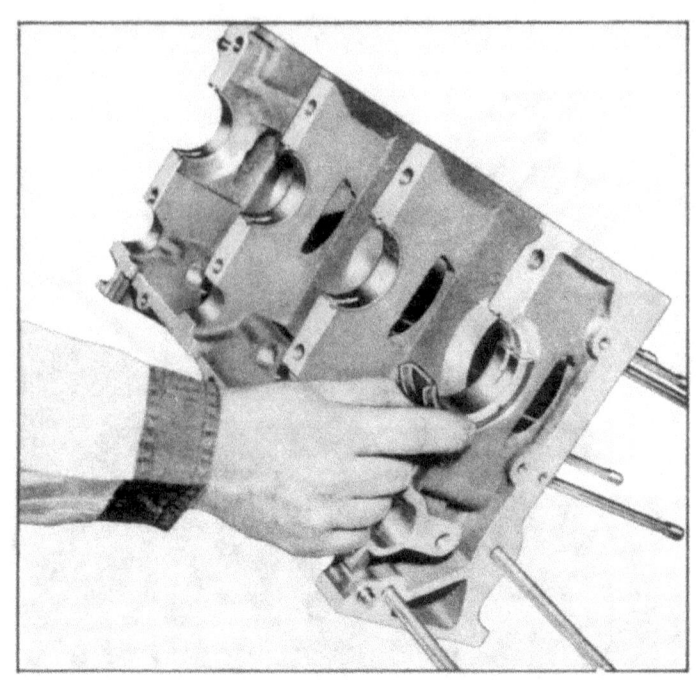

Removing and Installing Main Bearings

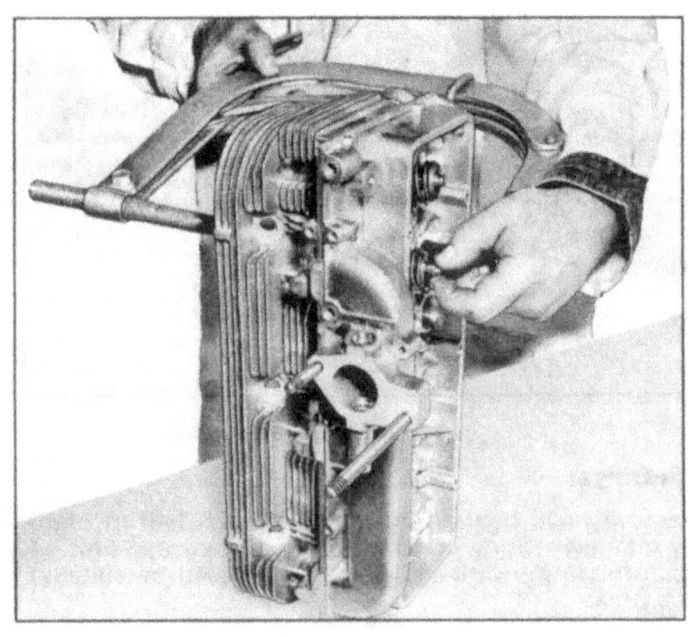

Removing Valves

REPAIRS — ENGINE COMPONENTS

Repairs to engine components, preceeding engine assembly are outlined below for cylinder heads, pistons and connecting rods, and main bearings.

CYLINDER HEADS

> NOTE: Always use extreme care to avoid damage to cooling fins.

Disassembly

1. Place cylinder head assembly on one end of a bench, compress valve spring and remove valve locks.
2. Remove valve spring cap, spring, shim and valve. Repeat this operation on each valve assembly.

Cleaning

1. Clean carbon from combustion chambers and ports using fine wire brush.

   > CAUTION: Avoid injury to cylinder sealing face surface head. Injury will cause premature combustion chamber leaks.

2. Thoroughly clean valve guide bores.
3. Clean valve stems and valve heads on a buffing wheel.

Removal and Assembly of Valves

A. Lock   B. Cap   C. Spring   D. Shim   E. Valve

4. Wash all parts in cleaning solvent and dry them thoroughly.

Inspection

1. Inspect cylinder heads for damage. Check fit of exhaust manifold sleeve assembly; if loose or cracked, replace.
2. Inspect the valves for burned seats, excessive seat pound in cracked faces or badly scuffed or worn stems.
3. Inspect valve seat inserts for cracks or burnt seats. Inspect valve guides for cracks or excessive wear.

   NOTE: If valve seat inserts or valve guides are beyond repair, cylinder head replacement is necessary.

   NOTE: Excessive valve to bore clearance may cause lack of power, oil comsumption, rough idling and noisy valves. Insufficient clearance will result in noisy and sticky functioning of the valve and disturb engine smoothness of operation.

4. Valve Stem clearance may be accurately determined by two methods:

   a. **Micrometer and Telescope Gage**
   Intake valve stem to bore clearance should be .001" to .0027" (new) and .001" to .004" (worn) while exhaust stem clearance should be .0015" to .0032" (new) and .002" to .005" (worn). Using a micrometer and a suitable telescope hole gage, check the diameter of the valve stem in three places; top center and bottom. Insert telescope hole gage in valve guide bore, measuring at the center. Subtract highest reading of valve stem diameter from valve guide bore center diameter to obtain valve to guide clearance. If clearance is not within .002" of above limits, use next oversize valve and ream valve bore to fit.

   b. **Using a Dial Indicator**
   Intake valve stem to bore clearance should be .001" to .0027" (new) and .001" to .004" (worn) while exhaust stem clearance should be .0015" to .0032" (new) and .002" to .005" (worn). Using a Last Word Indicator, clamp the indicator on one side of cylinder head rocker cover gasket rail, arranging the indicator so that movement of the valve stem from side to side (crosswise to the head) will cause a direct movement of the indicator stem. The indicator stem must contact the side of the valve stem just above the cylinder guide. With the valve head dropped about 1/16" off the valve seat, move the stem of the valve from side to side with light pressure to obtain the clearance. By trying new valves in the old bores it can be determined whether the valves should be replaced, or the bores reamed and oversized valves installed.

   NOTE: Valves with oversize stems are available in the following sizes, .003" and .010".

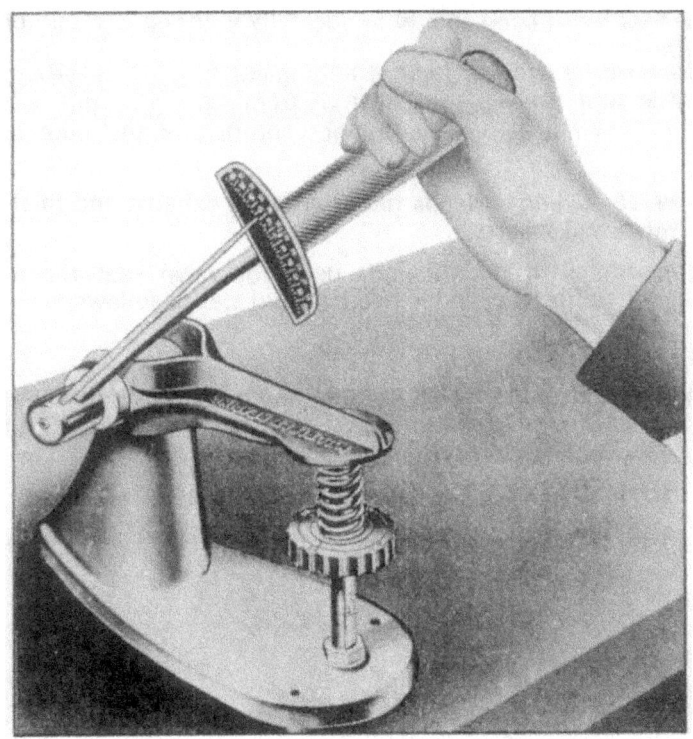

Checking Valve Spring Tension

5. Check valve spring tension.

Turbo Air Engine:
   Spring should be compressed to 1½" at which height it should check 58 to 64 lbs.

Super Turbo Air Engine:
   (R.P.O. 649)
   Spring should be compressed to 1 11/16" at which height it should check 71 to 81 lbs.
   Weak springs affect power and economy and should be replaced if not within 5 lbs. of the above limits.

Reseating Valve Seats

Reconditioning the valve seats is very important, because the seating of the valves must be perfect for the engine to deliver the power and performance built into it.

Another important factor is the cooling of the valve heads. Good contact between each valve and its seat in the head is imperative to insure that the heat in the valve head will be properly carried away.

Several different types of equipment are available for reseating valve seats; the recommendations of the manufacturer of the equipment being used should be carefully followed to attain proper results.

Regardless of what type of equipment is used, however, it is essential that valve guides be free from carbon or dirt and not worn excessively to insure proper centering of the pilot in the guide.

NOTE: Cylinder Heads have hardened exhaust and inlet valve seat inserts.

Regardless of the methods used for valve seat repair, the final seat width in cylinder head should be as follows:
Inlet 1/32" to 3/32"
Exhaust 1/16" to 1/8"

Valve seat angle on all valves should be 44° and should be concentric within .002" indicator reading. Always dress stones to proper angle before grinding valve seat.

NOTE: Valve face to seat angles should be as shown.

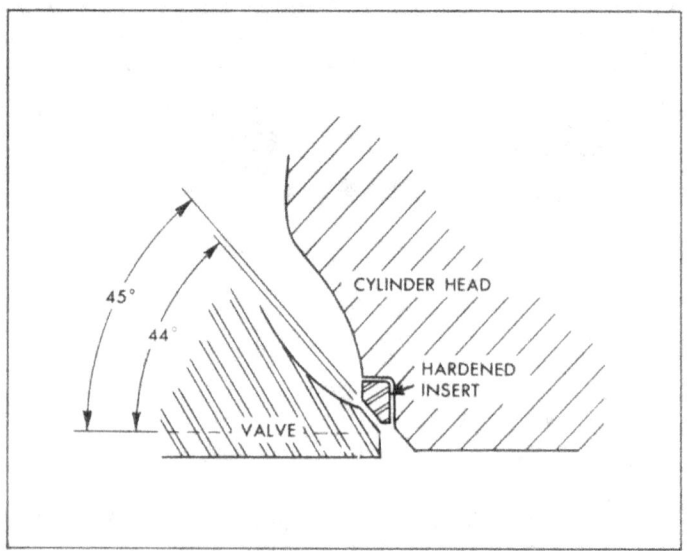

Relation of Valve and Seat Angles

Refacing Valves

Valves that are pitted can be refaced to the proper angle, insuring correct relation between the head and stem on a valve refacing machine. Valve stems which show excessive wear, or valves that are pounded in or warped excessively should be replaced. When a valve head which is pounded in or warped excessively is refaced, a knife edge will be ground on part or all of the valve head due to the amount of metal that must be removed to completely reface. Knife edges lead to premature breakage, burning and pre-ignition due to heat localizing on this knife edge. If the edge of the valve head is less than 1/32" thick after grind-

Removing Exhaust Manifold Sleeves

ing, replace the valve.

1. If necessary, dress the valve refacing machine grinding wheel to make sure it is true and smooth.
2. Set chuck angle at 44° mark for grinding valves.
3. After setting chuck angle, insert valve and grind carefully.

Exhaust Valve Seat Inserts

When reconditioning valves, the inserts in the cylinder head should be inspected. If either valve inserts or valve guides are beyond repair, cylinder head will need to be replaced as a unit.

Cylinder Head Assembly

1. To install carburetor attaching studs if replacement is necessary, coat threads with Permatex anti-seize compound #404 or equivalent and install long stud 5/16"-18-24 x 4 13/16", in intake manifold flange at "A" on left and right bank cylinder heads to a length of 4 3/16".
2. Install short stud 5/16"-18 x 24 x 2¼", in intake manifold flange at "B" on left and right bank cylinder heads to a length of 1 5/8".
3. If necessary to replace exhaust manifold studs coat new stud with anti-seize compound and install to a length of 31/32".
   NOTE: Cylinder Heads are identical except for location of vacuum balance tube hose connector "E" which is on one side of carburetor mounting pad on the right bank and the other side on the left bank.
4. Install each valve coated with SAE #30 engine oil or moly-

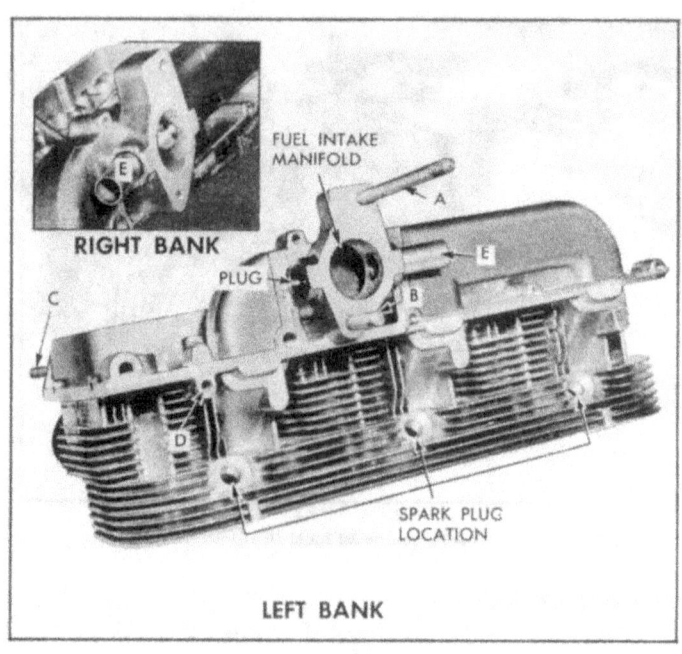

Carburetor Attaching Studs, and Vacuum Balance Tube

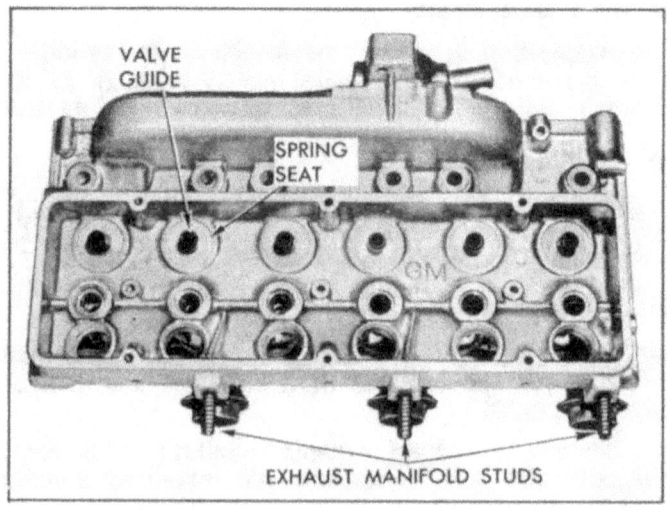

Top View of Cylinder Head (Right Bank Shown)

kote solution in the valve guide from which it was removed or to valve guide it was fitted. Lightly coat valve spring shim with petrolatum (this will hold shim in place for assembly) and place on valve spring seat.

5. Set valve spring in place on shim in cylinder head. Place cap in position and compress valve spring.

   NOTE: **Super Turbo-Air engines incorporate valve spring dampers.**

6. Install valve locks and release spring compressor tool, making sure locks seat properly in valve groove on stem.

7. Assemble the remaining valves, valve springs, shims, spring caps and valve locks in cylinder head in the same manner.
   NOTE: **Each valve spring must have a hardened shim (minimum of .020") under it, to protect aluminum sur-**

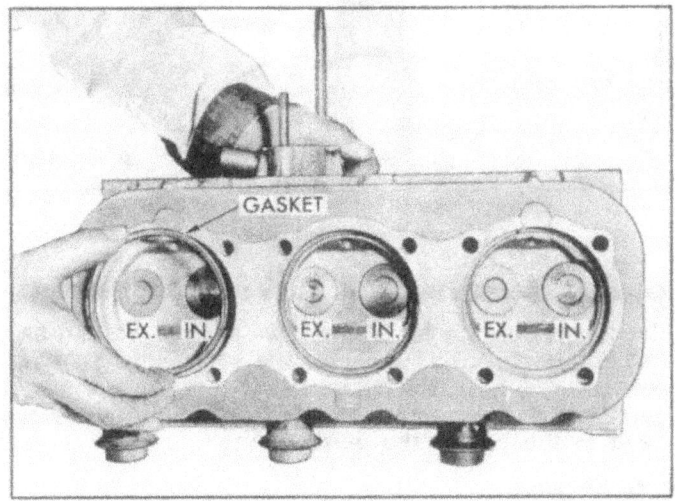

Installation of Cylinder Head Gasket

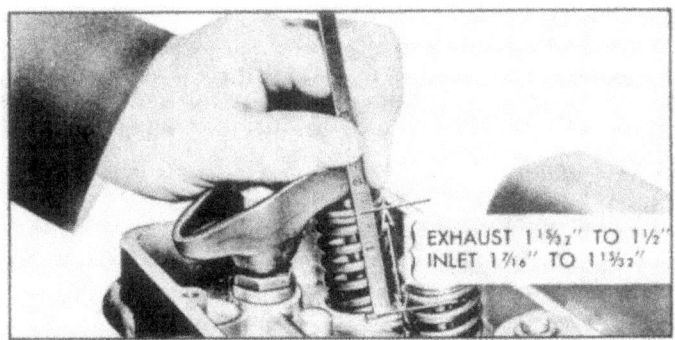

Checking Installed Height of Valve Springs

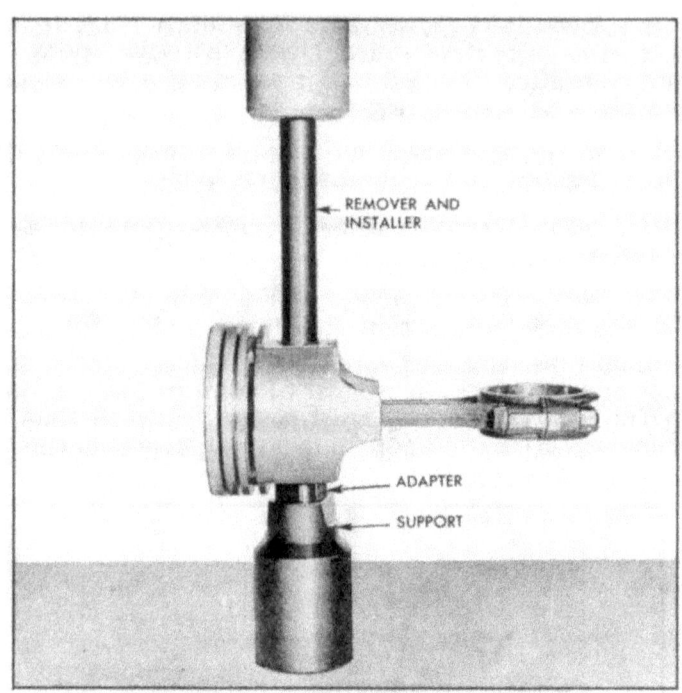

Removing and Installing Piston Pin

face. Shims are available for service in .030" thickness.

8. Check installed height of the valve springs. Reseating valves raises the installed height of the valve springs and, if excessive, will have the effect of weak valve springs. Use a narrow, thin scale and measure from the spring seat in the head to the top of the valve spring.

Turbo-Air Engine:
    1 1/2" exhaust valve springs.
    1 15/32" inlet valve springs.

Super Turbo-Air Engine:
    1 11/16" exhaust and inlet valve springs.

If readings are found in excess of the above readings, install a valve spring shim, approximately .030" thick. At no time should the spring be shimmed to give an installed height of less than:

Turbo-Air Engine:
    1 15/16" exhaust valve springs.
    1 7/16" inlet valve springs.

Super Turbo-Air Engine:
    1 21/32" exhaust and inlet valve springs.

9. Coat cylinder head, cylinder counterbore pilot with a light coat of petrolatum (this will retain gasket for assembly) and install new cylinder head gaskets in place.

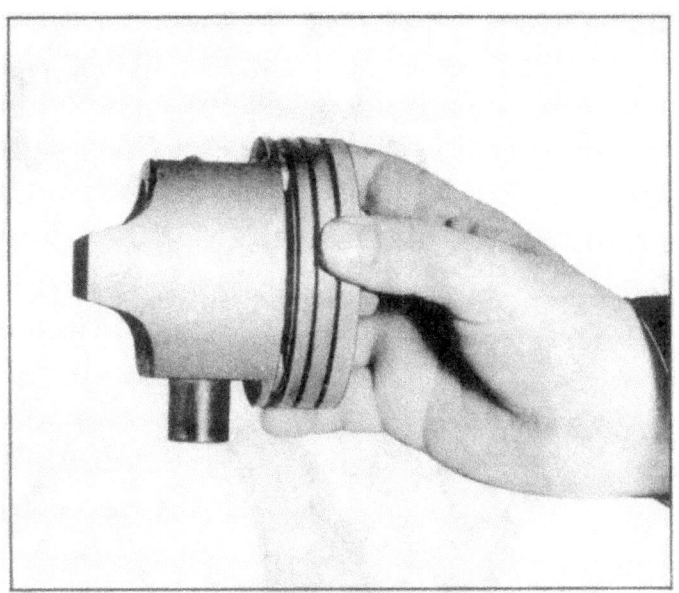
Checking Piston Pin Fit

PISTONS AND CONNECTING RODS
Disassembly
1. Remove all piston rings by expanding them and sliding them off the top of the pistons.
2. Install piston and connecting rod assembly. Place assembly in an arbor press. Press pin out of connecting rod.
3. Remove from press and remove piston pin from support and remove tool from piston and rod.

PISTON FIT PIN
Piston pins should be capable of supporting their own weight in either pin boss when coated with light engine oil and at 70°F. Higher or lower temperatures will cause false indications. Pistons, pins and cylinders are serviced as assemblies.

PISTONS, RINGS AND CYLINDER ASSEMBLY
Cylinders
1. Using a block of wood for a fixture, drill two holes, spaced to provide a location for two long bolts, holes should be small enough to require driving the bolts into the block of wood.
2. Clamp wood block fixture in a suitable vise.
3. Install cylinder over bolts on wood fixture. Holding cylinder with one hand, insert ridge reamer and remove ridge and/or carbon from cylinder.

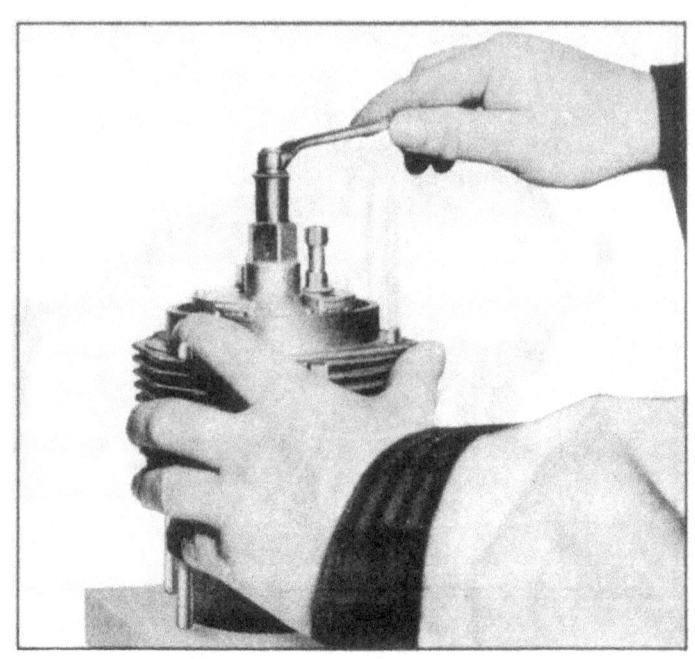

Removing Ridge and/or Carbon from Cylinder

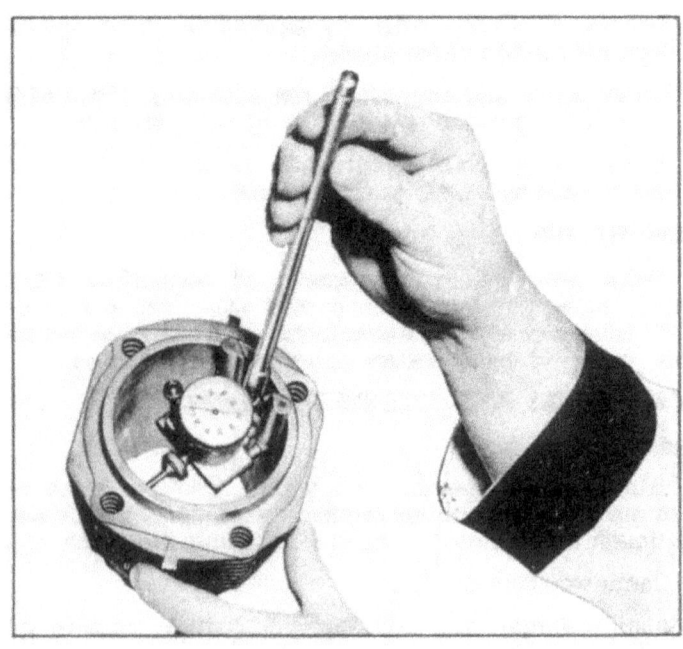

Checking Cylinder Bore

4. Check the cylinder walls for taper, out-of-round or excessive ridge at the top of ring travel. Set gauge so that thrust pin must be forced in about ¼" to enter gauge in cylinder bore. Center gauge in cylinder and turn dial to "0." Carefully work gauge up and down cylinder to determine taper and turn it to different points around cylinder wall to determine the out-of-round condition.

If the cylinders were found to have taper or wear in excess of .005" the cylinder and piston must be replaced.

NOTE: Cylinders and pistons are serviced as a unit.

Checking Ring Gap

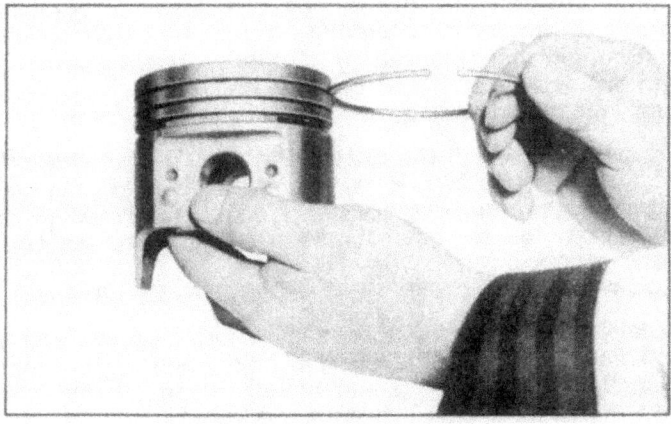

Rolling Ring in Groove

Piston Rings

All compression rings are marked with the letters "G.M." or "TOP" on the upper side of the ring.

When installing compression rings, make sure the face with the bevel is assembled away from the top of the piston. The face with markings is to top of piston.

NOTE: Piston rings are furnished in standard size only.

The oil control ring consists of a flexible expander with six horizontal slots, for a one piece cast iron constructed oil ring, with slots equally spaced, and the entire piston ring outside diameter having an undercut, leaving two wiping surfaces.

1. Slip a piston ring in the cylinder bore; then using the head of a piston, press the ring down into the cylinder bore about two inches.

   NOTE: Using a piston this way will place the ring square with the cylinder walls.

2. Check the space or gap between the ends of the ring with a feeler gauge. This should be from .010" to .020".

3. If the gap between the ends of the ring is less than .010", remove the ring and try another for fit, or file the ends for the proper gap.

4. New pistons, rings and cylinder bores wear considerably during seating and gaps widen quickly; however, engine operation will not become seriously affected if ring gaps do not become greater than 1/32".

5. Carefully remove all particles of carbon from the ring grooves in the piston and inspect the grooves carefully for burrs or nicks that might cause the rings to hang up.

6. Slip the outer surface of the compression ring into the piston ring groove and roll the ring entirely around the groove to make sure that the ring is free and does not bind in the groove at any point. If binding occurs, the cause should be determined and removed by carefully dressing with a fine cut file. However, if the binding is caused by a distorted ring, install a new ring.

7. Proper clearance of the piston ring in its piston ring groove is very important in maintaining engine performance and in preventing excessive oil consumption. Therefore, when fitting new rings, the clearance between the top and bottom surfaces of the ring grooves should be .0012" to .0032" for compression rings and .002" to .0035" for oil rings.

8. Install the oil ring expander in the oil ring groove and position gap in line with piston pin hole. Using ring expander expand oil control ring, and install in the oil ring groove, with the gap toward the top of the engine.

9. Flex the oil ring assembly in its groove to make sure ring

Checking Groove Clearance

is free and does not bind in the groove at any point. If binding occurs, the cause should be determined and removed by carefully dressing with a fine cut file. However, if the binding is caused by a distorted ring, install a new ring.

PISTON AND CONNECTING ROD

Assembly

1. Lubricate piston pin holes in piston and connecting rod to facilitate installation of pin.
2. Position connecting rod in its respective piston.
3. Install piston pin on installer J-8355-3 and pilot spring, adapter J-8355-1 and pilot in support.
4. Install piston and rod on support, indexing pilot through piston and rod.

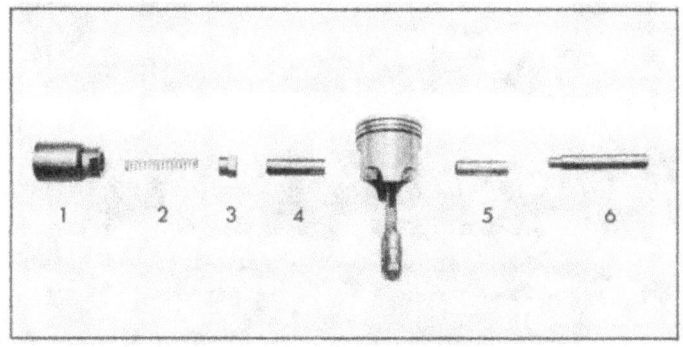

Piston Pin Assembly

1. Support (J-6994)
2. Spring
3. Adapter (J-8355-1)
4. Pilot (J-8355-2)
5. Piston Pin
6. Installer and Remover (J-8355-3)

5. Place support on an arbor press, start pin into piston and press on installer until piston pin pilot bottoms.
6. Remove installer and support assembly and adapter from piston and connecting rod assembly.
7. Check piston pin for freedom of movement in piston bore.

NOTE: Piston pins are a matched fit to each piston and are not available separately.

MAIN BEARINGS

Bearing and Journal Inspection

Whenever the crankcase is parted, the bearing inserts and the crankshaft journals should be inspected.

If upon inspection one half shows evidence of fatigue, distress, abrasion, erosion, scoring or the like, both halves should be replaced. Never should one-half be replaced without replacing the other half.

If the running clearance of a bearing is too great with used inserts, it will be necessary to install both bearing halves. Should this become necessary, the crankshaft journal should be checked with a micrometer for out-of-round, taper or undersize dimensions.

Crankcase Tightening Sequence

Measuring Plastigage on Crankshaft Journals

Experience has shown that clearance increase from wear in main bearings is not only due to bearing wear, but is also due in part to crankshaft journal wear.

Main Bearing Clearance (Using Plastigage)

Plastigage consists of a wax-like plastic material which will compress evenly between the bearing and journal surfaces without damaging either surface. To obtain the most accurate results with Plastigage, certain precautions should be observed.

> NOTE: To assure the proper seating of the bearings, all crankcase bolts must be at their specified torque. Eight long bolts 7/16"-20, 42 to 48 ft. lbs. and one 5/16"-18, 7 to 13 ft. lbs. torque. Hold bolt head, on crankcase bolts 7/16"-20" while tightening the nut. Do not tighten at bolt head. Figure shows tightening sequence. One 5/16" bolt (#9) is used to fasten the oil suction tube retaining bracket. In addition, preparatory to checking fit of bearings, the surface of the crankshaft journal and bearings should be wiped clean of oil.

1. Remove one half of the crankcase, while the other is supported on its side, wipe oil from journal and bearings with a soft clean cloth.

2. Place a piece of Plastigage the full width of the bearing (parallel to the crankshaft on the journal).

   NOTE: Crankcase split line surfaces must be free of nicks and foreign matter.

3. Install other half of crankcase with bearings and evenly tighten the crankcase bolts to proper torque.
   CAUTION: Do not rotate the crankshaft while the Plastigage is between the bearing and journal.

4. Remove one half of crankcase. The flattened Plastigage will be found adhering to either the bearing shells or journals. On the edge of Plastigage packing envelope there is a graduated scale which is correlated in thousandths of an inch.

5. Without removing the Plastigage, check its compressed width (at the widest point) with the graduations on the Plastigage envelope.

   NOTE: Normally, main bearing journals wear evenly and are not out-of-round. However, if a bearing is being fitted to an out-of-round journal be sure to fit to the maximum diameter of the journal. If the bearing is fitted to the minimum diameter of the journal and the journal is out-of-round .001" or more, interference between the bearing and journal will result in rapid bearing failure. If the flattened Plastigage tapers toward the middle or ends, there is a difference in clearance indicating a taper, low spot or other irregularity of the bearing or journal. Be sure to check the journal with a micrometer if the flattened Plastigage indicates more than .001" difference.

   NOTE: 1961-62 crankshaft journal diameters are 2.0978" to 2.0988" for No. 1 and 2. For No. 3 and 4 2.20993"-20983".

   NOTE: 1960 Crankshaft journal diameters are 2.0978" to 2.0988".

6. If the bearing clearance is not over .004" (worn), or .003" (new) or less than .001" the bearing insert is satisfactory. If the clearance is not within these limits replace the insert.

REPLACEMENT BEARINGS

If clearance with plastigage is	Install bearing sets
.0010	.000 (Std.)
.0015	.001 U/S
.0020	.001 U/S
.0025	.002 U/S
.0030	.002 U/S
.0035	.003 U/S
.0040	.003 U/S

If these undersize bearings do not produce the proper clearance, it will be necessary to regrind the crankshaft journal for use with the next undersize bearing.

Checking Crankshaft End Play

CAUTION: Do not install No. 4 main bearing in No. 2 or No. 3 bearing locations. The No. 4 main bearing halves are .0015" thicker than No. 2 and No.3 main bearings at the ends which are located at the top half of the crankcase and are thinner by the same amount at the opposite ends. This has the effect of lowering the center line of the bearing .0015".

The No. 4 main bearing is identified by a brown dye on edges of the bearing shell.

NOTE: Bearings are available in standard sizes and .001", .002", .003", .010" and .020" undersize.

7. Proceed to each bearing. After all bearings have been checked and installed, rotate the crankshaft to see that there is no excessive drag.

8. Check the end play by forcing the crankshaft to its extreme front position. Check with a dial indicator. This clearance should be from .002" to .006".

CONNECTING ROD BEARINGS

Bearing Clearance

Connecting rod bearing inserts are available in standard sizes and undersizes of .001", .002", .010" and .020". These bearings are not shimmed and when clearance becomes excessive the next undersized bearing insert should be used. Do not file rod or rod caps.

1. Remove the connecting rod bearing cap.

   NOTE: Install a piece of plastic hose with at least 5/16" I.D. over each bolt as shown in Figure 6A-85.

2. Wipe bearing insert shell and crankpin clean of oil.
3. Place a piece of Plastigage the full width of the bearing or crankpin (parallel to the crankshaft).
4. Reinstall the bearing cap and evenly tighten the retaining bolts to 20 to 26 ft. lbs. torque.

   CAUTION: Do not turn crankshaft with the Plastigage installed.

5. Remove the bearing cap and without removing the Plastigage, check its width at the widest point with the Plastigage scale.

   NOTE: If the crankpin is out-of-round be sure to fit the bearing to the maximum diameter of the crankpin. If the flattened plastic is not uniform from end to end in its

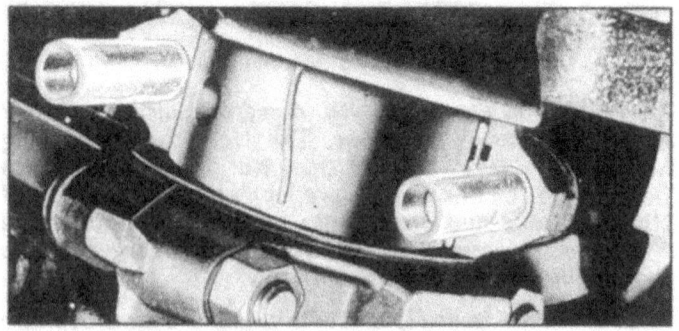

Plastigage on Crankpin

Measuring Plastigage

Connecting Rod Side Clearance

width, the crankpin or bearing is tapered, as a low spot or some other irregularity. Check the crankpin with a micrometer for taper if the flattened Plastigage indicates more than a .001" difference.

6. If the reading is not over .003" (worn), or .002" (new) or not less than .001" the fit is satisfactory. If however, the clearances are not within these limits, replace the bearing with the proper undersize bearings.

NOTE: The insert bearing shells are not adjustable and no attempt should be made to adjust by filing the bearing caps.

7. Rotate the crankshaft after bearing adjustment to be sure the bearings are not too tight.
8. Check connecting rod side clearance between upper half of connecting rod and side of crank pin. This clearance should be .005" to .010".

Flywheel Housing Seal Replacement

1. Tap seal out of flywheel housing with a wood or fibre drift.
2. Clean flywheel housing seal surface with a suitable solvent and check this surface for nicks or damage.
3. Lubricate seal outer surface (beaded area) with lubriplate or petrolatum and install with a suitable tool.

NOTE: Flywheel Housing Seal, sealing lips are coated with high melting (350°F) cup grease for the life of the seal. If seal is removed and still usable, pack sealing lips with a good grade of cup grease, with a melting point of 350°F minimum.

ENGINE ASSEMBLY

Crankshaft

1. To assemble the crankshaft gear to the crankshaft, proceed as follows:

    a. Firmly support crankshaft between front crankshaft throw and front journal with a support in on a hydraulic press.

    NOTE: Since the crankshaft gear to crankshaft uses a high press tolerance, a hydraulic press is required for removal and installation.

    Note: Support must clear thrust face on No. 6 crankpin.

    b. Lubricate crankshaft with hypoid lubricant, and install woodruff key in shaft keyway.

    c. Install crankshaft gear and press into place.

    d. Install woodruff keys (two) on rear end of crankshaft

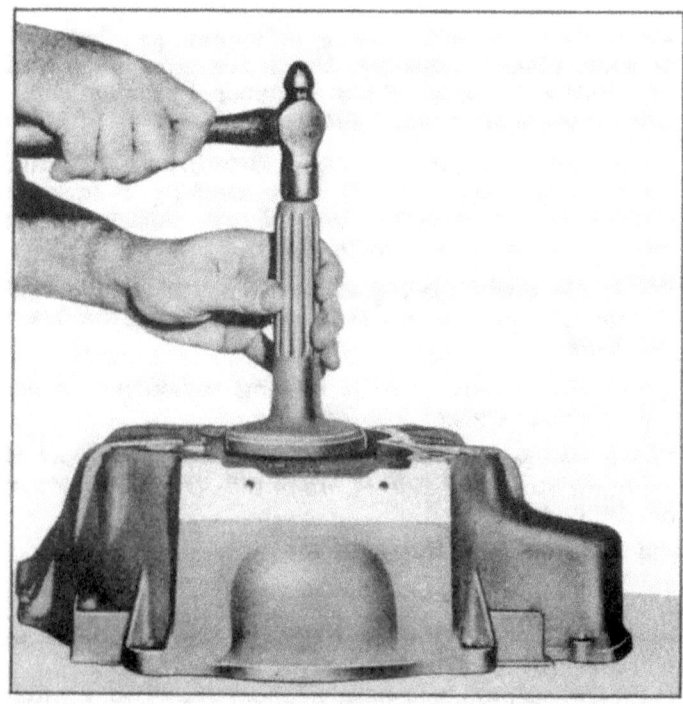

Installing Flywheel Housing Seal

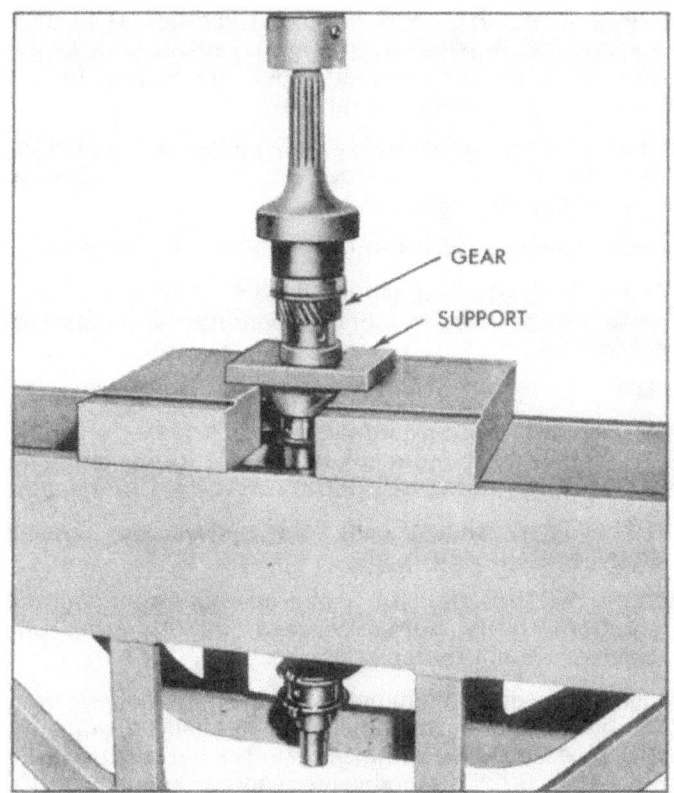

Installing Crankshaft Gear

(Engine Rear Housing End), one for the fuel pump eccentric distributor drive gear and the other for the crankshaft pulley. Position fuel pump eccentric and spacer on crankshaft. Lubricate crankshaft and distributor drive gear with engine oil and install distributor drive gear until it bottoms. Install oil slinger with concave side away from distributor drive gear.

2. If crankshaft main bearing journals have been refinished to

Crankshaft Installed

definite undersize, install the correct undersize bearings. Be sure the bearing inserts and crankcase bearing bores are clean. Foreign material under the inserts may distort the bearings and cause a failure.

3. Place one half of crankcase on a block of wood (preferably the left side) and install bearing insert and lubricate with a light coat of engine oil.
4. Install bearing insert in other half (right side) of crankcase.
5. Install crankshaft assembly in the crankcase (left side), being careful not to damage bearings and lubricate with engine oil.

Camshaft

The camshaft bearing journals are 1.2005"—1.1995" in diameter for the front intermediate, rear intermediate and rear journal. The front journal is 1.4405"—1.4395" in diameter.

NOTE: Each exhaust cam lobe serves two exhaust lifters, one on each bank.

6. Check the journals with a micrometer for an out-of-round condition. If the journals exceed .001" out-of-round, the camshaft should be replaced.
7. Check camshaft alignment. The best method is by use of "V" blocks and a dial indicator. The dial indicator will indicate the exact amount the camshaft is out of true. If it is out more than .002" dial indicator reading, the camshaft should be replaced.

Installing Camshaft in Crankcase

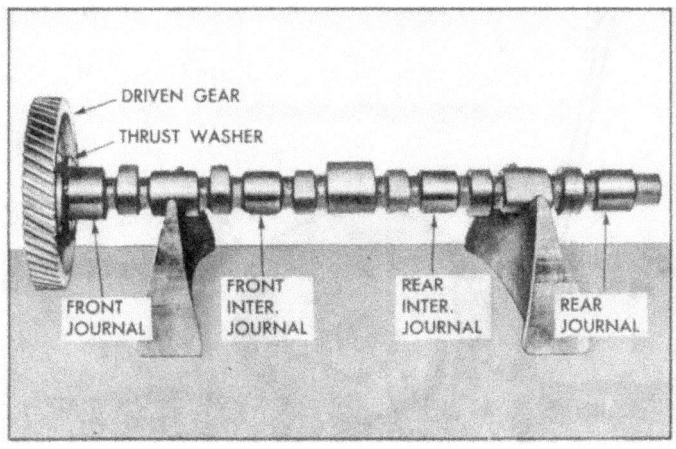
Camshaft Assembly

NOTE: Camshaft journal clearance should be .0015" to .0035" (new) and .002" to .004" (used). If camshaft clearance is beyond these limits either the crankcase or camshaft should be replaced.

8. To assemble camshaft driven gear and thrust washer to camshaft, proceed as follows:

   a. Firmly support shaft at back of the front journal in an arbor press.
   b. Place thrust washer over end of shaft, and install woodruff key in shaft keyway.
   c. Lubricate camshaft with hypoid lubricant.
   d. Install camshaft driven gear on camshaft and press into place, supporting gear until it bottoms against the thrust washer.

Timing Gear Marks

9. Install camshaft assembly guiding camshaft thrust washer into grove in crankcase while indexing camshaft driven gear to crankshaft gear, so that valve timing marks line up. Lubricate camshaft bearings and drive gear.

10. Install other half of crankcase and main bearing assembly onto crankshaft and camshaft. Seal crankcase parting line ends with sealer. Install all crankcase bolts, flat washers and nuts. Torque the eight long bolts 7/16"-20, 42 to 48 ft. lbs. and one small bolt 5/16"-18, 7 to 13 ft. lbs. Figure shows crankcase tightening sequence.

Camshaft End Play

11. Install a dial indicator so that indicator point touches the end of the camshaft. Zero dial indicator and push camshaft one direction then the other. Dial indicator reading should be .002" to .007".

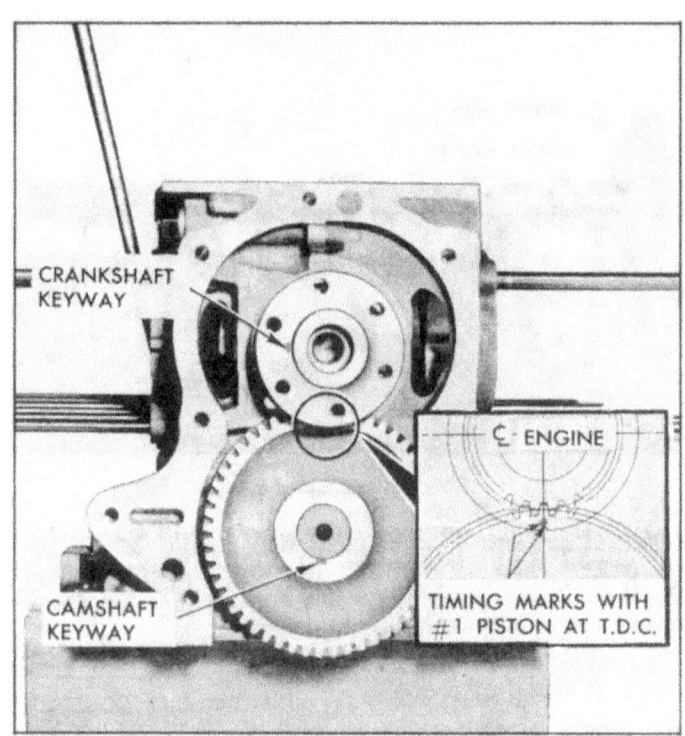

Timing Marks

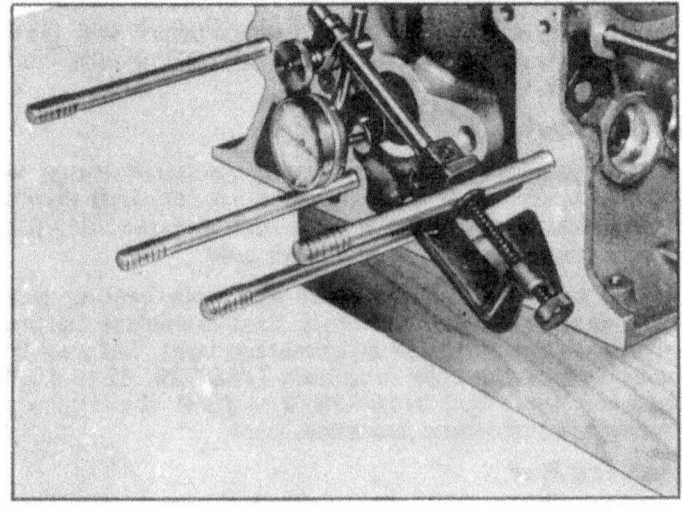

Checking Camshaft End Play

Timing Gear Backlash

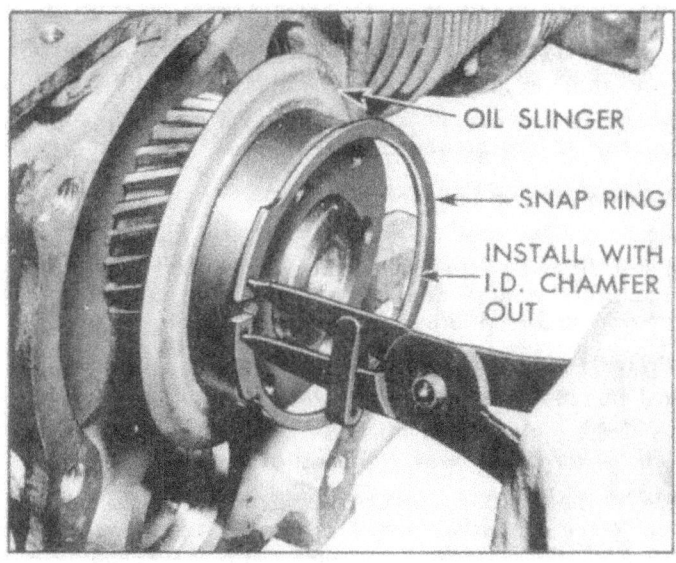

Installing Front Oil Slinger Retainer Snap Ring

12. If the end play is excessive, check the thrust washer and/or crankcase groove for wear. Replace timing gears in matched set and/or thrust washer.

Timing Gear Backlash

13. Check timing gear backlash by installing a dial indicator. Backlash should be .002" to .004".
14. Install the 1960 front crankshaft oil slinger on crankshaft gear with flange side toward crankcase. Install crankshaft oil slinger retaining ring in snap ring groove.

   NOTE: Be careful when installing snap ring. Avoid scratching sealing surface.

   Install main oil gallery plugs, with "Permatex Anti-seize Compound #404 or its equivalent.

Flywheel and Clutch Housing

15. Install a new gasket between the flywheel or clutch housing and crankcase. Install flywheel or clutch housing with bolts and flat washers and torque bolts 20-30 ft. lbs.

   NOTE: Total indicator runout for flywheel or clutch housing pilot is .015".

Flywheel

16. Install flywheel or flex plate on crankshaft flange with sealer between flywheel and crankshaft. Install spacer and bolts with sealer on bolt threads. Torque bolts 20 to 26 ft. lbs.

   NOTE: Flywheel face runout installed and torqued on crankshaft is .020" T.I.R. Flywheel O.D., T.I.R. .010".

17. Mount engine crankcase and flywheel or clutch housing assembly, to engine stand and adapter.

Piston, Cylinders and Connecting Rods

18. Apply a light coat of engine oil to the piston rings. Install piston rings by expanding them. Position oil ring gap towards the top of engine and compression ring gap 45° from the oil ring gap location.

   NOTE: 1960 Piston rings must be installed with marking and inside bevel toward top of piston.

   1961-62 piston rings must be installed with markings and inside bevel away from top of piston.

19. Install piston ring compressor over the piston and rings. Tighten snugly and insert piston and connecting rod assembly into the respective cylinder bore. (Corresponding number.
20. Push piston assembly in with a hammer handle, while holding cylinder bore in one hand until it is slightly below the

Installing Piston Assembly

top of the cylinder bore.

NOTE: Notch on piston top must be installed towards the front of engine (flywheel end) on both banks.

21. With piston assemblies in the cylinder bores, place connecting rod bearing inserts in place on connecting rods and caps.
22. Position crankcase pins, by turning crankshaft with crankshaft pulley, so that crankshaft journal is in line with piston and rod to be installed.
23. Place a piece of plastic hose with at least a 5/16" I.D. over each connecting rod bolt (this will protect the bearing surface on the crankshaft journal).
24. Install a new (copper) cylinder gasket over cylinder pilot. Push piston assembly with a hammer handle, while guiding cylinder bore pilot into crankcase. Remove plastic hose sections from connecting rod bolts. Install connecting rod, bearing cap and nuts. Torque connecting rod nuts 20 to 26 ft. lbs. Install cylinder holding fixture tubes (used previously on engine disassembly), one long and one short of cylinder studs to hold cylinder in place. Continue procedure until all cylinders and pistons are installed.

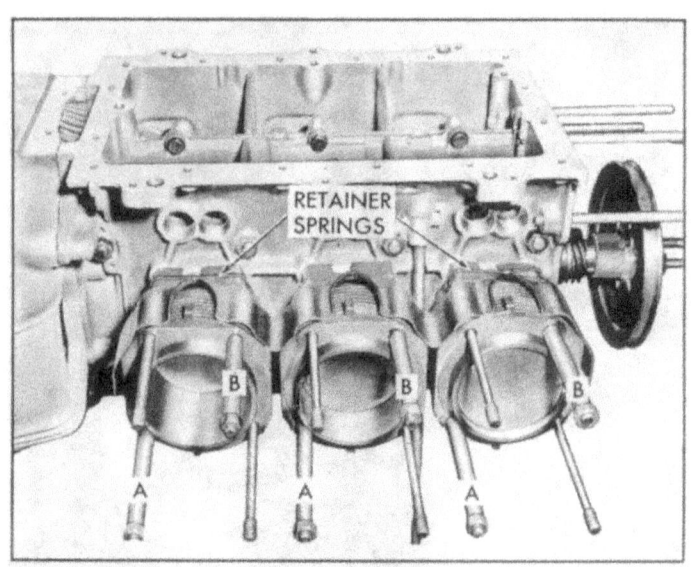

Installing Cylinder, Piston and Rod

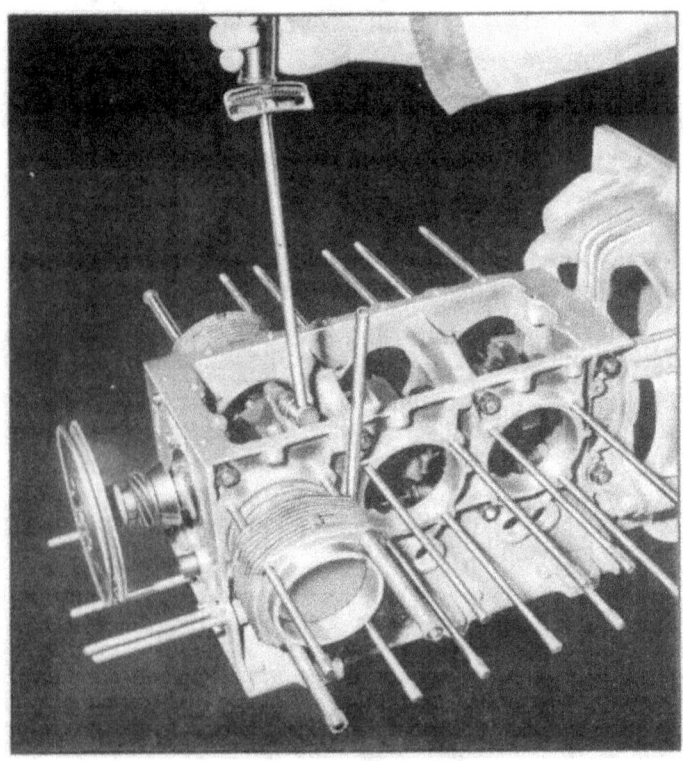

Torquing Connecting Rods—Showing Tubes Holding Opposite Cylinder

25. After all piston and connecting rod assemblies have been installed, check the side clearance between the connecting rod on each crankshaft journal. This clearance should be .005" to .010".
26. Install cylinder air baffles with retaining springs.

   NOTE: Air baffles are not interchangeable. Right side air baffle has a hole for crankcase vent tube.

Crankcase Cover and Blower Bearing

27. Install a new crankcase cover gasket on crankcase. Install crankcase vent and another crankcase gasket. Install crankcase cover and blower bearing assembly in place and install washers and bolts using anti-seize compound and torque bolts 7 to 13 ft. lbs. Install crankcase vent tube and gasket.

Oil Pump Screen and Tube

28. Invert the engine assembly on the work stand.

   NOTE: If the original or a new oil pump screen and tube assembly is to be installed in the original crankcase, the outside diameter of the end of the tube will have to be tinned with solder before installing in the crankcase.

Installing Oil Pump, Screen and Pickup Tube

Install oil pump, screen and pickup tube assembly into the cylinder case with the pickup screen positioned parallel to the oil pan rails. Install pickup tube retaining clamp to tube and crankcase.

29. Coat threads on engine temperature and oil pressure sending units, with anti-seize compound such as Permatex #404D

Installation of Cylinder Head

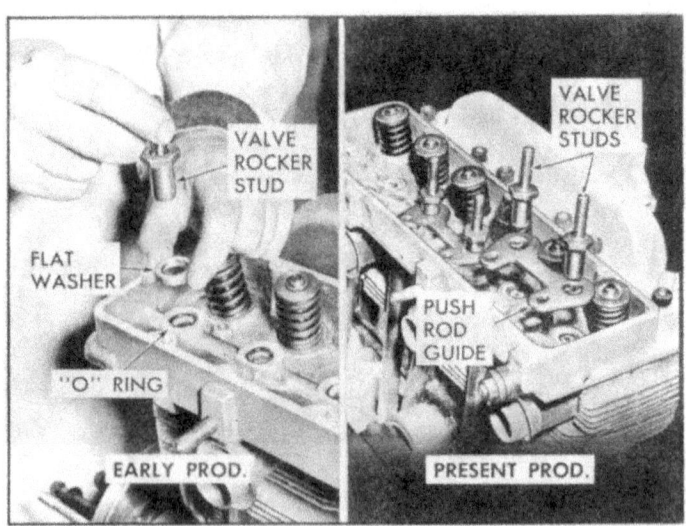

Installation of Valve Rocker Studs

Cylinder Head Tightening Sequence

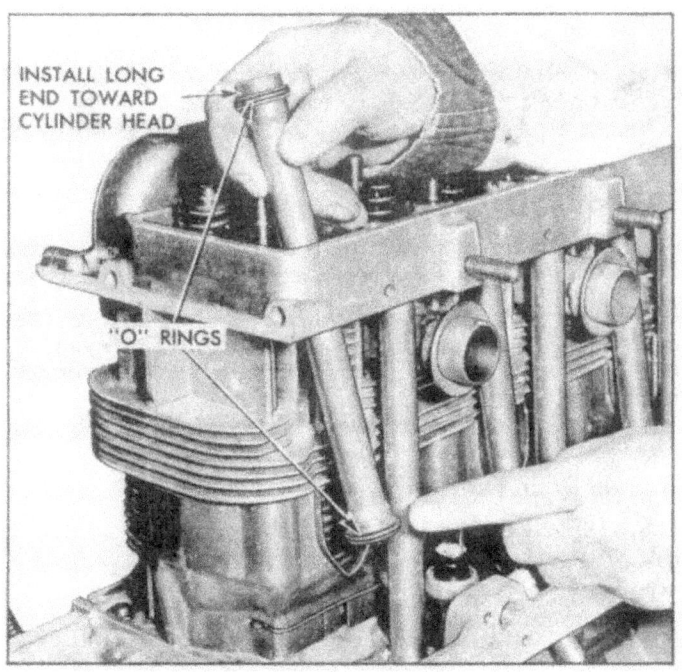

Installation of Push Rod Drain Tubes

Push Rod Installation

or its equivalent. Install oil temperature sending unit in cylinder head and torque 10 to 15 ft. lbs.

Install oil pressure sending unit and torque 45 to 65 in. lbs.

Cylinder Head

30. Position engine with cylinders up in a vertical position so that cylinder head may be lowered over the cylinder studs.

    NOTE: Be sure all cylinder head gaskets are in the cylinder head combustion chamber. Remove all cylinder retaining tubes from cylinder bank to which cylinder head is to be installed.

    Install cylinder head over studs and carefully lower in place.

Push Rod Oil Drain Tube

31. Lightly oil hydraulic lifters and install in their proper bores. Install push rod oil drain tubes through cylinder head. Place "O" rings, one on each end of drain tube. Oil "O" rings with motor oil and push into place, at lifter bore in crankcase and cylinder head.

    NOTE: Long end of push rod oil drain tube must be installed up towards cylinder head.

32. Install six flat washers and nuts on long studs, adjacent to the intake manifold. Install six new "O" rings lubricated with lubriplate in counterbore of cylinder head (location for

valve rocker studs) and coat rocker stud bore with anti-seize compound. Install push rod guides and valve rocker studs, with the threads coated with anti-seize compound.

Early 1960, install six flat washers and nuts on long studs, adjacent to the intake manifold. Install six new "O" rings lubricated with lubriplate in counterbore of cylinder head (location for valve rocker studs) and coat rocker stub bore with anti-seize compound. Install valve rocker studs, with the threads coated with anti-seize compound, with flat washer as shown. (Early production engines, install push rod guides **under** valve rocker studs.)

NOTE: Flat washer used under valve rocker stud, locates stud height for all valve rocker studs. DO NOT interchange with an ordinary flat washer.

33. Tighten the nuts and valve rocker studs in the sequence shown. Two sizes of sockets will be required when tightening cylinder head, a 13/16" deep socket for the valve rocker studs and a 9/16" socket on the cylinder head nuts. Torque nuts 27 to 33 ft. lbs. and valve rocker studs 27 to 33 ft. lbs.

34. Install push rods with the side oil hole up into the valve rocker arm socket. A ½" band of blue ink for identification is marked on the push rod at the .050" side oil hole end of the push rod.

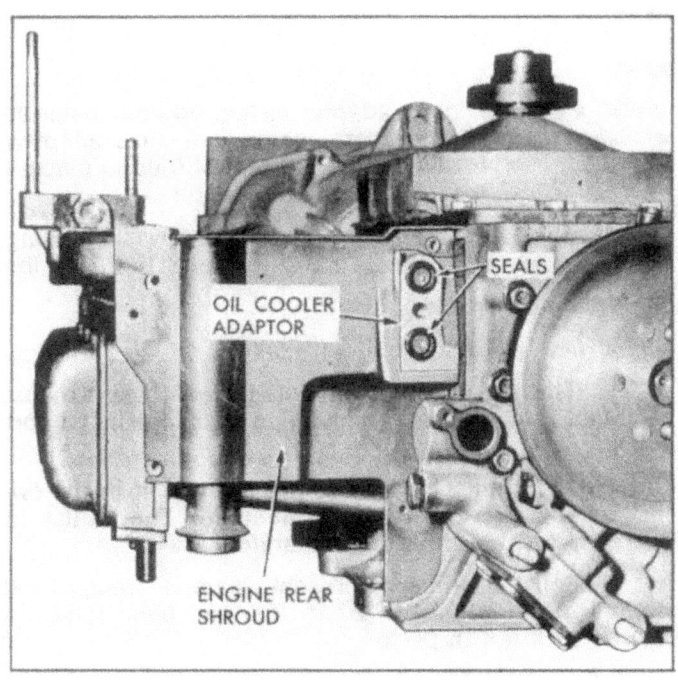

Installation of Oil Cooler Adapter and Seals

NOTE: Push rod guides are installed under the valve rocker studs in most models, early production was vice versa, replace as found.

35. Install valve rocker arms, balls and nuts loosely in place. Install remaining cylinder head and valve rocker arms, balls and nuts.

Engine Rear Housing

36. Install a new engine rear housing gasket and position engine rear housing in place. Coat bolt threads with anti-seize compound such as "Permatex" #404 or its equivalent. Install flat washers and bolts and torque bolts 7 to 13 ft. lbs.

Crankshaft Pulley

37. Block crankshaft from rotating with a wooden wedge. Coat crankshaft pulley seal surface with oil. Place crankshaft pulley on crankshaft and insert heavy flat washer and retaining bolt. Draw crankshaft pulley into place on crankshaft, by turning retaining bolt until crankshaft pulley bottoms in place. Back crankshaft pulley retaining bolt off one turn and torque 40 to 50 ft. lbs. Remove wooden wedge from crankshaft.

NOTE: Do not drive crankshaft pulley on crankshaft, this will damage crankshaft thrust bearing and crankcase.

Oil Cooler

38. Install a new oil cooler adapter gasket and oil cooler adapter with bolts and flat washers, using anti-seize adapter bolts 7 to 13 ft. lbs. Install engine left rear shroud in place. Install new oil cooler seals in oil cooler adapter.

39. Install oil cooler retaining bolt and flat washer using anti-seize compound on threads and torque 8 to 12 ft. lbs.

Exhaust Manifolds

40. Install new exhaust manifold gaskets.

NOTE: The steel flange on small steel type exhaust manifold gaskets must be installed next to exhaust port tubes.

CAUTION: Exhaust port tubes are a press fit in the cylinder head and the exhaust manifold. They must fit correctly to prevent exhaust manifold leaks.

Install heat tube, if present, clamps, french locks and nuts. Torque nuts 23 to 27 ft. lbs. and bend tab on french lock to lock nut in place.

Valve Lash Adjustment

41. Refer to "Electrical System" for distributor, cylinder firing

Adjusting Valve Lash

positions. Install distributor on engine rear housing with hold down clamp and nut. Turn crankshaft counter clockwise to set engine distributor firing No. 1 cylinder and crankshaft pulley notch at 0° on timing pad. Lash valves No. 1 Intake, No. 1 Exhaust, No. 3 Intake and No. 5 Exhaust on the right bank and No. 4 Exhaust and No. 6 Intake on the left bank.

Valves are to be lashed in the following manner: Turn down rocker arm adjusting nut using a 5/8" deep socket and ratchet wrench, until there is no axial movement of the push rod, felt with the fingers, then turn adjusting nut a 3/4 turn more on Turbo-Air engines and 1 1/4 turn more on Super Turbo-Air (R.P.O. 649) engine.

Turn crankshaft counter clockwise and set engine distributor firing on No. 2 cylinder and cranshaft pulley notch at 0° on timing pad. Lash valves No. 3 Exhaust and No. 5 Intake on the right bank and No. 2 Intake, No. 2 Exhaust, No. 4 Intake and No. 6 Exhaust on the Left Bank.

42. Install new gaskets in valve covers and carefully attach valve cover and gasket to the cylinder heads, torque valve cover screws 30 to 50 in. lbs.

Oil Filter and Generator Adapter

43. Install a new oil filter and generating adapter gasket on the engine rear housing. Install oil filter and generator adapter on the engine rear housing. Install all bolts and flat washers using anti-seize compound and torque bolts 7 to 13 ft. lbs. Install a new oil filter cartridge and torque oil filter bolt 9 to 15 ft. lbs. Install engine rear right shroud.

44. Install engine skid plate and rear mounting bracket with retaining nuts. Torque nuts 20 to 30 ft. lbs. Install lifting adapter and mount to rear engine mount.

45. Install blower and blower pulley to crankcase cover blower

bearing hub assembly.

46. Install front shrouds (and exhaust ducts—1960). Install left and right side shields.
47. Install upper shroud assembly. Turn blower and check clearance while tightening upper shrould retaining screws.
48. Install fuel lines and oil level gauge. Install lower engine shroud and exhaust ducts (and cooling air throttle valve assembly—1960).
49. Install idler bracket and pulley assembly in place on oil filter and generator adapter, with adjusting slot towards the flywheel end of engine.
50. Install coil bracket, coil and generator brace on cylinder head. Install generator and torque bolts. Install blower belt and adjust.

NOTE: Sequence of tightening mounting, is to prevent misalignment of brackets to generator and frames.

Spark Plugs

51. Install spark plugs and gaskets and torque 20 to 25 ft. lbs. Install wire harness to spark plugs and distributor. Install coil and wires. Install carburetors.

NOTE: Spark plugs are long reach plugs especially designed for aluminum threads. Substitutes should not be used.

52. Invert engine on stand and install oil pan with a new gasket. Check parting line to see if flywheel housing gasket is far enough up for good sealing. Torque oil pan bolts 40 to 60 ft. lbs.

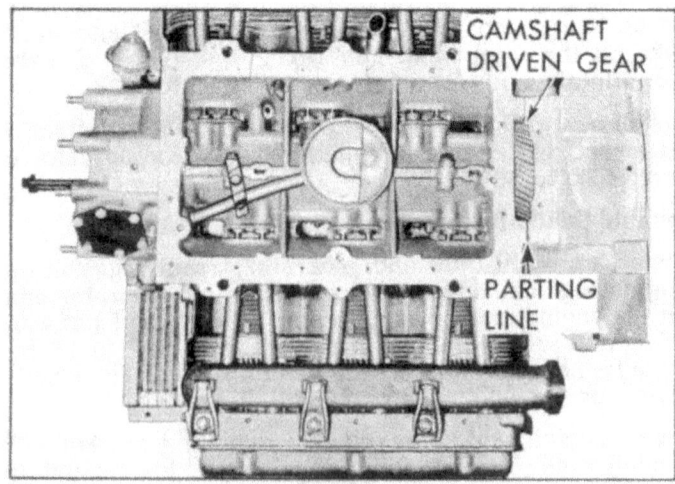

Oil Pan Rails

53. Attach a chain and shackle to lifting adapter and at the flywheel housing lifting eye. Remove bolts at flywheel housing adapter.
54. Lift engine with chain sling off of engine stand and onto lifting jack. Remove chain and adapter from rear mounting bracket.

Fuel Pump

55. Install fuel pump push rod return spring (large diameter down) into oil filter and generator adapter. Install fuel pump push rod well lubricated with oil in adapter and install fuel pump with a new "O" ring seal. Turn set screw finding hole in fuel pump and tighten 9 to 15 ft. lbs. Tighten locknut 9 to 15 ft. lbs. torque.
56. Connect fuel lines to carburetors and fuel pump. Install engine front shield and support strap, connect vacuum balance tube to both carburetors. (Connect choke heat tube and choke fresh air tube—1960.)
57. Install carburetor cross-shaft and choke assembly. Install carburetor air cleaner.
58. Refer to "Cooling System Exhaust Adjustment," for cooling air damper valve and thermostat adjustment.

Engine Oil

59. Add oil before or after installation of engine to vehicle. Add 5½ quarts of oil to a dry engine (overhauled engine) and 4 quarts to a wet engine (oil change).

TROUBLES AND REMEDIES

Symptom and Probable Cause   **Probable Remedy**

Lack of Power

1. **Poor Compression**
   - a. Incorrect valve lash
   - b. Leaky valves
   - c. Valve stems or lifters sticking
   - d. Valve springs weak or broken
   - e. Valve timing incorrect
   - f. Leaking cylinder head gasket
   - g. Piston ring broken
   - h. Poor fits between pistons, rings and cylinders

   - a. Adjust valve lash according to instructions under "Valve Lash Adjustment"
   - b. Remove cylinder head and grind valves
   - c. Free up or replace
   - d. Replace springs
   - e. Correct valve timing
   - f. Replace gaskets
   - g. Replace rings
   - h. Overhaul engine

2. **Ignition System Improperly Adjusted**
   - a. Ignition not properly timed
   - b. Spark plugs faulty
   - c. Distributor points not set correctly

   - a. Set ignition according to instructions under "Engine Tune-Up"
   - b. Replace or clean, adjust and test spark plugs
   - c. Set distributor points and time engine

3. **Lack of Fuel**
   - a. Dirt or water in carburetor
   - b. Gas lines partly plugged
   - c. Dirt in gas tank
   - d. Air leaks in gas line
   - e. Fuel pump not functioning properly

   - a. Clean carburetor and fuel pump
   - b. Clean gas lines
   - c. Clean gas tank
   - d. Tighten and check gas lines
   - e. Replace or repair fuel pump

4. **Carburetor Air Inlet Restricted**
   - a. Air cleaner dirty
   - b. Carburetor choke partly closed
   - c. Improperly installed and/or torn side and front shields, seals

   - a. Clean air cleaner or replace element
   - b. Adjust or replace choke mechanism
   - c. Adjust or replace

5. **Overheating**
   - a. Oil cooler dirty
   - b. Blower belt loose
   - c. Blower belt worn or oil soaked
   - d. Thermostat sticking closed
   - e. Incorrect cooling air valve opening
   - f. Engine cooling fins plugged
   - g. Incorrect ignition or valve timing
   - h. Brakes dragging
   - i. Improper grade and viscosity oil being used
   - j. Fuel mixture too lean
   - k. Valves improperly adjusted
   - l. Defective ignition system
   - m. Exhaust system partly restricted
   - n. Loose shield seals
   - p. Spark plug boots loose
   - r. Sheet metal loose

   - a. Clean oil cooler
   - b. Adjust or replace
   - c. Replace belt
   - d. Replace thermostat
   - e. Adjust thermostat
   - f. Clean engine
   - g. Retime engine
   - h. Adjust brakes
   - i. Change to correct oil
   - j. Overhaul or adjust carburetor
   - k. Adjust valves
   - l. See "Engine Tune-Up"
   - m. Clean or replace
   - n. Tighten or replace
   - p. Install properly
   - r. Tighten

Symptom and Probable Cause	Probable Remedy

6. Overcooling
   a. Thermostat holding wide open   a. Replace or adjust thermostat

Excessive Oil Consumption

1. Leaking Oil

a. Oil pan drain plug loose	a. Tighten drain plug
b. Oil pan retainer bolts loose	b. Tighten oil pan bolts
c. Oil pan gaskets damaged	c. Replace pan gaskets
d. Rear housing loose or gasket damaged	d. Tighten housing bolts or replace gasket
e. Rocker arm cover gaskets damaged or loose	e. Tighten covers or replace gaskets
f. Fuel pump loose or seal damaged	f. Tighten fuel pump or replace "O" ring seal
g. Crankshaft seal leaking oil into clutch housing or flywheel housing	g. Replace oil seal
h. Oil drain slots in crankcase cover vent closed	h. Remove crankcase cover and clean slots

2. Burning Oil

a. Broken piston rings	a. Replace rings
b. Rings not correctly seated to cylinder walls	b. Give sufficient time for rings to seat. Replace if necessary
c. Piston rings worn excessively or stuck in ring grooves	c. Replace rings
d. Piston ring oil return holes clogged with carbon	d. Replace rings
e. Excessive clearance between piston and cylinder wall due to wear or improper fitting	e. Replace piston and cylinder bore as a unit
f. Cylinder walls scored, excessive tapered or out-of-round	f. Replace cylinders and new pistons as a unit

Hard Starting

1. Slow Cranking

a. Heavy engine oil	a. Change to lighter oil
b. Partially discharged battery	b. Charge battery
c. Faulty or undercapacity battery	c. Replace battery
d. Poor battery connections	d. Clean and tighten or replace connections
e. Faulty starter switch	e. Replace switch
f. Faulty starting motor or drive	f. Overhaul starting motor

2. Ignition Trouble

a. Distributor points burned or corroded	a. Clean or replace points
b. Points improperly adjusted	b. Readjust points to .016", adjust new points to .019"
c. Spark plugs improperly gapped	c. Set plug gap at .035"
d. Spark plug wires loose and corroded in distributor cap	d. Clean wire and cap terminals
e. Loose connections in primary circuit	e. Tighten all connections in primary circuit
f. Series resistance in condenser circuit	f. Clean all connections in condenser circuit
g. Low capacity condenser	g. Install proper condenser
h. Ballast resister faulty or out of circuit	h. Inspect and correct

Symptom and Probable Cause	Probable Remedy

3. Engine Condition

    a. Valves holding open
    b. Valves burned
    c. Leaking exhaust manifold gasket
    d. Loose carburetor mounting
    e. Faulty pistons, rings or cylinders

    a. Adjust valves
    b. Grind valves
    c. Tighten manifold nuts or replace gasket
    d. Tighten carburetor
    e. See "Poor Compression"

4. Carburetion

    a. Choke not operating properly
    b. Throttle not set properly
    c. Carburetor dirty and passages restricted

    a. Adjust or repair choke mechanism
    b. Set throttle
    c. Overhaul carburetor

Popping, Spitting and Detonation

1. Ignition Trouble

    a. Loose wiring connections
    b. Faulty wiring
    c. Faulty spark plugs
    d. Incorrect ignition timing, fuel 92 octane or better.
    e. Fuel below 92 octane rating

    a. Tighten all wire connections
    b. Replace faulty wiring
    c. Clean or replace and adjust plugs
    d. Adjust timing to 4° BTC
    e. Retard timing towards 0 degrees

2. Carburetor

    a. Lean combustion mixture
    b. Dirt in carburetor
    c. Restricted gas supply to carburetor
    d. Leaking carburetor or intake manifold gaskets

    a. Clean and adjust carburetor
    b. Clean carburetor
    c. Clean gas lines and check for restrictions
    d. Tighten carburetor to manifold and manifold to head bolts or replace gaskets

3. Valves

    a. Valves adjusted too tight
    b. Valves sticking
    c. Exhaust valves thin and heads overheating
    d. Weak valve springs
    e. Valves timed early

    a. Adjust valve lash
    b. Lubricate and free up. Grind valves if necessary
    c. Replace valves
    d. Replace valve springs
    e. Retime

4. Cylinder Head

    a. Excessive carbon deposits in combustion chamber
    b. Partly restricted exhaust ports in cylinder head
    c. Cylinder head gaskets blown between cylinders

    a. Remove head and clean carbon
    b. Remove cylinder head and clean exhaust ports
    c. Replace cylinder head gaskets

5. Spark Plugs

    a. Spark plugs glazed
    b. Wrong heat range plug being used

    a. Clean or replace spark plugs
    b. Change to correct spark plugs

6. Exhaust System

    a. Exhaust manifold or muffler restricted causing back pressure

    a. Clean or replace manifold or muffler

7. Cooling System

    b. See Overheating Section

| Symptom and Probable Cause | Probable Remedy |

Rough Engine Idle

1. **Carburetor**
   a. Improper idling adjustment
   b. Carburetor float needle valve not seating

   a. Adjust according to instructions
   b. Clean or replace

2. **Air Leaks**
   a. Carburetor to manifold gasket leaks
   b. Exhaust manifold to head gasket leaks

   a. Tighten carburetor to manifold nuts or gasket
   b. Tighten manifold to head clamp nuts or replace gaskets

3. **Pistons or Pins Loose**
   a. Excessive cylinder wear
   b. Improperly fitted pistons or pins
   c. Contaminated oil
   d. Faulty fuel or ignition system causing unburned fuel to flush the oil from cylinder walls
   e. Piston pin or bore wear

   a. Replace cylinder and piston
   b. Replace pistons or pins
   c. Make necessary replacements, flush oiling system and use new oil
   d. Make necessary repairs to fuel or ignition system, replace worn parts and change oil
   e. Replace pistons and pins

4. **Engine Noise—General**
   a. Bent connecting rod
   b. Excessive end play in camshaft
   c. Excessive crankshaft end play
   d. Broken piston ring
   e. Loose timing gears
   f. Dry push rod sockets
   g. Improperly adjusted valve lash
   h. Sticking valves

   a. Replace rod
   b. Replace camshaft thrust plate, or correct end play by pressing gear on further
   c. Replace main bearings
   d. Replace broken ring and check condition of cylinder wall
   e. Replace timing gears
   f. Polish and lubricate push rod sockets
   g. Adjust valve lash
   h. Free or grind valves

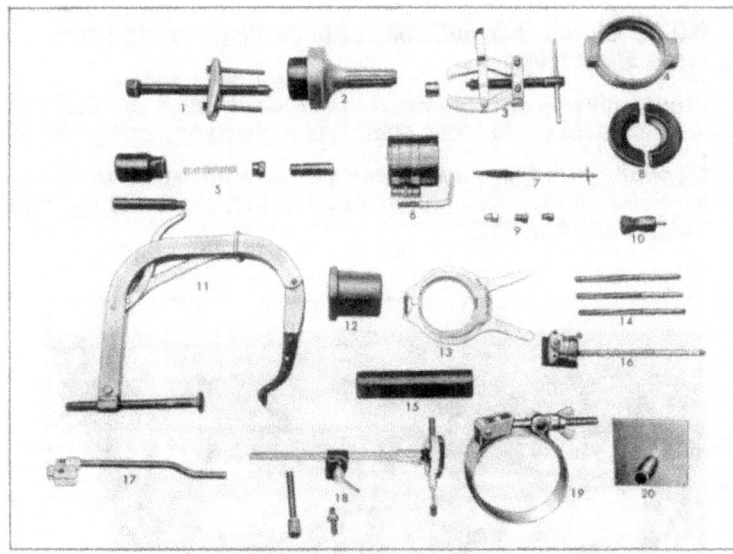

Engine Special Tools

1. J-8105 Crankshaft Pulley Remover
2. J-6175 Differential Side Bearing Installer
3. J-7112-2 Adapter
   J-7112 Side Bearing Remover
4. J-358-1 Press Plate Holder
5. J-8355 Piston Pin Assembly Adapter, used with Tool J-6994
6. J-8037 Piston Ring Compressor
7. J-8101 Valve Guide Cleaner
8. J-7028 Rear Pinion Bearing Remover
9. J-8354-1 (⅝-24)
   J-8354-2 (½-24)
   J-8354-3 (⅜-16)
10. J-8358 Carbon Remover Brush
11. J-8062 Valve Spring Compressor
12. J-0971 Camshaft Gear Remover and Installer
13. J-8014 Piston Ring Expander
14. J-5830 Valve Bore Reamer Set
15. J-5590 Transmission Front Bearing Installer
16. J-8087 Cylinder Bore Checking Gauge
17. J-8369 Oil Suction Pipe Installer
18. J-8520 Camshaft Lobe Indicator
19. J-8356 Ring Compressor
20. J-8280 Engine Stand Adapter

CLUTCH

A diaphragm spring clutch is used with the standard transmission. The clutch consists of two basic assemblies.

The clutch is attached at the front of the engine to the flywheel and is completely enclosed by the flywheel housing. The driven disc is solid mounted. The input shaft from the clutch to the transmission is flexible torsionally; thus eliminating the need for springs in the clutch disc.

The clutch is operated with a conventional clutch fork, except that it is shorter and operates by pulling instead of pushing. The clutch fork engages the throwout bearing which is piloted on the axle housing. A clutch lever control rod (6) is attached to the end of the clutch fork and to the clutch lever control cable cross shaft (1).

One end of the clutch lever control cable cross shaft, is attached to the cross-member and the other end to the body. Three pulleys are used to route the cable from the front to the rear.

MAINTENANCE AND ADJUSTMENTS

CLUTCH LINKAGE ADJUSTMENT

The pedal should have at least ¾" travel before the clutch release bearing engages the diaphragm spring. Check clutch control cable and make sure that it is well anchored, at the clutch pedal and engaged in each pulley.

1. Attach return spring to the clutch lever control cable cross shaft, outboard lever lower hole.

   NOTE: Clutch fork pull rod must be disconnected from cross shaft lever.

2. Adjust clevis swivel until the outboard lever on the clutch lever control cable cross shaft has a clearance of ½" to ¾".

3. Manually pull the clutch fork pull rod until slack is taken up at clutch fork. (The clutch release bearing touching clutch diaphragm fingers.)

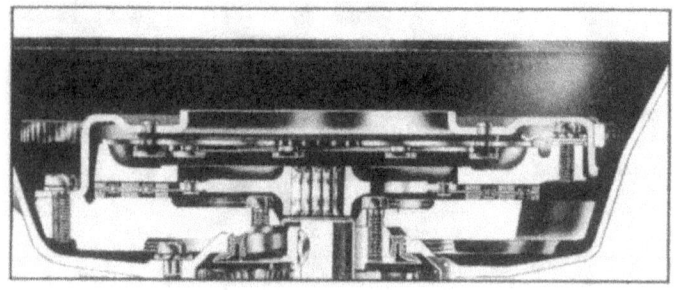

Clutch Cross-Section

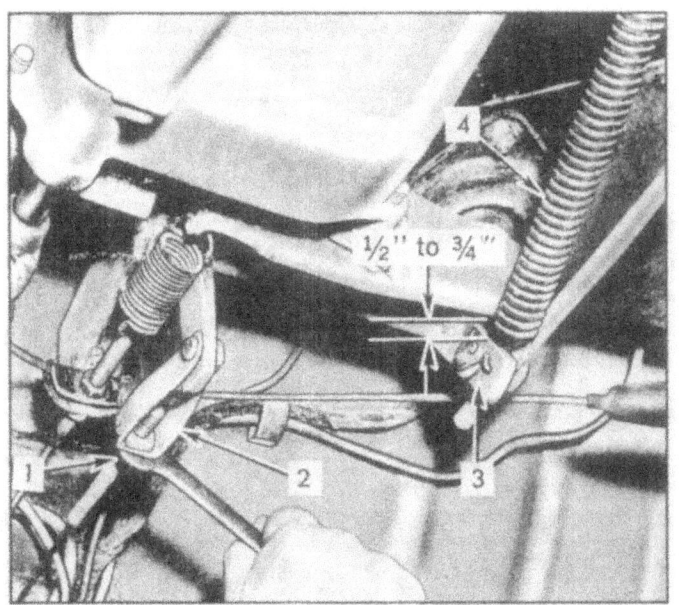

Adjusting Clutch Cable

1. Locking Nut
2. Cable Clevis
3. Control Cross Shaft, Outboard Lever
4. Return Spring

Adjusting Clutch Fork Pull Rod

1. Control Cross-Shaft Assembly
2. Control Cross-Shaft Out-Board Lever
3. Clutch Fork Pull Rod Swivel
4. Clutch Fork Pull Rod

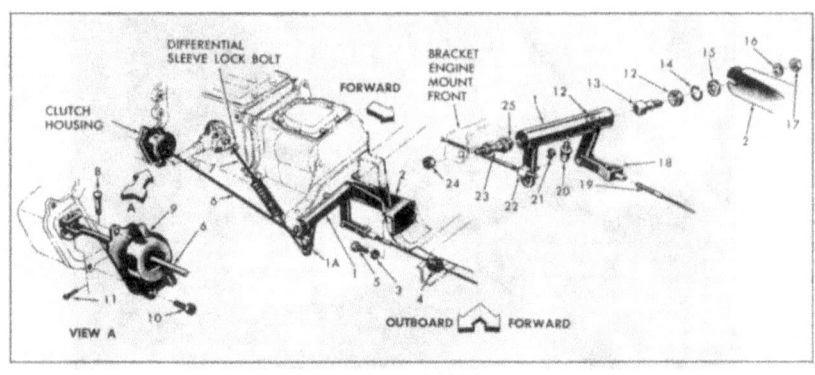

Clutch Linkage Exploded

1. Clutch Lever Control Cable Cross-Shaft
2. Shaft Mounting Bracket
3. Lockwasher
4. Cable Seal
5. Bolt
6. Clutch Fork Pull Rod
7. Return Spring
8. Clevis Pin
9. Dust Seal Assembly
10. Bolt
11. Cotter Pin
12. Ball Stud Seat
13. Ball Stud
14. Retainer Spring
15. Flat Washer
16. Lockwasher
17. Nut
18. Clevis Assembly
19. Control Cable
20. Lube Fitting
21. Cotter Key
22. Swivel
23. Ball Stud
24. Lock Nut
25. Items to be Lubricated before assembly with Lubriplate

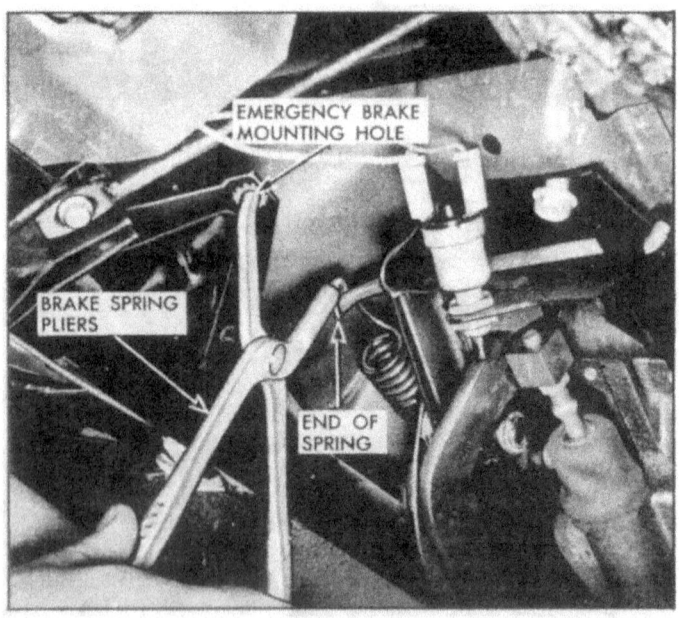

Clutch Pedal Assist Spring—Removal and Installation

4. With the clutch fork pull rod in this position, align swivel with the upper hole of the outboard lever. Back off swivel three complete turns and assemble to lever with retaining clip.

CLUTCH PEDAL ASSIST SPRING

Removal and Installation

1. Remove the retaining bolts from the emergency hand brake.

2. Depress the clutch pedal (to relieve some of the spring force).
3. Using a pair of brake spring pliers unhook the clutch pedal assist spring.
4. To replace clutch pedal assist spring, install one end of the assist spring into clutch pedal bracket.
5. Hook one end of brake spring pliers, on the emergency brake mounting hole and the other at the end of the spring.
6. Depress clutch pedal while squeezing the pliers to hook spring in place.

CLUTCH PEDAL AND SLEEVE BUSHING
Removal
1. Remove clutch pedal assist spring.
2. Remove snap ring from clutch pedal shaft.
3. Remove three retaining bolts from the bumper support bracket, and the clutch pedal shaft support bushing assembly.
4. Remove clutch pedal shaft from support assembly.

   NOTE: It is not necessary to remove the clutch pedal support assembly when master cylinder brake support is removed from the vehicle as a unit.
5. Check nylon sleeve bushings for wear and damage and replace if necessary.

Installation
1. If master brake cylinder support is mounted in vehicle, then install clutch pedal shaft in clutch shaft support, using a little lubricate on the nylon sleeve bushings.
2. Install snap ring on clutch pedal shaft.
3. Bolt clutch pedal bumper support and clutch shaft support, to the master brake cylinder support.
4. Install the clutch pedal assist spring and cable assembly as previously outlined.
5. Adjust clutch linkage.

CLUTCH CABLE AND PULLEY ASSEMBLY
Removal and Installation
1. Remove return spring from the clutch lever control cable cross-shaft.
2. Remove cotter key from swivel on clutch pull rod and remove swivel from clutch cross-shaft lever.
3. Remove cable clevis assembly at the inboard lever of the

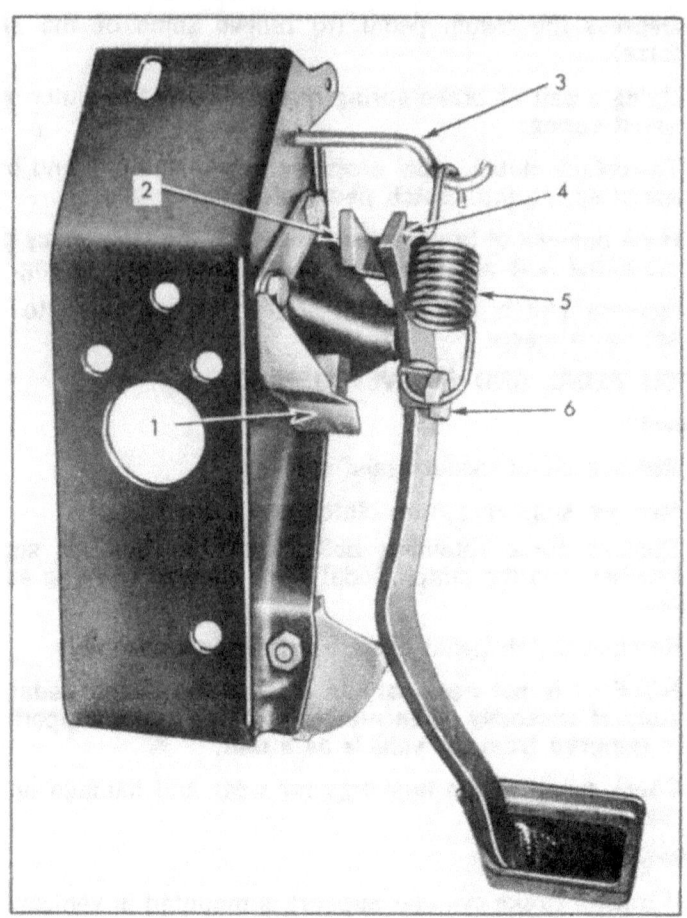

Clutch Pedal Components

1. Bumper
2. Pedal Stop
3. Clutch Assist Spring Hook
4. Clutch Pedal Cable Retainer Hook
5. Clutch Pedal Assist Spring
6. Clutch Pedal Assist Spring Bracket

    clutch cross-shaft.

4. Remove body tunnel, front and rear cover access to cables.
5. Remove retaining nut, bolt and pulley spacer from clutch pulley. Remove pulley and spacer from parking brake bracket.
6. Remove parking brake and clutch pulley assembly from dash and toe panel.
7. Unhook cable from clutch pedal and remove complete cable assembly.
8. To install cable and pulley assemblies, reverse the above steps and adjust clutch.

TROUBLES AND REMEDIES

| Symptom and Probable Cause | Probable Remedy |

Slipping
- a. Improper adjustment
- b. Oil soaked
- c. Worn splines on clutch gear
- d. Facing torn loose from disc
- e. Warped pressure plate of flywheel
- f. Weak diaphragm spring

- a. Adjust clutch linkage
- b. Install new disc
- c. Replace clutch gear shaft
- d. Install new disc
- e. Replace pressure plate or flywheel
- f. Replace cover assembly

Grabbing
- a. Oil on facing or burned or glazed facings
- b. Worn splines on clutch gear
- c. Loose engine mountings
- d. Warped pressure plate or flywheel

- a. Install new disc
- b. Replace clutch gear shaft
- c. Tighten or replace mountings
- d. Replace pressure plate or flywheel

Rattling
- a. Weak retracting springs
- b. Throwout fork loose on ball stud or in bearing groove

- a. Replace springs
- b. Check ball stud and retaining spring and replace if necessary

Release Bearing Spinning with Clutch Fully Engaged
- a. Improper adjustment
- b. Release bearing binding on axle release bearing shaft
- c. Insufficient tension between clutch fork spring and ball stud

- a. Adjust clutch linkage
- b. Clean, relubricate, check for burrs, nicks, etc.
- c. Replace fork

Noisy
- a. Worn release bearing

- a. Replace bearing

Pedal Tension
- a. Clutch pedal not contacting rubber stop bumper
- b. Clutch lever compressing rubber stop bumper
- c. Pedal low
- d. Pedal effort high

- a. Adjust clutch linkage
- b. Adjust clutch linkage
- c. Cable adjustment
- d. Check for binding of pulleys, and other pivot points. Check linkage for proper adjustment

Insufficient Clutch Release
- a. Improper lash adjustment
- b. Clutch fork pull rod movement

- a. Adjust linkage
- b. Check clutch fork pull rod movement. Must be .825" minimum with full clutch pedal travel. If less than .825" check linkage for total pedal travel (5.6"), broken pulleys, supports, etc. If more than .825" remove clutch and check for failed material.

REAR AXLE

The "Corvair" rear axle is of the straddle mounted hypoid gear type which embodies a differential carrier mounted rigidly to the engine; no rear axle housing is used. Independently suspended axle shafts are attached to universal joints which, in turn, are splined into the differential side gears. Axle driving torque is transmitted by the lower control arms and lateral forces are absorbed by the wheel bearings and rubber bushings at the lower control arm attachment to the rear crossmember.

A hollow shaft is used with the drive pinion to permit passage of the engine output shaft forward to the transmission. To permit the axial hole in the pinion shaft, the drive pinion and gear are two pieces coupled by a shrink fit. Currently, the pinion gear and shaft are serviced only as an assembly. The drive pinion shaft is directly connected to the transmission output member. Preloaded tapered roller bearings support the drive pinion at fore and aft locations in the differential carrier. The hypoid ring gear is bolted to the differential case which is mounted by preloaded tapered roller bearings on each side of the differential carrier.

Components of the differential assembly are conventional with the exception of the side gears which have integral elongated splined hubs which project to the outboard extremity of the differential case and cover to receive the axle shaft universal joints.

Axle ratios of 3.27-to-1 are used as standard with three speed, four speed and automatic transmissions through application of an eleven tooth pinion and 36 tooth ring gear. All transmissions can be used with the optional 3-55 - 1 ratio provided by a 9-32 tooth combination pinion and ring gear.

The speedometer drive gear is now pressed onto the drive pinion shaft as compared to the integral gear which was machined into the pinion shaft in 1960. Service replacement drive pinions will have the speedometer drive gear installed in production. The nylon driven gear is mounted in the differential carrier.

Rear axle assemblies used with three or four speed transmissions and those used with automatic transmissions have fundamental differences in lubrication, drive pinion design, and mounting hub provisions for the clutch release bearings or converter stator, respectively.

Lubricant requirements for the manual transmission and rear axle are identical. Therefore, when this driveline is used, the lubricant, Multipurpose Lubricant SAE 80, cycles between the axle and transmission. Although the lubricant is common, individual filler plugs are provided in both the axle and transmission as a lubricant dam is formed between the two units which prohibits a common sump.

Automatic transmission rear axles are sealed to prevent axle lubricant from entering the transmission. The automatic transmission rear axle uses Multipurpose Lubricant SAE 80 where the automatic transmission requires Automatic Transmission Fluid, Type "A," common in most automatic transmissions.

Drive pinion design for the two rear axle assemblies varies mostly in overall length, splining for adaptation to the transmis-

Three Speed Transmission Rear Axle—Sectional Plan View

1. Clutch Shaft (Transmission Input)
2. Washer
3. Clutch Release Bearing Shaft Inner Seal
4. Clutch Release Bearing Shaft
5. Clutch Release Bearing Shaft Outer Seal
6. Differential Carrier
7. Pinion Rear Bearing and Race
8. Pinion Gear
9. Differential Side Bearing Adjusting Sleeve
10. Axle Shaft
11. Universal Joint
12. Pinion Shaft
13. Speedometer Driven Gear Assembly
14. Speedometer Drive Gear (Integral with Pinion Shaft)
15. Pinion Front Bearing and Race
16. Pinion Bearing Adjusting Sleeve
17. Pinion Adjusting Sleeve Seal Ring
18. Transmission Output Shaft
19. Differential Pinion Gear Shaft
20. Differential Pinion Gear
21. Differential Side Bearing and Race
22. Differential Side Gear (Short)
23. Differential Side Bearing Adjusting Sleeve Seal
24. Differential Cover
25. Ring Gear

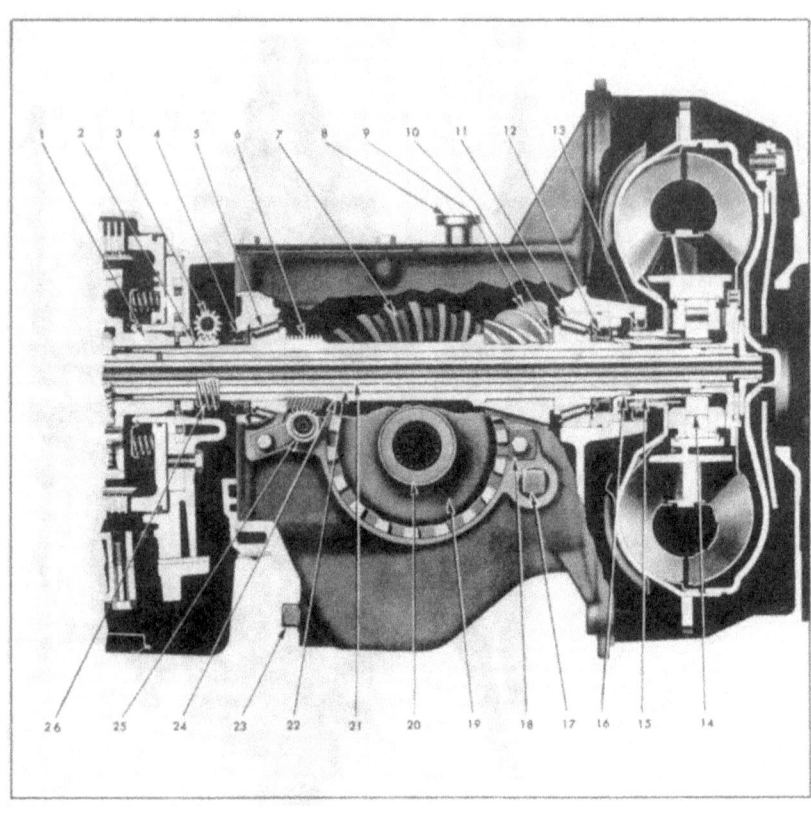

Automatic Transmission Rear Axle—Sectional Side View

1. Planet Carrier Hub (Transmission Output)
2. Rear Selective End Play Spacers
3. Governor Driven Gear
4. Pinion Shaft Front Seal
5. Pinion Front Bearing and Race
6. Speedometer Drive Gear (Integral Part of Pinion Shaft)
7. Ring Gear
8. Vent
9. Pinion Gear
10. Selective Pinion Depth Shim
11. Pinion Rear Bearing and Race
12. Pinion Shaft Rear Seal
13. Converter Hub Seal
14. Stator Assembly
15. Stator Shaft
16. Pinion Shaft Seal Ring (Cast Iron)
17. Differential Carrier Filler Plug
18. Side Bearing Adjusting Sleeve Lock Tab
19. Side Bearing Adjusting Sleeve
20. Side Bearing Adjusting Sleeve Seal
21. Transmission Front Pump Shaft
22. Transmission Turbine Shaft
23. Drain Plug
24. Pinion Shaft
25. Speedometer Driven Gear Assembly
26. Governor Drive Gear

sion, and sealing. The manual transmission axle pinion shaft extends forward only to the pinion bearing adjusting sleeve and is internally splined to receive the transmission output shaft. On automatic transmission versions, the pinion shaft extends forward beyond the pinion bearing adjusting sleeve and is externally splined to index with the transmission planetary carrier. A seal is mounted in the pinion bearing adjusting sleeve to prevent lubricant from transferring between the rear axle and automatic transmission.

Because of its location between the engine and transmission, the "Corvair" rear axle provides mounting elements usually incorporated on the transmission in conventional designs. On manual transmission models, the rear of the differential carrier mounts the shaft for the clutch release bearing where as a stator shaft for the converter is carried by the automatic transmission rear axle. The clutch release bearing shaft has a lip seal in the inner diameter to prevent lubricant from flowing rearward onto the clutch. The stator shaft is externally splined and lip-type seals are used at the contact of the pinion shaft and the inside diameter of the stator shaft to prevent transfer of lubricants. A converter hub seal is mounted in the differential carrier adjacent to the stator shaft to prevent loss of automatic transmission fluid. Both the clutch release bearing shaft and the stator shaft use an "O" ring seal at their mating surface with the differential carrier.

POSITRACTION DIFFERENTIAL

The Corvair Positraction differential, available on all vehicle series, in a multiplate clutch unit incorporated into the right hand side of the differential case. The purpose of this unit is to eliminate a major amount of one-wheel slip and afford better all around traction.

A Belleville spring located in the clutch pack is compressed during assembly of the differential case and cover, and provides a constant pre-load on the clutch pack. This pre-load is in addition to the load resulting from the differential side gear separating forces. The total clutch pack load provides the non-slip action of the differential under road conditions which would normally cause one wheel to slip. The assembly will act as a standard differential under cornering and straight ahead driving conditions.

MANUAL TRANSMISSIONS

In essence, the Corvair manual three speed transmission is a conventional synchromesh type except for the use of concentric input and output shafts and its mounting on the differential carrier.

Because of its attachment to the differential carrier, the main shaft is hollow to permit passage of the clutch shaft to the front of the transmission to the clutch gear. The clutch gear drives a counter gear and the remaining power flow sequence is identical to the conventional three speed transmission.

1960 gear ratios are 3.22:1 in first, 1.84:1 in second, and 1:1 in third. Reverse ratio is 3.65:1.

On 1961 models gear ratios are 3.50:1 in first, 1.99:1 in second, and 1:1 in third. Reverse ratio is 3.97:1. The increased multiplication in first and second offsets the reduced rear axle ratio of 3.27:1 (standard) so that total torque multiplication (transmission times rear axle) remains virtually unchanged in the first two gears.

The shift mechanism used is basically a single shift rod system. From the transmission, the single shift rod is connected by a rubber sleeve coupling to the main shift rod which is mounted in the tunnel by two nylon bushed brackets. A 90-degree ball socket is integral to the front of the tunnel shaft which receives the ball-end of the gearshift lever, which is floor mounted in the passenger compartment. By this arrangement, the shift rod can be moved both fore-and-aft and laterally.

In the transmission, the shift rod carries a finger which extends upward to engage either the first and reverse fork or the second and third fork, depending on shift lever position. As the two forks are parallel to each other, a slight rotational motion of the shift rod places the actuating finger in the proper fork and permits the desired shift. An interlock between the two fork shafts holds the fork not being actuated in the neutral cross-over position.

SHIFT LINKAGE ADJUSTMENT

After any service operation in which the shift control rod in the tunnel has been replaced or it has been found that transmission response is improper to the shift pattern, adjust the shift linkage.

It should be noted that the "Corvair" shift lever position can be "tailored" to the driver. For example, if the driver is tall and drives with the seat full rearward, the shift linkage can be adjusted so as to minimize the reach for second and reverse by adjusting the linkage as follows with the seat in the driver's normal driving position:

1. Shift the transmission to first, then loosen the coupling clamp nut on the transmission shift shaft.

2. Move the gearshift lever rearward in first until it is resting against the edge of the seat, then tighten the coupling clamp nut. The shift lever will not touch when a person's weight is on the seat and it should also be noted that the shift throw is longer from neutral to first than neutral to third.

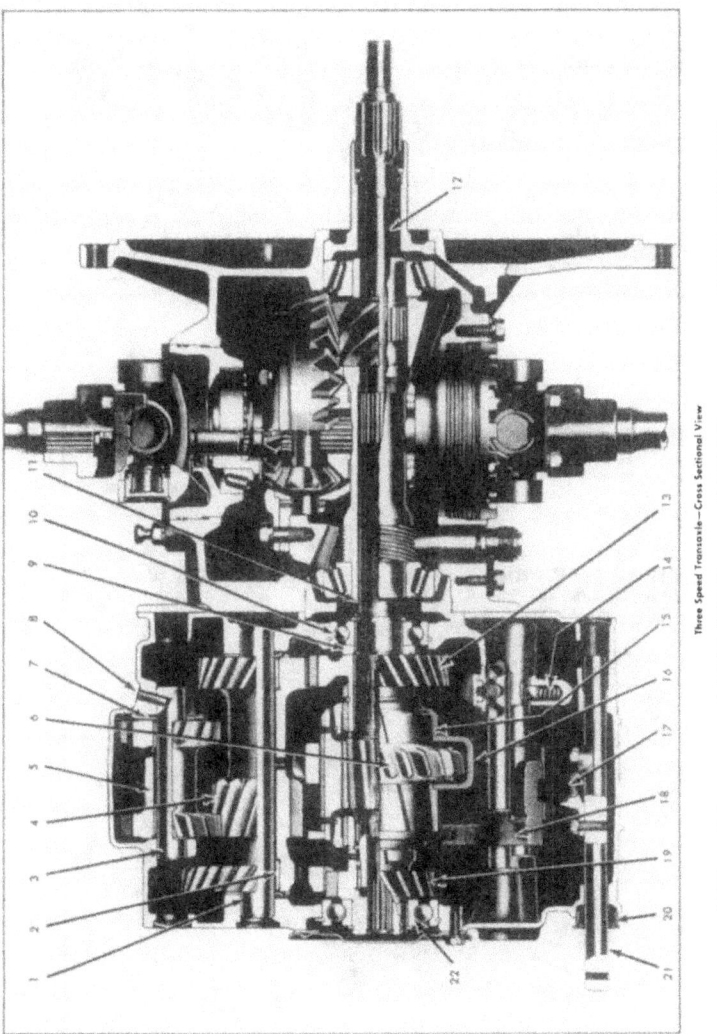

Three Speed Transaxle—Cross Sectional View

1. Countergear Shaft
2. Countergear Needle Bearings (Torrington)
3. Reverse Idler Gear Shaft
4. Countergear
5. Reverse Idler Gear
6. First and Reverse Sliding Gear
7. Radial Needle Bearing (Torrington)
8. Reverse Idler Shaft Retaining Pin
9. Thrust Washer
10. Mainshaft Bearing
11. Mainshaft
12. Clutch Shaft
13. Second-speed Gear
14. First and Reverse Detent Spring and Ball
15. Second and Third Speed Clutch
16. First and Reverse Shift Fork
17. Manual Shift Shaft Finger
18. Second and Third Speed Shift Fork
19. Clutch Gear
20. Manual Shift Shaft Seal
21. Manual Shift Shaft
22. Clutch Gear Bearing

3. Test shifts in all ranges.

GEARSHIFT LEVER ASSEMBLY

Removal from Vehicle

1. Remove tunnel front plate.
2. Remove four nuts securing gearshift lever assembly to floor pan.

   NOTE: **Two nuts also secure the shift control shaft front mounting bracket. On early production vehicles, the two rear nuts retain the bracket; on later vehicles, the two front nuts will retain the bracket.**
3. From the driver's compartment, lift the gearshift lever assembly up until its studs clear the floor pan, then remove the unit by lifting the floor mat at the center of seat.

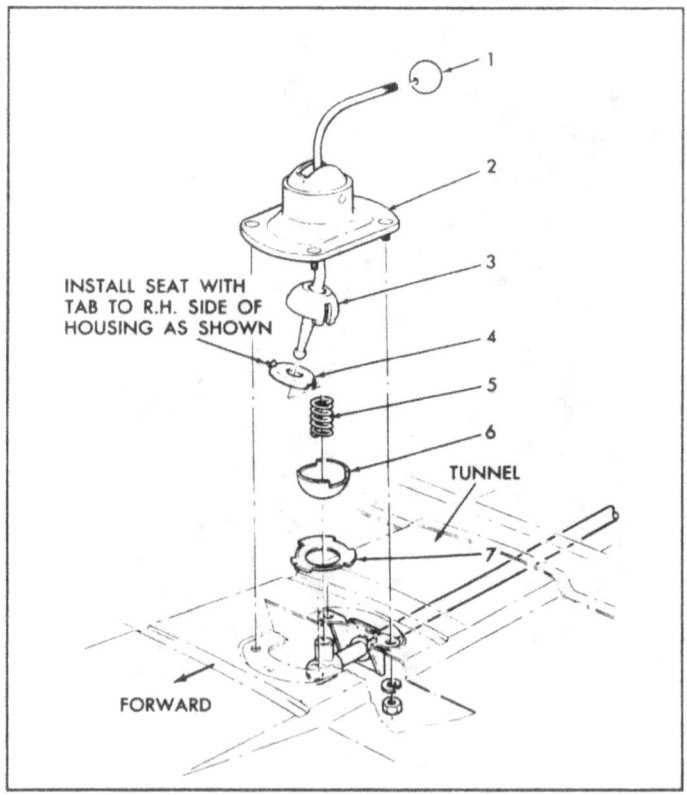

Gearshift Lever Assembly—Exploded View

1. Knob
2. Housing
3. Gearshift Lever Assy.
4. Seat
5. Spring
6. Spherical Joint
7. Retainer

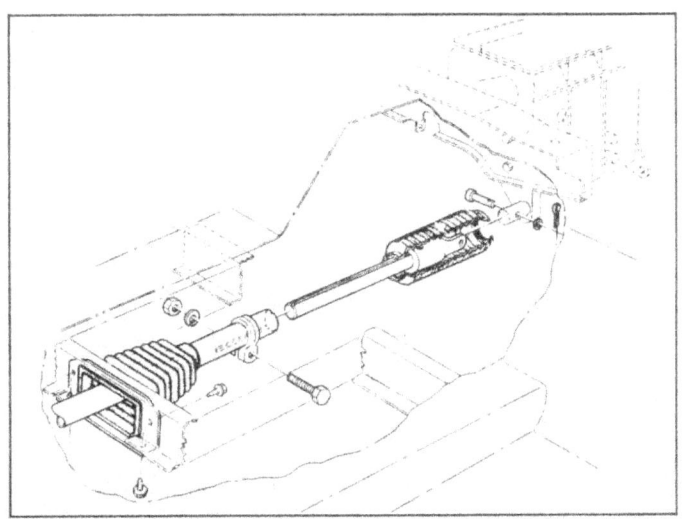

Tunnel Shaft Components—Exploded

Disassembly of Gearshift Lever Assembly

1. Unscrew the knob to remove, then clamp the gearshift housing in a vise.
2. Using a length of 1½" pipe, depress the retainer plate and rotate until its three lugs clear the lands in the gearshift housing, then remove the retainer.
3. Remove the lower spherical joint, spring, and seat, then pull lever out of housing.

Inspection and Repair

Inspect all working surfaces for wear and roughness. Repair or replace pieces as required. If broken, replace the spring.

Assembly of Gearshift Lever Assembly

1. Apply Lubriplate generously to all working surfaces.
2. Place retainer plate on lower spherical and place the housing in a vise.
3. Place seat on gearshift lever with tab to right side of housing.
4. Place spring and lower spherical joint on seat in housing.
5. Place retainer plate on lower spherical joint, then compress the retainer and rotate laterally to engage its lugs in the housing with a length of 1½" pipe.
6. Complete assembly by installing knob on shift lever.

SHIFT CONTROL ROD

Removal of Control Shaft from Vehicle

1. With tunnel cover removed, fold back rubber boot covering control shaft oil seal at transmission end of shaft sufficiently to expose the connecting pin.
2. To remove connecting pin, first remove cotter then remove pin by pushing out with channel lock pliers.
3. Separate the control shaft coupling from the transmission shifter shaft by pushing the control shaft toward the front of the car.
4. Complete removal of control shaft by removing two nuts attaching control shaft front mounting bracket, then remove control shaft, coupling, and mounting bracket as an assembly.

Inspection and Repair

Coupling Replacement

1. To insure maintaining shift control adjustment, scribe the control shaft adjacent to the end of the coupling, then loosen the clamp bolt and remove old coupling and rubber boot.
2. Insert new coupling with rubber boot installed in shift control shaft until the end of the coupling is aligned with the mark scribed in Step 1. Rotate coupling so attaching pin hole at transmission end is vertical, then tighten clamp bolt.

Control Shaft Front Mounting Bracket or Bushing Replacement

1. Remove the coupling as previously described.
2. Slide bracket off control shaft. Nylon bushing in bracket is of the push-in type.
3. Reinstall bracket with reinforced side toward rear of shaft, then install U-joint as previously covered.

Installation of Control Shaft in Vehicle

1. Center the shift lever ball, position and align the control shaft front bracket with the shift lever studs (rear on early vehicles, front on later vehicles), then insert the bracket on its studs simultaneously with insertion of the control shaft ball socket onto the shift lever ball. The control shaft socket should be well coated with Lubriplate prior to installation in vehicle.
2. Secure shaft bracket with two nuts.
3. Align control shaft coupling with transmission shifter shaft, then pull coupling over shifter shaft and install connecting pin and secure with cotter pin. Cover with boot.
4. Snap boot of shifter seal into place in tunnel rear plate and install tunnel covers.

1962

The 1962 3-speed transmission service procedures are basically the same except for a change in the shift linkage adjustment procedure.

The rod support bracket now has a delrin bushing instead of a nylon bushing.

Shift Linkage Adjustment

500 and 700 Series

After any operation in which the shift control rod in the tunnel has been replaced or it has been found that transmission response is improper to the shift pattern, adjust the shift linkage.

> **NOTE: Before making adjustment, lash in system is to be taken up by moving the shift control rod to the rear.**

1. With seat in full forward position, shift transmission to the first gear (500 and 700 models), then loosen the coupling nut on the transmission shift control rod.
2. Adjust the gearshift lever to .50 inch from edge of seat, then tighten the coupling clamp nut.
3. Test shift in all ranges.

900 Series

Shift linkage adjustment procedure for the 900 model is similar to the above except shift transmission to the reverse gear and adjust the gearshift lever a distance of 2.25 inches from the center of the gearshift lever housing, rearward, to the center of the gearshift lever knob.

CORVAIR – 500, 700 AND 900 SERIES FOUR SPEED TRANSMISSION

The Corvair four-speed transmission (1961 and later) is of the helical gear, constant mesh type to provide full synchronization in all forward gears. Spur gears on the mainshaft and countershaft are engaged by a small sliding spur gear to provide reverse. Reverse is not synchronized.

Like the Corvair three-speed, the four-speed mainshaft is hollow to permit passage of the clutch shaft forward to the clutch gear. The mainshaft is supported at the front in a double row of needle bearings carried by the clutch gear and at the rear by a ball bearing race. In turn, the clutch gear is carried in the front of the case by an identical ball bearing race.

The countergear is of single piece construction and is carried on double rows of needle bearings at each end. Thrust washers are used both front and rear between the countergear and the transmission case. A slight press fit is used at the front of the countershaft to retain the shaft and to prevent lubrication loss at this point.

Vehicle shift components are comparable to those used with the Corvair three-speed transmission. A long shift tube supported by nylon bushed brackets in the tunnel spans the distance between the driver's compartment and the front of the transmission. At the front, the tunnel shift tube carries a ball socket at 90-degrees to receive the lower end of the gearshift lever. A rubber sleeved coupling is secured by a clamp nut to the tunnel shift tube at the rear to provide attachment to the transmission shift rod and to provide a means of adjusting the length of the tunnel tube for linkage adjustment. Thus, by moving the gearshift lever, shift tube motion is provided both fore and aft and laterally.

In the transmission, three shift fork rods are mounted parallel above the transmission shift rod which is attached to the tunnel shift tube. The transmission shift rod carries a finger which extends upward to engage the shift forks. As the three forks are mounted on parallel rods, a slight rotation of the shift rod moves the shift finger from the 1-2 fork in the center to the 3-4 fork which is outboard. To engage the reverse shifter head, which is mounted on the inboard shaft, the shift finger must be moved laterally against a spring-loaded plunger at the neutral crossover point. The plunger is required to prevent accidental shifting into reverse while in motion as the 1-2 fork has a gate to permit passage of the shift finger through it to reach reverse.

Gear ratios are 3.65:1 in first, 2.35:1 in second, 1.44:1 in third, and 1:1 in fourth. Reverse is 3.66:1.

The same lubrication procedure is recommended as for 3-speed transmission.

SERVICE OPERATIONS

Gearshift Lever Assembly

The removal, overhaul, and installation procedures for the

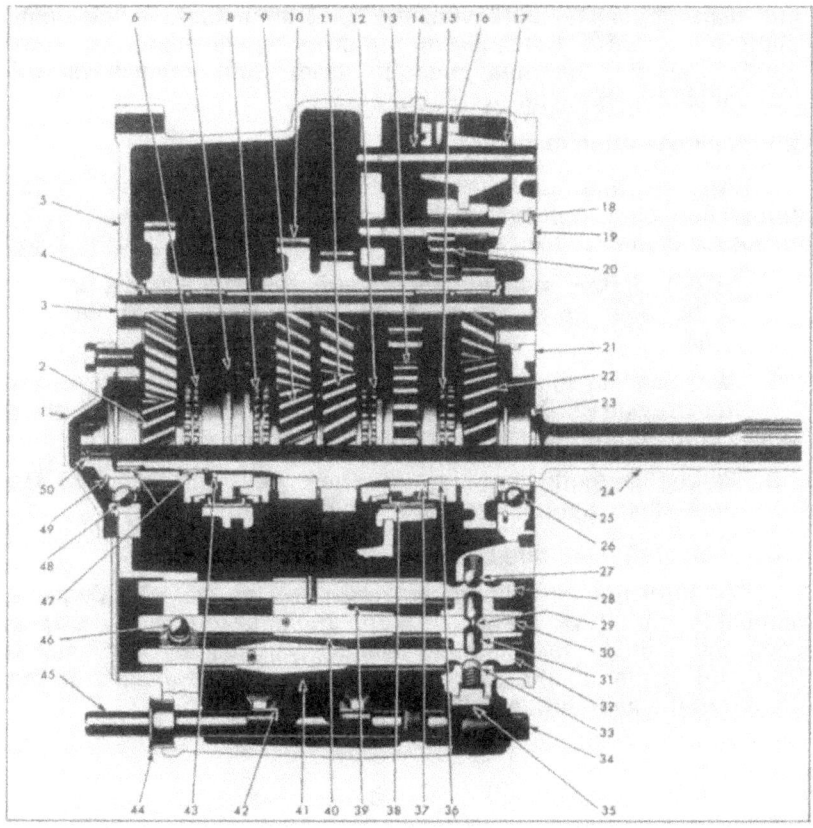

Corvair Four Speed Transmission—Cross Sectional View

1. Front Bearing Retainer
2. Clutch Gear
3. Countershaft
4. Countergear Thrust Washer
5. Transmission Case
6. 3-4 Blocker Ring
7. 3-4 Shift Collar
8. 3-4 Blocker Ring
9. Third Gear
10. Countergear
11. Second Gear
12. 1-2 Blocker Ring
13. 1-2 Shift Collar (with Integral Reverse Spur Gear)
14. Reverse Shift Fork Shaft
15. 1-2 Blocker Ring
16. Reverse Shifter Lever
17. Reverse Shift Fork
18. Woodruff Key
19. Reverse Idler Gear Shaft
20. Reverse Idler Gear
21. Rear Bearing Retainer
22. First Gear
23. Rear Bearing Selective Snap Ring
24. Mainshaft
25. First Gear Thrust Washer
26. Rear Bearing
27. Reverse Shifter Head Shaft Detent Ball and Spring
28. Reverse Shifter Head Shaft
29. Interlock Pin
30. 1-2 Shift Fork Shaft
31. Interlock
32. 3-4 Shift Fork Shaft
33. 3-4 Shift Fork Shaft Detent Ball and Spring
34. Drain Plug
35. 3-4 Detent and Interlock Channel Cap
36. First Gear Sleeve
37. 1-2 Synchronizer Hub
38. Synchronizer Key
39. Reverse Shifter Head
40. 1-2 Shift Fork
41. 3-4 Shift Fork
42. Shift Finger
43. Special Snap Ring
44. Shifter Shaft Seal
45. Shifter Shaft
46. 1-2 Shift Fork Shaft Detent Ball and Spring
47. Clutch Gear Roller Bearings (33 Front—37 Rear)
48. Clutch Gear Bearing
49. Clutch Gear Bearing Selective Snap Ring
50. Snap Ring (Clutch Shaft Bottoming Stop)

four-speed gearshift lever are identical to those provided earlier in this section for the three-speed transmission. However, the four-speed gearshift lever does not embody the seat used in three-speed gearshift levers.

500, 700 and 900 Series

The 1962 4-speed transmission service procedures are basically the same as 1961 except for a change in the shift linkage adjustment procedure.

The transmission reverse inhibitor mechanism has been redesigned. Also the distance between the shoulder and the third and fourth speed snap ring groove on the mainshaft has been increased. To accommodate this change on the mainshaft, a new clutch gear needle bearings are required. The new clutch gear and bearings can be used with the 1961 mainshaft. If the mainshaft on a 1961 transmission requires replacement, the new clutch gear and bearings must be used. Both mainshafts will be available for service.

Shift Linkage Adjustment

After any operation in which the shift control rod in the tunner has been replaced or it has been found that transmission response is improper to the shift pattern, adjust the shift linkage.

> **NOTE: Before making adjustment, lash in system is to be taken up by removing the shift control rod to the rear.**

1. With seat in full forward position, shift transmission to the fourth gear (500 and 700 Models), then loosen the coupling clamp nut on the transmission shift control rod.
2. Adjust gearshift lever to .50 inch from the edge of the seat, then tighten the coupling clamp nut.
3. Test shift in all ranges.

The shift linkage adjustment procedure for the 900 Model is similar to the above except shift the transmission to the reverse gear and adjust the gearshift lever a distance of 3.25 inches from the center of the gearshift lever housing, rearward, to the center of the gearshift lever knob.

TROUBLES AND REMEDIES

Symptom and Probable Cause   **Probable Remedy**

Slips Out of High Gear
- a. Transmission loose on differential carrier.
- b. Control linkage does not work freely, binds.

- c. Does not fully engage.

- d. Damaged mainshaft pilot bearing.
- e. Clutch gear bearing retainer broken or loose.
- f. Dirt between transmission case and differential carrier.

a. Tighten mounting bolts.
b. Adjust and free up shift linkage. Torque reactions of engine should not cause the lever on transmission to move. The movement of transmission with respect to body should be transferred to the control linkage.
c. Measure length of engagement pattern on clutching teeth. If less than $7/64''$, check for bent levers, shifter shafts, detent cam plates, control rods and other shift linkage. Replace or straighten defective parts.
d. Replace pilot bearing.
e. Replace clutch gear bearing retainer.
f. Clean mating surfaces.

Slips Out of Low and/or Reverse
- a. First and/or Reverse gears damaged from operating at part engagement.
- b. Improper mated splines on inside of first and reverse gear and/or external spline on 2nd and 3rd clutch sleeve.

- c. Improperly adjusted linkage.

a. Determine cause, for example, worn shift fork & control lever or rod interference. Replace worn or bent parts.
b. Replace 2nd or 3rd speed clutch sleeve and/or first, and reverse sliding gear. Possible correction is to change index of gear on clutch sleeve approximately 180° and/or turning the rear side of first and reverse gear to the front of the transmission.
c. Adjust linkage.

Noisy in All Gears
- a. Insufficient lubricant.
- b. Worn countergear bearings.
- c. Worn or damaged clutch gear and countershaft drive gear.
- d. Damaged clutch gear or mainshaft ball bearings.
- e. Damaged speedometer gears.

a. Fill to correct level.
b. Replace countergear bearings and shaft.
c. Replace worn or damaged gears.
d. Replace damaged bearings.
e. Replace damaged gears.

Noisy in High Gear
- a. Damaged Clutch gear bearing.
- b. Damaged mainshaft bearing.

a. Replace damaged bearing.
b. Replace damaged bearing.

Noisy in Neutral with Engine Running
- a. Damaged clutch gear bearing.
- b. Damaged mainshaft pilot bearing roller.

a. Replace damaged bearing.
b. Replace damaged bearing roller.

Noisy in All Reduction Gears
- a. Insufficient lubricant.
- b. Worn or damaged clutch gear or counter drive gear.

a. Fill to correct level.
b. Replace faulty or damaged gears.

| Symptom and Probable Cause | Probable Remedy |

Noisy in Second Only
  a. Damaged or worn second speed constant mesh gears.
  b. Worn or damaged countergear rear bearings.

  a. Replace damaged gears.
  b. Replace countergear bearings and shaft.

Noisy in Low and Reverse Only
  a. Worn or damaged first and reverse sliding gear.
  b. Damaged or worn low and reverse countergear.

  a. Replace worn gear.
  b. Replace countergear assembly.

Noisy in Reverse Only
  a. Worn or damaged reverse idler.
  b. Worn reverse idler bushings.
  c. Damaged or worn reverse countergear.

  a. Replace reverse idler.
  b. Replace reverse idler.
  c. Replace countergear assembly.

Excessive Backlash in Second Only
  a. Second speed gear thrust washer worn.
  b. Mainshaft rear bearing not properly installed in case.
  c. Worn countergear rear bearing.

  a. Replace thrust washer.
  b. Replace bearing or case, as necessary.
  c. Replace countergear bearings and shaft.

Excessive Backlash in All Reduction Gears
  a. Worn countergear bushings.
  b. Excessive end play in countergear.

  a. Replace countergear.
  b. Replace countergear thrust washers.

Leaks Lubricant
  a. Excessive amount of lubricant in transmission.
  b. Loose or broken clutch gear bearing cover.
  c. Clutch gear bearing retainer gasket damaged.
  d. Cover loose or gasket damaged.
  e. Operating shaft seal leaks.
  f. Idler shaft expansion plugs loose.
  g. Countershaft loose in case.

  a. Drain to correct level.
  b. Tighten or replace cover.
  c. Replace gasket.
  d. Tighten cover or replace gasket.
  e. Replace operating shaft seal.
  f. Replace expansion plugs.
  g. Replace case.

AUTOMATIC TRANSMISSION

The "Corvair" Powerglide consists of an air cooled, three element torque converter which drives through an automatic shift, two-speed planetary transmission.

As illustrated, the Powerglide transmission is integrated to the differential carrier to form a Transaxle. As a result, the converter is remote from the main transmission assembly, being separated by the differential carrier. Two shafts run axially through the hollow pinion shaft; one from the converter cover hub to the front pump and the other from the turbine to the input sun gear to transmit converter torque to the transmission gear box.

Excepting the converter location, mechanical components of the "Corvair" Powerglide are generally scaled-down versions of comparable parts in conventional Powerglides. The use of a plate-type reverse clutch and a welded converter with integral starter driven gear are obvious exceptions. Gear ratios are 1.82:1 in low and reverse and 1:1 in high gear. Automatic low is also 1.82:1.

Selector lever positions from top to bottom are Reverse, Neutral, Drive and Low. No Park position is provided. Power flow sequences in each range are identical to conventional Powerglide transmissions.

Two innovations have been added to the Low range in this design, these being the addition of a manual low inhibitor and and extended part throttle downshift.

The manual low inhibiting feature is designed to protect the transmission from damage which could result from moving the selector lever into Low while the vehicle is traveling more than approximately 45 mph. For example, if the driver moved the selector lever into "low" at 70 mph, the transmission would remain in "high" until vehicle speed was reduced to approximately 45 mph, and then the downshift would occur.

Part throttle downshifts are provided to provide better low speed acceleration characteristics. At speeds below 25 mph, a downshift to Low will occur if the accelerator is moved to one-half throttle or more. The subsequent upshift will occur at 34-41 mph. As with the conventional Powerglide, wide-open throttle downshifts are possible with the speed limitations being 38-44 mph.

MAINTENANCE

OIL REQUIREMENTS

The Powerglide transmission requires an oil known as Automatic Transmission Fluid, "Type A" bearing a "AQ-ATF" mark. This oil is available through Chevrolet dealers and oil company filling stations in sealed containers.

OIL LEVEL

The transmission oil level should be checked every 1000 miles. Oil should be added only when the lever is near the "ADD" mark on the dip stick with oil at normal operating temperature. The oil level dip stick is located in the right-front of the engine com-

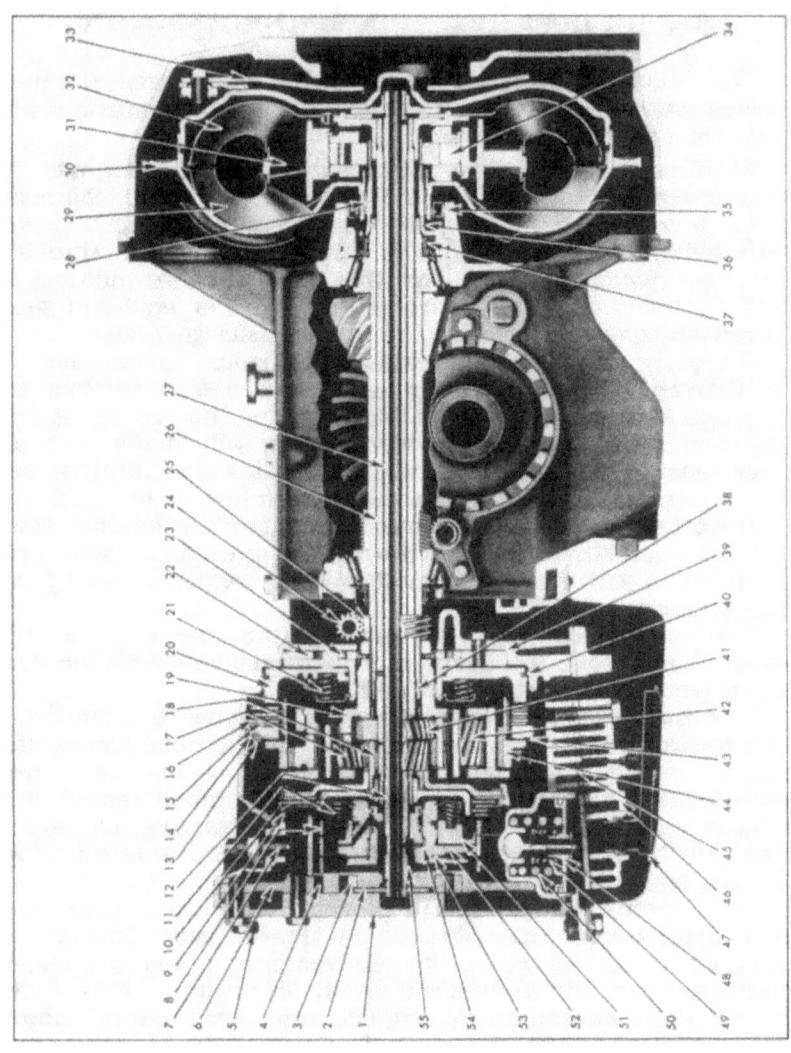

1. Front Pump Cover
2. Front Pump Shaft Drive Hub
3. Front Pump Drive Gear
4. Front Pump Driven Gear
5. Transmission Vent
6. Front Pump Body
7. Low Band Adjusting Screw and Lock Nut
8. Low Band
9. Clutch Drum Reaction Plate (3 Used)
10. Clutch Drum Faced Plate (15 Used)
11. Clutch Piston Return Spring
12. Turbine Shaft Front Bushing
13. Reverse Clutch Retaining Ring Clip
14. Reverse Clutch Front Reaction Plate (Thick)
15. Reverse Clutch Faced Plates (3 Used)
16. Reverse Clutch Reaction Plate (3 Used)
17. Short Pinion
18. Low Sun Gear Bushing
19. Planet Carrier Hub (Transmission Output)
20. Reverse Piston
21. Reverse Piston Return Spring (17 Used)
22. Rear Pump Driven Gear
23. Rear Pump Drive Gear
24. Governor Driven Gear
25. Governor Drive Gear
26. Turbine Shaft
27. Front Pump Shaft
28. Converter Hub Bushing
29. Converter Pump
30. Starter Gear
31. Stator
32. Turbine
33. Engine Flex Plate
34. Stator Cam Race
35. Converter Hub Seal
36. Stator Shaft
37. Pinion Shaft Rear Oil Seal
38. Pinion Shaft Bushing
39. Rear Pump Wear Plate
40. Reverse Piston Outer Seal
41. Planet Carrier Input Sun Gear
42. Long Pinion Gear
43. Reverse Clutch Plate Retaining Ring
44. Ring Gear
45. Valve Body Ditch Plate
46. Valve Body
47. Oil Pick-up Pipe
48. Low Servo Piston
49. Low Servo Piston Cushion Spring
50. Low Servo Piston Return Spring
51. Clutch Drum Piston
52. Clutch Drum Hub
53. Clutch Drum Selective Thrust Washer
54. Clutch Drum Bushing
55. Front Pump Body Bushing

182

partment.

NOTE: The difference in oil level between Full and Add is one (1) pint.

In order to check oil level accurately, the engine should be idled with the transmission oil at normal temperature and the control lever in neutral (N) position.

It is important that the oil level be maintained no higher than the "FULL" mark on the transmission oil level gauge. DO NOT OVERFILL, for when the oil level is at the full mark on the dip stick, it is just slightly below the planetary gear unit. If oil is added which brings the oil level above the full mark, the planetary unit will run in the oil, foaming and aerating the oil. This may cause malfunction of the transmission assembly due to improper application of the band or clutches.

If the transmission is found consistently low on oil, a thorough inspection should be made to find and correct all external oil leaks. Transmission oil leakage is easily identified as all automatic transmission fluid used in Chevrolet production is dyed red.

All mating surfaces such as the front pump, oil pan rail, filler tube, governor, and the attachment to the differential carrier should be carefully examined for signs of leakage. The vacuum modulator must also be checked to insure that the diaphragm has not ruptured as this would allow transmission oil to be drawn into the intake manifold. Usually, the exhaust will be excessively smoky if the diaphragm ruptures due to the transmission oil added to the combustion.

DRAINING AND REFILLING

No periodic draining of the transmission oil is recommended.

When the transmission requires repair, drain the oil by loosening the filler tube attaching nut in the oil pan and allow oil to drain; no drain plug is provided.

To refill the transmission, tighten the filler tube attaching nut and add four (4) points transmission fluid using filler tube and funnel. Start engine and allow engine to idle in Neutral 3-5 minutes to warm oil, then check oil and add as required to raise to the level of the "FULL" mark. Assuming that the converter was not drained (since it is welded) and allowing for a normal spillage or draindown, approximately six (6) pints of oil will be required for refill.

CAUTION: Do not over-fill!

The dry capacity of the transmission, including converter, is 12 pints. Normal refills require 6 pints.

DIAGNOSIS GUIDE

No drive in any selector position; cannot load engine.
* Low oil level.
* Clogged oil section pipe screen.
* Broken or disconnected manual valve cable.
* Defective pressure regulator valve.
* Defective line pressure limit valve.
* Front pump defective.
* Rear pump check valve and rear pump priming ball not seating. Both must occur for possible malfunction.
* Front pump shaft disengaged at either converter or pump gear.
* Front pump priming ball not seating.

Engine speed flares on standstill starts but acceleration lags.
* Low Band Partially Applied:
   a. Low oil level.
   b. Clogged pickup pipe screen.
   c. Improper band adjustment.
   d. Servo piston apply passage blocked.
   e. Servo piston ring broken or leaking.
   f. Band facing worn.
   g. Low band apply linkage disengaged or broken.
   h. Converter stator not holding (rare).

Engine speed flares on upshift.
* Low oil level.
* Clogged oil section screen or pipe.
* High clutch partially applied—blocked feed orifice.
* Clutch plates worn.
* Clutch seals leak.
* Clutch piston hung up.
* Clutch drum relief ball not seating.
* Vacuum modulator hose collapsed.

Transmission will not upshift.
* Low band not releasing, probably due to:
   a. Stuck low-drive valve.
   b. Defective governor.
   c. No rear pump output such as stuck priming ball, drive pins not engaged, or defective pump.
   d. TV valve stuck or maladjusted.
   e. Maladjusted manual valve lever.

Upshifts harsh.
* Incorrect carburetor-to-transmission TV rod adjustment.
* Improper low band adjustment.
* Vacuum modulator hose broken or disconnected.
* Vacuum modulator diaphragm leaks.
* Vacuum modulator valve stuck.
* Hydraulic modulator valve stuck.

Closed throttle (coast) downshifts harsh.
* Improper low band adjustment.
* Vacuum modulator hose disconnected, broken.
* Vacuum modulator diaphragm ruptured.
* Vacuum modulator valve stuck.
* Engine idle speed too high.
* Sticking valves in valve body (pressure regulator or hydraulic modulator valves).

Car creeps excessively in Drive.
* Idle speed too high.

Car creeps in Neutral.
* Incorrect manual valve lever adjustment.
* High clutch or low band not released.

No drive in Reverse.
* Manual valve lever improperly adjusted.
* Cable linkage adjustment.
* Reverse clutch piston stuck.
* Reverse clutch plates worn out.
* Reverse clutch leaking excessively.
* Blocked reverse clutch apply orifice.

Improper shift points (see Shift-MPH Chart).
* Incorrectly adjusted carburetor-to-transmission.
* Incorrectly adjusted TV valve.
* Governor defective.
* Rear pump priming ball stuck.

Oil forced out of filler tube.
* Oil level too high causing planet carrier to run in oil and cause foam.
* Oil pickup pipe split or not sealed causing air entrainment.

Unable to push start.
* Rear pump drive gear not engaged with drive pins on planet carrier hub.
* Rear pump defective.
* Rear pump priming ball not seating.

CORVAIR POWERGLIDE
SHIFT POINT—MPH CHART

UPSHIFTS	MPH
Minimum Throttle	10-12½
Full Throttle	41-47
Part Throttle (Detent Touch)	34-41
DOWNSHIFTS	
Closed Throttle	8-12
Full Throttle	38-44
Part Throttle (Detent Touch)	23-30
Manual Low (Inhibited)	41-46

ENGINE TUNE-UP

The engine tune-up has become increasingly important to the modern automotive engine with its vastly improved power and performance. With the higher compression ratios, improved electrical systems and other advances in design, today's engines have become more sensitive to usage and operating conditions, all of which have a decided effect on power and performance.

Since the modern engine is admittedly more temperamental and sensitive to adjustments, some means must be devised to put back into the engine the standard of performance and economy of which it is capable.

Since it is seldom advisable to attempt an improvement in performance by correction of one or two items only, time will normally be saved and more lasting results assured if the tuner will follow a definite and thorough procedure of analysis and correction of all items affecting power, performance, and economy.

The tune-up will be performed in two parts. The first part will consist of visual and mechanical checks and adjustments, while the second part will consist of an instrument checkout that can be performed with any one of the modern compact units of service equipment available for this purpose. Always follow the instructions provided by the manufacturer of the particular equipment to be used.

Additional checks and adjustments are included in the latter part of this section for use as required. Many of these operations would normally be used to isolate and correct trouble located during the tune-up.

All operations included herein will be performed on the vehicle. Illustrations depicting bench operations have been employed for convenience only and are intended only to clarify the operations which will be performed on the vehicle. Since it is impractical to illustrate all possible installations that may be encountered, only a typical installation will be used to illustrate the point in question.

MECHANICAL CHECKS AND ADJUSTMENTS

The mechanical checks and adjustments described below are performed with the engine off. Except where noted, the car may be at either room temperature or operating temperature.

1. **REMOVE SPARK PLUGS AND TEST COMPRESSION**

    a. Remove spark plug wires.

    b. Remove any foreign matter from around spark plugs by blowing out with compressed air then loosen all plugs one turn.

    NOTE: To remove or loosen center spark plugs, it will be necessary to disconnect or remove carburetor throttle rod and use a universal drive on spark plug socket.

c. Start engine and accelerate to 1000 rpm to blow out loosened carbon.

NOTE: Clearing out carbon in this manner is important in preventing false compression readings due to chips or carbon being lodged under the valves.

d. Stop engine and remove spark plugs.

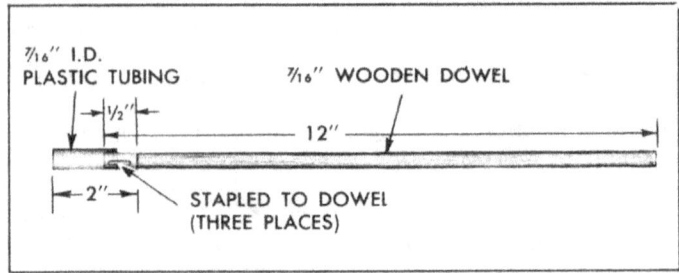

Spark Plug Holding Tool

NOTE: It may be desirable to use a special spark plug socket that is equipped with an internal "O" ring seal to grip the spark plug or fabricate a tool as shown to grip plug after loosening with socket to avoid the possibility of dropping plug into engine shroud assembly.

Checking Compression

e. Remove air cleaner and block throttle and choke in wide open position.
   f. Hook up starter remote control cable and insert compression gauge firmly in spark plug port.

   NOTE: Unless special adapters are available, it will be necessary to remove both carburetors to perform the compression test.

   g. Crank engine through at least four compression strokes to obtain highest possible reading.
   h. Check and record compression of each cylinder. Compression should read as indicated below and variation between highest and lowest reading cylinders should be less than 20 pounds. The minimum pressure should be 130 pounds.
   i. To determine whether rings, valves, or head gasket are at fault, if one or more cylinders are low or uneven, oil would ordinarily be injected into each cylinder and compression rechecked. Due to the design of this engine (horizontal-opposed) the oil would lay in the bottom (along the cylinder wall) of each cylinder, thus preventing an accurate check. A careful diagnosis with a vacuum gauge, oscilloscope, etc., should be used with this compression test to determine what (if anything) is at fault.

The compression check is important because an engine with low or uneven compression cannot be tuned successfully to give peak performance. Therefore, it is essential that improper compression be corrected before proceeding with an engine tune-up.

2. **CLEAN, SERVICE AND INSTALL SPARK PLUGS**
   a. Inspect each plug individually for badly worn electrodes, glazed, broken or blistered porcelains and replace plugs where necessary. Refer to spark plug diagnosis information for an analysis of plug conditions.
   b. Clean serviceable spark plug thoroughly, using an abrasive-type cleaner such as sand blast. File the center electrode flat.
   c. Inspect each spark plug for make and heat range. All Plugs must be of the same make and number or heat range (AC 44FF which has ½" thread reach).
   d. Adjust plug gaps to .035" using a round feeler gauge.

   CAUTION: Never bend the center electrode to adjust gap. Always adjust by bending ground or side electrode.

   e. If available, test plugs with a spark plug tester.
   f. Inspect spark plug hole threads and clean before installing plugs. Corrosion deposits can be removed with a 14 mm. x 1.25 SAE spark plug tap (available through local job-

bers) or by using a small wire brush in an electric drill. Use plenty of grease on tap to catch any chips.

CAUTION: Use extreme care when using tap to prevent cross threading. Also, crank engine several times to blow out any material dislodged during cleaning operation.

g. Install spark plugs to engine with new gaskets and tighten to 20-25 lbs. torque. Spark plug gaskets thread onto spark plug.

NOTE: Do not use any "anti-seize" compound on spark plug threads as this will act as an insulator and not allow proper spark plug cooling. It may be desirous to use a spark plug wrench that is equipped with an internal "O" ring seal to grip the spark plug and avoid the possibility of dropping spark plugs into engine shroud assembly or to fabricate a tool to start the plug into the cylinder head.

h. Secure wires and spark plug covers.

NOTE: Be certain spark plug covers are tightly in place. If as many as two are loose, all air pressure in cooling system will be lost and engine will overheat. In addition, a whistling sound may develop that could be difficult to locate.

i. Reconnect carburetor linkage.

Improper installation is one of the greatest single causes of unsatisfactory spark plug performance. Improper installation is the result of one or more of the following practices:

1. Installation of plugs with insufficient torque to fully seat the gasket.
2. Installation of the plugs using excessive torque which changes gap settings.
3. Installation of plugs on dirty gasket seal.
4. Installation of plugs to corroded spark plug hole threads.

Failure to install plugs properly will cause them to operate at excessively high temperatures and result in reduced operating life under mild operation or complete destruction under severe operation where the intense heat cannot be dissipated rapidly enough.

Always remove corrosion deposits in hole threads before installing plugs. When corrosion is present in threads, normal torque is not sufficient to compress the plug gasket and early failure from overheating will result.

Always use a new gasket and wipe seats in head clean. The gasket must be fully compressed on clean seats to complete heat transfer and provide a gas-tight seal in the cylinder. For

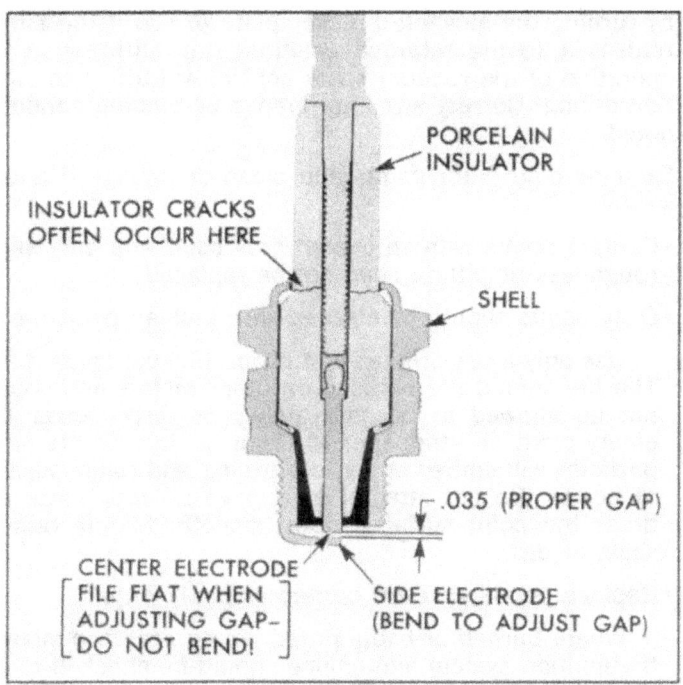

Spark Plug Detail

this reason as well as the necessity of maintaining correct plug gap, the use of correct torque is extremely important during installation.

3. SERVICE IGNITION SYSTEM AND MAKE NECESSARY REPAIRS

    a. Replace brittle or damaged spark plug wires. Install all wires to proper spark plugs.

    b. Tighten all ignition system connections.

    c. Replace or repair any wires that are frayed, loose or damaged.

    d. Remove distributor cap, clean cap and inspect for cracks, carbon tracks and burned or corroded terminals. Replace cap where necessary.

    e. Clean rotor and inspect for damage or deterioration. Replace rotor where necessary.

    f. Check the distributor centrifugal advance mechanism by turning the distributor rotor to see if the springs return it to its retarded position. If the rotor does not return readily, the distributor must be disassembled and the cause of the trouble corrected.

    g. Check to see that the vacuum spark control operates freely by turning the movable breaker plate to see if the spring returns it to the retarded position. Any stiffness in the operation of the vacuum spark control will affect the ignition timing. Correct any interference or binding condition noted.

h. Examine distributor points and clean or replace if necessary.

- Contact points with an overall gray color and only slight roughness or pitting need not be replaced.
- Dirty points should be cleaned with a clean point file.

Use only a few strokes of a clean, fine-cut contact file. The file should not be used on other metals and should not be allowed to become greasy or dirty. Never use emery cloth or sandpaper to clean contact points since particles will embed and cause arcing and rapid burning of points. Do not attempt to remove all roughness nor dress the point surfaces down smooth. Merely remove scale or dirt.

- Replace points that are burned or badly pitted.

Where burned or badly pitted points are encountered, the ignition system and engine should be checked to de-

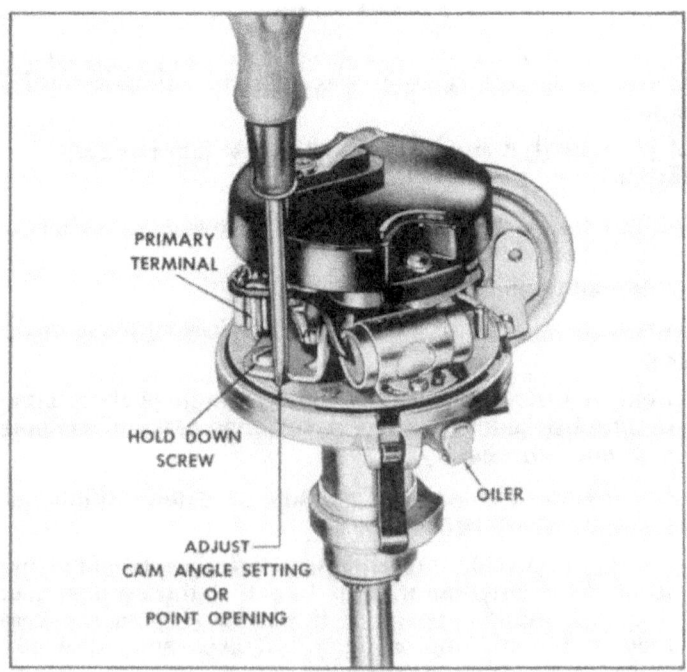

Point Adjustment

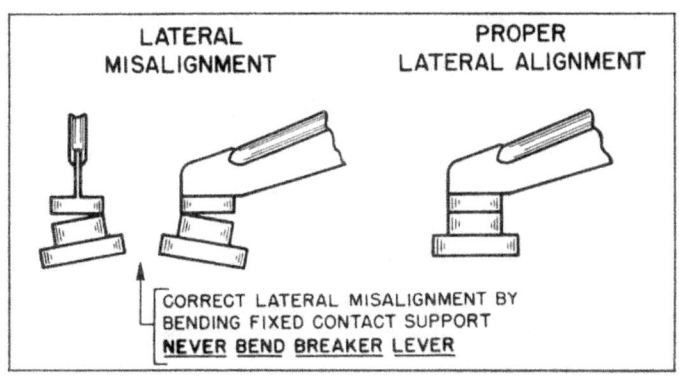

Alignment of Points

termine the cause of trouble so it can be eliminated. Unless the condition causing point burning or pitting is corrected, new points will provide no better service than the old points.

i. Adjust distributor contact point gap to .019" new points) or .016" (used points), using a feeler gauge or dial indicator. Breaker arm rubbing block should be on extreme top of cam lobe during adjustment.

NOTE: Contact points should be cleaned before adjusting with a feeler gauge if they have been in service.

- Check alignment of distributor points with points closed. Align new points where necessary, but do not attempt to align used points. Instead, replace used points where serious misalignment is observed.
- Align points by bending fixed contact support if necessary, using an alignment tool if available. Do not bend breaker arm.
- After adjusting alignment, readjust point gap.

j. Make sure all distributor wire terminals are clean and tight.

k. Lubricate distributor.

- Fill hinge cap oiler with light engine oil.
- Apply a thin film of Delco-Remy Cam and Ball Bearing Lubricant, Lubriplate or other similar high melting point, non-bleeding grease to the cam.
- Apply one small drop of light engine oil on the breaker lever pivot.

l. Install rotor and distributor cap. Press all wires firmly into cap towers.

To Replace Distributor Points and Condenser — 1962

1. Loosen hold-down screws and remove cap.
2. Lift off primary and condenser wire leads at clip "A".
3. Remove condenser bracket screw and condenser.
4. Remove contact point hold-down screw and remove points as a unit.
5. Reverse Steps 2-4 to install.

   NOTE: Primary and condenser leads must be installed between insulator and contact point spring arm.

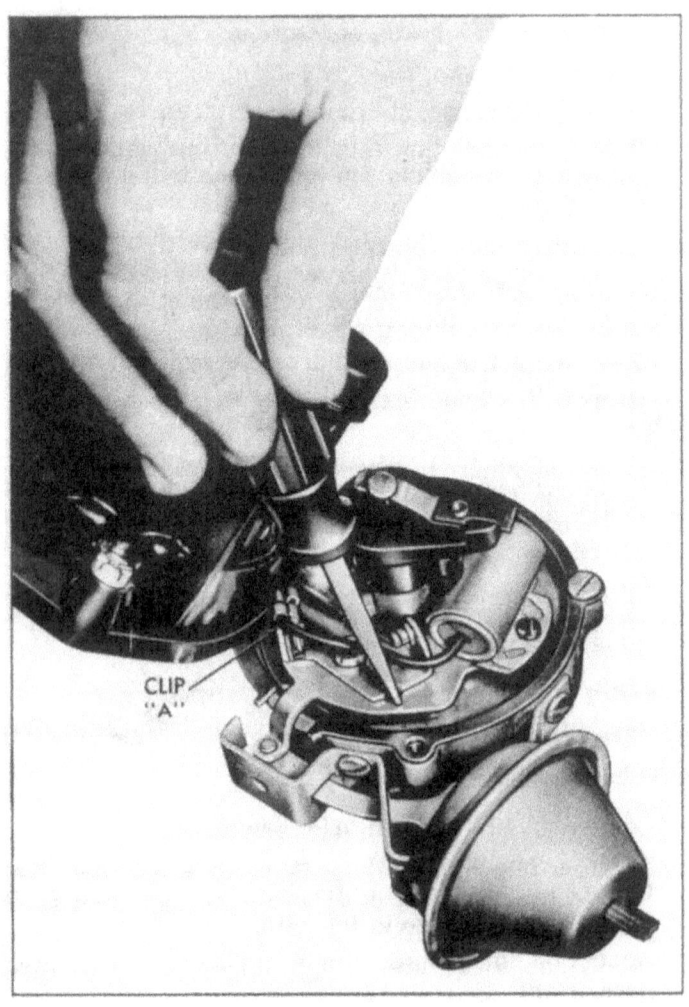

Point Adjustment

6. Adjust points to .019" new or .016" used, and lock stationary point. Check arm spring tension.
7. Install distributor cap and tighten screws.

   NOTE: Cap must be installed with notch to vacuum advance lever opening on housing.

4. SERVICE BATTERY AND BATTERY CABLES

Inspect battery and cables and perform necessary service on these components.

Inspect for signs of corrosion on battery, cables and surrounding area, loose or broken carriers, cracked or bulged cases, dirt and acid, electrolyte leakage and low electrolyte lever. Fill cells to proper level with distilled water or water passed through a "demineralizer."

The top of the battery should be clean and the battery hold-down bolts properly tightened. Particular care should be taken to see that the tops of the 12-volt batteries are kept clean of acid film and dirt because of the high voltage between the battery terminals. For best results when cleaning batteries, wash first with a dilute ammonia or soda solution to neutralize any acid present and then flush off with clean water. Care must be taken to keep vent plugs tight so that the neutralizing solution does not enter the cell. The hold-down bolts should be kept tight enough to prevent the battery from shaking around in the holder, but they should not be tightened to the point where the battery case will be placed under a severe strain.

To insure good contact, the battery cables should be tight on the battery posts and fully bottomed. To remove or install the new spring type cable clamps, a suitable pliers must be used to spread the ends of the clamps. Oil battery terminal felt washer. If the battery posts or cable terminals are corroded, the cables should be cleaned separately with a soda solution and a wire brush. It is NOT recommended that the battery posts and cable clamps be greased prior to installing cables to battery as this may contribute to slippage of the clamps from the battery posts.

If battery has remained undercharged, check for loose (worn) generator belt, defective generator, high resistance in the charging circuit, oxidized regulator contact points, or a low voltage setting.

If the battery has been using too much water, the voltage regulator setting is too high.

5. SERVICE BLOWER BELT AND GENERATOR

a. Inspect blower belt condition and check deflection of belt.

   1. If belt damage is noted, replace the belt. A slightly damaged belt **must** be replaced to prevent premature failure.

   2. Adjust belt (if necessary) to give a $\frac{3}{8}$ deflection between blower and idler pulley under a 15 pound load.

If a new belt is installed, adjust deflection as described above, then operate the engine at 1500 rpm for at least one minute to "seat" the new belt. Recheck deflection, or:

Use a strand tension gauge and adjust idler pulley to give a reading of 70 lbs. on a new belt and 50 lbs. on a used belt.

NOTE: A belt is considered new until it has been used approximately 1000 miles.

NOTE: If there is any preload on generator, front end frame will break. To avoid this condition, follow the generator mounting procedure.

b. Inspect generator commutator and brushes for cleanliness and wear. The commutator should be cleaned if dirty and the brushes should be replaced if worn down to less than half their original length.

The commutator may be cleaned by holding No. 00 sandpaper or a cleaning stone against it while the generator is operating.

c. Replace or repair frayed or broken generator wires and tighten all wire connections.

d. Lubricate generator by filling hinge cap oilers with light engine oil.

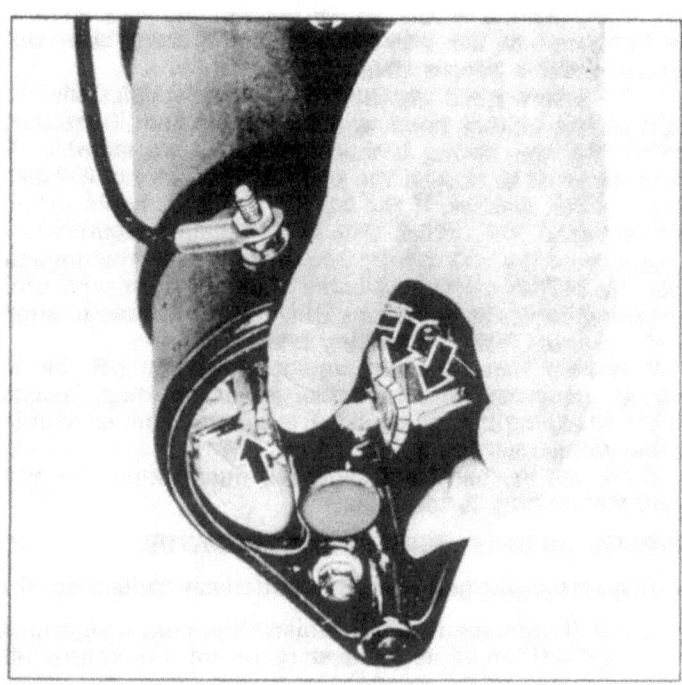

Inspecting Generator Brushes and Commutator

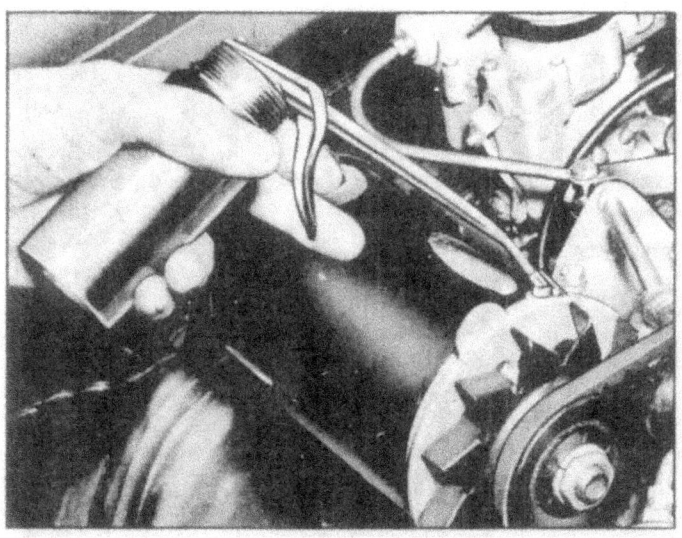

Lubricating Generator

6. CHECK FUEL LINES AND FUEL FILTER

Inspect fuel lines for kinks, bends or leaks and clean fuel filter.

NOTE: If poor high speed performance exists on the vehicle, fuel pump tests should be performed.

7. CLEAN AND SERVICE AIR CLEANER

Do not attempt to perform any operational adjustments on the carburetor (idle speed, mixture, etc.) without first servicing the air cleaner.

SYNCHRONIZING CARBURETORS — 1960

NOTE: Float level and float drop checks and adjustments will not be covered in this section but may require checking.

1. Remove wing nut attaching air cleaner to air cleaner air horn assembly and "Corbin" clamps attaching air hoses to carburetors. Lift off air cleaner and air hoses as a unit and place on a clean surface.

2. Disconnect throttle rods from each carburetor as follows:

    a. Right carburetor — remove retainer clip and disconnect throttle rod from carburetor throttle shaft lever.

    b. Left carburetor — remove retainer clip and detach throttle rod swivel from left hand cross shaft lever. Be certain that throttle lever stop on fast idle linkage is off cam.

3. Fully back off the idle speed screw on each carburetor so

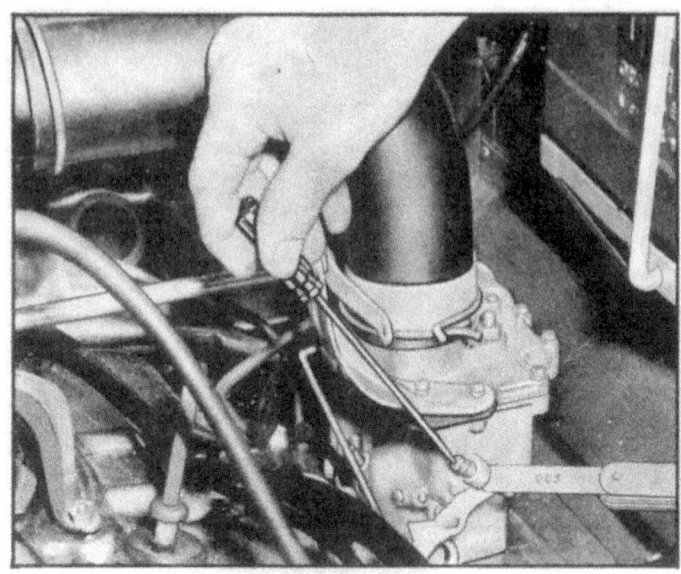

Synchronizing Carburetors

that each throttle valve is fully closed.

4. Place a .003" feeler gauge between the idle speed screw and the throttle lever. Turn the screw down until it just holds the gauge. Remove the gauge and turn the screw one more complete turn. Perform this operation on each carburetor.

5. On the right hand carburetor, using the retainer clip, connect the throttle rod to the carburetor throttle shaft lever.

6. Be certain the left hand cross shaft lever is turned fully clockwise to insure that the right hand carburetor throttle valve is fully closed. Lifting up on the left hand carburetor throttle rod (to insure that the throttle valve is fully closed),

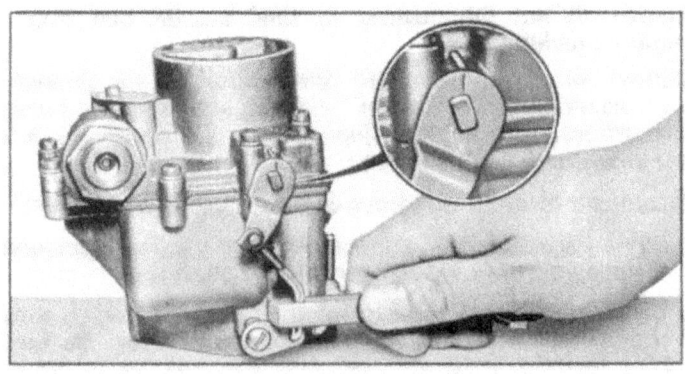

Pump Rod Adjustment

adjust the swivel at the top of the rod so that it freely enters the hole in the cross shaft lever. Attach it with the retainer clip.

7. The two carburetors are now synchronized. Any further curb idle speed screw adjustment must be duplicated on both carburetors.

8. Replace air cleaner and air hoses.

Pump Rod Adjustment

1. Back off idle screw until throttle valve is completely closed.

2. Holding throttle valve closed, check to see that the scribe mark on the accelerator pump is aligned with the mark cast into the bowl cover.

3. The accelerator pump rod may be carefully bent, using a carburetor rod bending tool, to obtain the correct adjustment, if necessary.

4. Synchronize and re-adjust carburetors.

Fast Idle Adjustment

The fast idle adjustment is located on the air horn/air cleaner assembly linkage.

1. Place a ⅛" spacer between the throttle lever and the adjusting screw at the left hand carburetor.

2. Remove the clip attaching the fast idle link swivel to the fast idle lever.

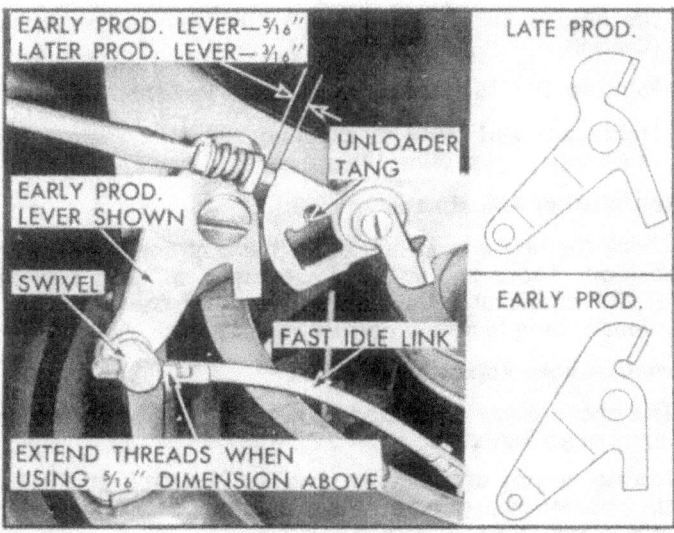

Fast Idle Adjustment

Choke Mechanism—Exploded View

1. Choke Cover Retaining Screws
2. Choke Cover Retainers
3. Choke Modifier Lever
4. Choke Modifier Pointer
5. Choke Thermostat and Cover Assembly
6. Choke Thermostat Baffle Plate
7. Choke Shaft Lever and Link Assembly
8. Choke Valve Retaining Screws
9. Choke Valve
10. Choke Housing Retaining Screws
11. Choke Housing
12. Air Horn Assembly
13. Throttle Lever Assembly
14. Throttle Lever Retaining Screw
15. Fast Idle Cam
16. Washer
17. Choke Trip Lever
18. Fast Idle Cam Retaining Screw

3. Turn down the fast idle adjusting screw until approximately 5/16" (early models) or 3/16" (late models) projects past the fast idle lever.

4. Rotate the fast idle cam counter-clockwise (viewed from left of vehicle) until the fast idle screw can be brought to bear on the highest portion of the cam.

5. Holding screw and fast idle lever in this position, turn the swivel on the fast idle link until the swivel pin will just enter the hole in the fast idle lever. Clip the swivel and link in position.

6. Remove the 1/8" spacer which was installed in step 1.

7. Hold cam and lever in position and then adjust the fast idle screw to just allow the spacer to slip out.

Choke Unloader Adjustment

Check the choke unloader adjustment at the wide open throttle position. There should be a clearance of .25" between the top of the choke and the adjacent wall of the air horn. Bend the unloader tang to obtain correct adjustment.

Automatic Choke Adjustment

The choke cover is located in proper position on the housing by means of an index tab.

Normal setting of the choke modifier is such that with throttles in idle position the pointer is set at index mark scribed on the choke housing cover.

The choke modifier is adjusted as follows:

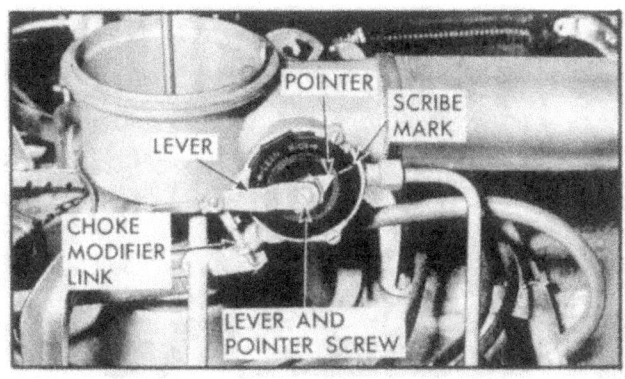

Choke Modifier Adjustment

1. The choke modifier lever must be attached to cross shaft lever by means of the modifier link. Carburetors must be in curb idle position.
2. Loosen lever and pointer screw.
3. Rotate pointer to the index mark.

   NOTE: Lever must point toward rear of vehicle.
4. Turn down on screw to lock the lever and pointer and pointer in this direction.

SYNCHRONIZING CARBURETORS — 1961

1. **Initial Adjustments**

   Perform the following adjustments, in sequence, with both throttle rods disconnected at the carburetor cross-shaft levers and with engine off.

   NOTE: Adjustments must be made on each carburetor.
   a. Back the curb idle speed and fast idle speed adjustment screws away from carburetor throttle shaft lever.

   b. **Curb Idle Speed** — Place a .003" feeler gauge between the curb idle speed screw and the carburetor throttle shaft lever. Turn the screw until it just contacts the gauge, then remove the gauge and turn the screw 1½ more turns to set the throttle valve.

   c. **Fast Idle—(choke fully open)** — Place a feeler gauge (.010" on automatic and .030" on synchromesh transmission) between fast idle speed screw and pad (tang) on throttle lever and adjust the screw until it contacts (or holds) the gauge.

   d. Turn the idle mixture screw lightly to its seat and back out 1½ turns.

   CAUTION: Do not turn idle mixture screws tightly

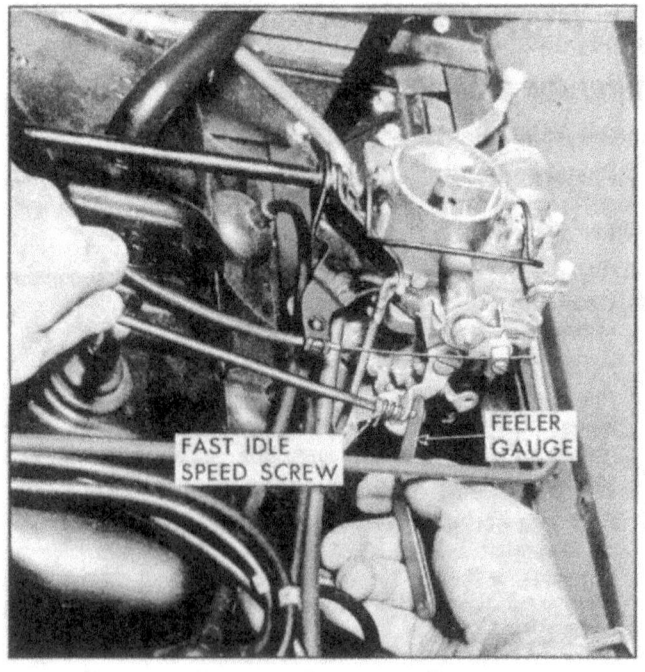

against seats or damage to needle seat will result.

2. Connect Throttle Rods as Follows:

   a. Right Carburetor — Connect throttle rod to carburetor cross-shaft lever using retainer clip.

   b. Left Carburetor — Rotate carburetor cross-shaft (with accelerator rod) to ensure positive closing of the right carburetor throttle valve. Adjust throttle rod length in swivel until rod freely enters hole on carburetor cross-shaft lever and secure rod with retainer clip.

   NOTE: The carburetors are now mechanically synchronized. Any further curb idle speed screw adjustment must be duplicated on both carburetors.

3. Preliminary Curb Idle Speed and Mixture Adjustment

   a. Start engine and normalize.

   b. Check timing.

   c. Connect vacuum gauge to adapter on vacuum balance tube. (Remove transmission vacuum line on automatic transmission and cap on synchromesh from balance tube adapter.)

   d. Connect tachometer to engine.

   e. Adjust curb idle speed (duplicate adjustment on both carburetors) to attain approximately 500 rpm (automatic trainsmission in drive and synchromesh in neutral, hand

Idle Mixture Adjustment

Spark Port Vacuum Connections

brake applied). Adjust idle mixture screws on both carburetors to obtain peak steady vacuum at given idle speed.

f. Remove vacuum gauge and close adapter as required for given transmission model.

4. **Carburetor Balance — Vacuum Check**

   a. Remove distributor vacuum advance hose from right hand carburetor and plastic cap from left hand carburetor spark port adapter tubes.

   b. Connect vacuum gauge to adapter tube ot each carburetor (best results will be obtained using 2 equally calibrated gauges).

   c. Move accelerator lever to obtain 1200 rpm (all transmissions in neutral).

   d. Check vacuum readings at each carburetor and note difference is one inch or less, the carburetors are satisfactorily synchronized. If difference is more than one inch, return engine to idle and adjust **left** carburetor throttle rod one turn (up to increase left carburetor vacuum and down to decrease) and recheck carburetor vacuum difference at 1200 rpm. Make adjustment by disconnecting rod at cross-shaft end and rotating in swivel. Repeat adjustment until difference is within one inch of vacuum.

   NOTE: It is preferable to have higher reading on right carburetor (distributor advance side).

CAUTION: When making linkage adjustments, accelerate engine by moving accelerator rod only. Do not open throttle by grasping other portions of linkage or this may upset geometry and synchronization.

e. Remove vacuum gauge/or gauges, replace distributor advance hose on spark port adapter tube of right carburetor and plastic cap on left carburetor spark port adapter tube.

5. Final Curb Idle Speed and Mixture Adjustment Check

NOTE: Always make final idle speed mixture adjustment with air cleaners installed.

a. Replace air cleaners.

b. Reconnect vacuum gauge to vacuum balance tube adapter.

c. Read vacuum at idle speed of 500 rpm.
If necessary, adjust curb idle speed and mixture screws to highest steady vacuum reading between 14-18 inches.

CAUTION: Any necessary adjustment must be duplicated at each carburetor.

6. Recheck Fast Idle Setting as Outlined in Step 1c.
(This setting depends upon final curb idle 500 rpm setting.)

Synchronizing Carburetors — 1962

1. Initial Adjustment
Perform the following adjustments on each carburetor, in sequence, with both throttle rods disconnected at the cross-shaft, choke control rods disconnected at choke levers and with engine off.

    a. Back idle speed screw away from throttle lever. Open the choke valve so throttle lever does not ride fast idle cam. Place a .003" feeler gauge between idle speed screw and throttle lever. Turn the screw until it just contacts the gauge and then turn 1½ more turns to set the throttle valve.

    b. Turn idle mixture screw lightly to its seat and back out 1½ turns.

    CAUTION: Do not turn idle mixture screws tightly against seats or damage to needle and seat will result.

2. Connect Throttle Rods as Follows:

    a. Right Carburetor-Connect throttle rod to carburetor cross-shaft lever using retainer clip.

    b. Left Carburetor-Rotate cross-shaft (with accelerator rod) to ensure positive closing of right carburetor throttle valve. Adjust throttle rod length in swivel until rod freely enters

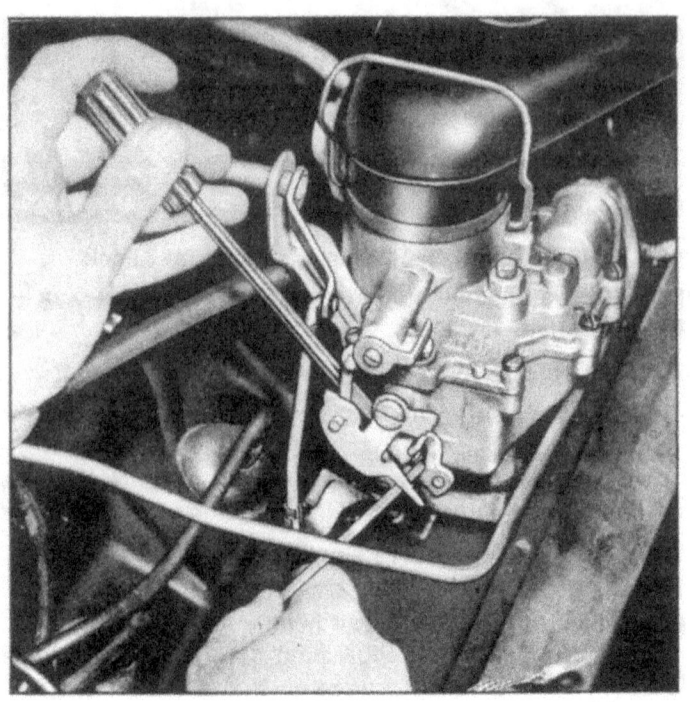

Idle Adjustments

hole on carburetor cross-shaft lever, then shorten rod one more turn in swivel. Secure rod with retainer clip.

NOTE: It may be necessary to hold the choke valve open so fast idle cam is clear of throttle lever.

NOTE: The carburetors are now mechanically synchronized. Any further idle speed or mixture adjustment must be duplicated on both carburetors.

3. Preliminary Curb Idle Speed and Mixture Adjustment.

   a. Start engine and normalize.

   b. Check timing.

   c. Connect vacuum gauge to adapter (fig. 7-4) or vacuum balance tube. (Remove transmission vacuum line on automatic transmission and cap on synchromesh from balance tube adapter.)

   d. Connect tachometer to engine.

   e. Adjust curb idle speed (duplicate adjustment on both carburetors) to attain approximate idle speed shown in chart for each engine. Adjust idle mixture screws on both carburetors to obtain peak steady vacuum at given idle speed.

   f. Remove vacuum gauge and close adapter as required for

given transmission model.

4. Carburetor Balance — Vacuum Check.

   NOTE: Ordinarily carburetors are satisfactorily synchronized at this point, and Step 4 is merely a vacuum test comparing the two banks.

   a. Remove choke diaphragm hose from each carburetor base adapter and connect vacuum gauge to the adapter. (Best results can be obtained using 2 equally calibrated gauges.)

   CAUTION: Do not turn tubing in carburetor body.

   NOTE: One gauge can be used by constructing a "T" line to both carburetors from the gauge. Pinch hose closed between gauge and one carburetor and read vacuum of opposite carburetor.

   b. Operate engine at idle speed. Check vacuum at each carburetor and note difference. If difference is one inch or less, the carburetors are satisfactorily synchronized. If difference is more than one inch, adjust left carburetor throttle rod one turn (up to increase left carburetor vacuum and down to decrease) and recheck vacuum readings. Make the adjustment by disconnecting rod at cross-shaft and rotating it in the swivel.

   NOTE: It is preferable to have higher reading on right carburetor (spark advance side).

   CAUTION: When making linkage adjustments, move the cross-shaft by grasping accelerator rod only. Do not open throttle by grasping other portions of linkage as this might upset geometry and synchronization.

   c. Remove gauge/or gauges and replace choke diaphragm hoses.

5. Final Curb Idle Speed and Mixture Adjustment Check.

   NOTE: Always make final idle speed mixture adjustment with air cleaners installed.

   a. Replace air cleaners.

   b. Reconnect vacuum gauge to vacuum balance tube adapter.

   c. Read vacuum at idle speed.

If necessary, adjust curb idle speed and mixture screws to highest steady vacuum reading between 14-18 inches.

   CAUTION: Any necessary adjustment must be duplicated at each carburetor.

ADJUST FAST IDLE CAM CLEARANCE

   NOTE: This adjustment must be made after curb idle

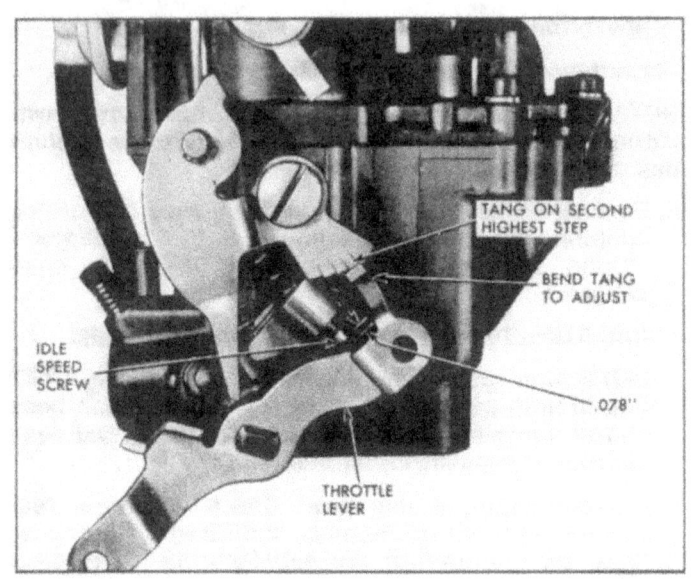

Fast Idle Cam Clearance

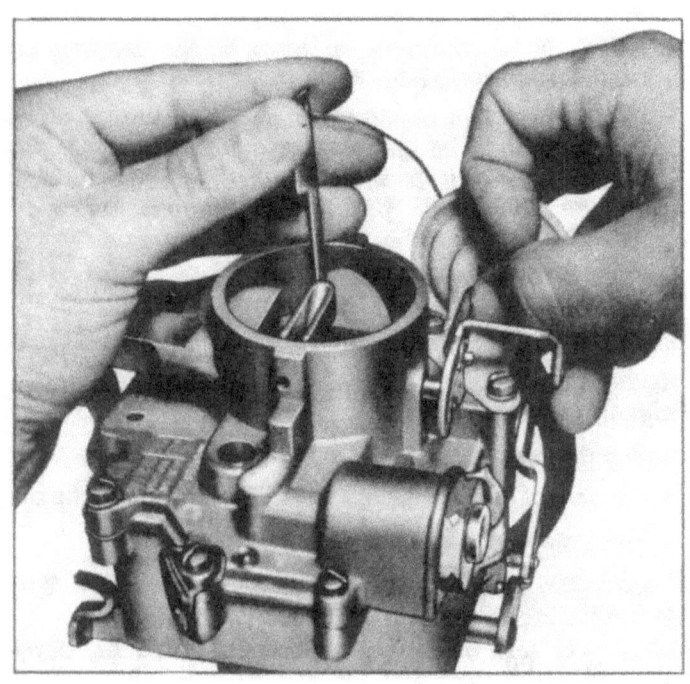

Vacuum Diaphragm Adjustment

speed has been set.

a. Stop engine.

b. With throttle lever on second highest step of fast idle cam, bend tang to obtain .078" clearance between idle speed screw and throttle lever.

c. Start engine and recheck speed as above.

VACUUM DIAPHRAGM ADJUSTMENT

a. Hold vacuum diaphragm arm squarely against diaphragm.

b. Measure clearance between lower edge of choke valve and wall of air horn. Clearance should be .145" to .170".

c. At this setting, throttle lever fast idle tang should rest on second highest step of fast idle cam. If not, adjust by bending outer choke shaft lever tang.

CHOKE ADJUSTMENT (1961)

1. With the slide ¼" from the rear of the mounting bracket and choke knob on dashboard out approximately ⅛", tighten the slide screw onto main choke cable wire.

2. Assembly cable and housing assemblies loose at both carburetor mounting brackets. Extend cable housing approximately ¼" beyond mounting bracket clamps and tighten clamp at each carburetor.

3. With slide approximately ¼" from rear of mounting bracket slot, tighten swivels at choke valve shaft levers with choke valve fully open. Cut the cable wire so about ¼" extends past the swivel. Do not bend the cable wire.

CAUTION: Hold swivel with a wrench when tightening the screw, to avoid kinking the choke cable wire.

4. Pull choke knob and check for proper operation.
   a. Pull knob approximately ⅜" to ½" out and check to see that choke valve just begins to move.

   NOTE: During the first ⅜" to ½" choke knob travel, the fast idle cam raises idle speed without moving the choke valve.
   Pull knob full out and choke valve should be closed.

   c. Check ease of operation. (Kinks cause sticking.)

AUTOMATIC CHOKE ADJUSTMENT 1962

Perform adjustment with engine off.

1. Disconnect choke control rod at choke shaft lever.
2. Hold choke valve closed and, while holding the control rod up against the stop in choke thermostat bracket, adjust upper

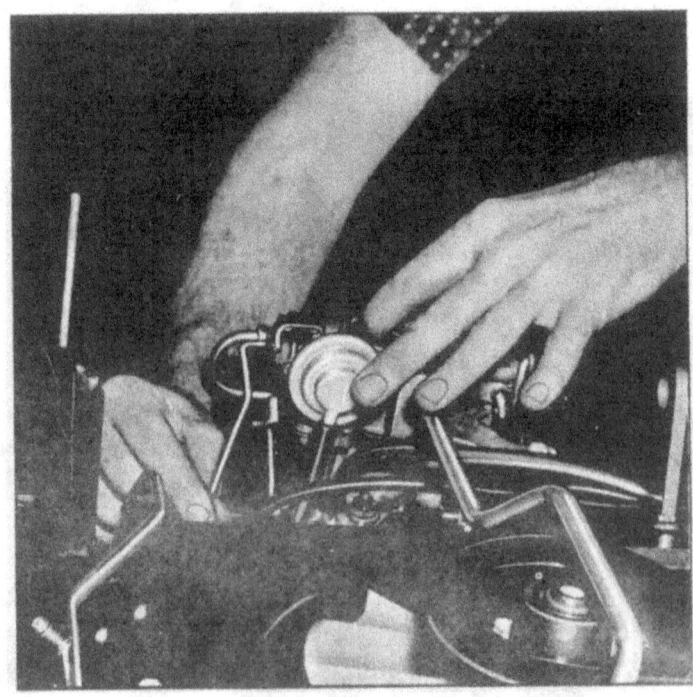

Choke Control Rod Adjustment

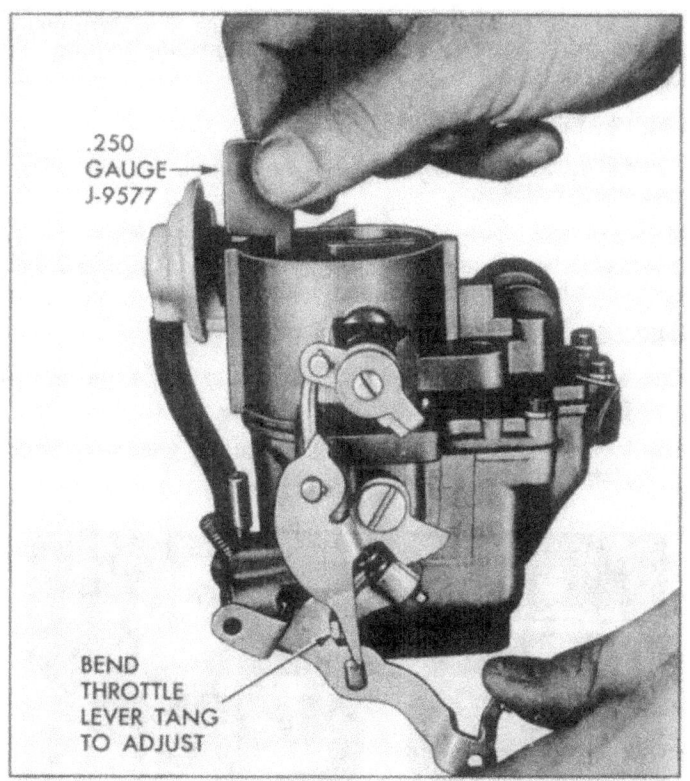

Unloader Adjustment

choke control rod until it freely enters hole in choke shaft lever.

CAUTION: To minimize the possibility of deforming the control rod while adjusting, always turn the vertical portion. Do not "crank" the rod using offset portion.

3. Start engine and warm up — check choke position after warm up. Choke valve should be open and fast idle cam should clear the throttle lever.

UNLOADER ADJUSTMENT

Check unloader adjustment by holding throttle valve in wide open position and insert a .250" wire gauge between choke valve lower edge and wall of air horn. To adjust, if necessary, bend tang on throttle lever.

> **NOTE: Unloader adjustment should be checked especially if it has been necessary to adjust the choke shaft outer lever tang during choke diaphragm link check.**

10. **CHECK OPERATION OF COOLING DAMPERS —**
    1961 & later

With the engine at operating temperature, the dampers must move freely from open to closed position without binding. Check and adjust as outlined below.

With Engine at Operating Temperature:

1. Open the damper door until the bellows is stopped within its mounting bracket.
2. Measure the opening of the damper door from its upper edge, and, if necessary adjust swivel to produce a 2.36 (approximately 2 11/32 inch opening.

10. INSPECT AND SERVICE COOLING SYSTEM

- Be certain that all metal shrouds are in place and are properly fitted so as to prevent air leaks.
- Be certain that blower belt is properly tensioned and that blower assembly is in good condition.

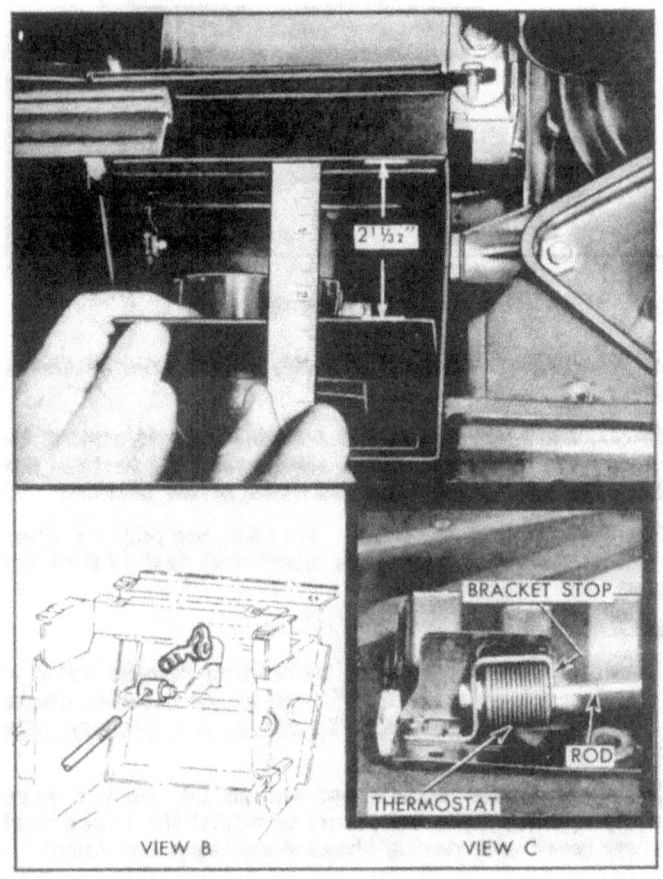

Adjusting Cooling Air Damper

11. **CHECK LUBRICANT LEVEL AND INSPECT FOR OIL LEAKS**

    Check level of lubricant in crankcase and inspect engine for oil leaks.

12. **NORMALIZE ENGINE**

    Set parking brake and place transmission in Neutral, then start engine and run until normal operating temperature is reached. This should be approximately 3-5 minutes with a cold engine.

    NOTE: If disturbed, throttle stop screws and point gap will have to be reset.

    Warmup will insure that proper lubricant viscosity is provided at each engine component and that each component will be at operating temperature and size.

13. **PERFORM FOLLOWING CLEANING AND CHECKING OPERATIONS DURING WARMUP**

    Check the following for proper operation:

    a. Windshield wipers

    b. Headlights

    c. Parking lights

    d. Tail lights

    e. Stop lights

    f. Directional signals

    g. Horn

    h. Instruments and indicator lights

    i. Brake and clutch pedal adjustment

    j. Accessories

14. **CYLINDER HEAD BOLTS**

    The cylinder head bolts should **not** be retorqued

INSTRUMENT CHECK-OUT

The instrument check-out may be performed with any one of several excellent pieces of equipment on the market by following the specific operating instructions of the equipment manufacturer.

15. **TEST CRANKING VOLTAGE**

    a. Disconnect coil to distributor high voltage lead at the coil to prevent engine from firing during cranking.

    b. Connect voltmeter between primary terminal on resistance wire side of coil and ground (fig. 19).

    c. Operate starting motor, using ignition-starter switch.

    - If voltage is 9 volts or more and cranking speed is

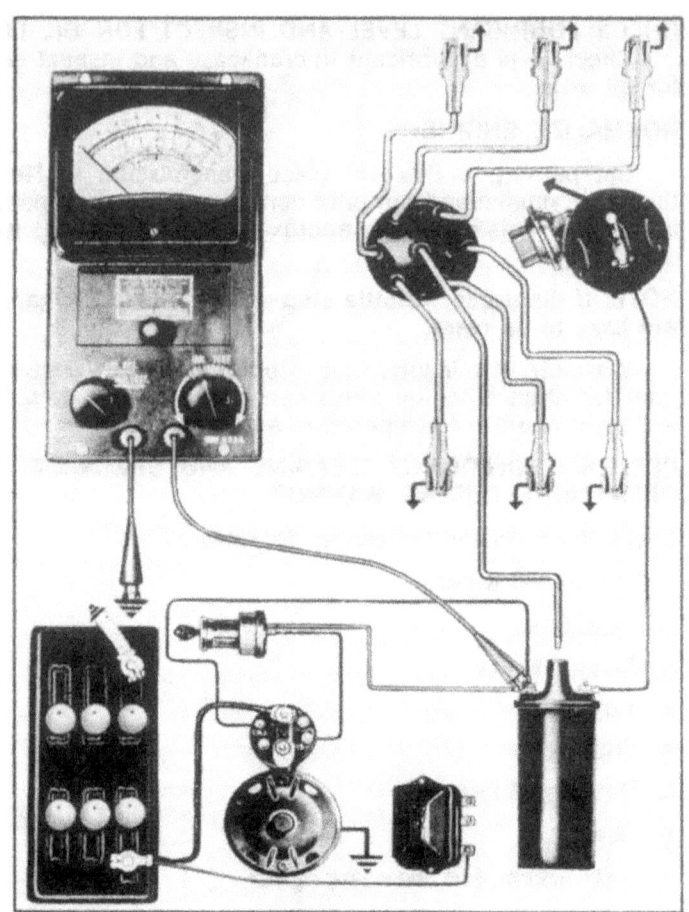

Checking Cranking Voltage

satisfactory, the battery, starter, cables, starter switch and ignition circuit to coil (bypassing resistance wire) are in good condition.

- If below 9 volts, check circuit until difficulty is located. Meter reading below specification — Weak battery; defective cables, connections, switch or starter, defective ignition circuit to coil. Cranking speed below normal — Excessive resistance in cables or starting motor; excessive mechanical friction in engine.
Uneven cranking speed — Uneven compression, defective starter or starter drive.

16. **TEST IGNITION RESISTANCE BY-PASS**

    a. With voltmeter connected as described for the Cranking Voltage Test (fig. 7-19), turn ignition switch to ON. Voltage should drop to $4\frac{1}{2}$ to $6\frac{1}{2}$ volts as current is now passing through ignition resistance wire.

NOTE: No external ignition resistor is used. Resistance is incorporated into the harness.

If battery voltage of 12 volts is obtained, the starter solenoid is by-passing the resistance wire and the starter solenoid is not functioning properly to by-pass the ignition resistance wire or the ignition circuit is incorrectly wired.

    b. Connect coil to distributor high voltage lead and disconnect meter.

17. **TEST DISTRIBUTOR RESISTANCE**

Use equipment as directed by manufacturer. Excessive resistance in primary circuit must be eliminated before continuing with test procedure.

15. **TEST DWELL AND DWELL VARIATION**

    a. Use dwell meter as directed by manufacturer. Dwell should be 31° to 35°.

    If dwell reading is not within specifications, recheck point gap, then check for wrong point assembly, defective or misaligned point rubbing block, or worn distributor cam.

    b. Slowly accelerate engine to 1500 rpm and note dwell reading. Dwell reading at no time should vary more than 3 degrees. If dwell reading varies more than 3 degrees, check for worn distributor shaft, bushings or breaker plate or loose breaker plate.

    c. Stop engine.

Ignition Timing

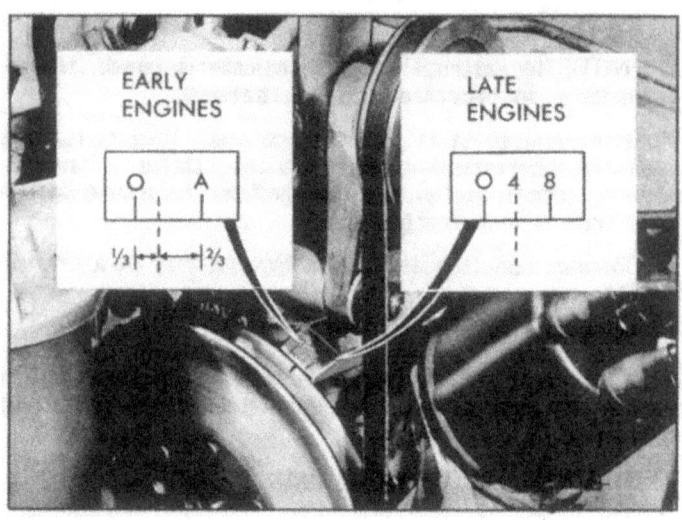

Ignition Timing

16. TEST IGNITION TIMING AND ADVANCE

a. Connect a distributor tester and/or timing light to No. 1 spark plug and battery, using extension at plug.

b. Start engine and run at idling speed.

c. Aim timing light at timing mark on top of crankshaft pulley. For correct timing mark on pulley should line up with $4° \pm 1°$ BTDC mark on timing tab for models with manual transmissions and $13°$ BTDC on Powerglide models.

d. Adjust timing as required by loosening distributor clamp bolt and rotating distributor body until correct timing is indicated, then tighten distributor clamp bolt.

e. Check distributor advance and compare against distributor specifications. If total advance is not within limits, disconnect vacuum line to obtain centrifugal advance only. If centrifugal advance is satisfactory, the difficulty is in the vacuum system.

An unsteady position of the timing mark during either timing or advance test is generally caused by pitted or misaligned distributor points, improper distributor point spring tension, worn or loose vacuum breaker plate, worn distributor shaft or bushings.

CYLINDER BALANCE TEST

It is often difficult to locate a weak cylinder. A compression test, for example, will not locate a leaky intake manifold, a valve not opening properly due to a worn camshaft, or a defective spark plug.

With the cylinder balance test, the power output of one cylin-

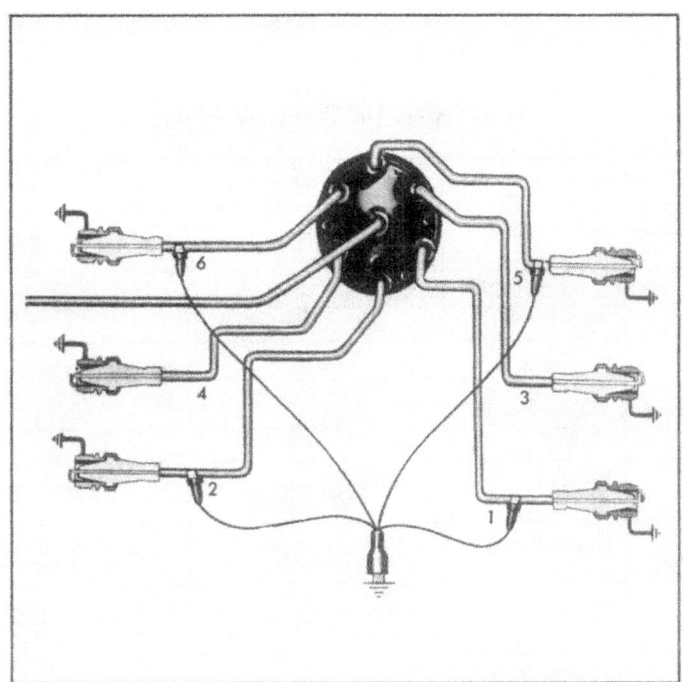

Cylinder Balance Test

der may be checked against another, using a set of grounding leads. When the power output of each cylinder is not equal, the engine will lose power and run roughly.

Perform a cylinder balance test as follows:

1. Connect the tachometer and vacuum gauge.
2. Start engine and run at 1500 rpm.
3. Ground large clip of grounding leads and connect individual leads to all spark plugs except the pair being tested. Divide the firing order in half and arrange one-half over the other.

The cylinders to be tested together appear one over the other, i.e.,
Firing Order = 1-4-5-2-3-6 =

     1-4-5
     2-3-6

= 1-2, 4-3, 5-6.

4. Operate engine on each pair of cylinders in turn and note engine rpm and manifold vacuum for each pair. A variation of more than 1 inch of vacuum or 40 rpm between pairs of cylinders beting tested indicates that the cylinders are off balance.
5. To isolate a weak cylinder, short out one bank at a time — the one giving the lower reading will include the weak cylinder.

1961 TUNE-UP SPECIFICATIONS

ENGINE		TURBO-AIR	SUPER TURBO-AIR
Compression Pressure (Cranking)		130 lbs. Variation—20 lbs.	130 lbs. Variation—20 lbs.
Spark Plugs	Make and Number	AC—46FF	AC—46FF
	Gap and Torque	.035"—20-25 ft. lb.	.035"—20-25 ft. lb.
Ignition Distributor	Cam Angle	31° — 36°	31° — 36°
	Point Gap	.019 new—.016 used	.019 new—.016 used
	Arm Spring Tension	19-23 oz.	19-23 oz.
	Condenser	.18-.25 mfd.	.18-.25 mfd.
Ignition Timing	See Note 1	4° BTDC Synchromesh 13° BTDC Automatic	Synchromesh only 13° BTDC
Tappet Clearance	Inlet and Exhaust	Hydraulic—¾ turn to center lifter	Hydraulic—1¼ turn to center lifter
Fuel Pump	Pressure	4 to 5 lbs. @ idle to 1000 RPM	4 to 5 lbs. @ idle to 1000 RPM
	Volume	1 Pint in 30 to 45 seconds	1 Pint in 30 to 45 seconds
Engine Idle RPM	Automatic (In Drive)	500	500
	Synchromesh	500	500
Air Cleaners		Oil wetted—to be cleaned and reoiled aprox. 2000 mile intervals	Oil wetted—to be cleaned and reoiled aprox. 2000 mile intervals
Blower Belt Adjustment		⅜" deflection (with 15 lb. push midway between blower and idler pulleys)	⅜" deflection (with 15 lb. push midway between blower and idler pulleys)
Carburetor		Rochester model H with manual choke	Rochester model H with manual choke
Fuel Filter		Backwash in fuel and blow out with compressed air	Backwash in fuel and blow out with compressed air
Exhaust Damper Door Adjustment		Approx. 2¹¹⁄₃₂" from door top to opening top with door open against bellow stop	Approx. 2¹¹⁄₃₂" from door top to opening top with door open against bellow stop

NOTE 1—At idle speed without disconnecting vacuum advance hose

1962 TUNE-UP SPECIFICATIONS

ENGINE		TURBO-AIR	MONZA POWERGLIDE	SUPER TURBO-AIR
Compression Pressure (See Note 1)		130 Lbs. Variation—20 Lbs.		
Spark Plugs	Make and Number	AC-46FF	AC-44FF	AC-44FF
	Gap and Torque	.035″—20-25 Ft. Lbs.		
Ignition Distributor	Cam Angle	31°—36°		
	Point Gap	.019 New—.016 Used		
	Arm Spring Tension	19—23 ounces		
	Condenser	.18-.25 mfd.		
Ignition Timing	See Note 2	4° BTDC Synchromesh / 13° BTDC Automatic	13° BTDC	13° BTDC
Tappet Clearance	Inlet and Exhaust	Hydraulic 1 Turn to Center Lifter		
Fuel Pump	Pressure	colspan: 4 to 5 lbs. @ Idle 1000 RPM		
	Volume	1 Pint in 30 to 45 Seconds		
Engine Idle RPM	Automatic (In Drive)	500	500	500
	Synchromesh	500	—	600
Air Cleaners		Oil wetted—to be cleaned and reoiled approx.—2000 mile intervals		
Blower Belt Adjustment	Tension Gauge	70 lbs. new—50 lbs. used / Aprox. 1000 miles is considered used		
Carburetor		colspan: 2 Rochester Model "H" with Automatic Choke		
Exhaust Damper Door Adjustment		Approx. 2⅜″ from door top to top of opening with control rod against bellows stop		

NOTE 1—At cranking speed with all plugs removed and throttle wide open.
NOTE 2—With Vacuum advance disconnected.

ELECTRICAL SYSTEM

GENERAL TROUBLE SHOOTING

The wiring diagram for the engine electrical system is included with body and chassis electrical circuit diagrams.

Described below are a series of quick checks, which are designed to assist in locating trouble within the various components of the engine electrical system.

BATTERY

Identifying Deficient Batteries

1. With battery in vehicle and coil secondary lead disconnected, turn on headlamps (Hi Beam), radio, heater (Hi Blower), and crank engine for four 30 second periods allowing 30 seconds between cranks for starter to cool.

    CAUTION: Prolonged continuous cranking can result in permanent damage to starting motor — be sure to follow above sequence of alternate cranking and cooling periods.

2. Check electrolyte for perceptible changes in color — if one or more cells appear "murky," battery is in some stage of failure and should be replaced. If electrolyte remains clear, continue with step No. 3.

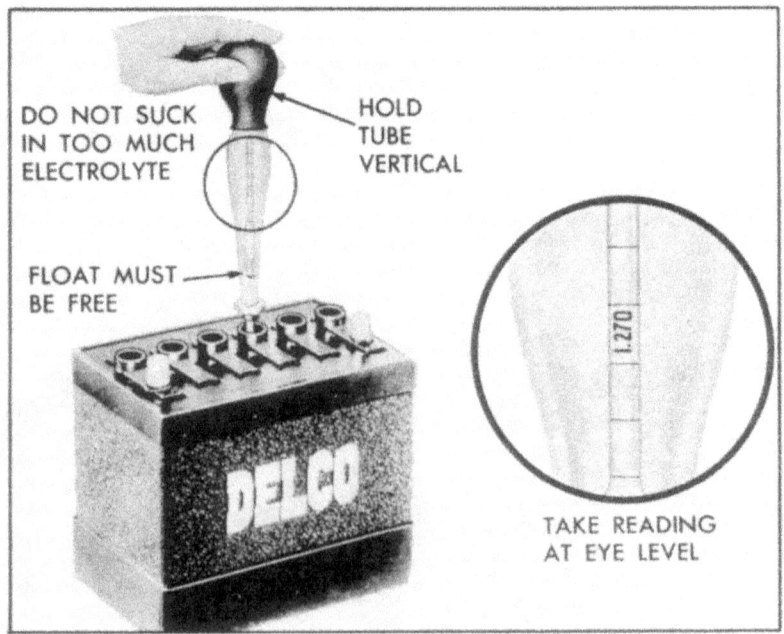

Testing Specific Gravity of Battery (Typical)

3. Connect a battery charger to battery and proceed with a "boost" charge, i.e., 35 amperes for one hour or until electrolyte reaches 125°F, checking occasionally for indications of "murkiness."
4. If electrolyte does not become "murky" during the "boost" charge, battery can be assumed to be in good condition.

1. Quick In-the-Car Battery Test

Inspection

Check outside of battery for damage or signs of serious abuse such as broken case or broken covers. Check inside of battery by removing the vent caps and inspecting for signs of abuse such as electrolyte level too low to see, or bad or unusual odors.

If battery shows signs of serious damage or abuse, it should be replaced. If not, make Light Load Test.

Light Load Test

Check electrical condition of battery cells as follows:

1. First, place load on battery by cranking engine. If engine starts, turn off ignition immediately. If engine does not start, hold starter switch "ON" for 3 seconds, then release.
2. Then, turn on headlights (low beam). After 1 minute, with lights still "ON" read individual cell voltage of battery with voltmeter (.01 volt division). Compare readings with the following:

   - Uniform Readings
   If one or more cells read 1.95 volts or more and the difference between the highest and lowest cells is less than .05 volts, battery is good and ready for service.

     However, if any cell reads less than 1.95 volts and difference between the highest and lowest cell is less than .05 volts, battery is good but should be fully recharged for good performance. See "Charging After Light Load Test."

   - Non-Uniform Readings
   If any cell reads 1.95 volts or more and there is a difference of .05 volts or more between the highest and lowest cell, the battery should be replaced.

   - Low Readings
   If all cells read less than 1.95 volts, battery is too low to test properly. FAILURE OF THE METER TO REGISTER ON ALL CELLS DOES NOT INDICATE A DEFECTIVE BATTERY. Boost charge battery and repeat Light Load Test. (See Boost Charging for Light Load Test.) If battery is found to be good after boosting, it should be fully recharged for good performance.

     If none of the cells come up to 1.95 volts after the first boost charge, the battery should be given a second boost. Batteries which do not come up after second boost charge should be replaced.

NOTE: If any battery found to be good by the Light Load Test does not perform satisfactorily in subsequent service, it should again be tested by the Light Load Test and if it still tests "good" it should be removed from the car and tested.

Other Quick Checks

1. Connect a voltmeter across the battery terminals and measure the terminal voltage of the battery during cranking (remove the coil secondary lead during this check to prevent engine from firing). If the terminal voltage is less than 9.0 volts at room temperature (approx. $80\pm20°F$), the battery should be further checked.
2. If the battery remains undercharged, check for loose generator belt, defective generator, high resistance in the charging circuit, oxidized regulator contact points, or a low voltage setting.

GENERATOR

1. Check belt tension and adjust at idler pulley as required.
2. Remove wires from BAT terminal of regulator and hook an ammeter between these wires and the regulator BAT terminal. With the engine operating at medium speed, momentarily ground the "F" terminal of the generator. Generator output should increase. If it doesn't, make a complete check of the generator.
3. If output is high and is not affected by grounding the "F" terminal of the generator, disconnect the lead from the "F"

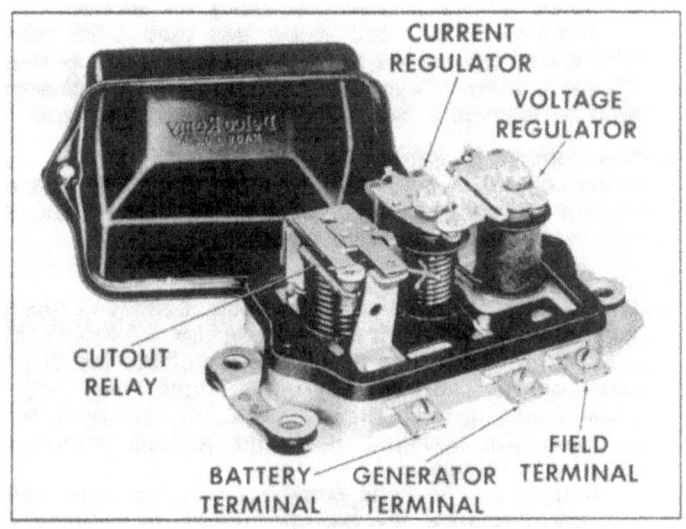

Generator Regulator

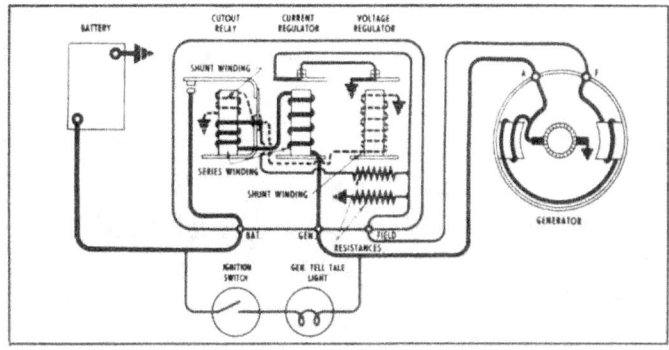

terminal of the generator. Generator output should fall off. If it does not, remove the generator and check it for a grounded field.

REGULATOR

Voltage Regulator

Measure the voltage between the "BAT" terminal of the regulator and ground at (1) idle speed, and (2) medium engine speed. The voltage should be higher at a medium engine speed than it is at idle speed. If it is not and the generator passes its tests above, make a complete check of the regulator. If voltage is higher at medium speed, the voltage regulator setting still may require adjustments as discussed previously under Steps 2 and 3 of "OTHER QUICK CHECKS" if the battery remains undercharged or uses too much water.

STARTING MOTOR AND SOLENOID

The following checks may be made:

1. If the solenoid does not pull in, measure the voltage between the switch (S) terminal of the solenoid and ground with the starting switch closed.

   CAUTION: If the solenoid feels warm, allow to cool before checking.

   If the voltage is less than 7.7 volts, check for excessive resistance in the solenoid control circuit. If the voltage exceeds 7.7 volts, remove the starting motor and check (1) solenoid current draw, (2) starting motor pinion clearance, and (3) freedom of shift lever linkage.

2. If the solenoid "chatters" but does not hold in, check the solenoid for an open "hold-in" winding. Whenever it is necessary to replace a starting motor solenoid, always check starting motor pinion clearance.

3. If motor engages but does not crank or cranks slowly, check for excessive resistance in the external starting circuit,

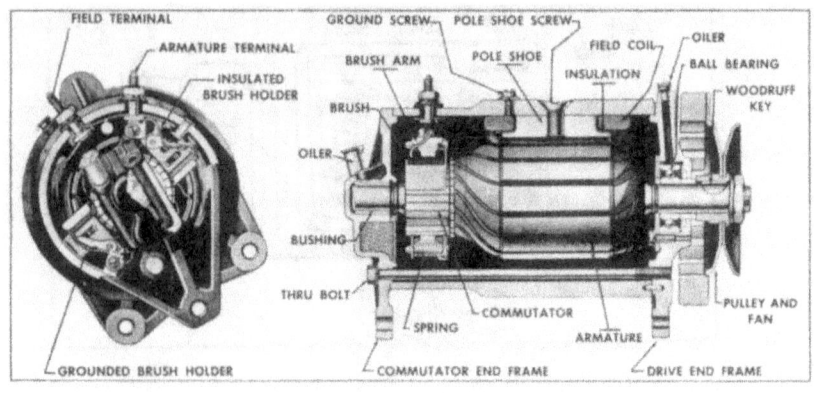

Generator Cross-Section

trouble within the starting motor, or excessive engine resistance to cranking.

IGNITION SYSTEM

If the engine does not run, the ignition system may be at fault if:

1. There is no spark, during cranking, when a spark plug is held ¼ inch from the engine.
2. The engine starts but immediately stops when the ignition switch is released from the START position.

If these checks indicate trouble in the ignition system, follow the procedure outlined under Ignition Circuit—Checks and Adjustments on the Vehicle. This procedure may also be helpful in locating trouble in the ignition system if the car runs but not satisfactorily.

BATTERY

A 7 plate (per cell), 35 ampere hour battery was used for the standard production models in 1960-61. An optional battery was offered and is of 9 plate (per cell), 40 ampere hour capacity. A 9 plate 42AH is standard for 1962.

Liquid level in the battery should be checked at least every 1,000 miles or once every two weeks. If the liquid level is found to be low, water should be added to each cell until the liquid level rises to the bottom of the vent well. **Do not overfill!** Distilled water, or water passed through a "demineralizer" should be used for this purpose in order to eliminate the possibility of harmful impurities being added to the electrolyte. Many common impurities will greatly shorten battery life. **Do not add any substance to the electrolyte except water.**

The external condition of the battery and the battery cables should be checked periodically. The top of the battery should be kept clean and the battery hold-down bolts should be kept properly tightened. Particular care should be taken to see that the tops of 12-volt batteries are kept clean of acid film and dirt because of the high voltage between the battery terminals. For best results when cleaning batteries, wash first with a dilute ammonia or soda solution to neutralize any acid present and then flush off with clean water. Care must be taken to keep vent plugs tight so that the neutralizing solution does not enter the cell. The holddown bolts should be kept tight enough to prevent the battery from shaking around in its holder, but they should not be tightened to the point where the battery case will be placed under a severe strain.

To insure good contact, the battery cables should be tight and bottomed on the battery posts. The new spring type battery cable clamps require that the ends of the clamps must be spread with a suitable pliers to remove or install. **It is important that the clamps be fully bottomed during installation.** If the battery posts or cable terminals are corroded, the cables should be disconnected and the terminals and clamps cleaned separately with a soda solution and a wire brush. **It is not recommended that lubrication be applied to the terminals** and cable clamps as it may contribute to slippage of the new type cable clamps from the terminals.

The positive terminal felt washer should be lubricated every 1000 miles with engine oil.

BATTERY

If a battery failure is encountered, the cause may lie outside the battery itself. DO NOT BE SATISFIED MERELY TO RECHARGE

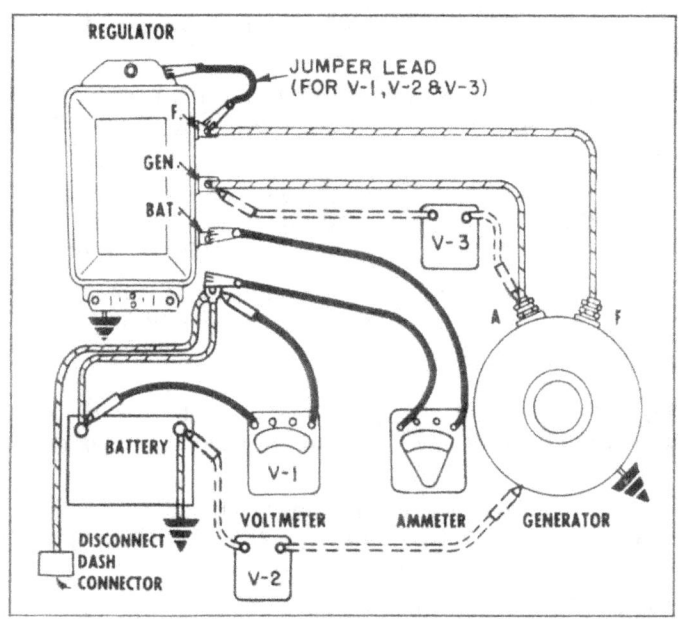

Checking Generator Circuit Resistances

OR REPLACE IT. FIND THE CAUSE OF FAILURE AND PREVENT RECURRENCE OF TROUBLE.

REGULATOR

> **NOTE:** The external grounding strap on the Corvair regulator is copper colored to identify it from other regulators. Check to see that correct regulator is installed.

Four regulator electrical checks can be made on the car; the settings of the cutout relay, voltage regulator, and current regulator, and a check for oxidized regulator contact points.

The regulator must have the cover in place and must be at operating temperature when the electrical settings are checked. Operating temperature shall be assumed to exist after not less than 15 minutes of operation at a charging rate of 8-10 amperes. For best results, the electrical checks should be made in the following order:

1. Voltage regulator setting.
2. Cutout relay closing voltage.
3. Current regulator setting.
4. Check for Oxidized Regulator Contact Points.

HEADLAMPS

Sealed Beam Unit Replacement

1. Remove four headlamp door retaining screws and remove door.
2. With long nosed pliers remove the retaining spring from the retaining ring. Remove the retaining ring attaching screws. Do not disturb the adjusting screws.
3. The retaining ring may now be removed and the sealed beam unit and mounting ring pulled forward. Disconnect connector plug from the sealed beam unit and remove the unit.
4. Replace mounting ring. Attach connector to new sealed beam unit and place unit in position in the mounting ring, being certain that the number molded into the lens face is at the top.

   > **NOTE:** In the dual headlight installation, the inboard unit is designated "1". The outboard unit is designated "2".

5. Set the retaining ring in place and replace the retaining ring attaching screws, then use long nosed pliers to engage retaining spring in hole in retaining ring.
6. Replace the headlamp door and four retaining screws.

   > **NOTE:** Remove and replace any of the four headlights in the same manner.

Low Battery and No Charging Rate
(Gen. Ind. Light "ON")

Blower belt broken or loose	Replace or tighten blower belt
Charging circuit open between regulator and battery	Locate open circuit and make necessary repairs
Cut-out voltage winding open circuited	Replace regulator unit
Corroded points in current and voltage regulator	Clean points and readjust regulator
Open circuit between generator and regulator	Locate open circuit and make necessary repairs to wiring
Internal trouble in generator	Overhaul generator

IGNITION CIRCUIT

Engine Will Not Start
(See Starting & Fuel System Troubles)

Weak battery	Charge battery
Excessive moisture on high tension wiring or spark plugs	Dry parts
Cracked distributor cap	Replace cap
Faulty coil or condenser	Replace faulty unit
Coil to distributor high tension wire not in place	Properly install wire
Loose connections or broken wire in low tension circuit	Tighten or replace wires
Improperly adjusted or faulty distributor points	Clean and adjust or replace points

Hard Starting
(See Starting and Fuel System Troubles)

Faulty or improperly set spark plugs	Clean and adjust or replace spark plugs
Improperly adjusted or faulty distributor points	Clean or replace and adjust points
Loose connections in primary circuit	Tighten loose connections
Worn or oil soaked high tension wires	Replace high tension wires
Low capacity condenser	Replace condenser
Low capacity coil	Replace coil
Faulty distributor cap or rotor	Replace faulty part

Engine Misfires

Dirty or worn spark plugs	Clean or replace plugs
Damaged insulation on high tension wires or wires disconnected	Connect or replace wires
Distributor cap cracked	Replace cap
Poor cylinder compression	See Engine Troubles and Remedies
Improper distributor point adjustment	Adjust distributor points

Noise And/Or Engine Overheats
(See Engine)

Loose Spark Plug Covers	Secure Covers

TROUBLES AND REMEDIES

Symptom & Probable Cause	Probable Remedy

BATTERY AND STARTING CIRCUIT

Slow Engine Cranking Speed

Partially discharged battery	Charge or change battery & determine cause of battery condition
Low Capacity battery	Cycle battery to improve capacity or replace it
Faulty battery cell	Replace battery
Loose or corroded terminals	Clean and tighten terminals
Under capacity cables	Replace battery cables
Burned starter solenoid switch contacts	Replace solenoid
Internal starting motor trouble	Overhaul starting motor
Heavy oil or other engine trouble causing undue load	Make necessary repairs to engine

Starter Engages but Will Not Crank Engine

Partially discharged battery	Charge or change battery
Faulty battery cells	Replace battery
Bent armature shaft or damaged drive mechanism	Overhaul starter
Faulty armature or fields	Overhaul starter

Starter Will Not Run

Battery fully discharged	Replace or charge battery
Disconnected Battery cables	Replace faulty cables
Shorted or open starter circuit	Make necessary repairs

GENERATING CIRCUIT

Low Charging Rate

Fully charged battery & low charging rate	This is a normal condition with a fully charged battery
Blower belt slipping	Replace or adjust belt
Generator commutator dirty	Clean commutator
High resistance in charging circuit	Check charging circuit progressively & make necessary repairs to remove high resistance
Too low voltage setting of voltage regulator unit	Adjust voltage regulator
Oxidized voltage regulator points	Clean and adjust points
Partially shorted field coils	Overhaul generator

High Charging Rate With Fully Charged Battery

Voltage regulator setting too high	Adjust voltage regulator
Voltage regulator points stuck	Clean and adjust points and readjust regulator
Regulator unit improperly grounded	Remove regulator and clean connections. Readjust regulator
Generator field circuit to regulator short circuited	Test to locate short circuit and make necessary repairs
Shunt field circuit short circuited within regulator	Replace regulator

WINDSHIELD WIPER
GENERAL DESCRIPTION

The regular production, single-speed electric windshield wiper assembly available on the 1962 Corvair incorporates a new design, non-depressed type (blades park approximately 2" above windshield moulding) motor and gear train. The rectangular, 12 volt, shunt wound motor is similar to 1961 models, but is coupled to a new type gear train consisting of a helical drive gear at the end of the motor armature shaft, an intermediate gear and pinion assembly, and an output gear and shaft assembly. The crank arm is attached to the output gear shaft.

The optionally available two-speed, non-depressed wiper and washer assembly is of a new design incorporating a rectangular, compound wound (series and shunt field) motor adapted to the same type gear train as that used with the new single-speed wipers.

Two switches, connected in parallel, control the starting, stopping and parking of both types of wiper motors. The manually operated start, stop switch is located on the dash panel, while the cam operated park switch is located in the wiper gear box.

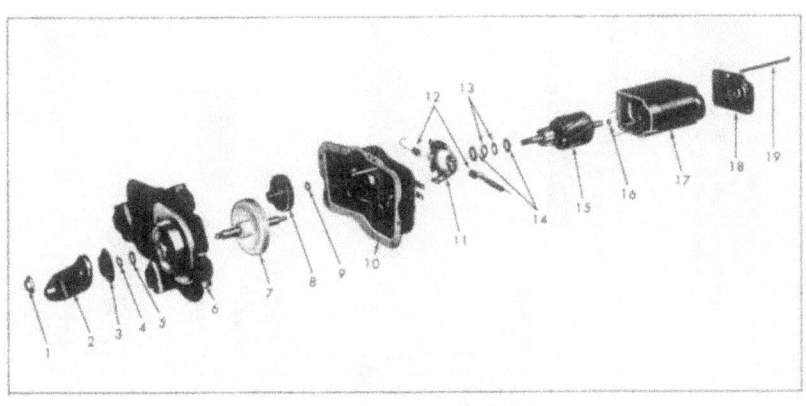

Wiper Motor and Gear Box Exploded View (Typical)

1. Nut
2. Crank Arm
3. Seal Cap
4. Retaining Ring
5. Washer
6. Gear Box Cover
7. Output Gear and Shaft Assembly
8. Intermediate Gear
9. Wave Washer
10. Gear Box Housing
11. Brush Plate Assembly and Mounting Brackets
12. Brushes
13. Wave Washers
14. Flat Washers
15. Armature
16. Thrust Plug
17. Frame and Field
18. End Plate
19. Tie Bolts (Two required)

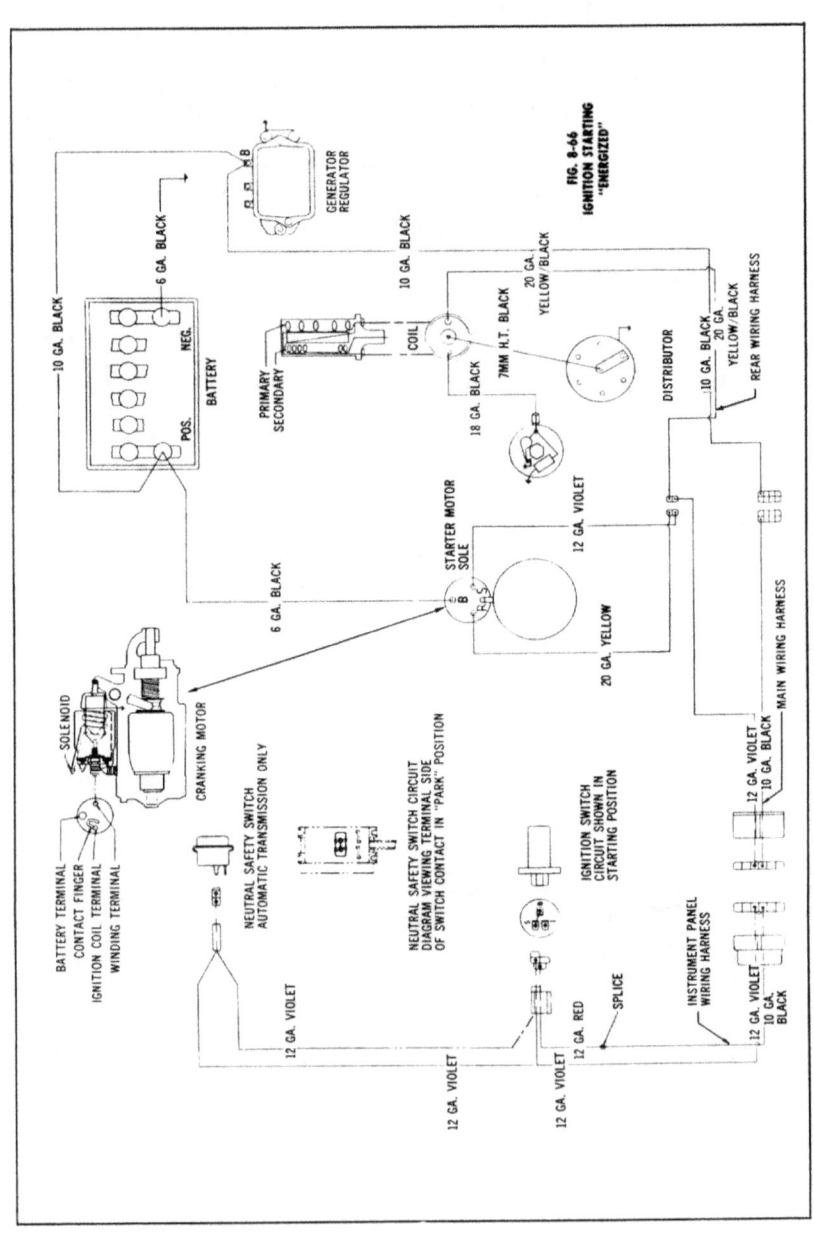

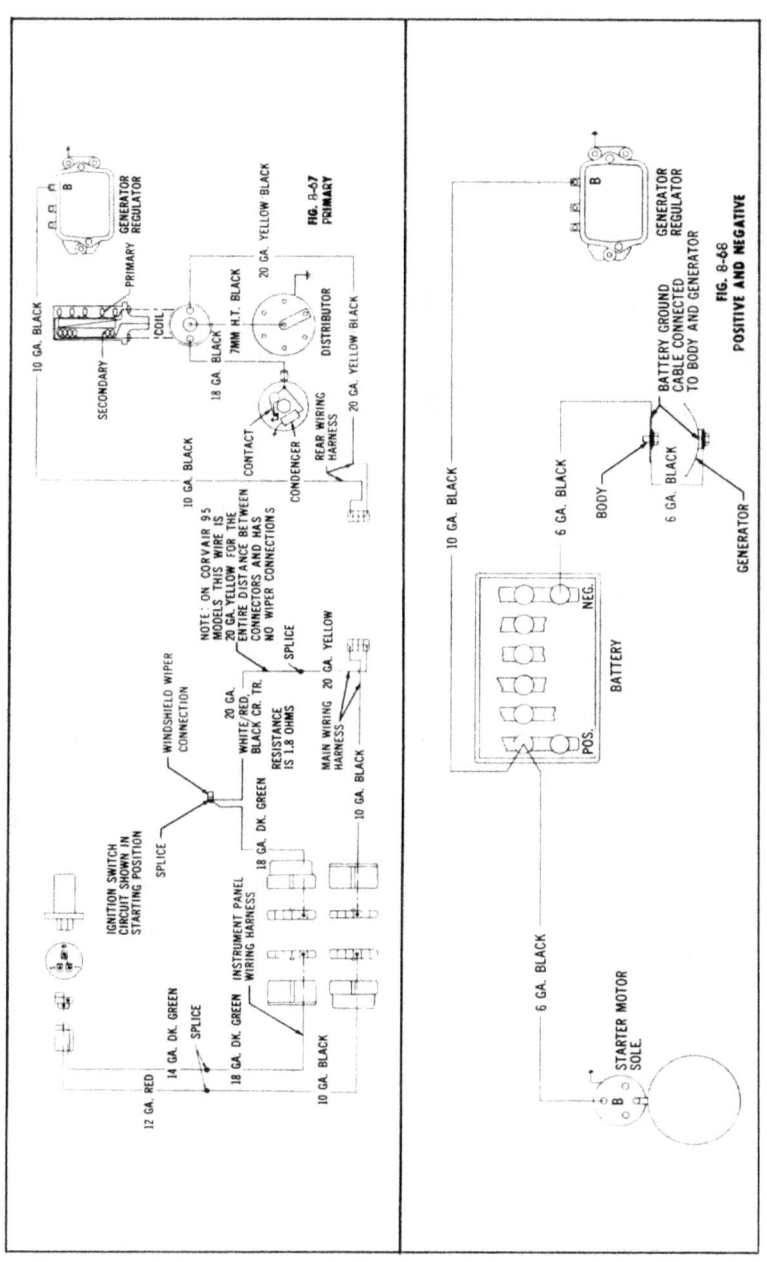

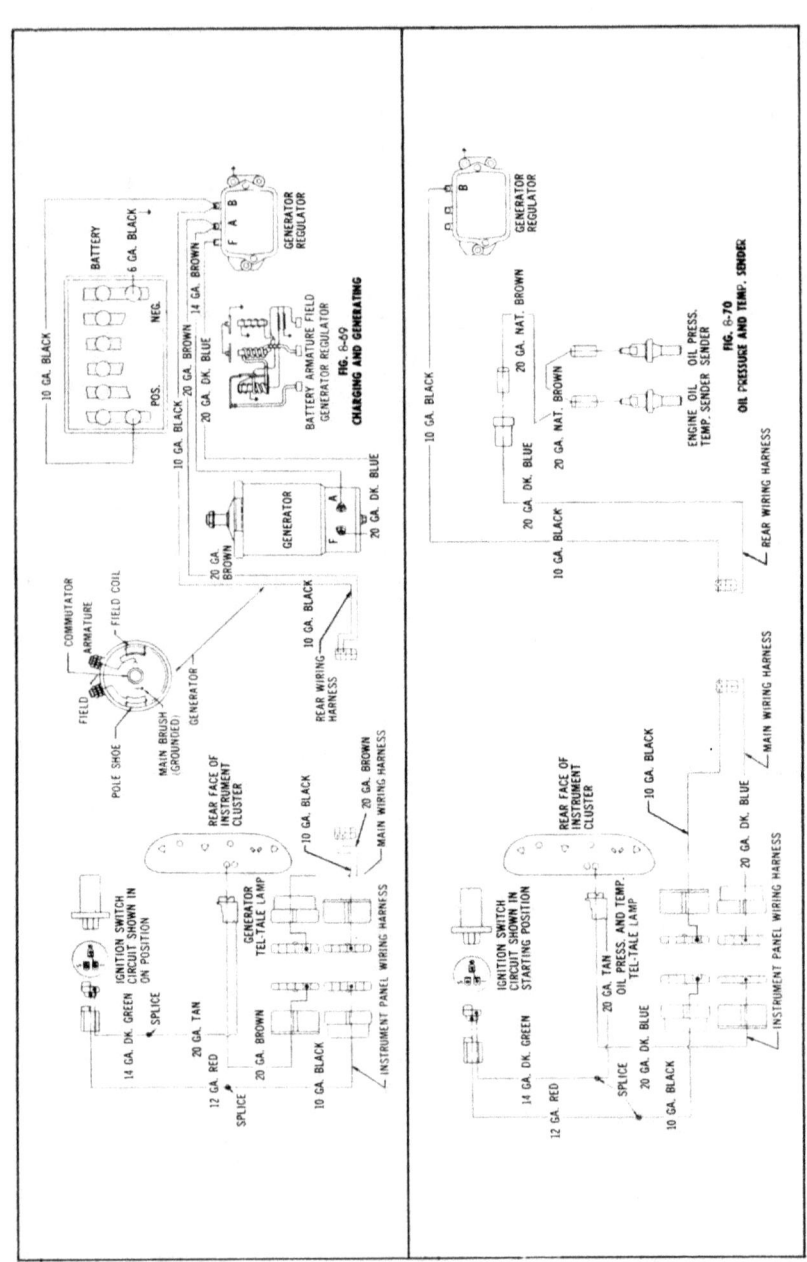

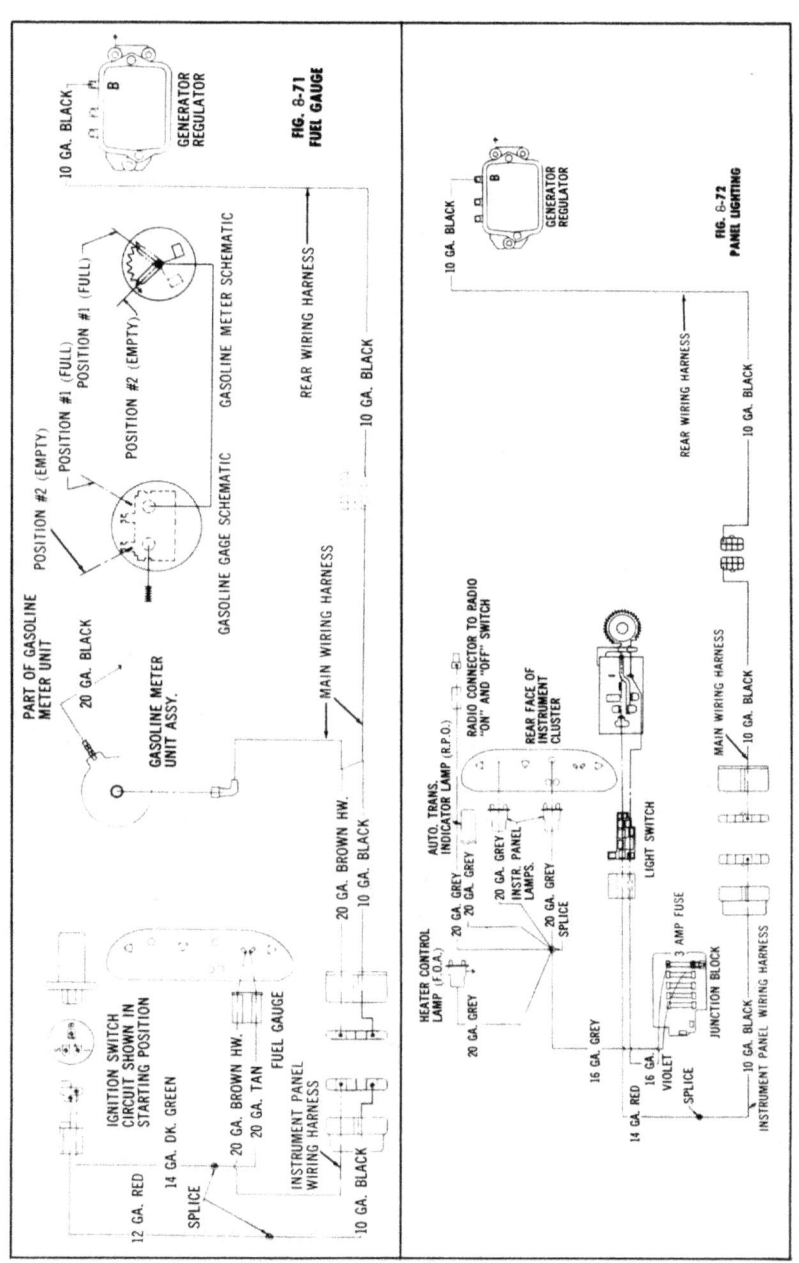

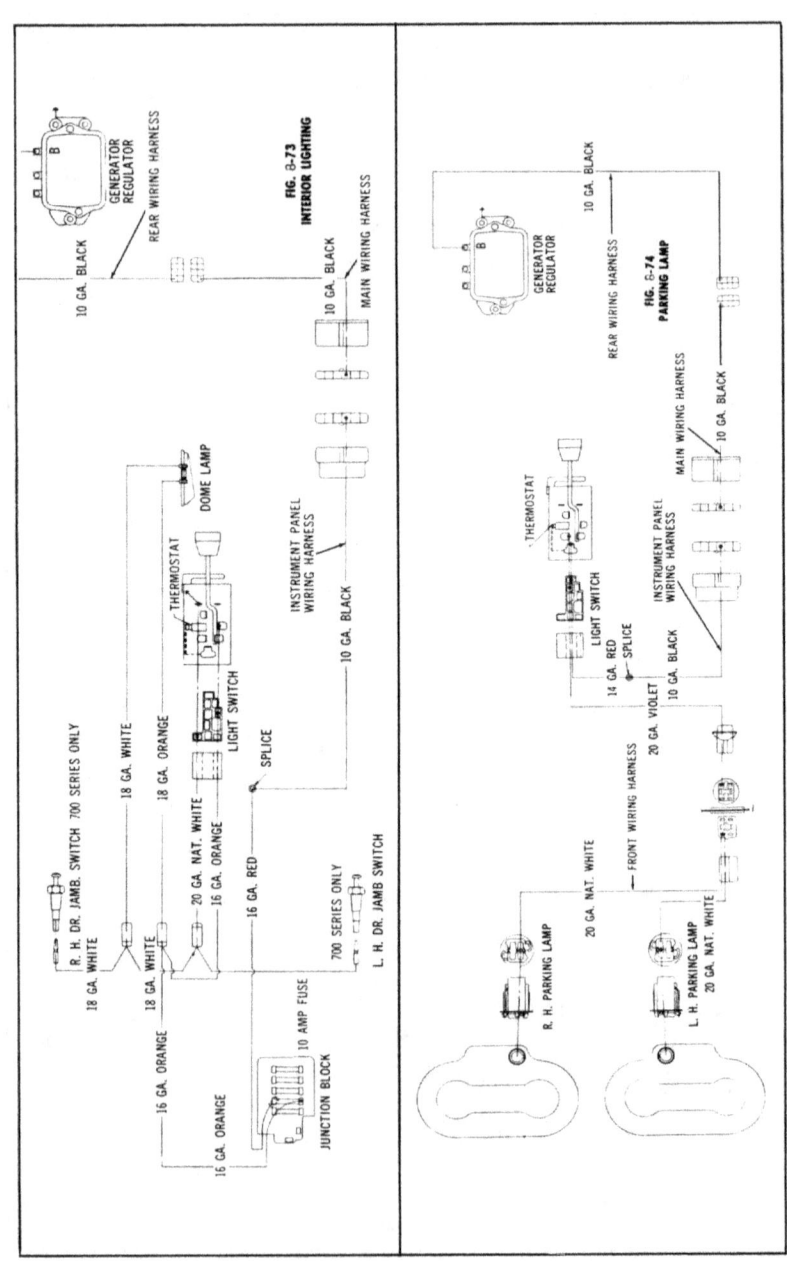

FIG. 8-73 INTERIOR LIGHTING

FIG. 8-74 PARKING LAMP

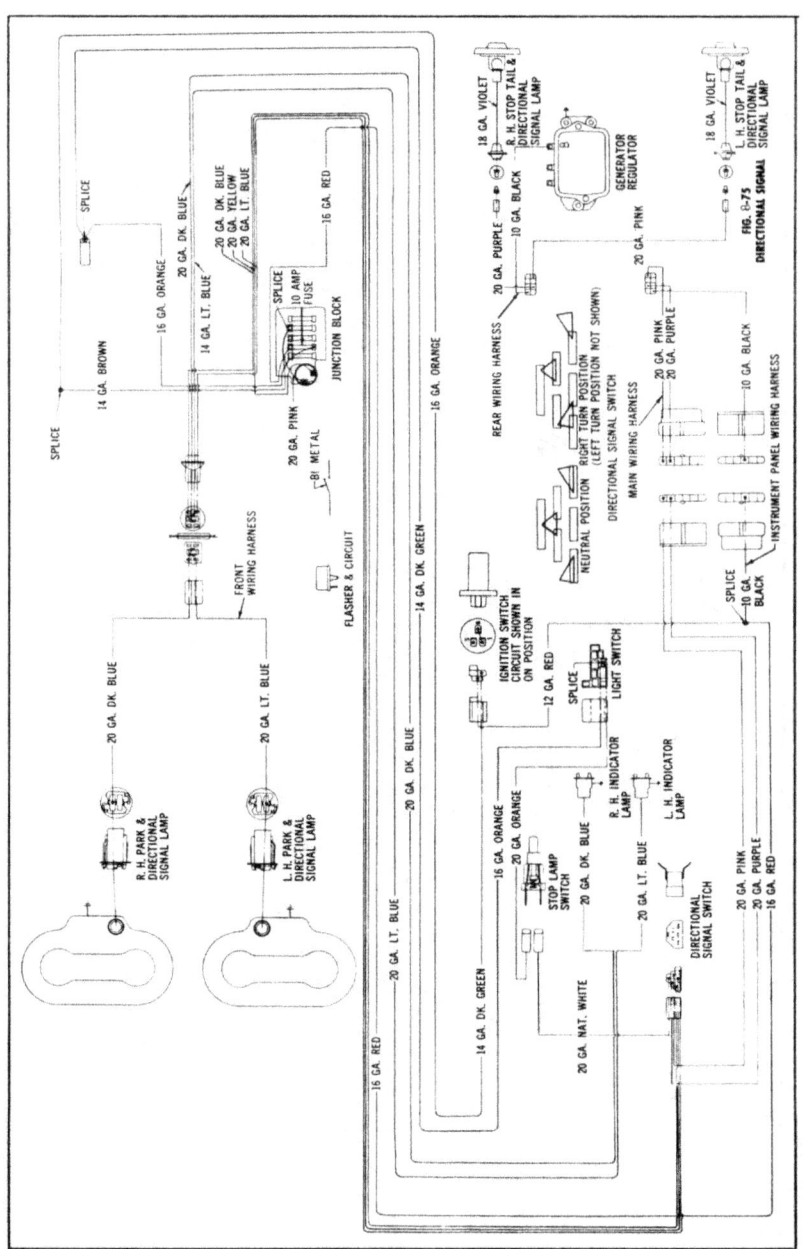

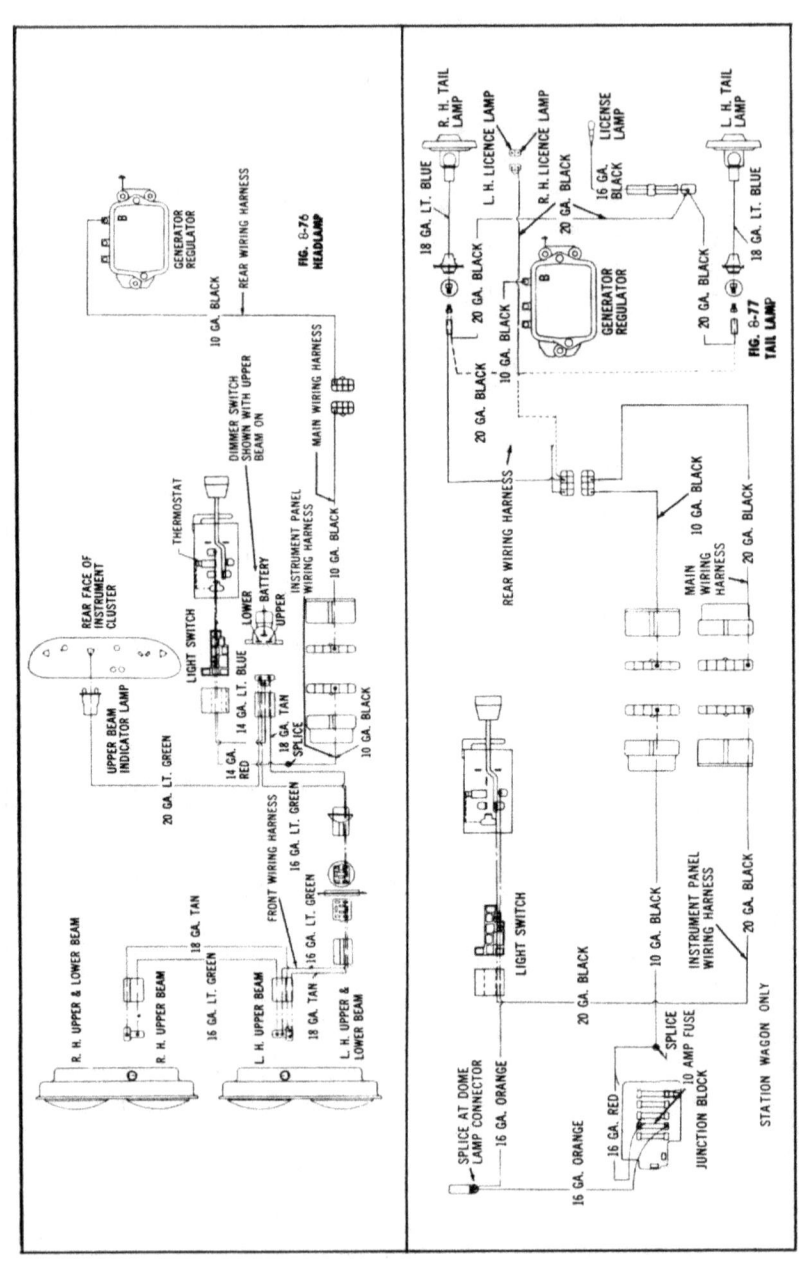

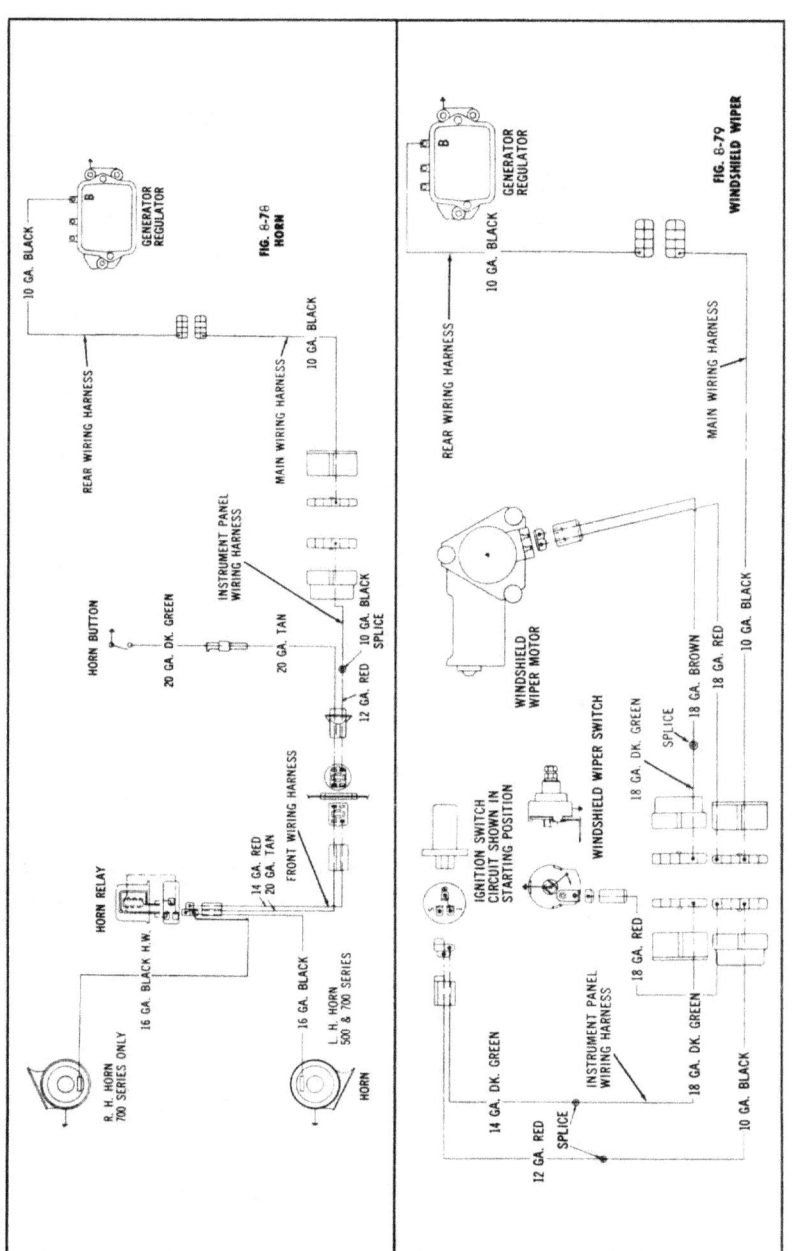

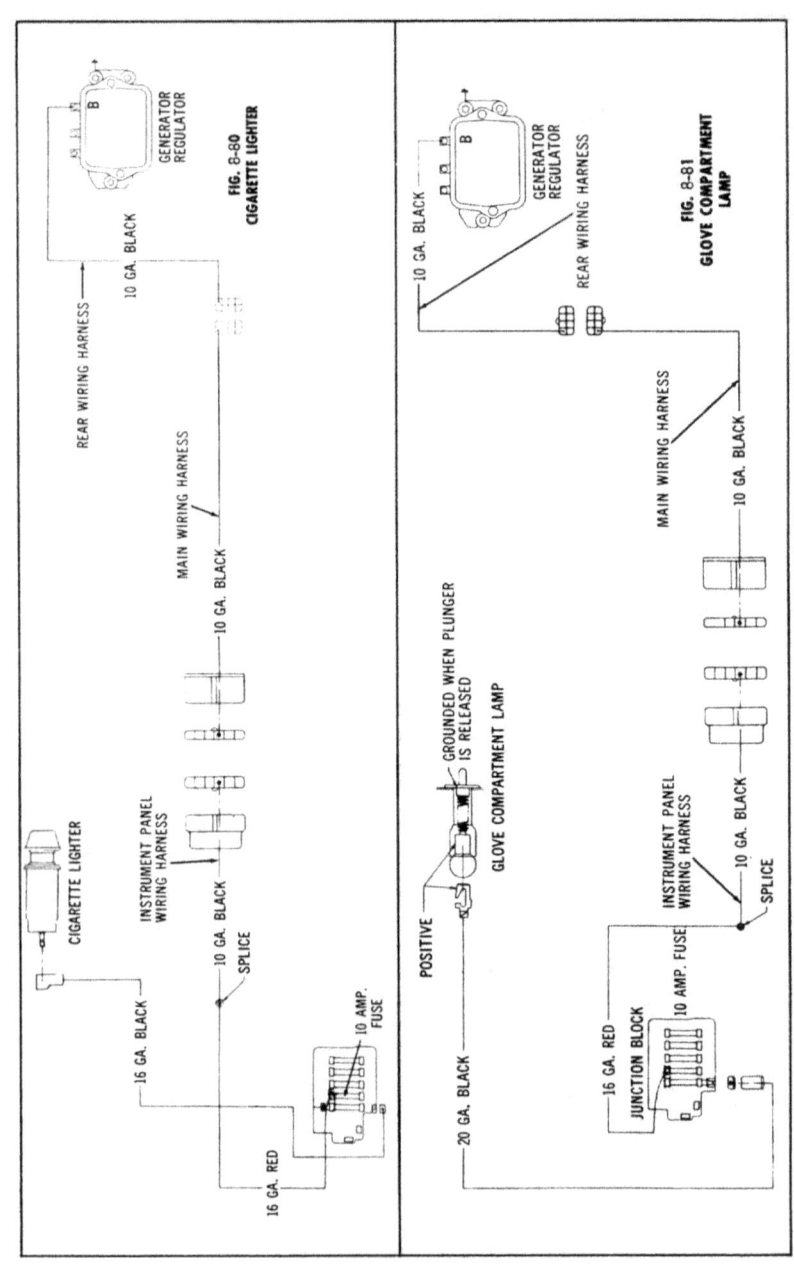

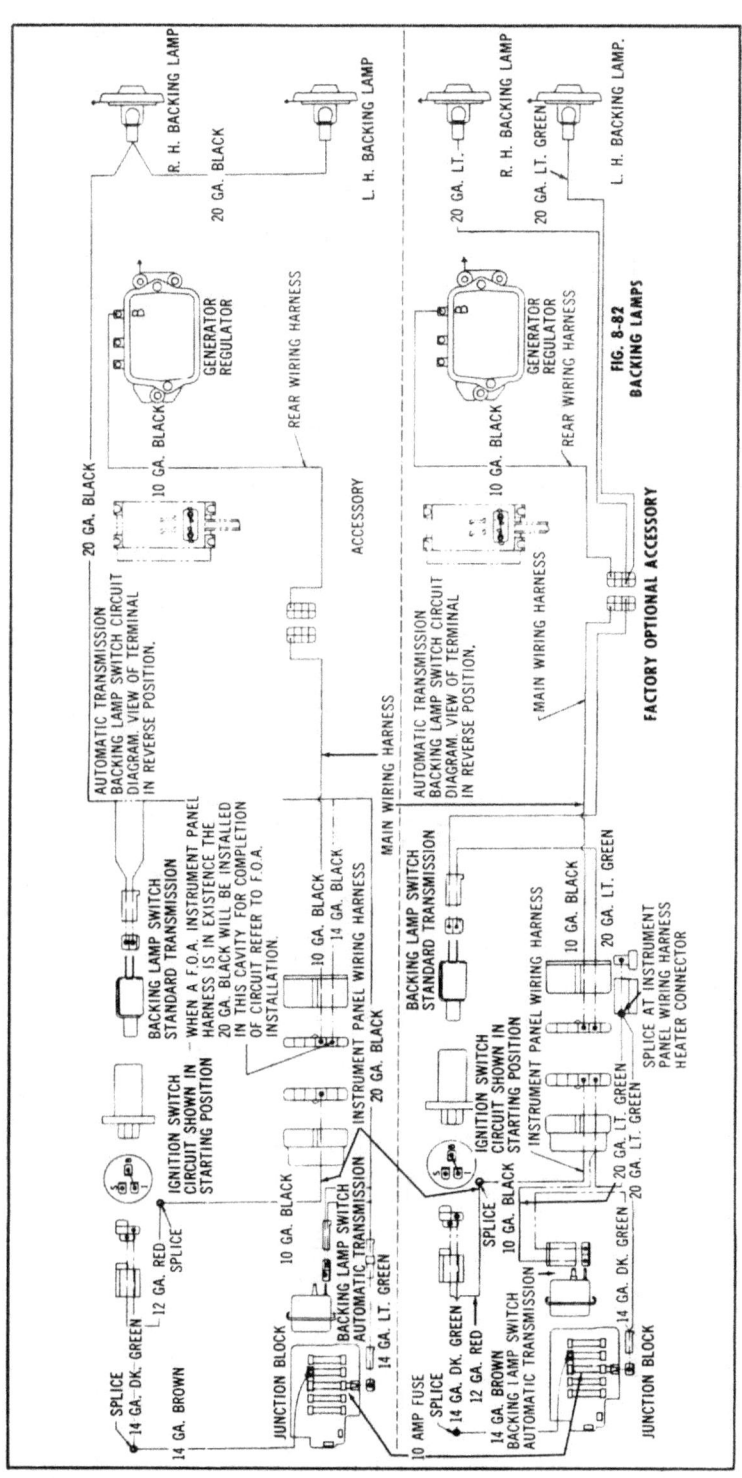

FIG. 8-82 BACKING LAMPS

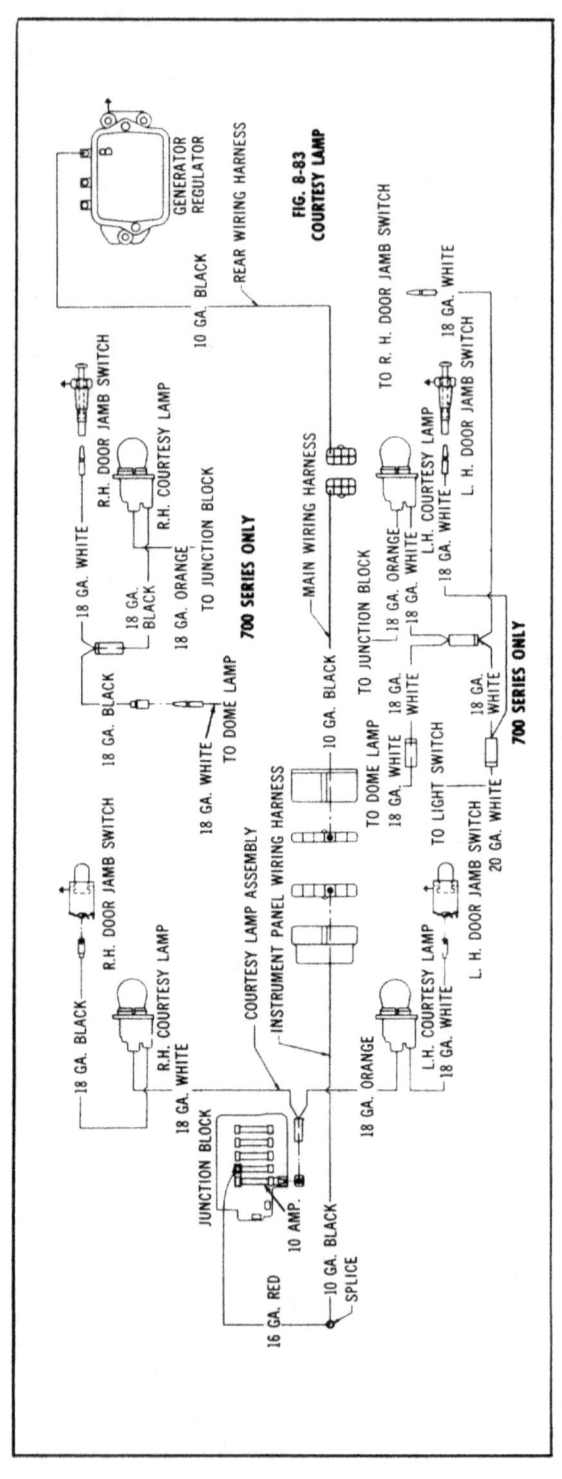

FIG. 8-83 COURTESY LAMP

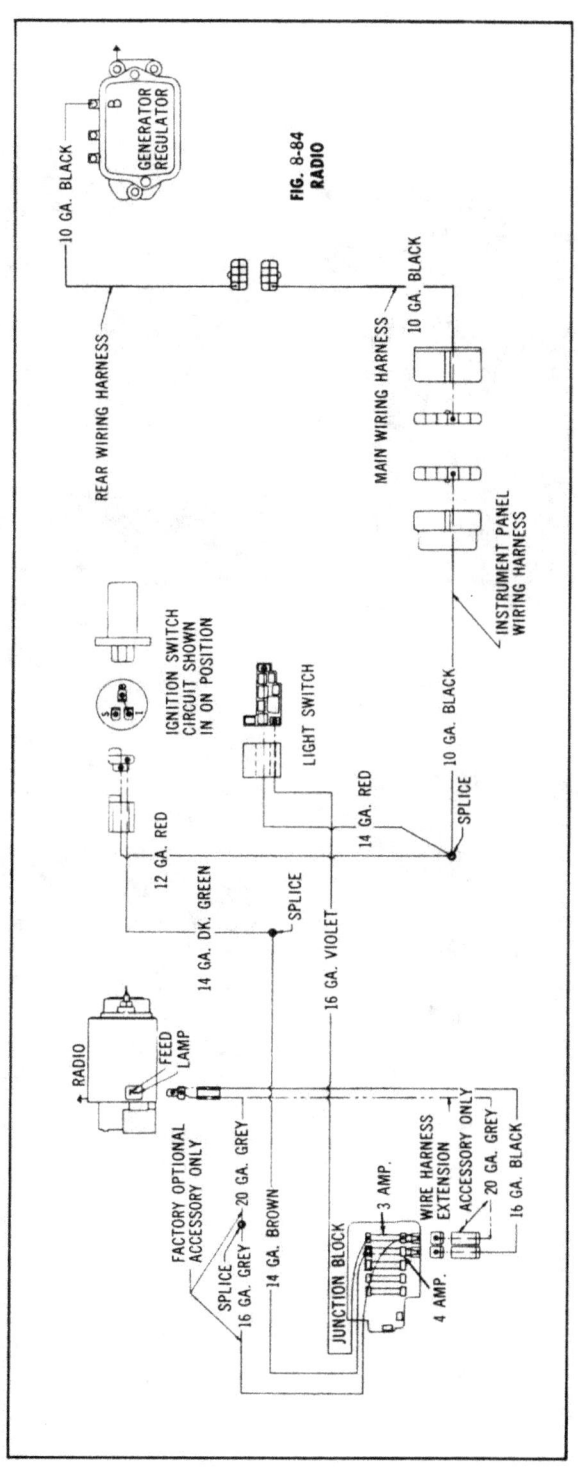

FIG. 8-84
RADIO

Junction Block

Retaining Ring Attaching Screws

Removing Retaining Ring, Sealed Beam Unit and Mounting Ring

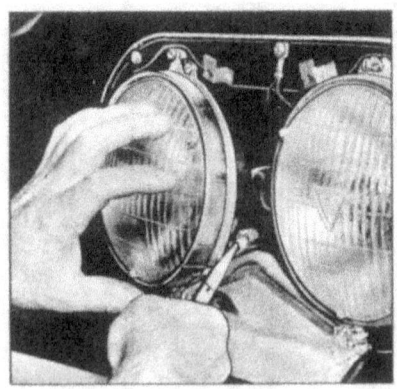

Removing Retaining Ring Spring

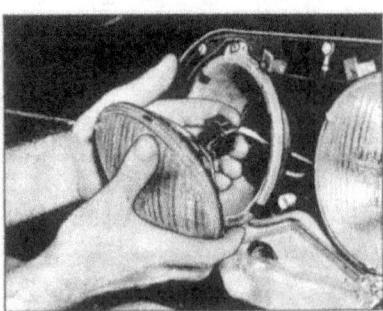

Connecting Sealed Beam Unit

FUEL SYSTEM

The Corvair engine uses two identical Rochester Model "H" single-barrel downdraft carburetors, one located on each intake manifold. Each carburetor is separated from the engine manifold by an insulator block. On 1961 models each carburetor is equipped with a manual choke controlled by a choke cable pull knob, located at the left of the steering column. 1960 and 1962 have automatic chokes.

1962 automatic choke mechanism consists of: a thermostatic control coil mounted to the lower side of the cylinder head, linked directly to the carburetor choke valve shaft; a vacuum diaphragm mounted on the air horn, replacing conventional choke vacuum piston, to provide the start and run position of the choke valve; a fast idle cam to control engine speed during warm-up.

The two carburetor throttle shaft levers are connected by a cross-shaft which is actuated by the accelerator linkage. Careful adjustment must be made to insure that the carburetors are properly synchronized (See "Tune Up").

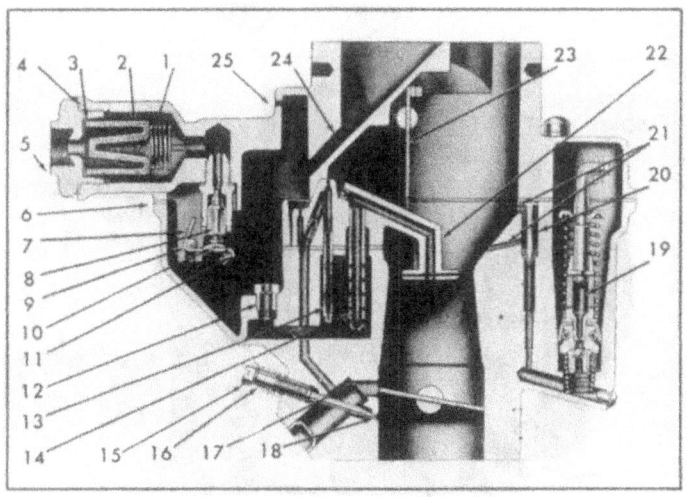

Carburetor Schematic Cross-Section

1. Filter Spring
2. Filter
3. Filter Gasket
4. Inlet Nut Gasket
5. Inlet Nut
6. Float Seal Gasket
7. Float Drop Adjusting Tang
8. Float Needle
9. Float Hinge Pin
10. Float Level Adjusting Tang
11. Float Hanger Arm
12. Main Metering Jet
13. Idle Tube
14. Main Well Tube
15. Idle Mixture Adjusting Screw
16. Idle Mixture Adjusting Spring
17. Secondary Idle Port
18. Primary Idle Port
19. Accelerator Pump
20. Pump Discharge Valve
21. Pump Discharge Ports
22. Venturi Cluster
23. Choke Valve
24. Bowl Internal Vent
25. Bowl External Vent

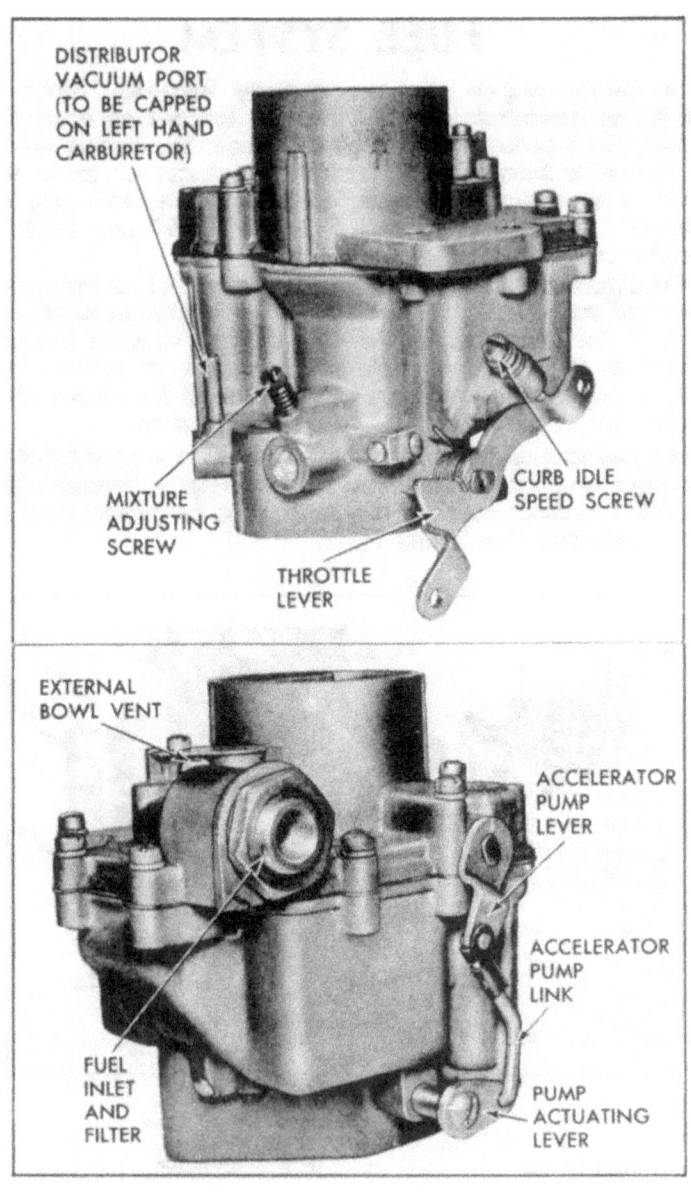

Type "H" Carburetor

Inlet Fuel Filter

The inlet fuel filter, one located at the fuel inlet of each carburetor, should be cleaned regularly and replaced after each 15,000 miles of operation, or sooner if carburetor flooding occurs.

Remove the filter element, and clean by washing in solvent and blowing dry with compressed air. When replacing the element,

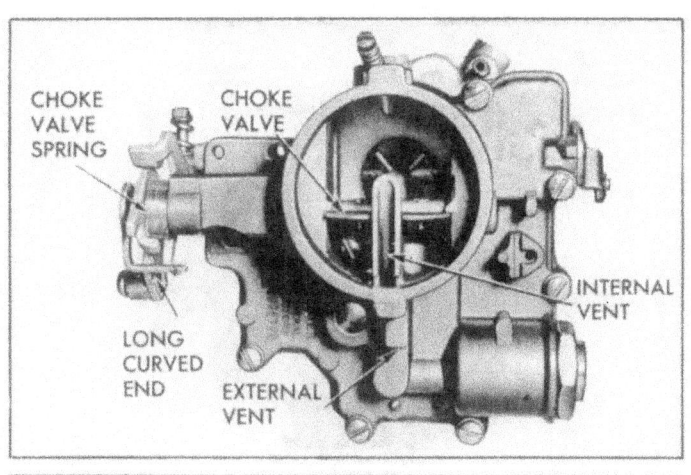

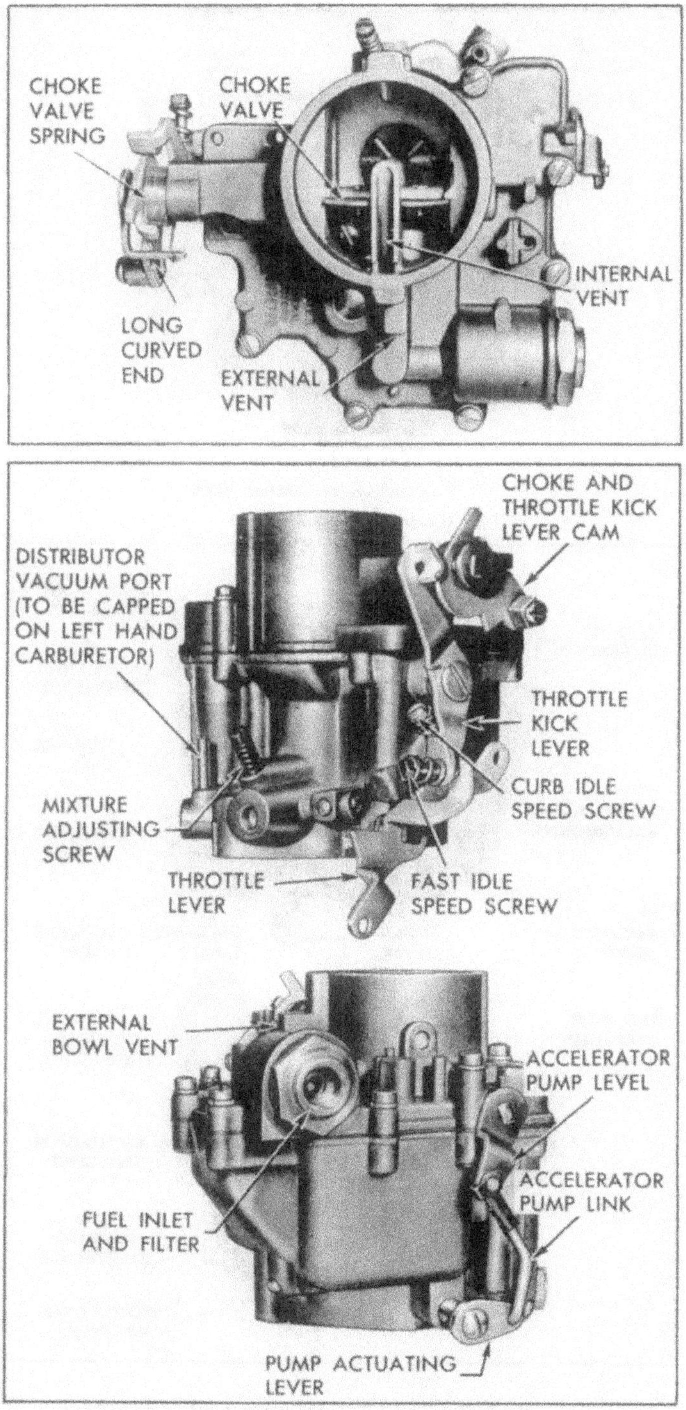

Rochester Model 'H' manual choke carburetor — 1961

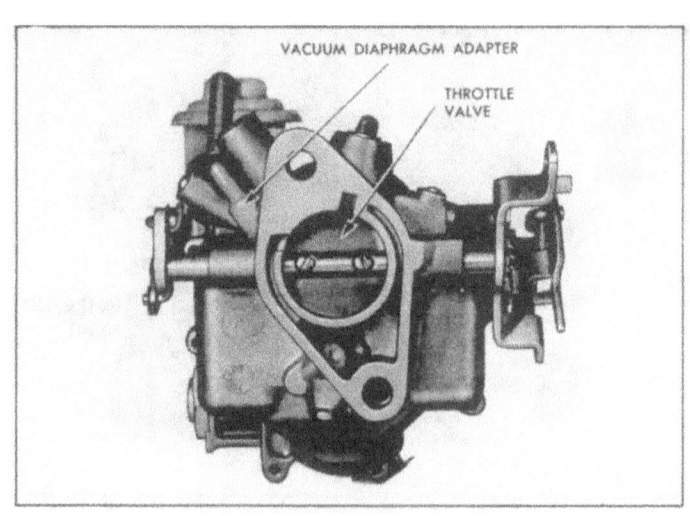

—Carburetor—Bottom View

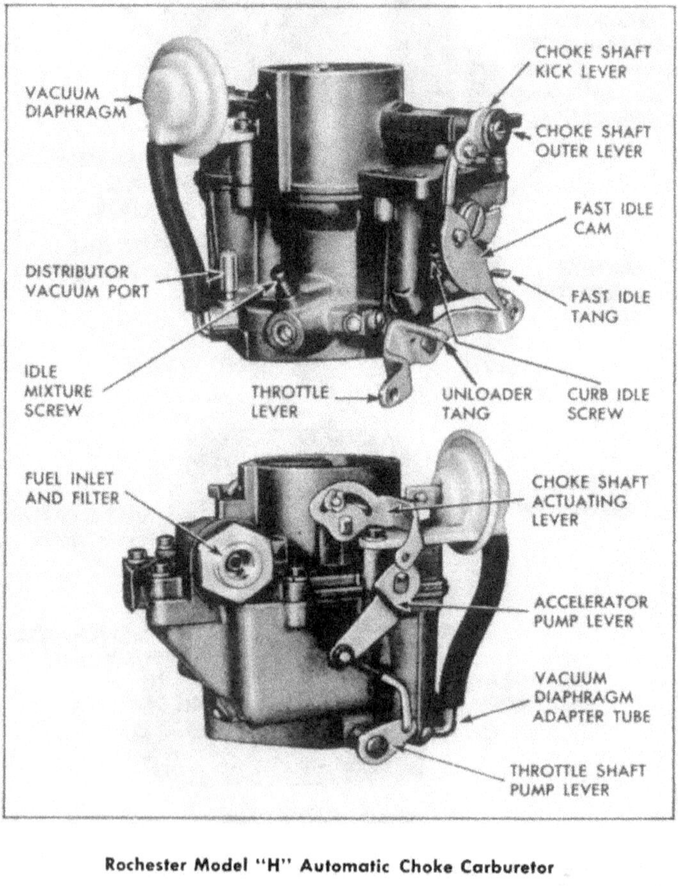

Rochester Model "H" Automatic Choke Carburetor

Choke Thermostat Mounting

be sure that all gaskets are in place and that the 'point" of the cone faces the inlet line.

The filter should be cleaned regularly, since the pressure relief spring, located under the filter element, will allow fuel to by-pass the filter should the filter become clogged, thus allowing impurities into the carburetor bowl.

Accelerator Pedal

Disassembly of the accelerator pedal is self explanatory. Assembly procedure is equally simple except that extra precautions are necessary during the assembly operation.

When assembling the pedal assembly, it is necessary to insert a spacer between the sides of the pedal bracket to keep the sides from collapsing. Apply Lubriplate to the rod before assembly.

The correct relationship between the accelerator pedal and pedal rod is very important. If the pedal is too close to the floor, full throttle position cannot be obtained or in the other extreme the pedal will be in almost a vertical position at idle.

The following procedure explains how the proper position of the pedal can be obtained on a bench prior to installation.

1. Position pedal and rod as shown with serrations on rod held firmly against the pedal bracket. Rotate the rod until a dimension of 1 11/16" is obtained between the bench and the underside of the pin.

2. Mark rod and bracket so the same position can be maintained when the parts are assembled in a press.

3. Before pressing rod into pedal install rod support assembly and two bushings.

4. The inner leg of the pedal should seat against the nylon sleeve after the parts are pressed together.

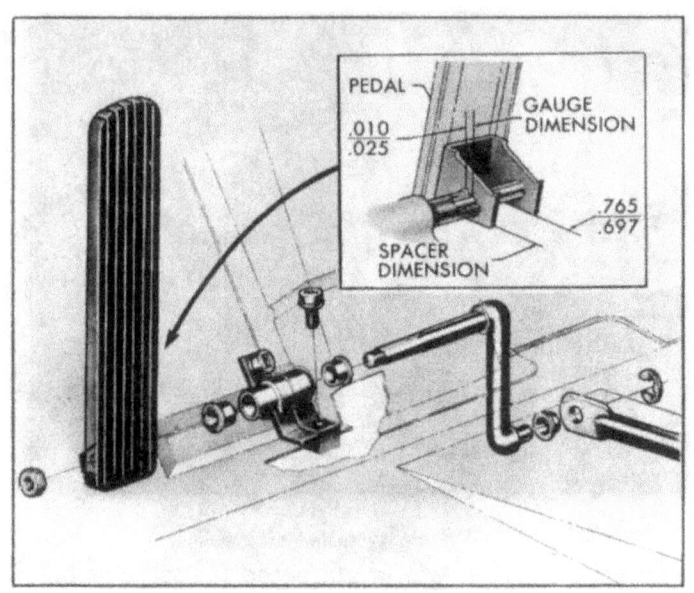

Accelerator Pedal

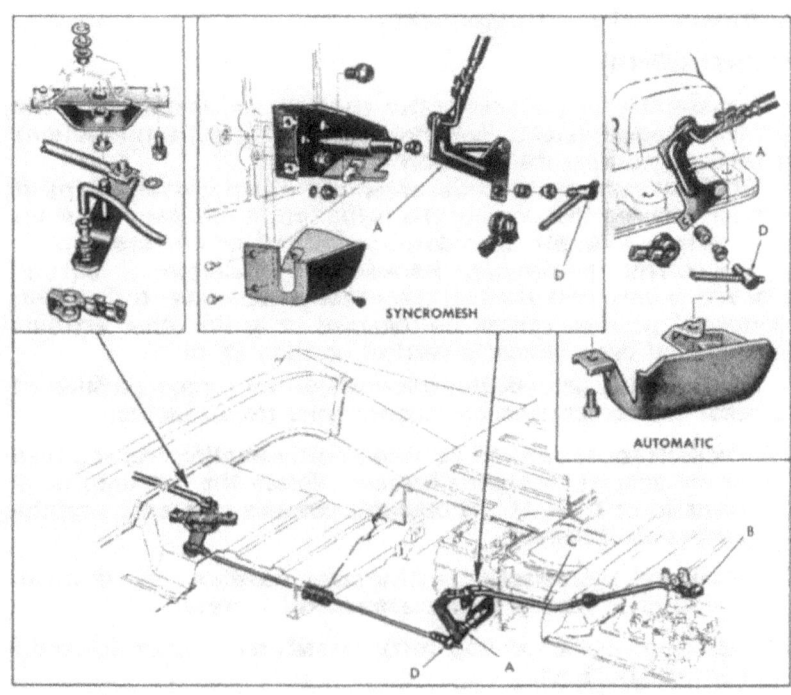

Accelerator Linkage

5. Install self locking nut. Torque the nut until a gap of from .010 to .025 is attained between the pedal assembly and the bushing.

The figure indicates the size of the spacer needed between the sides of the pedal bracket and shows where to gauge the spacing between the bracket and the bushing. After assembly the pedal and rod assembly must operate freely in the support.

Accelerator Control Linkage Adjustments

1. Disconnect swivel "D" from lever "A."
2. Disconnect swivel "B" from the left carburetor cross shaft lever "E."
3. Pull accelerator rod "C" to wide open throttle (through detent) and turn lever "E" to wide open throttle position (carburetor throttle lever against the stop). Adjust swivel "B" to align with hole in lever "E," then lengthen accelerator rod "C" by backing off swivel five full turns.

   NOTE: With this adjustment the transmission is in detent position when the carburetor is in wide open throttle position.

4. Position accelerator pedal 1" from floor mat (3-speed) or 1¼" from floor mat (automatic) by placing a block of wood between pedal and floor mat.
5. Hold lever "A" in wide open throttle position (through detent) turn swivel "O" to align with hole in lever "A."

   NOTE: This adjustment provides the proper clearance between the accelerator pedal and floor mat at wide open throttle.

CARBURETOR ASSEMBLY

Removal from Engine

1. Remove air cleaner assemblies.
2. Disconnect choke wire at each carburetor swivel and cable housing from support bracket. (1961)
3. Disconnect accelerator return spring and accelerator rod. Remove carburetor rods at cross-shaft.
4. Remove all cross-shaft retainer screws and remove cross-shaft assembly.
5. Remove gas inlet line from carburetors.
6. Remove two nuts and washers attaching carburetor to intake manifold studs.
7. Remove vacuum advance hose from right carburetor.
8. Remove carburetor from the mounting studs.

Removing Carburetor

Disassembly

1. Detach clip attaching pump rod to pump lever, remove clip and detach rod from pump lever.

2. Remove fuel inlet nut and gasket and remove filter element and spring.

3. Remove six remaining bowl cover attaching screws and lockwashers, then remove bowl cover assembly and gasket. **NOTE: Take note of the location of screws as removed. Two screws located on either side of pump are longer than the other 4 screws.**

4. Remove pin attaching floats to bowl cover assembly.

5. Lift out float needle. Check seat for dirt or corrosion.

6. If necessary, needle seat and gasket may be removed by using a large size screwdriver. It may then be cleaned or replaced as needed.

7. Accelerator pump may be removed if necessary. Remove "C" clip and pump. Remove shaft and lever, if desired, by removing clip, shaft and lever.

8. Remove the two screws and lockwashers attaching venturi cluster to the bowl assembly and lift out the cluster, gasket and main well insert.

9. Remove the pump discharge valve.

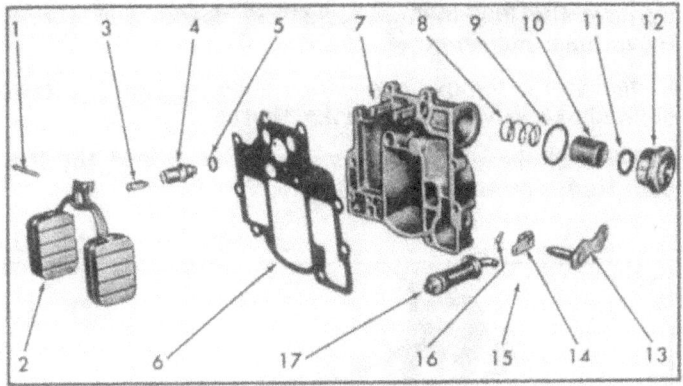

Bowl Cover—Exploded

1. Float Pin
2. Floats
3. Float Needle
4. Needle Seat
5. Needle Seat Gasket
6. Bowl Cover Gasket
7. Bowl Cover
8. Fuel Filter Spring
9. Inlet Nut Gasket
10. Fuel Filter
11. Fuel Filter Gasket
12. Inlet Nut
13. Accelerator Pump Lever and Shaft
14. Inner Accelerator Pump Lever
15. Accelerator Pump Attaching Clip
16. Accelerator Pump
17. Accelerator Pump

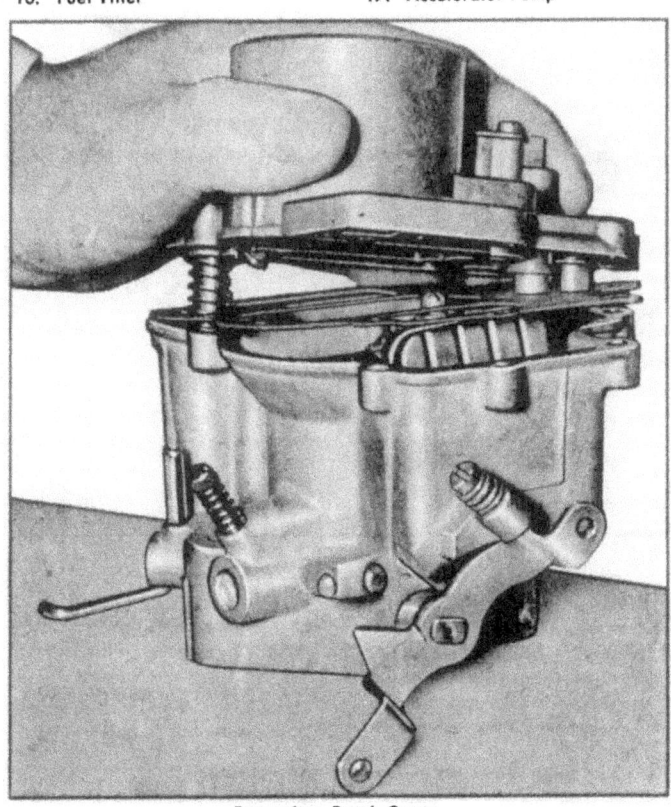

Removing Bowl Cover

10. Remove the idle mixture adjusting needle and spring. Remove main metering jet.
11. If necessary, remove two choke valve retaining screws and slide choke valve out of choke shaft.
12. Remove choke shaft, spring, choke lever and throttle kick cam from carburetor air horn.

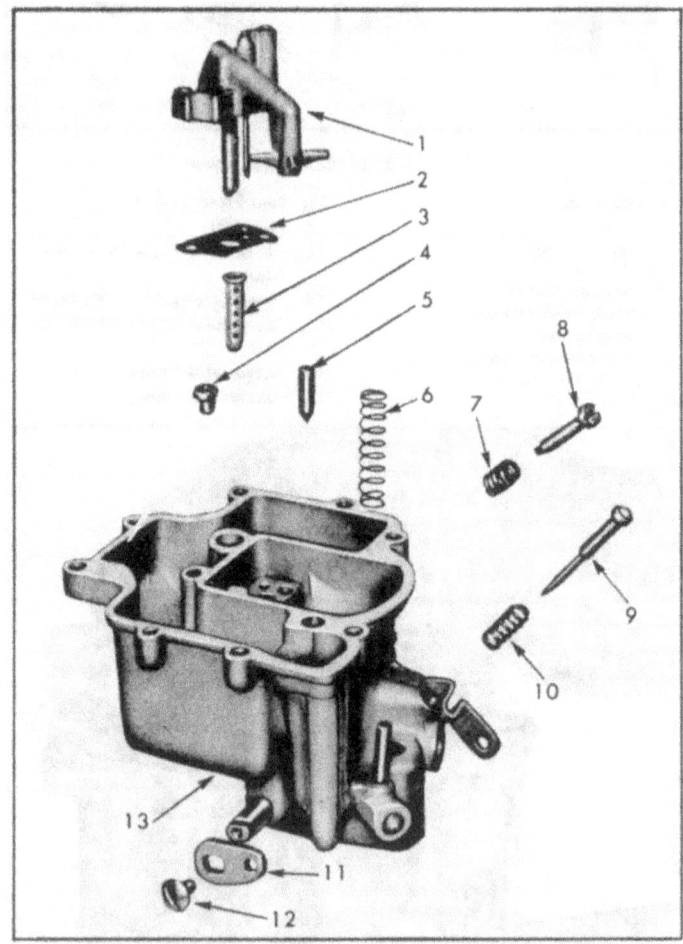

Carburetor Bowl Exploded

1. Venturi Cluster
2. Venturi Gasket
3. Main Well Insert
4. Main Metering Jet
5. Pump Discharge Valve
6. Accelerator Pump Return Spring
7. Idle Adjusting Screw Spring
8. Idle Adjusting Screw
9. Idle Mixture Adjusting Screw
10. Idle Mixture Adjusting Screw Spring
11. Accelerator Pump Actuating Lever
12. Accelerator Pump Actuating Lever Screw
13. Float Bowl

Removing Float Needle

13. Remove fast idle cam attaching screw, spring and throttle kick lever.

14. If necessary, invert carburetor bowl and remove throttle valve retaining screws and remove throttle valve and shaft assembly.

Cleaning and Inspection

Dirt, gum, water or carbon contamination in the carburetor or on the exterior moving parts are often responsible for unsatisfactory performance. For this reason, efficient carburetion depends upon careful cleaning and inspection while servicing.

1. Thoroughly clean carburetor castings and metal parts in clean cleaning solvent.

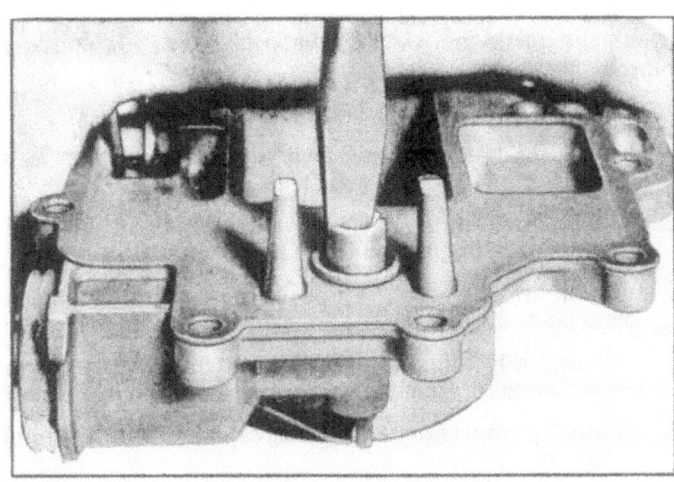

Removing Needle Seat

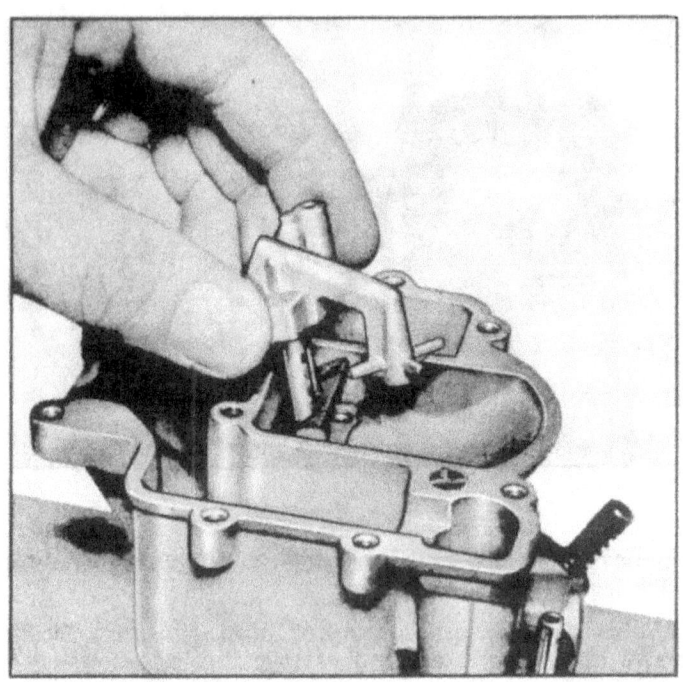

Removing Radial Cluster

CAUTION: Pump plunger and gaskets should never be immersed in carburetor cleaner.

2. Blow out all passages in castings, dry with compressed air and blow out all parts until they are dry. Make sure all jets and passages are clean. Do not use wires or drills for cleaning fuel passages or air bleeds.

3. Check all parts for wear. If wear is noted, defective parts must be replaced.

   NOTE ESPECIALLY THE FOLLOWING:

   A. Check float needle and seat for wear. If wear is noted the assembly must be replaced.

   B. Check float hinge pin for wear and float for dents or distortion. Check floats for fuel leaks by shaking.

   C. Check throttle shaft for wear and out-of-round in the throttle body section of the bowl casting.

   D. Inspect idle adjusting needles for burrs or grooves and misalignment. Such a condition requires replacement.

   E. Inspect pump plunger leather; replace pump if damaged or worn.

   F. Inspect pump well in fuel bowl for wear or being scored.

G. Check that main well nozzle and idle tube is not bent. Should be exactly 90° from body.

H. Check choke shaft for wear and choke valve for nicks.

4. Inspect gaskets to see if they appear hard or brittle or if the edges are torn or distorted. If any such condition is noted they must be replaced.

5. Check filter element for dirt or lint. Clean and if it is distorted or remains plugged, replace.

6. If for any reason parts have become loose or damaged in the cluster casting, it must be replaced.

Float Level and Drop Adjustments

1. Remove bowl cover with gasket from carburetor.

2. The float level dimension (top of float to gasket) should be 1 13/64" if measured without the gauge. Bend Tang as necessary.

3. Hold bowl cover in an upright position and measure the distance from the gasket to the bottom of the float. This dimension should be 1¾". Bend the tang at the end of the float hinge arm to obtain the correct drop, recheck setting after this adjustment.

4. Install the bowl cover.

5. Synchronize and readjust carburetors.

Assembly

1. Install throttle shaft and throttle valve, if removed, with two screws, carefully center and seat valve in shaft end bore.

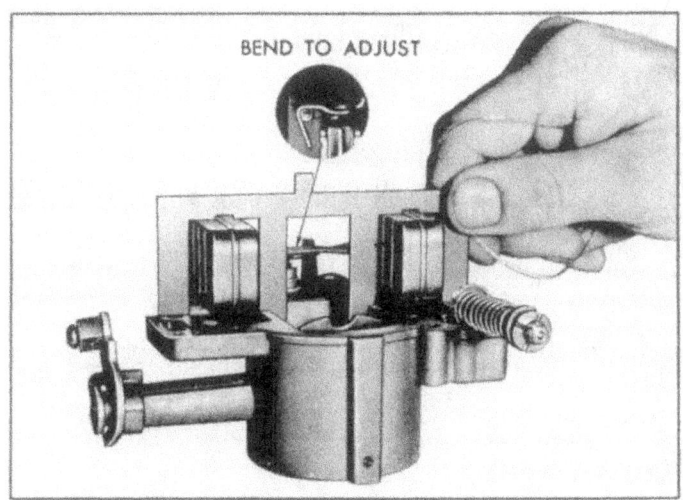

Checking Float Level

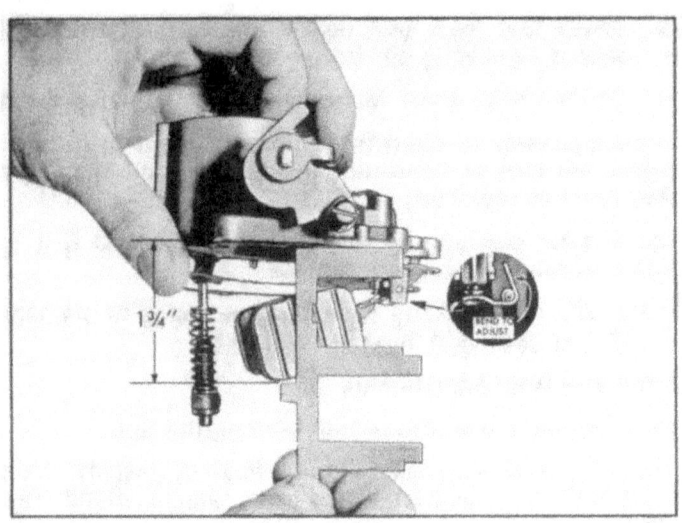

Checking Float Drop

2. Install venturi cluster and gasket in bowl assembly, and install the two screws and lockwashers.

3. If accelerator pump has been removed, replace pump assembly and install "C" clip.

   NOTE: Be sure that the pump return spring is in place in bowl assembly.

4. Install pump discharge needle.

5. Install choke valve spring with long curved end under lever. Then install shaft, valve, choke lever and throttle kick cam. Retain choke valve with two screws. (Choke shaft assembly should rotate freely without binds).

6. Install float needle seat if previously removed from bowl cover.

7. Carefully replace float needle.

8. Install a new gasket and replace float and pin. Check float level and float drop.

9. Carefully place bowl cover assembly and new gasket on bowl assembly and install the six screws and lockwashers in original positions.

10. Replace filter return spring, filter gasket, gasket and inlet nut.

11. Install pump rod in pump lever and retain with clip.

Installation on Engine.

1. Install insulator block in place, install carburetor on intake manifold studs. Install two attaching nuts and washers and

tighten evenly. On right carburetor, replace vacuum advance line with other end to distributor advance. On the left carburetor, the vacuum port tube is capped with a plastic cap.

2. Replace cross-shaft lever support and install three hex head attaching screws at each carburetor.

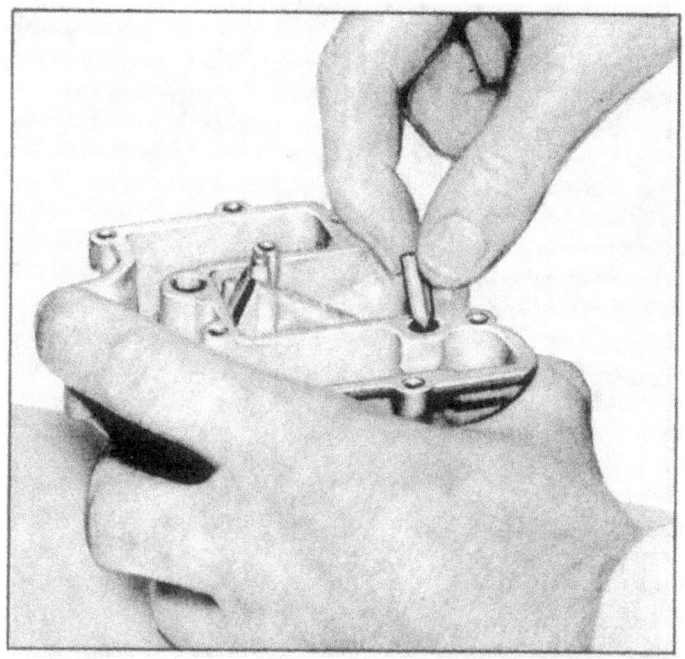

Installing Pump Discharge Valve

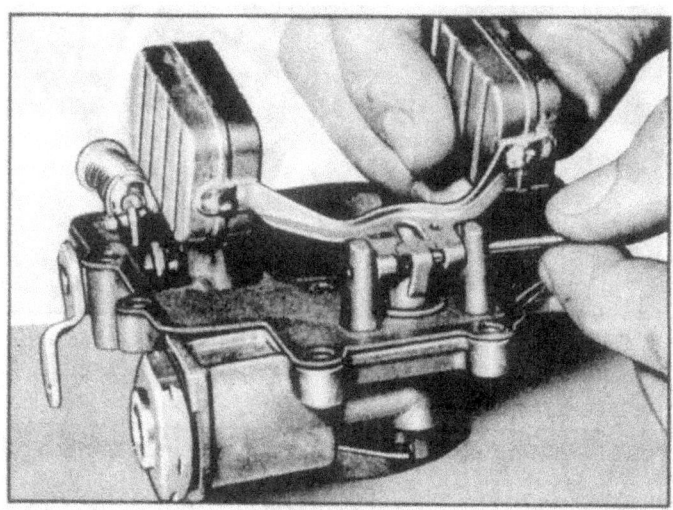

Replacing Floats

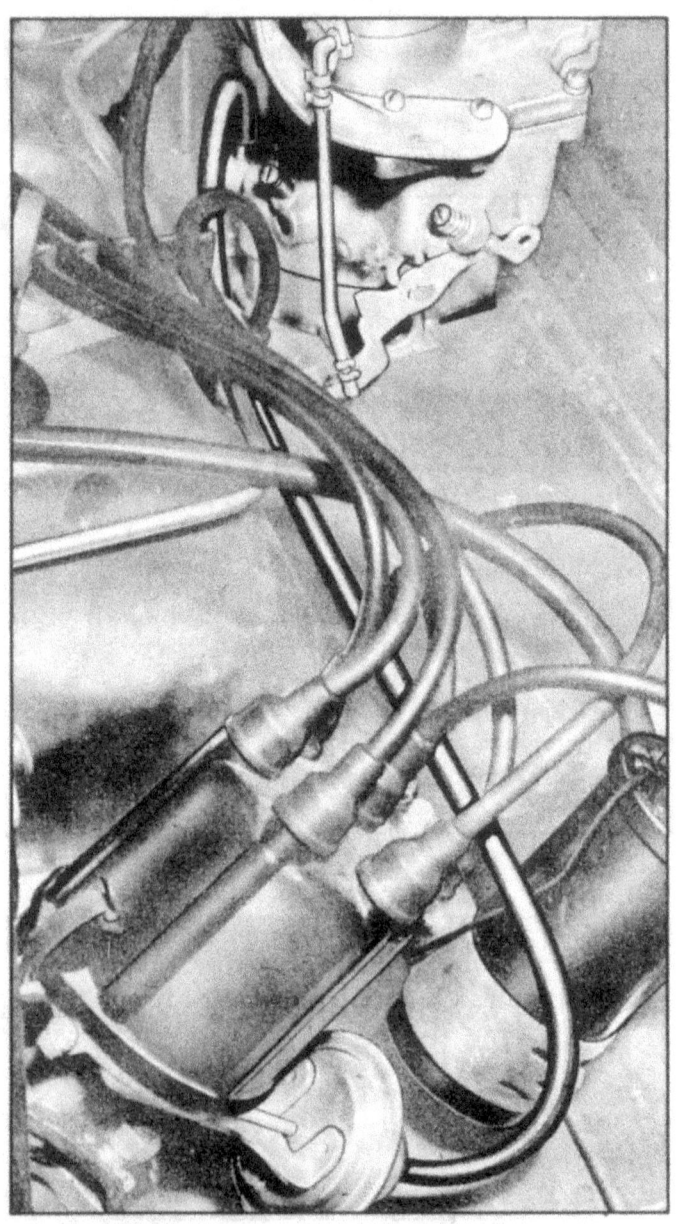

Vacuum Advance Line

3. Replace gas inlet lines.
4. Replace accelerator rod and return spring. Connect throttle rods to cross-shaft.
5. Install choke cable and wire to each carburetor bracket and choke swivel or individual choke rods—1962. Adjust as out-

lined under "Choke Adjustment."
6. Check carburetors for "Carburetor Synchronization."
7. Clean air cleaner elements if necessary.
8. Install air cleaners, gaskets and connector.

TROUBLE SHOOTING CHART

(MODEL "H" CARBURETOR)

ALWAYS CHECK FIRST:
Heat Insulator, Carburetor Mounting Nuts, Compression, Ignition System.

FLOODING	ROUGH IDLE	ECONOMY	HESITATION	ACCELERATION FLATNESS	SURGE	LOW TOP SPEED OR POWER	COLD OPERATION	STALLING	HARD HOT STARTING	CHECK POINTS*	WHAT TO LOOK FOR
1	★	★				★	1		★	IDLE ADJUSTMENT	Correct speed and mixture
1a	★	★			1	1	1a			CARBURETOR SYNCHRONIZATION	Improper linkage adjustments / Air leakage at vacuum hoses
2	3		★	3	2			3	1	FLOAT ADJUSTMENT	Use correct gauge
			1	★			★			PUMP ROD ADJUSTMENT	Use correct dimension, throttle valves closed
★	★								★	EXTERNAL VENT	Dirty or plugged (must be open)
	★				4		1a	★	★	CHOKE ADJ.	Cable adjustment not opening or not closing fully
							1b	★		FAST IDLE ADJUSTMENT	Improper clearance
★	★	★								CHOKE VALVE	Sticking choke valve—loose cable
	4		2	1	3	★				METERING JET	Loose, plugged, incorrect part
1	★	★						2		NEEDLE & SEAT	Worn, damaged, dirty, incorrect part
★	★	5	3	2	★		2			VENTURI CLUSTER	Dirty, loose screws, incorrect part
3	★			★			★	★		FLOAT	Bent, leaky
3							★			IDLE NEEDLE	Worn, damaged
4		★	★		★	★	★			THROTTLE VALVES	Sticking open or closed, damaged
4	★	★	★	★	★	★	★	★		GASKETS	Improper seal, hard or brittle material, loose screws
2							★			IDLE PASSAGES	Dirty
★	★									PUMP BODY	Crack or loose fit on plunger shaft
		3				★				PUMP PLUNGER	Hard or worn leather, distorted spring, stuck vent ball check
		4				★				PUMP INLET CHECK	Out-of-round, damaged seat, stuck
★	★			★	★			★		PUMP DISCHARGE NEEDLE	Out-of-round, damaged seat, stuck needle
		1			2				3	DRIVER	Driving habits, correct procedures
		2	1							PUMP DISCHARGE JETS (4)	Dirt, must be open

Numbers under each complaint heading indicate probable order of trouble.
★ Star indicates other possible troubles.

EXHAUST SYSTEM

The exhaust system on all Corvairs is a single unit which includes the exhaust pipes, muffler and tail pipe. The exhaust pipes are packing flange connected to the exhaust manifolds. Both pipes turn towards the right side of the vehicle, combine into a single pipe and thence into the muffler. The muffler is located to the right of the engine and is attached by means of a bracket to the engine. The close proximity to the engine helps reduce condensation problems and contributes to longer muffler life. The flanges at the exhaust manifolds and the bracket at the engine comprise the entire exhaust system mounting.

The muffler is cylindrical and of the reverse flow type. An asbestos wrap, over the steel single wrap inner shell, is covered by a single outside plated steel shell, providing extra long life.

NOTE: 1962 system is not interchangeable with older models.

Exhaust System and Mounting

Removal and Installation

1. Remove the four mounting nuts "A".
2. Remove bolt "B".
3. Carefully pull muffler and exhaust pipe assembly from under car.
4. Install in the same manner removed, being sure that the packing is in place between the exhaust pipe and each manifold.
5. Torque nuts "A" to 15 to 20 ft. lbs. and bolt "B" to 8 to 10 ft. lbs.

Repairs

When replacing the muffler, cut the old muffler off as close to the muffler as possible. The service muffler will have a flange over which the cut end of the exhaust pipe can be clamped.

1962 CORVAIR MONZA SPYDER

The Monza Convertible or Monza Club Coupe together with Regular Production Option 690 constitutes the new Corvair Spyder. The Spyder features a special instrument cluster with complete instrumentation, and is equipped with a Turbocharged engine. Four-speed transmission (RPO 651), 3.55:1 ratio rear axle (RPO 693), heavy-duty suspension (RPO 696) and sintered metallic brakes (RPO 686) are required equipment with the Spyder.

In addition to regular Monza appointments "Spyder" nameplates are added to fender and glove box door immediately beneath the Monza emblem. Emblems designating the Turbocharged engine are located on the rear deck lid beneath the Corvair nameplate and on the steering wheel hub.

Similar in basic configuration to the regular instrument cluster, the cluster face plate is finished in satin chrome and has circular gauges. Instruments include 120 mph speedometer with regular and trip odometer; electric tachometer graduated to 6000 rpm; manifold pressure gauge; cylinder head temperature gauge; fuel level gauge and circular direction signals. Generator-Fan and Temperature-Pressure (oil) warning lights are retained from the regular production cluster. Headlight and ignition switches and high-beam indicator complete the instrument cluster. The cigarette lighter and windshield wiper controls are located on a separate painted panel below the instrument cluster and to the left of the steering column.

The horizontally opposed Corvair engine is extensively changed to provide increased output for the Spyder models. The power increase is as much as 87 percent over the base Corvair engine, and as much as 47 percent over the high performance RPO 649 engine.

Basically, the Spyder engine differs from other Corvair engines in that a turbo-supercharger (turbine driven) is used to charge the bores. Although important internal revisions are necessary, the more obvious changes occur in the external parts of the induction system. Single air cleaner, single side draft carburetor and an induction crossover tube replace the dual carburetor-air cleaner arrangement of the regular Corvair engine. Mounted between the carburetor and induction crossover is the turbo-supercharger. This supercharger consists of an exhaust driven turbine which drives a centrifugal impeller, drawing fuel-air mixture from the carburetor and forcing it through the crossover which supplies either cylinder bank.

Bore and stroke of the new engine are not changed, consequently, piston displacement remains 145 cubic inches. The engine peak power rating is 150 horsepower at 4400 rpm, slightly more than one horsepower per cubic inch of displacement. Peak torque is 210 pounds-feet and occurs through a range of 3200 to 3400 engine revolutions per minute. The compression ratio is 8.0:1, however, it is necessary to use premium grade fuels because of the super volumetric efficiency achieved during supercharger boost.

To withstand the power increase many internal engine parts are changed. The pistons, connecting rods and crankshaft are revised to provide greater structural strength, and exhaust valves and exhaust valve guides are made of high temperature alloys. A new engine cooling blower is utilized to reduce inertial forces and improve the generator-blower belt life. Parts such as valve springs, connecting rod bearings, crankshaft bearings and camshaft are the same as used for the 102 horsepower high performance engine.

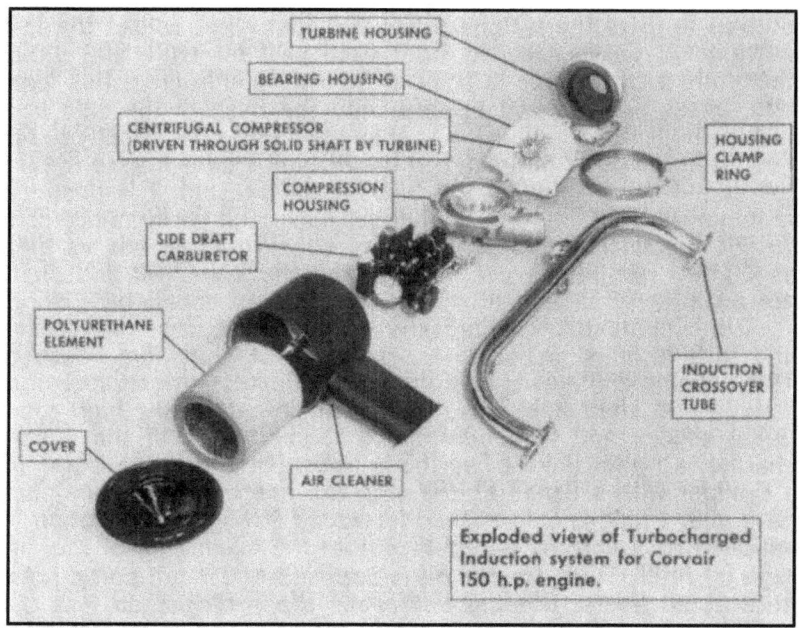

Exploded view of Turbocharged Induction system for Corvair 150 h.p. engine.

INDUCTION SYSTEM. The air cleaner houses a cylindrical oil-wetted polyurethane element mounted on the left side of the engine. Air enters the large air horn, passing from the outer perimeter of the filtering element to the inside, utilizing the maximum filtering area.

Good fuel-air diffusion and atomization is obtained by a single-throat side draft carburetor with a three-venturi arrangement. Engine heat and vacuum are used to operate the automatic choke. The control mechanisms are supplied filtered air from the air cleaner to insure operational accuracy and realiability. All carburetor levers, screws and bolts are chrome plated while the carburetor body is covered with black enamel. An in-line type paper element fuel filter is placed between the fuel pump and carburetor. The large filtering area and remote location, respective to the carburetor, helps prevent vapor lock and protects the carburetor from impurities. A three-bolt attachment is used to fasten the carburetor to the cast aluminum compressor housing of the supercharger.

To accelerate the fuel-air mixture and thereby increase manifold pressures, a centrifugal impeller is driven at very high speeds. Made of a three inch diameter aluminum die casting, the impeller has eleven evenly spaced blades, which draw in the fuel-air mixture and accelerate the particles by directing them radially outward into the diffuser ring of the housing. The compressor housing outlet attaches to the chrome plated induction crossover tube which feeds the two cylinder banks.

The compressor impeller is bolted directly to a solid shaft which is an integral part of the turbine so that a one-to-one drive ratio exists. The energy of engine exhaust gases is effectively utilized to drive the turbine wheel. Exhaust pipes collect the fast moving hot gases expelled from each cylinder bank and direct them into a single pipe in front of the right bank. From this location, gases are directed upward, into the base of the cast iron turbine housing. The housing is shaped so that high velocity gases flow from the outer perimeter of the turbine blades inward toward the center, thus spinning the turbine. A large outlet is provided to minimize back pressure, and under maximum performance conditions the turbine and compressor, will turn at speeds as high as 70,000 revolutions per minute. The turbine wheel and shaft are an integral casting of a high temperature cobalt base alloy.

To simplify disassembly and maintenance, the compressor and turbine housing bolt to a separate cast aluminum housing. This housing contains a bearing which supports the compressor, turbine and shaft assembly. Due to the exceptionally high rotational speeds and high operational temperatures of the supercharger, a rather unique bearing is used. Formed in the shape of a cylinder with a flange at one end, the bearing is an aluminum base alloy which is cold worked for added strength. Lubrication is supplied by a chrome plated line from the clean side of the engine oil filter. Thus, filtered oil is supplied under full pump pressure at all times. Bearing tolerances are arranged so that the complete system floats in oil and is cooled by oil. High rotational speeds cause oil foaming, therefore the oil outlet tube is more than 2.5 times as large as the oil inlet to assure proper lubricant flow.

ENGINE INTERNAL COMPONENTS. To withstand the increased output, all of the high performance and heavy duty components used for the optional 102 horsepower engine are incorporated, plus many more. Because of the exceptionally high temperatures in the exhaust valve area, all exhaust valves are a two-piece welded construction. The valve head and neck are made of an alloy generally found in jet aircraft engines. The material is a nickle base alloy known as Nimonic 80A. The weld-on stem is a nickle silicon alloy of steel which provides excellent scuff resistant qualities.

The exhaust valve guide is designed of a nickle, aluminum and bronze alloy to provide good heat conductivity away from the valve stem as well as a good high temperature bearing surface. To improve valve life, both inlet and exhaust valves are provided with a beaded lock device to retain the valve cap and spring. The beaded locks help reduce the force on the stem at the point of minimum load so that small amounts of valve rotation may take place.

The piston upper compression ring is chrome plated to improve durability, and the connecting rod shank cross section is increased for greater strength. Material for the forged crankshaft has been changed from carbon steel to a steel alloy of nickle and silicon. The new material provides increased and more uniform depth of hardenability which increases the crankshaft strength and toughness sufficiently to withstand the additional forces placed upon it.

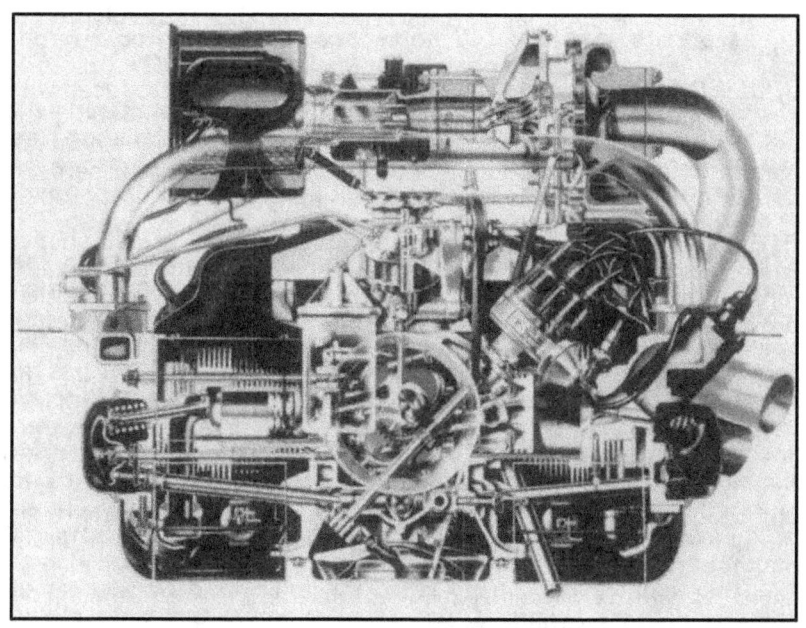

IGNITION SYSTEM. The ignition system has also undergone revisions. A high capacity ignition coil with approximately 20 percent greater output is used in conjunction with a block type resistor to provide a hotter spark at the plugs. The distributor has been revised to include an automatic pressure retard device, in place of a vacuum advance, to change the spark timing.

Initial spark setting is 24 degrees before the piston reaches top center. Since there is no vacuum advance, the spark remains at this point until the pressure retard device or centrifugal advance alters it. The centrifugal advance is set so that it does not change the spark setting below 3900 engine revolutions per minute. As speed increased beyond 3900 rpm, the spark is advanced a maximum of 12 additional degrees when 4500 rpm is reached. Operation of the pressure retard device begins at a manifold pressure of one pound per square inch, and reaches a maximum of 9 degrees retard at two pounds per square inch manifold pressure. Under wide open throttle conditions one psi manifold pressure occurs at approximately 2500 rpm, and 2 psi, or full retard, at approximately 2750 rpm. Spark advance under full throttle will remain at 24 degrees up to approximately 2500 rpm engine speed. Under conditions of partial to full throttle the setting will vary between 15 and 36 degrees.

This spark arrangement is necessary to prevent severe detonation during supercharged operation. Due to the increase in initial cylinder pressures during supercharger boost periods, the resulting compressed fuel charge at the top of the piston stroke is increased in density. This density increase is sufficient to cause such rapid burning of the fuel mixture that the spark must be retarded to prevent severe detonation.

As with the optional 102 horsepower engine, the colder running AC44FF spark plugs are used in place of the AC46FF.

COOLING SYSTEM. A new engine cooling blower is introduced with the Spyder engine. Rather unique for this type of installation, the new blower is made of an acetal resin plastic. The lighter weight material reduces fan and generator belt peak loads by 40 percent, thus improving reliability as well as durability.

EXHAUST SYSTEM. To protect the spare tire, a bullet shaped heat shield of polished stainless steel covers the turbine exhaust tube. A unique double-walled construction with louvered outlets provides highly efficient cooling by the heat convection principle. The turbine exhaust pipe and muffler inlet are 2½ inches in diameter. The muffler is somewhat unique in that the outlet and all major internal passages are also 2½ inches in diameter. Specifically designed for the Turbo-charged engine, the muffler is oval with a reverse gas flow internal configuration. Divided into four compartments, the large passages and strategically placed bulkheads provide a freedom of gas flow comparable to a straight through muffler with greatly superior sound and vibration damping. The shell, or main body structure, is covered by a sheet of asbestos with an aluminized metal outer wrap. A chrome plated tail pipe completes the exhaust assembly.

CLUTCH. Clutch revisions consist of a thicker pressure plate to increase driven plate cooling, and a 16 percent greater effective plate load to absorb the increased engine output.

Optional equipment recommended by the factory for use with Spyder models includes Positraction Rear Axle (RPO 480), and Seat Belts (FOA 148).

TURBOCHARGED ENGINE SPECIFICATIONS

Type . . . . Horizontal Opposed, 6-Cylinder

Bore 3.437

Stroke 2.60

Displacement (Cu. In.) 145

Compression Ratio 8.0:1

Output Ratings
    Horsepower (at RPM) . . . . 150 at 4400
    Torque (Ft. lb at RPM) . . . . 210 at 32 to 3400

Air Cleaner . . . . Oil Wetted Polyurethane Element

Carburetor . . . . Triple Venturi, Sidedraft

Choke . . . . Automatic

Fuel Filter . . . . In-line Paper Element

Super Charger
    Type . . . . Turbo-Supercharger
                                              (Turbine Driven Compressor)
    Turbine . . . . Single Stage, In-Flow Type
        Material . . . . High Temperature Cobalt Base Alloy
        Diameter (in) 2.97
        Blades . . . . 11, Equally Spaced
        Drive . . . . Engine Exhaust Gases

    Compressor . . . . Centrifugal Impeller
        Material . . . . Die Cast Aluminum Alloy
        Diameter (in.) 3.00
        Blades . . . . 14, Equally Spaced
        Drive . . . . Solid Shaft from Turbine

    Bearing . . . . One Piece Floating Bushing
        Material . . . . Aluminum Alloy
        Lubrication . . . . Engine Oil, Full Pressure

TURBOCHARGED ENGINE SPECIFICATIONS
(Continued)

Valve Springs .... Heavy Duty

Exhaust Valve Guides .... High Temperature
Aluminum Bronze Alloy

Exhaust Valves .... Two Piece welded
    Head and Neck .... Super Alloy (Nimonic 80A)
    Stems .... Silicon and Chromium Alloy Steel

Piston Top Ring .... Chromium Plate

Connecting Rod .... Heavy Duty

Crankshaft .... Forged Alloy Steel

Connecting Rod Bearings .... Heavy Duty

Crankshaft Main Bearings .... Heavy Duty

Electrical
    Distributor Control .... Centrifugal Advance and
        Diaphragm Pressure Retard
    Coil .... High Capacity
    Resistor .... Block Type
    Spark Plugs 44FF

Muffler
    Type .... Single, Reverse Flow
    Construction .... Oval, Lock Seam, welded
        Body covered with Asbestos
        and Aluminized Outer Wrap
    Inlet Diameter (in) 2.50

Clutch
    Effective Plate Load (lb) .... High Performance
    Driven Plate .... 1050 to 1250
    Pressure Plate .... Heavy Duty Facing

Cooling Blower
    Material .... Plastic, Acetal Resin
    Diameter (in) 11.19
    Blades .... 11, Unevenly Spaced

1965 SECTION

> On the following pages will be found details on service and repair to 1965 models which are substantially different from those outlined for earlier models. On this section will also be found the information relating to the 164 cubic inch engines used since 1964. Complete specifications are presented at the end of the section.

SPEEDOMETER CABLE

The speedometer drive is from the left front wheel in the 1965 Corvair rather than from the transmission output shaft as in past models. The speedometer cable runs to the inside of the wheel where it is bracket mounted to the steering nuckle. The cable then runs through a hole drilled in the spindle. The square end of the cable pilots into the square center hole of a plastic insert which is part of the hub grease cap. The usual cotter pin cannot be used to lock the spindle nut in place because of the cable through the spindle. In its place a special lock ring is used on the left spindle nut only. When performing the following service operations keep in mind these differences, especially the plastic insert in the hub grease cap. Removal and installation of the cap should be performed with care so as not to damage the insert.

Removal
1. Remove the two speedometer cable bracket to steering knuckle attaching screws and carefully pull the cable and seal from the spindle.

Installation
1. Remove the hub cap or wheel cover from the left front wheel and then carefully pry the grease cap from the wheel hub.
2. With the seal in place over the speedometer cable, carefully slide the cable into the hole in the spindle and attach the bracket to the steering knuckle with its two attaching screws (30-50 lbs. in. torque).
3. Reinstall the grease cap as follows: set the cap in place over the hub and rotate it with your fingers until you feel the speedometer cable enter the plastic grease cap insert. Then, using a screwdriver, carefully tap around the bead of the cap until it is seated. (If available, Tool J-6417 may be used to install the grease cap.)

REAR SUSPENSION

The 1965 independent four-link type rear suspension consists of a front and a rear strut rod with the drive shaft and the torque control arm forming four links at each wheel, and a full-coil spring mounted between the frame and torque arm.

The stamped-steel, welded, hat-section control arms are pin-jointed to the front mounting brackets through a rubber isolated bushing pressed into the arm. Rear wheel toe in angle is adjusted by positioning the horizontally slotted arm-to-body brackets to the proper setting. Wheel spindle and spindle support are attached to the torque arms through four studs which are pressed into the arm.

An adjustable bracket, attached to the transmission support, secures the inboard end of the rubber mounted front strut rod. The outboard end is rubber mounted and directly connected to the torque arm.

A rear strut is mounted laterally from a bracket bolted to lower surface of axle carrier to the torque arm. The strut rod to torque arm connection provides for rear wheel camber adjustment through an eccentric cam bolt adjustment.

The rear wheel spindles are driven through double universal jointed, tubular drive shafts, which are bolted to the differential yoke and drive spindle flange. Wheel spindle support houses the inner and outer tapered roller bearings. Bearing adjustment is made through the use of a spacer and variable thickness shims between the bearings.

The direct, double-acting shock absorbers upper end is secured to an underbody bracket and at the lower end to the torque arm bracket. A full coil spring is seated against the upper surface of the torque arm and the upper end rests against the underbody side rail.

MAINTENANCE AND ADJUSTMENTS

Periodic maintenance and adjustments are not required for the rear suspension components. The suspension system should be checked for shock absorber action, condition of suspension bushings, tightness of suspension attaching bolts and an overall visual inspection of components for defects.

WHEEL ALIGNMENT
Camber
Wheel camber angle is obtained by adjusting the eccentric cam and bolt assembly located at the outboard mounting of the rear strut rod. Place rear wheels on alignment machine and determine camber angle. Adjust camber by loosening the cam bolt and rotating cam and bolt assembly to obtain specified camber. Tighten nut securely and torque to specifications.

Toe-in

Wheel toe-in is adjusted by moving the torque arm to underbody bracket horizontally as required to obtain specified toe-in. To adjust wheel toe-in, loosen front strut rod inner bracket to transmission support bolts so that bracket is loose on slots, loosen bracket to underbody attaching bolts until bracket is free enough to be moved. Position torque arm to obtain specified toe-in. Tighten affected bolts securely and torque to specifications.

Camber Adjusting Cam Location

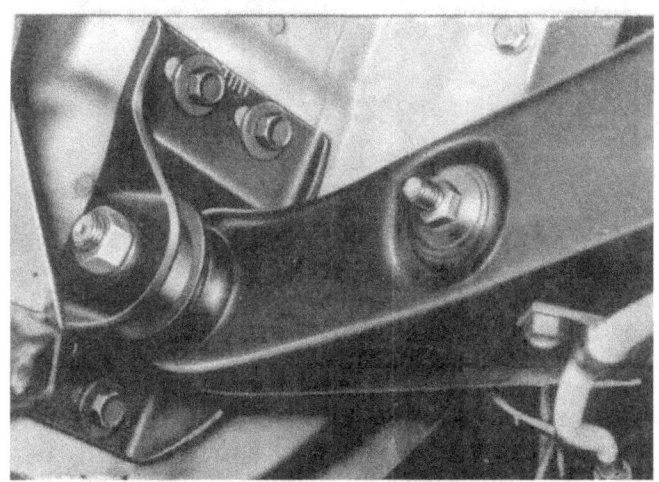

Toe-in Adjusting Bracket Location

RIDING HEIGHT AND REAR COIL SPRING SAG

In cases of vehicle riding height complaints, a rear coil spring height check will show if the rear suspension is at the proper height.

1. Position car on smooth, level floor. The vehicle should be at curb weight (a full tank of gasoline, but an empty front compart-

ment except for spare tire).

2. Bounce rear end several times and allow it to settle to its normal height.

3. Measure the distance from the floor to the bottom of the rocker panel 29" ahead of center line of rear wheel.

4. This measurement should be $8\frac{1}{2} + \frac{1}{2}$".

5. Measure the opposite side of the vehicle in a similar manner. It is essential that the two be within $\frac{1}{2}$".

6. To correct these heights, springs must be replaced. These springs do not have flat ends and shims should not be used.

NOTE: This check should be used in conjunction with the front coil spring check to be certain that overall "sag" (trim) is within $\frac{1}{2}$". (See "Specifications")

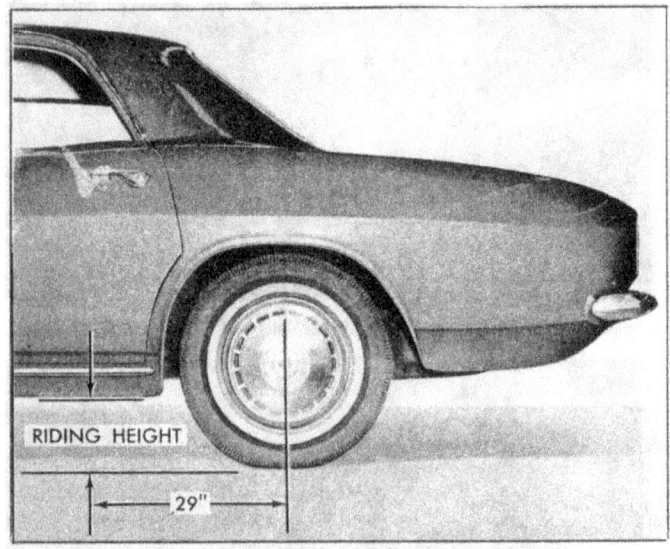

Rear Riding Height

SHOCK ABSORBER REPLACEMENT

1. Raise engine compartment lid and remove shock absorber upper attaching nut, retainer and grommet.

2. Raise rear of vehicle to obtain access to shock absorber attachment at rear of torque control arm.

3. Remove bolt securing shock absorber to torque arm bracket and withdraw shock from vehicle.

4. Extend upper portion of shock absorber into underbody bracket so that it protrudes into the engine compartment.

5. Install grommet, retainer and nut to shock absorber upper attaching rod in the engine compartment—torque nut to specifications.

6. Position shock absorber lower eye into torque arm bracket and install through bolt. Install lock washer and nut—torque nut to specifications.

7. Lower vehicle and test shock absorber action.

SPRING REPLACEMENT

1. Raise rear of vehicle, position stand jacks at jacking pads and remove wheel and tire assembly.
2. Position hydraulic jack under torque arm, raise torque arm and compress spring so that it is near curb height.
3. Disconnect rear strut rod bracket at the differential carrier.
4. Disconnect shock absorber at torque arm bracket, then slowly release hydraulic jack permitting spring to relax until it is fully expanded.
5. Remove spring, spring retainer and cushion from the vehicle.
6. Place spring retainer and cushion on spring so that spring end rest against stop on retainer, then place assembly between torque arm and under body bracket. Make sure spring is indexed in both the upper and lower seats.
7. Slowly raise hydraulic jack to partially compress spring, then connect shock absorber to torque arm bracket.
8. With shock absorber installed to torque arm, continue to raise hydraulic jack until spring is at curb position. Connect rear strut rod bracket to differential carrier.
9. Remove hydraulic jack and install wheel and tire assembly.
10. With weight of vehicle resting on suspension, torque affected attaching parts to specifications.

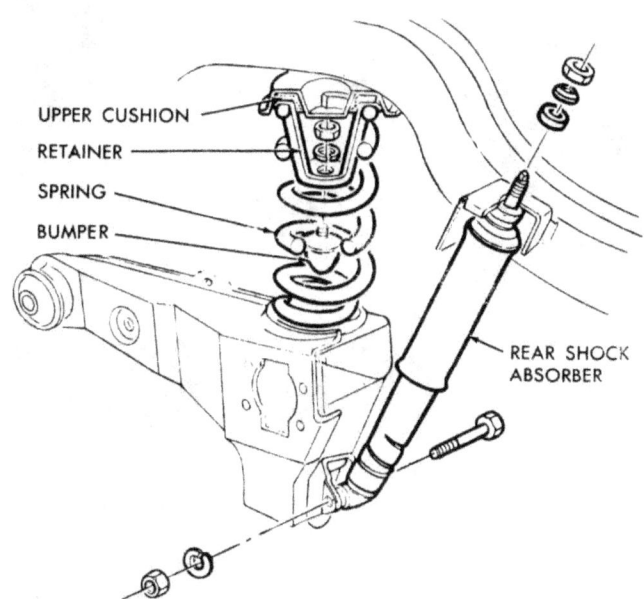

Spring and Shock Absorber Installation

BRAKES

The self-adjusting brakes used on both front and rear of all 1965 models are the Duo-Servo single anchor type which utilize the momentum of the vehicle to assist in the brake application. This self-energizing or self-actuating force is applied to both shoes at each wheel in both forward or reverse motion. The brake shoe facings are bonded to the shoes.

Wheel cylinders are the double piston type permitting even distribution of pressure to each brake shoe. To keep out dust and moisture, both ends of each wheel cylinder are sealed with a rubber boot. The wheel cylinders have no adjustments.

The main cylinder consists of a piston which receives mechanical pressure from the brake pedal and transmits it through the brake lines as hydraulic pressure to the wheel cylinders. The filler cap is accessible from inside the trunk compartment.

The parking brake lever is located to the left of the steering column. A cable type linkage, directed over pulleys and routed through the tunnel, connects this lever to an equalizer at the under body forward of the transmission.

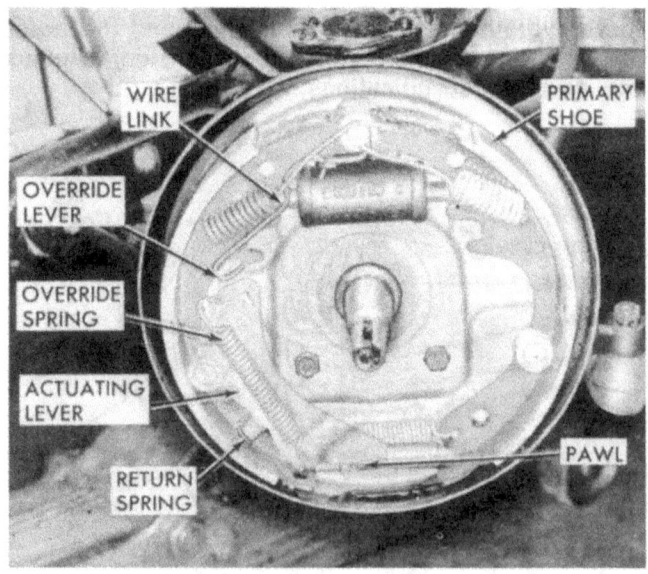

Self-Adjusting Brakes

Force applied at the parking brake lever is transmitted to both right and left rear brakes by means of a single actuating cable which passes through the equalizer and is connected at each end to an actuating lever within the brake assembly.

The parking brake lever is of the single stroke ratchet type and incorporates a trigger release which is located in the lever grip.

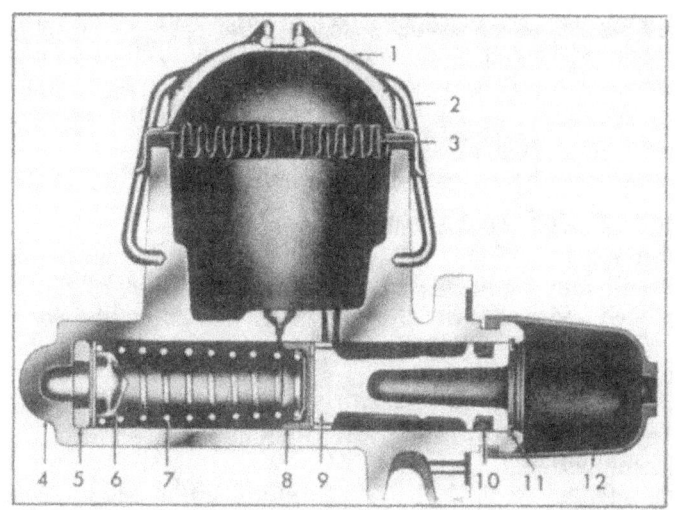

Main Cylinder

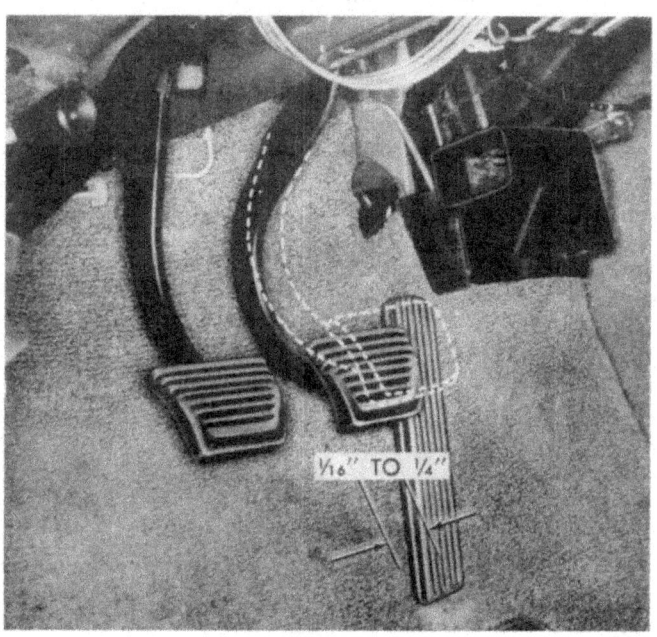

Brake Pedal Free Movement

PUSH ROD TO MAIN CYLINDER CLEARANCE

Brake pedal free movement is the upward movement of the brake pedal pad, with pedal in return position, before the pedal arm contacts the pedal stop. Since the pedal stop is permanently mounted and non-adjustable, it is essential that free movement be present—too much free movement results in pedal rattle while insufficient movement will tend to force undue pressure on main

cylinder piston, which would possibly close compensating port.
1. Loosen check nut on push rod sufficiently to allow adjustment.
2. Turn push rod in proper direction to obtain correct adjustment. Upward movement of the pedal pad before the pedal arm contacts the pedal stop must be 1/16 to 1/4 inch.
3. Tighten check nut against clevis, and recheck free movement.

SERVICE BRAKE ADJUSTMENT

Although the brakes are self-adjusting, a preliminary or initial adjustment may be necessary after the brakes have been relined or replaced, or whenever the length of the adjusting screw has been changed. The final adjustment is made by using the self-adjusting feature.
1. With brake drum off, disengage the actuator from the star wheel by spinning or turning with a small screw driver.
2. Recommended:
a. Use special Tool J-21177, Drum-to-Brake Shoe Clearance Gauge, to check the diameter of the drum inner surface.
b. Turn the tool to the opposite side and fit over the brake shoes by turning the star wheel until the gauge just slides over the linings.
3. Rotate the gauge around the brake shoe lining surface to assure proper clearance.

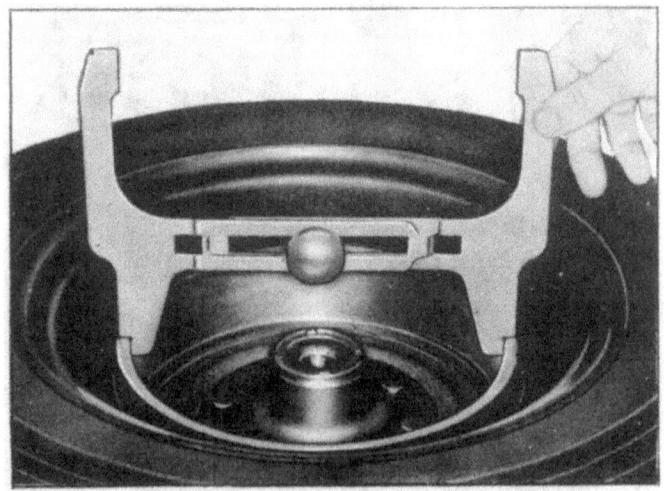

Using Drum-to-Brake Shoe Clearance Gauge

Alternate:
a. Using the brake drum as an adjustment fixture, turn the star wheel until the drum slides over the brake shoes with a slight drag.
b. Turn the star wheel 1-1/4 turns to retract the shoes. This will allow sufficient lining-to-drum clearance so final adjustment may be made as described in Step 4.
3. Install the drum and wheel.

NOTE: 1: If lanced area in brake drum was knocked out, be sure all metal has been removed from brake compartment. Install new hole cover in drum to prevent contamination of the brakes.

NOTE: 2: Make certain when installing drums that drums are installed in the same position as when removed with the drum locating tang in line with the locating hole in the axle shaft.

4. Make final adjustment by making numerous forward and reverse stops, applying brakes with a firm pedal effort until a satisfactory brake pedal height results.

NOTE: Frequent usage of an automatic transmission forward range to halt reverse vehicle motion may prevent the automatic adjusters from functioning, thereby inducing low pedal heights.

Checking Brake Shoe Lining Clearance

PARKING BRAKE

The service brake must be properly adjusted first as a base for the parking brake adjustment.

Adjustment
1. Jack up both rear wheels.
2. Pull parking brake lever up 1 notch from fully release position.
3. Loosen the forward check nut on the equalizer and tighten the rear one until a heavy drag is felt when rear wheels are rotated.
4. Tighten check nuts securely.
5. Fully release parking brake and rotate rear wheels; no drag should be present.

Aligning Drum Tang with Wheel Hub

ENGINE MECHANICAL

The six cylinder, overhead valve, engines covered in this section are the 164 cu. in. engines used in the Corvair 10100 and 10500 series vehicles. The engine is horizontally opposed, air cooled and has two opposing, aluminum heads that incorporate integral intake manifolds.

The aluminum crankcase is vertically divided into two halves, each having three pilot openings for individual cast iron cylinders. The crankshaft and camshaft are located between the split halves of the crankcase. The crankshaft, supported by the crankcase halves, has four main bearings. The camshaft journals, having no bearings, ride directly on the crankcase halves.

The cylinders are numbered rear to front: 1-3-5 on the right bank, and 2-4-6 on the left bank. Firing order is 1-4-5-2-3-6. Crankshaft rotation as viewed from the rear is counter-clockwise.

Full pressure lubrication, through a full flow oil filter and an air cooled oil cooler is furnished by a gear-type oil pump located in the engine rear housing. The distributor, driven by a helical gear on the crankshaft, drives the oil pump. The main oil gallery feeds oil through drilled passages to the camshaft and crankshaft journals. The main oil gallery also feeds the hydraulic valve lifters, which through hollow push rods feed the individually mounted rocker arms.

ENGINE SEAL AND SHIELDS

Seal and Retainer
Removal
1. Remove spare tire, then remove air cleaner assembly.
2. Remove retainer to body attaching screws.
3. Disconnect seal from engine shields by pushing groove of seal off seal flange.
4. Remove seal and retainer assembly.

Installation
1. Lubricate groove of seal with liquid soap or silicone and place seal and retainer assembly in position over engine shields.
2. While guiding groove of seal on shield flange, (with one hand), press seal in place using a block of wood or a hammer handle.
3. Install all retainer attaching screws finger tight, then tighten screws securely.

Front Shield
Removal
1. Disconnect battery positive cable.
2. Remove spare tire, then remove air cleaner assembly.
3. Remove vacuum balance tube.
4. Disconnect heater hose at **upper** shroud.
5. Remove grommet for **Powerglide** dip stick tube (if so equipped).

6. Disconnect seal from flange of front shield.
7. Remove grommet (for starter wiring and fuel line) from front shield.
8. Disconnect starter wiring (engine side).
9. From the underside of vehicle: disconnect accelerator rod at transmission bellcrank and disconnect fuel line at flexhose (plug fuel line from fuel tank), then disconnect axle dip stick tube at differential carrier.
10. Disconnect accelerator rod at carburetor cross shaft, then remove rod and bellows from front shield.
11. Disconnect grommet from front shield and remove axle dip stick tube assembly.
12. Disconnect fuel line at fuel pump, then remove fuel line from front shield.
13. Remove bolts attaching front shield, then remove front shield.

Installation
1. Install front shield by guiding shield over starter wiring and Powerglide dip stick tube (if so equipped).
2. Install all bolts attaching front shield finger tight, then tighten bolts securely.
3. Install fuel line through front shield, then connect fuel line at fuel pump.
4. Install accelerator rod through front shield, then connect bellows to front shield and connect accelerator rod at carburetor cross shaft.
5. Install axle dip stick tube assembly through front shield and connect grommet in front shield.
6. Connect starter wiring.
7. Install grommet (for starter wiring and fuel line) in front shield.
8. Lubricate groove of seal with liquid soap or silicone, then while guiding groove of seal onto shield flange (with one hand), press seal in place with a block of wood or a hammer handle.
9. Install grommet for Powerglide dip stick tube (if so equipped).
10. Connect heater hose at upper shroud.
11. Install vacuum balanced tube.
12. From the underside of vehicle: connect fuel line at flexhose, connect accelerator rod at transmission bellcrank and connect axle dip stick tube at differential carrier.
13. Connect battery positive cable.
14. Install air cleaner assembly, then install spare tire.

Left Shield
Removal
1. Remove bolts attaching left side of upper shroud and left shield to cylinder head.
2. Remove bolts attaching left shield to left exhaust duct.
3. Remove bolt attaching left shield and oil cooler to cylinder head.
4. Remove bolts attaching left shield to front shield and (if so

equipped) remove screw from ground strap.
5. Disconnect seal from flange of left shield.
6. Remove left shield, by pulling from under upper shroud, front shield and oil cooler flange.

Installation
1. Place left shield in position under upper shroud, front shield and oil cooler flange.
2. Install all bolts attaching left shield finger tight, then tighten bolts securely.
3. Lubricate groove of seal with liquid soap or silicone, then while guiding groove of seal onto shield flange (with one hand), press seal in place with a block of wood or a hammer handle.
4. Connect ground strap (if so equipped).

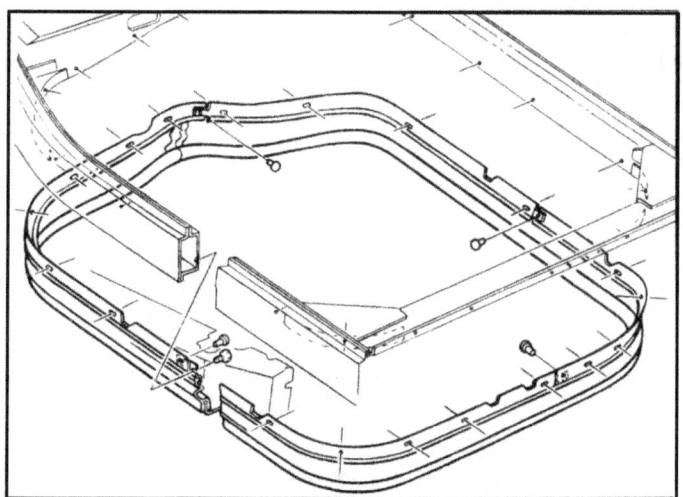

Engine Seal and Retainer

Right Shield
Removal
1. Remove spare tire then, remove bolts attaching right side of upper shroud and right shield to cylinder head.
2. Remove bolts attaching right shield to right exhaust duct.
3. Remove ignition coil and bracket.
4. Remove bolts attaching right shield to front shield and (if so equipped) remove screw from ground strap.
5. Disconnect seal from flange of right shield.
6. Remove bolt attaching muffler bracket to right shield.
7. Remove muffler.
8. Remove right shield by pulling from under upper shroud and front shield.

Installation
1. Place right shield in position under upper shroud and front

shield.

2. Install all bolts attaching right shield finger tight, then tighten bolts securely.

3. Lubricate groove of seal with liquid soap or silicone, then while guiding groove of seal onto shield flange (with one hand), press seal in place with a block of wood or a hammer handle.

4. Connect ground strap (if so equipped).

5. Install ignition coil and bracket, then install spare tire.

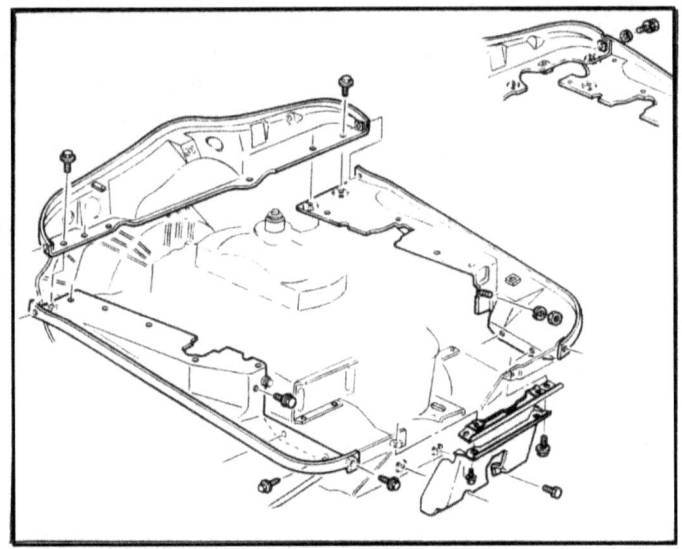

Engine Shields

Rear Center Shield

NOTE: The rear center shield is two pieces. The engine seal is connected to the upper half, which need not be removed under normal conditions.

Removal and Installation (Lower Half)

1. Remove bolts attaching rear center shield to skid plate and exhaust ducts.
2. Remove rear center shield.
3. Place rear center shield in position with attaching bolts finger tight, then tighten bolts securely.

Removal and Installation (Upper Half)

1. Remove lower half as outlined.
2. Disconnect seal from flange of rear center shield.
3. Remove bolts and remove upper half.
4. Install upper half and tighten securely.
5. Install lower half as outlined.
6. Lubricate groove of seal with liquid soap or silicone, then while guiding groove of seal onto shield flange (with one hand) press seal in place with a block of wood or a hammer handle.

MUFFLER HEAT SHIELD

Removal
1. Remove two bolts attaching heat shield to muffler hanger.

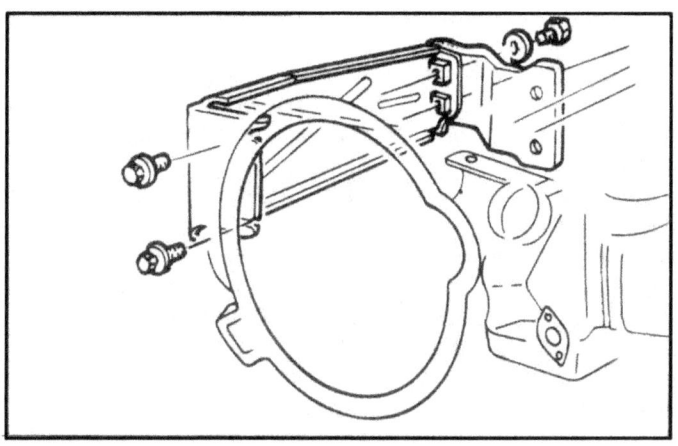

Muffler Heat Shield

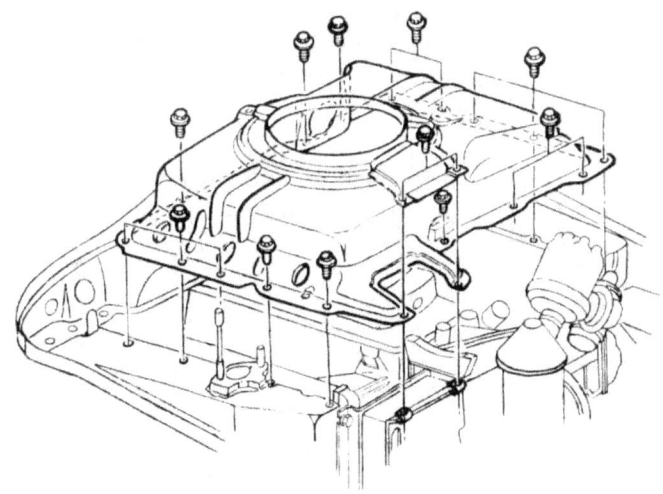

Upper Shroud

2. Loosen two bolts attaching rear of heat shield and right rear shroud to cylinder head.
3. Remove heat shield.

Installation
1. Install heat shield in position under head of two bolts and tighten securely.
3. Tighten two bolts attaching rear of heat shield and right rear shroud to cylinder head.

ENGINE COOLING COMPONENTS
UPPER SHROUD
Removal
1. Remove spare tire then remove air cleaner assembly.
2. Disconnect fuel lines at fuel pump and carburetors, then remove fuel lines to carburetors.
3. Disconnect vacuum advance hose at right carburetor.
4. Disconnect accelerator rod at carburetor cross shaft and disconnect choke control rods at choke levers then remove choke control rods.
5. Remove carburetors with cross shaft and linkage attached.
6. Remove blower belt.
7. Disconnect crankcase ventilation tube at upper shroud, then disconnect vacuum balance tube at bracket and cylinder heads.
8. Remove vacuum balance tube and crankcase ventilation tube and hoses as an assembly.
9. Remove Delcotron with bracket attached.
10. Disconnect heater hose at upper shroud.
11. Remove oil cooler access hole cover and oil dip stick.
12. Remove distributor cap, then remove spark plug wires and distributor cap as an assembly.
13. Remove bolts attaching upper shroud, then remove shroud by raising front of shroud and rotating clockwise to clear oil filter and Delcotron adapter.

Installation
1. Place upper shroud in position and install all attaching bolts finger tight then rotate blower checking clearance while tightening bolts securely.
2. Install oil cooler access hole cover and oil dip stick, then install spark plug wires and distributor cap assembly.
3. Connect heater hose at upper shroud.
4. Install Delcotron and Delcotron bracket.
5. Install vacuum balance tube and crankcase ventilation tube and hoses.
6. Install blower belt and adjust as outlined.
7. Install carburetors and cross shaft then connect vacuum advance hose at right carburetor.
8. Install, adjust and connect upper choke control rods, then adjust and connect accelerator rod as outlined in Engine Tune-Up.
9. Install and connect fuel lines.
10. Install air cleaner assembly, then install spare tire.

LOWER SHROUDS AND THERMOSTATS
Removal
1. Remove bolts attaching lower shroud to crankcase, cylinder head, front shroud and exhaust duct.
2. Drop lower shroud until swivel on thermostat rod can be disconnected from exhaust duct damper.

3. Disconnect swivel and remove lower shroud and thermostat assembly.

Thermostat Replacement
NOTE: In the event of a failed thermostat bellows, the exhaust duct damper will remain in the open position allowing a maximum air flow over the engine to prevent overheating.

1. Remove lower shroud as outlined.
2. Using an open end wrench, on the flat provided, hold thermostat and remove thermostat actuating rod and swivel assembly.
3. Remove nut attaching thermostat to bracket, then remove thermostat.
4. Install new thermostat and tighten securely.
5. Install thermostat actuating rod and swivel assembly and tighten securely.

CAUTION: To prevent damage to the thermostat bellows while tightening actuating rod, hold flat on thermostat with an open end wrench.

Thermostat Adjustment
1. Install lower shroud assembly with two bolts (one to crankcase and one to cylinder head).
2. Hold exhaust duct damper in the fully open position and pull the thermostat actuating rod out the maximum travel (thermostat against bracket stop).
3. Adjust the swivel until it just enters the hole provided in the exhaust duct damper.
4. Remove lower shroud assembly and connect retaining clip, then install lower shroud as outlined.

Installation
1. Connect swivel to exhaust duct damper then install all lower shroud attaching bolts and tighten securely.
2. Check adjustment verifying that thermostat bottoms at bracket before damper hits stop.

FRONT SHROUDS
Removal
1. Remove lower shroud as outlined.
2. Remove exhaust manifold as outlined.
3. Disconnect heater hose at elbow on front shroud.
4. Remove bolts attaching front shroud to cylinder head and upper shroud, then remove front shroud and heater elbow as an assembly.

NOTE: On left front shroud, one attaching bolt (to cylinder head) is reached through heater elbow.

Installation
1. Install front shroud and tighten securely.
2. Connect heater hose.

3. Install exhaust manifold as outlined.
4. Install lower shroud as outlined.

EXHAUST DUCTS
Removal
1. Disconnect seal from flange of exhaust duct and rear center shield.
2. Remove ignition coil and bracket (for right exhaust duct).
3. Remove grille, then, remove rear center shield as outlined.
4. Remove lower shroud as outlined.
5. Remove exhaust duct attaching bolts, then remove exhaust duct.

Installation
1. Install exhaust duct with all bolts finger tight, then tighten bolts securely.
2. Install lower shroud as outlined.
3. Install rear center shield as outlined, then, install grille.
4. Lubricate groove of seal with liquid soap or silicone, then, while guiding groove of seal onto rear center shield and exhaust duct flange (with one hand), press seal in place with a block of wood or a hammer handle.
5. Install ignition coil and bracket (if removed).

REAR SHROUDS
Removal
1. Remove oil cooler (for left rear shroud) or remove ignition coil and bracket (for right rear shroud).
2. Remove lower shroud as outlined.
3. Remove exhaust duct as outlined.

> **NOTE:** For right rear shroud it is necessary to disconnect the wiring at the cylinder head temperature and oil pressure sending units, then disconnect at harness quick-disconnect so harness may be removed with shroud.

Installation
1. Install rear shroud, then install exhaust duct and lower shroud as outlined.
2. Install oil cooler and/or ignition coil and bracket.

BLOWER BELT, IDLER PULLEY AND BELT GUIDES
Removal
1. Loosen nut and bolt at idler pulley and remove blower belt.
2. If necessary, remove bolt and remove idler pulley and rear belt guide as a unit.
3. If necessary, remove bolts attaching upper belt guide and remove upper guide.

Installation and Adjustment
1. If removed, install upper guide leaving bolts finger tight.

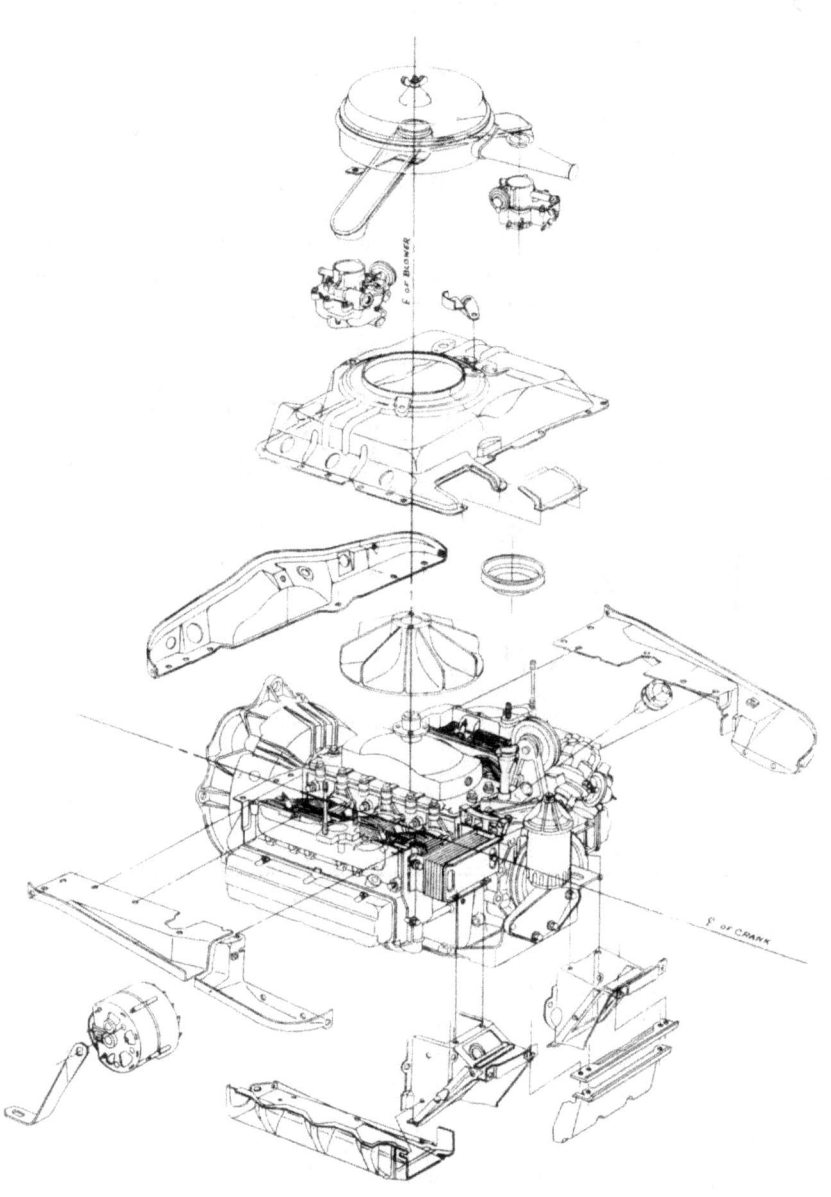

Engine Sheet Metal—Exploded View

2. If removed, install rear guide and idler pulley as a unit and leave bolt and nut finger tight.
3. Install blower belt over pulleys (Delcotron pulley last).
4. Adjust blower belt as follows:

Place a 1/16" shim between belt and rear guide then using a bar and a strand tension gauge adjust blower belt to 55 lb. ± 5 lb. (used belt), 75 lbs. ± 5 lb. (new belt) and tighten bolt and nut securely.

Remove shim from between blower belt and rear guide then using shim as a gauge adjust upper guide and tighten securely.

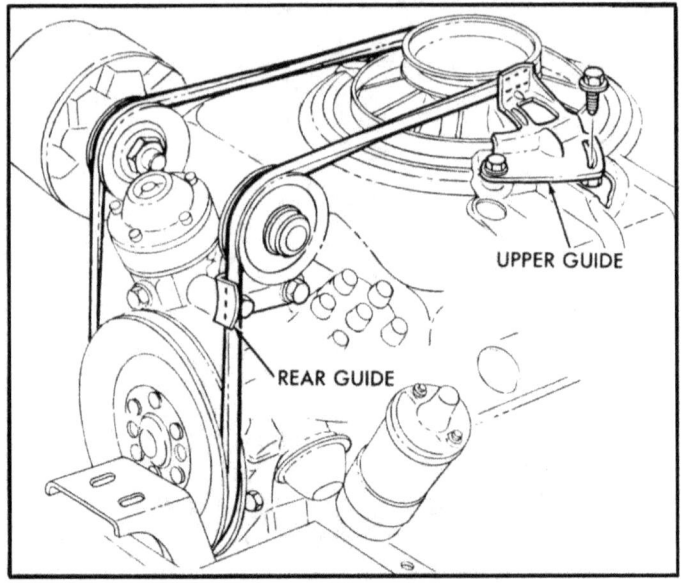

Blower Belt and Guides

Removal
1. Remove spare tire.
2. Disconnect heater hose at upper shroud.
3. Disconnect engine seal from engine shields.
   NOTE: Disconnect seal by grasping at lower edge, then pulling up and off the shield flange.
4. Remove axle dip stick.
5. Disconnect the following electrical items:

Battery positive cable terminal and 10 gauge red wire at terminal body side rail.
Battery negative cable at Delcotron bracket.
Starter wiring at quick disconnect.
Cylinder head temperature and oil pressure indicator wire at quick disconnect.
Positive wire at ignition coil.
If so equipped, radio ground straps at left and right engine shields.

Electrical Disconnect

6. Raise vehicle, then remove grille and rear center shield.
7. Disconnect fuel line at flexible hose then plug line from tank.
8. Disconnect heater hoses at elbows on left and right front shrouds.
9. Disconnect accelerator control rod at idler lever on transmission.
10. Index adjustment cam on outer end of rear strut rods, then loosen nut (do not turn bolt).
   NOTE: This will aid in disconnecting and connecting rear strut rod at differential carrier.
11. Disconnect left and right rear strut rod brackets from differential carrier, then swing rods down.
12. Disconnect inner universal joints.
13. On automatic transmission equipped vehicles, disconnect transmission shift cable.
   NOTE: Disconnect transmission shift cable by removing bolt retaining cable at transmission case, then rotate throttle lever its full limit clockwise and pull cable from transmission case.
14. On synchromesh transmission equipped vehicles: Disconnect shift tube coupling at transmission shifter shaft.
   Disconnect clutch return spring, then disconnect clutch rod from clutch cross shaft.
   If so equipped, disconnect back up lamp switch from 4-speed transmission.
15. Remove 3/8" bolt from bottom of skid plate then place engine lift, with Tool J-7894 attached, under engine and support weight of engine.
16. Remove nuts from engine rear mount, then remove bolts attaching front mount bracket to transmission case.
   CAUTION: Do not loose spacer on synchromesh transmission equipped vehicles. Spacer is located on right bolt between transmission case and front mount bracket.
17. Slowly lower power train being sure all disconnects have

Rear Strut Rod Lowered

been made and checking for interference, then remove power train from under vehicle.

18. Remove exhaust pipe and muffler as an assembly.
19. Remove transaxle (and clutch) as follows:

Rear Axle Disconnected

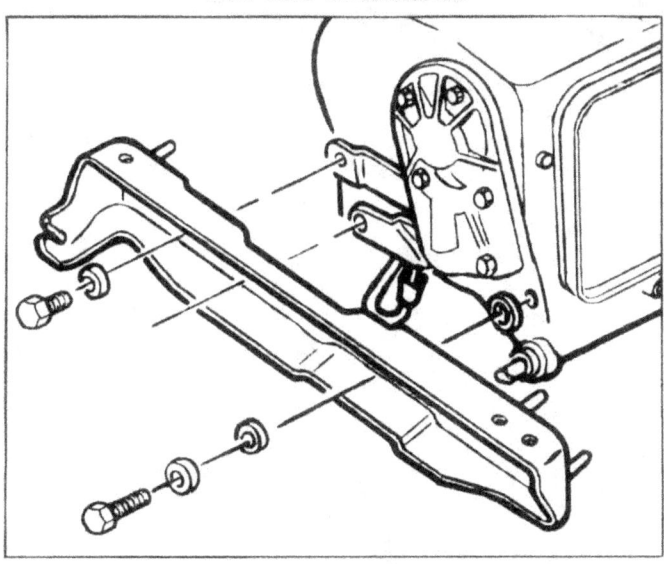

Front Mount Bracket Bolts

SYNCHROMESH

   a. Using the engine lift, lower power train until transaxle rests on suitable blocks to support weight of transaxle.
   b. Disconnect starter wiring and remove starter.

c. Remove the two bolts securing the clutch rod dust seal assembly, then remove the pin attaching the rod to the clutch fork.
   d. Separate the transaxle from the engine by removing the attaching bolts securing the differential carrier to the flywheel housing. Pull engine away horizontally.
   e. Loosen clutch mounting bolts a turn at a time (to prevent distortion of clutch cover) until the spring pressure is released. Remove all bolts, clutch disc and pressure plate assembly.

AUTOMATIC
   a. Drain transmission by disconnecting transmission filler tube.
   b. Disconnect hose from vacuum modulator.
   c. Disconnect starter wiring and remove starter.
   d. Disconnect the converter from the engine flex plate by removing the three attaching bolts through the access hole at the 12 o'clock position in the converter housing. The converter may be rotated by prying against the starter gear teeth on the converter housing with a screw driver.
   e. Using the engine lift, lower power train until transaxle rests on suitable blocks to support weight of transaxle.
   f. Separate the transaxle from the engine by removing the attaching bolts securing the differential carrier to the flywheel housing. Pull engine away horizontally.

Installation
1. Install transaxle (and clutch) on engine as follows:

SYNCHROMESH
   a. Install clutch on flywheel as outlined in Section 7.
   b. Position the engine (on engine lift) adjacent to the transaxle and with the clutch shaft in place in the transaxle align the clutch shaft to clutch splines and align the differential carrier and flywheel housing.
   c. Pilot the clutch shaft into the clutch and install all bolts securing transaxle to flywheel housing.
   d. Connect the clutch rod to the clutch fork with pin, then position and secure the clutch rod dust seal assembly to the clutch housing with two bolts.

AUTOMATIC
   a. Position the engine (on engine lift) adjacent to the transaxle and align the converter with the flex plate and align the differential carrier to the flywheel housing.
   b. Pilot the converter hub into crankshaft and install all bolts securing differential carrier to flywheel housing.
   c. Install converter-to-flex plate bolts through the access hole in the converter housing. The converter can be rotated to make the attaching points accessible by turning the converter with a screw driver against its starter gear teeth.

d. Install starter and connect wiring.
  e. Connect hose at vacuum modulator.
  f. Connect transmission filler tube.
2. Install exhaust pipe and muffler assembly.
3. Place power train under vehicle and raise into position.
4. Install bolts attaching front mount bracket to transmission case. Tighten bolts securely.

> **NOTE:** On synchromesh equipped vehicles be sure and install spacer between front mount bracket and transmission case.

5. Connect rear mount and install nuts and lock washers. Tighten nuts securely.
6. Remove engine lift and Tool J-7894 from under vehicle, then install ⅜" bolt in skid plate.
7. On synchromesh transmission equipped vehicles: Adjust and connect clutch rod and connect clutch return spring.

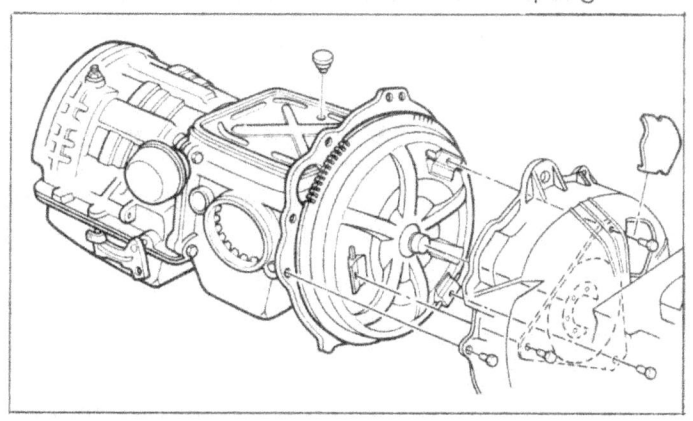

Transaxle Separated from Engine

Connect shift tube coupling at transmission shifter shaft.
8. On automatic transmission equipped vehicles, connect transmission shift cable.

> **NOTE:** Connect transmission shift cable by rotating throttle lever its full limit counterclockwise and inserting ball end of cable into transmission case until shoulder seats against transmission case, then lock in place with bolt.

9. Connect universal joints.
10. Connect left and right rear strut rod brackets to differential carrier.
11. Connect accelerator control rods at idler lever on transmission.
12. Connect heater hoses at elbows on left and right front shrouds.
13. Connect fuel line at flexible hose.
14. Install rear center shield and grille, then lower vehicle.

15. With vehicle sitting at curb height:
Check cam adjusters on outer end of rear rod and be sure they are in the same position as indexed, then tighten nut without turning bolt.
16. Connect the following electrical items:
If so equipped, radio ground straps at left and right engine shields.
Positive wire at ignition coil.
Cylinder head temperature and oil pressure indicator wire at quick disconnect.
Starter wiring at quick disconnect.
Battery positive cable at battery terminal and 10 gauge red wire at terminal on body side rail.
Battery negative cable at Delcotron bracket.
17. Install axle dip stick.
18. Lubricate groove of engine seal with liquid soap or silicone then connect seal.

NOTE: While guiding groove of seal on shield flange, (with one hand) press seal in place using block of wood or a hammer handle.

19. Connect heater hose at upper shroud, then install spare tire.
20. If necessary, fill engine with oil, fill transmission and fill axle.
21. Start engine, check for leaks and perform necessary adjustments.

10100 AND 10500 SERIES ENGINE TUNE-UP

All operations included herein will be performed on the vehicle. Illustrations depicting bench operations have been employed for convenience only and are intended only to clarify the operations which will be performed on the vehicle. Since it is impractical to illustrate all possible installations that may be encountered, only a typical installation will be used to illustrate the point in question.

Remove Spark Plugs
1. Remove spare tire.
2. Remove air cleaner assembly.
3. Disconnect spark plug wires at spark plugs.
4. Remove any foreign matter from around spark plugs by blowing out with compressed air then loosen all plugs one turn.
5. Start engine and accelerate to 1000 rpm to blow out loosened carbon.

NOTE: Clearing out carbon in this manner is important in preventing false compression readings due to chips of carbon being lodged under the valves.

6. Stop engine and remove spark plugs.

NOTE: A piece of 7/16 L.D. soft rubber or soft plastic tubing approximately 8" long may be used t o remove the spark plugs after they have been loosened.

Test Compression
1. Block throttle and choke in wide open position.
2. Hook up starter remote control cable and insert compression gauge firmly in spark plug port.

CAUTION: Whenever the engine is cranked remotely at the starter, with a special jumper cable or other means, the primary distributor lead must be disconnected from the negative post on the coil and the ignition switch must be in the "ON" position. Failure to do this will result in a damaged grounding circuit in the ignition switch.

NOTE: Unless special adapters are available, it will be necessary to remove carburetors to perform the compression test.

3. Crank engine through at least four compression strokes to obtain highest possible reading.

Clean and Inspect Spark Plugs

Inspect each plug individually for badly worn electrodes, glazed, broken or blistered porcelains and replace plugs where necessary. Refer to spark plug diagnosis information Section 6Y for an analysis of plug conditions. Use new spark plug gaskets with cleaned plugs.

Install Spark Plugs and Torque to Specifications
Service Ignition System
1. Replace brittle or damaged spark plug wires. Install all wires to proper spark plug.
2. Tighten all ignition system connections.
3. Replace or repair any wires that are frayed, loose or damaged.
4. Remove distributor cap, rotor, and dust shield. Clean cap and inspect for cracks, carbon tracks and burned or corroded terminals. Replace cap where necessary.
5. Clean rotor and inspect for damage or deterioration. Replace rotor where necessary.
6. Check the distributor centrifugal advance mechanism by turning the distributor cam to see if the springs return it to its retarded position. If the cam does not return readily, the distributor must be disassembled and the cause of the trouble corrected.
7. Check to see that the vacuum spark control operates freely by turning the movable breaker plate to see if the spring returns it to the retarded position. Any stiffness in the operation of the vacuum spark control will affect the ignition timing. Correct any interference or binding condition noted.
8. Examine distributor points and clean or replace if necessary.
    Contact points with an overall gray color and only slight roughness or pitting need not be replaced.
    Dirty points should be cleaned with a clean point file.
    Use only a few strokes of a clean, fine-cut contact file. The file should not be used on other metals and should not be allowed to become greasy or dirty. Never use emery cloth or sandpaper to clean contact points since particles will embed and cause arcing and rapid burning of points. Do not attempt to remove all roughness nor dress the point surfaces down smooth. Merely remove scale or dirt.
    Replace points that are burned or badly pitted.
9. Clean cam lobe with cleaning solvent, lubricate cam lobe with "Delco Remy Cam and Ball Bearing Lubricant" or its equivalent and rotate cam lubricator wick ½ turn.

    NOTE: Where prematurely burned or badly pitted points are encountered, the ignition system and engine should be checked to determine the cause of trouble so it can be eliminated. Unless the condition causing point burning or pitting is corrected, new points will provide no better service than the old points. Refer to Section 6Y for an analysis of point burning or pitting.

10. Adjust distributor contact point gap to .019" (new points) or .016" (used points), using a feeler gauge or dial indicator. Breaker arm rubbing block should be on extreme top of cam lobe during adjustment.

NOTE: If contact points have been in service they should be cleaned before adjusting with a feeler gauge.

Check alignment of distributor points with points closed. Align new points where necessary, but do not attempt to align used points. Instead, replace used points where serious misalignment is observed.

If necessary, align points by bending fixed contact support. Use an alignment tool if available. Do not bend breaker arm. After alignment, readjust point gap.

11. Make sure all distributor wire terminals are clean and tight.
12. Install dust shield, rotor and distributor cap. Press all wires firmly into cap towers.

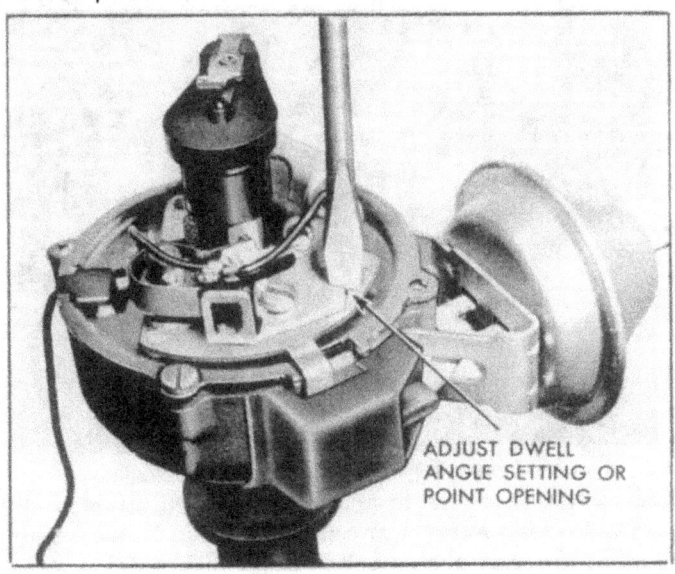

Point Adjustment

NOTE: Cap must be installed with notch to vacuum advance lever opening on housing.

Service Battery and Battery Cables

Inspect battery and cables and perform necessary service on these components. See Additional Checks and Adjustments for battery tests.

Inspect for signs of corrosion on battery, cables and surrounding area, loose or broken carriers, cracked or bulged cases, dirt and acid, electrolyte leakage and low electrolyte level. Fill cells to proper level with distilled water or water passed through a "demineralizer."

The top of the battery should be clean and the battery hold-down bolts properly tightened. Particular care should be taken to see that the tops of batteries are kept clean of acid film and dirt. For best results when cleaning batteries, wash first with a dilute

Blower Belt and Guide Adjustment

ammonia or soda solution to neutralize any acid present and then flush off with clean water. Care must be taken to keep vent plugs tight so that the neutralizing solution does not enter the cell. The hold-down bolts should be kept tight enough to prevent the battery from shaking around in the holder, but they should not be tightened to the point where the battery case will be placed under a severe strain.

To insure good contact, the battery cables should be tight on the battery posts and fully bottomed. To remove or install spring type cable clamps, a suitable pliers must be used to spread the ends of the clamps. Oil battery terminal felt washer. If the battery posts or cable terminals are corroded, the cables should be cleaned separately with a soda solution and a wire brush. It is NOT recommended that the battery posts and cable clambs be greased prior to installing cables to battery as this may contribute to slippage of the clamps from the battery posts.

If battery has remained undercharged, check for loose (worn) blower belt, defective Delcotron, high resistance in the charging circuit, exidized regulator contact points, or a low voltage setting.

If the battery has been using too much water the voltage output (regulator setting) of the Delcotron is too high.

Service Blower Belt and Delcotron
1. Inspect blower belt condition and check deflection of belt.
   If belt damage is noted, replace the belt. A slightly damaged belt must be replaced to prevent premature failure. Install blower belt over pulleys (Delcotron pulley last).
2. Adjust blower belt and guides as follows:
   Place a 1/16" shim between belt and rear guide, then using a bar and a strand tension gauge adjust blower belt. Fifty-five lbs. ± 5 lbs. (used belt), 75 lbs. ± 5 lbs. (new belt) and tighten securely.
   Remove shim from between blower belt and rear guide and using shim as a gauge adjust upper guide and tighten securely.

CARBURETOR SYNCHRONIZATION

1. Disconnect accelerator control rod swivel at cross shaft lever and connect accelerator pull back spring to swivel hole in cross shaft lever "A".

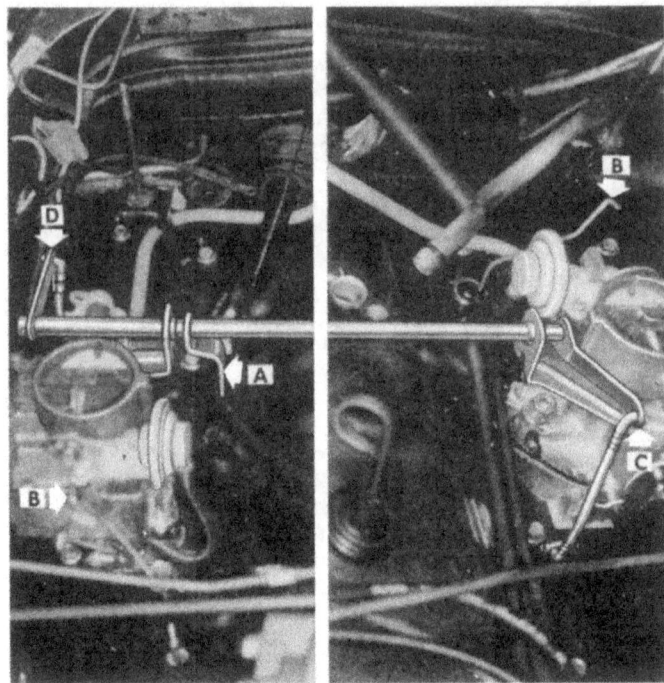

Carburetor Linkage

2. Disconnect choke rods at choke shaft levers on both carburetors and open choke valves "B", then tighten carburetor hold down nuts.
3. Back idle screws away from throttle shaft levers on both carburetors (2½ turns should be sufficient) to leave clearance between the throttle shaft levers and idle screws.
4. Disconnect throttle rod from cross shaft lever on R/H carburetor "C".

   NOTE: A strip of paper approximately ⅜" wide and 8" long should be used in the following step. Feeler gauge stock will not provide a SENSITIVE feel and should not be used.

5. Set idle screw on L/H carburetor by placing strip of paper between idle screw and throttle shaft lever and turning screw in until a firm drag is felt on the paper. Turn idle screw in 1½ additional turns.

   NOTE: This will give an initial idle speed of 500-600 rpm.

6. Connect throttle rod to cross shaft lever on R/H carburetor

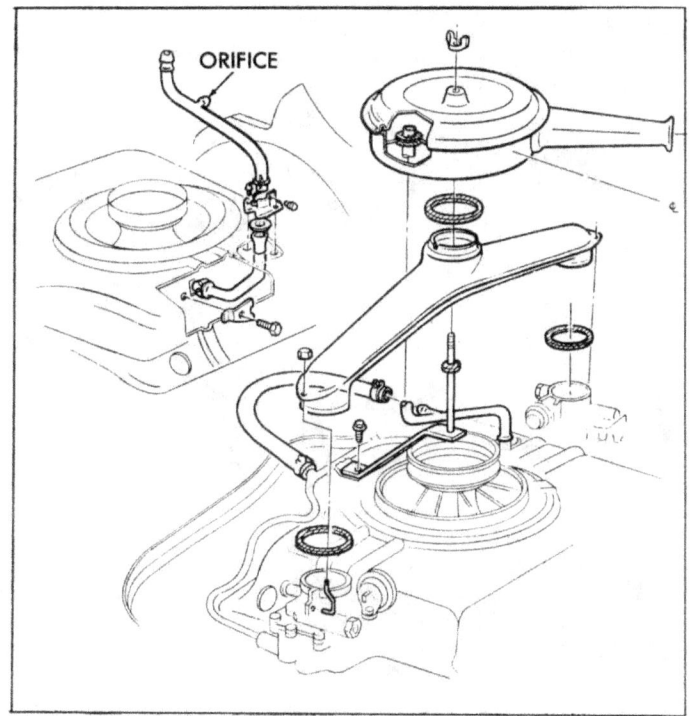

Crankcase Ventilation

and disconnect throttle rod from cross shaft lever on L/H carburetor "D".

7. Set idle screw on R/H carburetor in the same manner as L/H carburetor.

8. Adjust throttle rod on L/H carburetor by holding up on rod (so throttle shaft lever is against idle screw) and turning rod in lower swivel until rod freely enters hole in cross shaft lever.

9. Connect throttle rod on L/H carburetor to cross shaft lever.

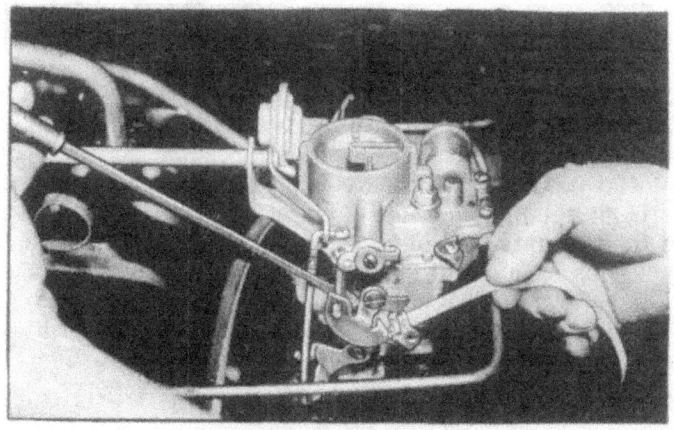

Adjusting Idle Speed Screw

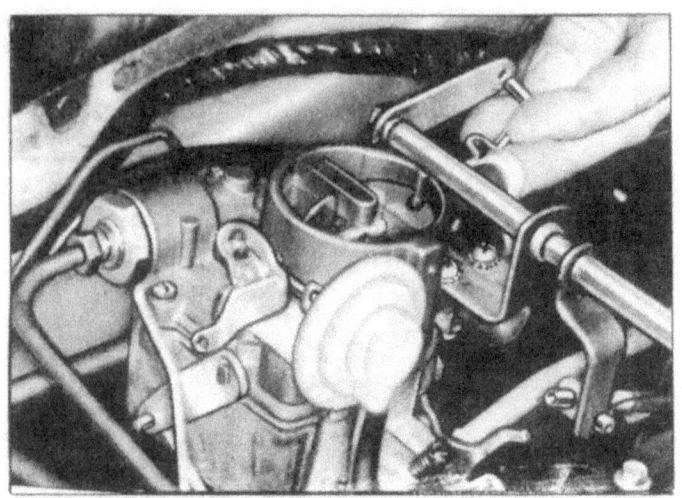

Adjusting Throttle Rod

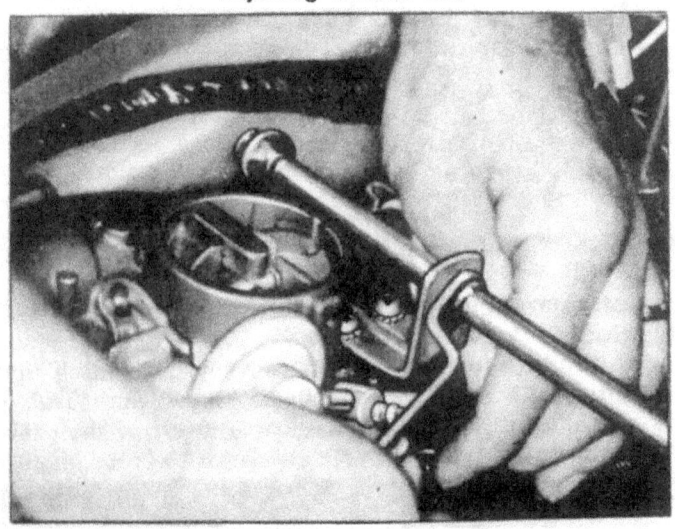

Adjusting Accelerator Rod

10. Remove accelerator pull back spring from cross shaft lever, hold cross shaft lever in the full throttle position and pull accelerator control rod rearward (on vehicles equipped with Powerglide, pull through detent), and adjust swivel on accelerator control rod until it freely enters hole in cross shaft lever. Then connect swivel and pull back spring and be sure carburetors return to idle position (idle screws against throttle levers).

11. Turn idle mixture screws on both carburetors lightly to its seat and back out 1½ turns.

INSTRUMENT CHECK-OUT

Instrument Hook-Up
1. Remove distributor vacuum advance hose from R/H carburetor spark port tube and plastic cap from L/H carburetor spark port tube.
2. Connect vacuum gauge, dwell meter, tachometer and timing light.

> **NOTE:** The vacuum gauge must be connected to both carburetor spark port tubes. A windshield washer tee makes this possible.

Ignition Dwell
1. Start engine and check ignition dwell.
   If dwell is not within specifications, recheck point gap, check for wrong point assembly, defective or misaligned point, worn rubbing block or worn distributor cam.
2. Check dwell variation.
   Slowly accelerate engine to 1500 rpm and note dwell reading. Return engine to idle and note dwell reading. If dwell variation exceeds specifications, check for worn distributor shaft, worn distributor shaft bushing or loose breaker plate.

> **CAUTION:** Accelerate engine at accelerator rod only. Do not open throttle by grasping other portions of linkage.

Set Ignition Timing
1. Adjust timing as required by loosening distributor clamp bolt and rotating distributor body until specified timing is indicated at tab, then tighten distributor clamp bolt.

> **NOTE:** Timing should be advanced as far as possible (within specifications) unless detonation (spark-knock) occurs.

2. Check operation of centrifugal advance mechanism by accelerating engine and watching clockwise (advance) movement of timing mark.

Check Carburetor Synchronization as Follows:
1. Accelerate engine 1100 to 1200 rpm and hold steady.

> **NOTE:** A tool to hold engine rpm steady may be manufactured with a small turn buckle and hooks. When this tool is installed between the accelerator rod and fuel line the rpm can be adjusted by turning turnbuckle.

2. With rpm set to 1100 to 1200 and steady, note vacuum reading. Pinch shut vacuum gauge hose to R/H carburetor and note vacuum reading. If vacuum decreases, return engine to idle and lengthen throttle rod (one turn) on L/H carburetor, then recheck.
   If vacuum increases, return engine to idle and shorten throttle rod (one turn) on L/H carburetor, then recheck.
   If vacuum remains steady ($\pm 1''$) open hose to R/H carburetor

and pinch shut vacuum gauge hose to L/H carburetor. Vacuum should remain steady ($\pm 1''$).
3. Disconnect vacuum gauge from spark port tubes and reinstall distributor vacuum advance hose on R/H carburetor and plastic cap on L/H carburetor.

Vacuum Advance
Check operation of vacuum advance by accelerating engine and watching movement of vacuum advance arm.

Idle Speed and Mixture Adjustment
1. Disconnect choke diaphragm hoses from both carburetor bases and connect vacuum gauge at these locations.
2. Adjust idle speed (duplicate adjustment on both carburetors) to obtain specified engine idle.
3. Adjust idle mixture screws on both carburetors to obtain peak, steady vacuum at specified idle speed.

Adjust Fast Idle Cam Clearance
1. Stop engine.
2. With throttle lever on next to the highest step of fast idle cam, bend tang to obtain .078" clearance between idle speed screw and throttle lever.

Adjust Vacuum Diaphragm
1. Hold choke valve closed with a rubber band.
2. Hold vacuum diaphragm arm squarely against diaphragm.
3. Measure clearance between lower edge of choke valve and wall of bowl cover. Clearance should be .180" to .195".
4. If necessary to adjust, disconnect and bend diaphragm link.
5. At this setting, throttle lever fast idle tang should rest on next to the highest step of fast idle cam. If not, adjust by bending outer choke shaft lever tang.

Adjust Vapor Vent
The vent should just start opening when idle screw is on high step of fast idle cam. The valve will then be open at idle setting. If necessary, adjust by bending throttle lever tang.

NOTE: It is hard to see this valve when carburetor is installed. A mirror will aid in making this adjustment.

Adjust Choke
Hold choke valve closed and, while holding the control rod up against the stop in choke thermostat bracket, adjust upper choke control rod until it freely enters hole in choke shaft lever, then lengthen rod two turns and connect.

CAUTION: To minimize the possibility of deforming the control rod while adjusting, always turn the vertical portion. Do not "crank" the rod using offset portion.

Adjust Choke Unloader

Check unloader adjustment by holding throttle valve in wide open position and insert a .312" wire gauge between choke valve lower edge and wall of bowl cover. To adjust, if necessary, bend tang on throttle lever.

Final Adjustment
1. Install air cleaner assembly.
2. Start engine, and if necessary, readjust carburetor idle speed and mixture.
3. Shut engine off, remove instruments, then connect choke vacuum hoses, and install spare tire.

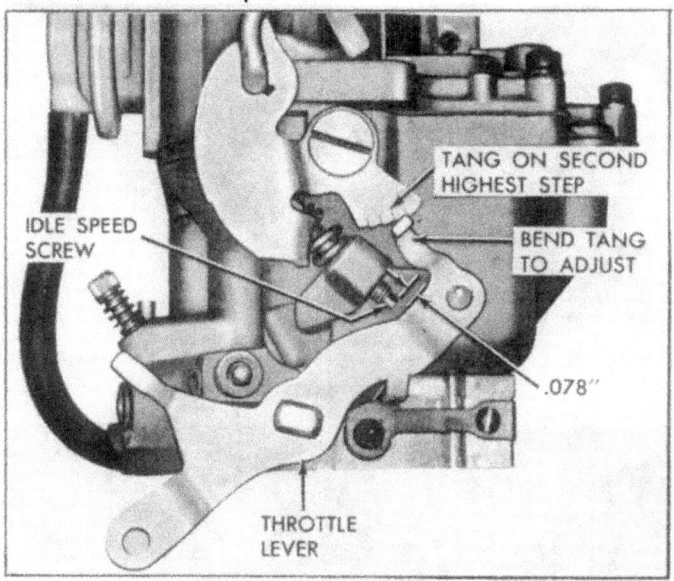

Fast Idle Cam Adjustment

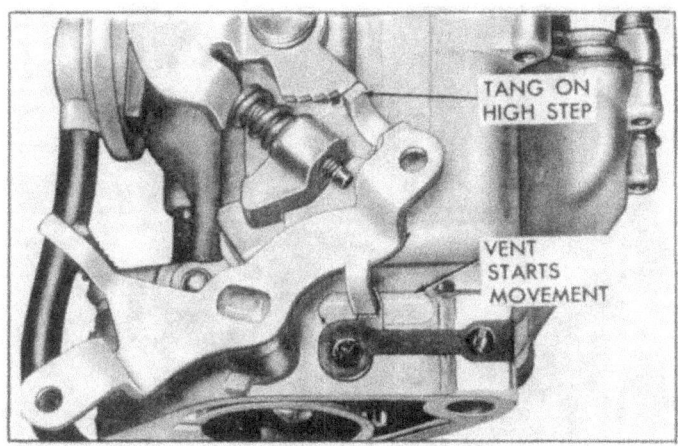

Vapor Vent Adjustment

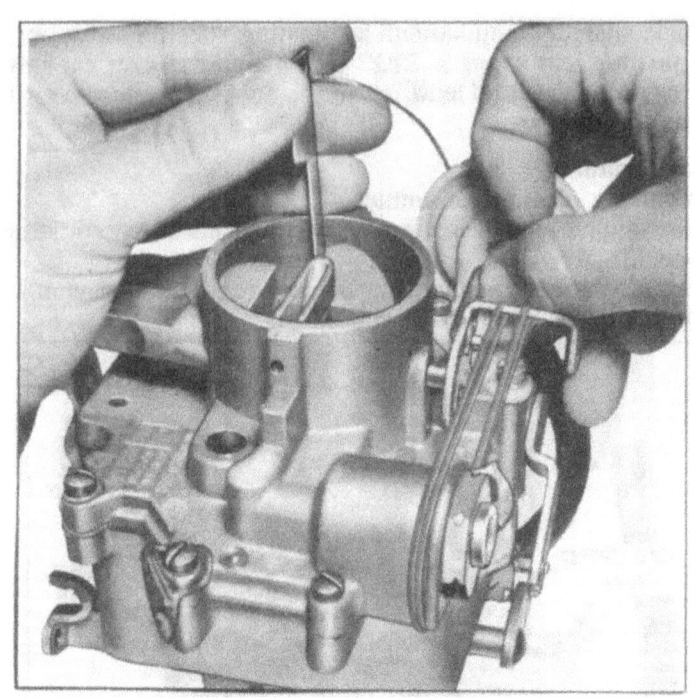

Vacuum Diaphragm Adjustment

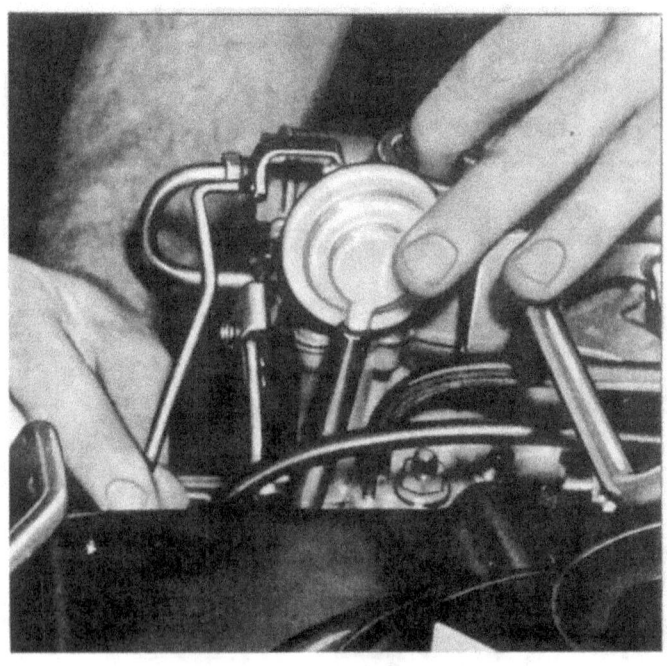

Choke Control Rod Adjustment

10700 SERIES AND R.P.O. L63
(4x1 CARBURETORS)

Corsa Engine (4 x 1 Carburetor)

The special hi-performance engine used on the Corvair 10700 series and optional on the 10100 and 10500 series Corvair has larger exhaust manifolds, a special camshaft and cylinder head with larger valves, larger exhaust port tubes and larger intake manifolds with cast mounting pads for four single barrel carburetors. The engine also has special piston rings and crankshaft (same as turbocharged engine) and a 12 plate oil cooler.

Service and repair procedures remain basically the same as for the 10100 and 10500 series Corvair, except for the service procedures outlined.

TUNE-UP

Tune-up procedures for the 10700 series Corvair engine (4x1 carburetors) are the same as outlined for the 10100 and 10500 series Corvair engine except for the mechanical carburetor synchronization.

Carburetor Synchronization

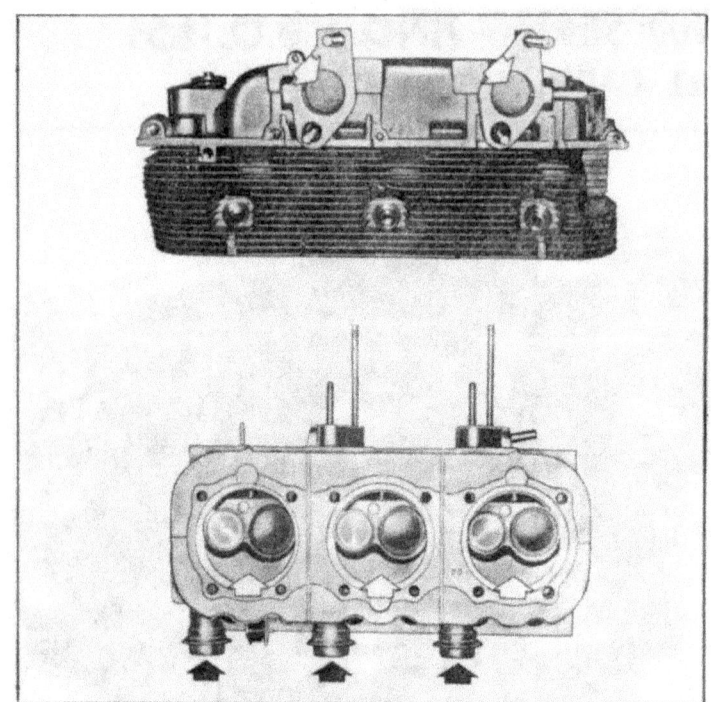

Cylinder Head

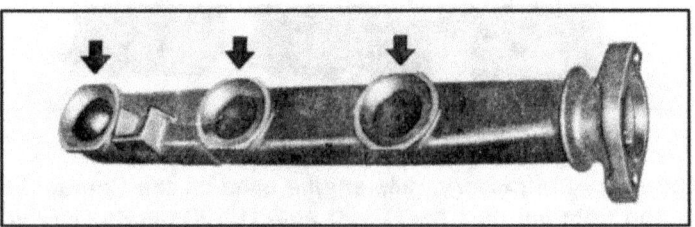

Exhaust Manifold

1. Synchronize the primary carburetors as outlined under Carburetor Synchronization, Mechanical Adjustments in Engine Tune-Up for the 10100 and 10500 series Corvair.

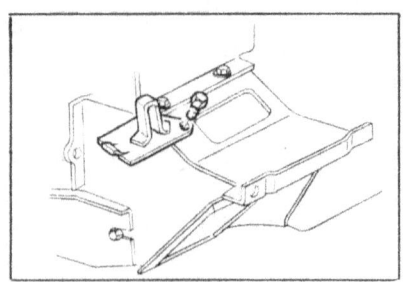

Air Circulating Plate

2. Disconnect left and right secondary carburetor actuating rods at the cross-shaft levers.

3. Disconnect the accelerator return spring and rotate accelerator control lever on cross-shaft until primary carburetors are at full throttle position.

> **CAUTION:** Do not actuate cross-shaft at any linkage point other than the accelerator control lever on the cross-shaft. To do so may disturb primary carburetor synchronization.

4. While holding primary carburetors at full throttle position, position left secondary carburetors at full throttle position, then adjust actuating rod by turning rod in swivel until rod will just enter front of slot in cross-shaft lever.

5. Repeat above step for the right secondary carburetor.

6. Return primary carburetors to the idle position, then connect left and right secondary carburetor actuating rods at the cross-shaft levers.

7. Slowly rotate cross-shaft towards full throttle position, checking for simultaneous engagement of the secondary carburetor actuating rods.

8. Continue to rotate cross-shaft to full throttle position checking that all carburetors reach full throttle position simultaneously.

AIR CIRCULATING PLATE

Air circulating plate (left side only); removed in winter—installed in summer.

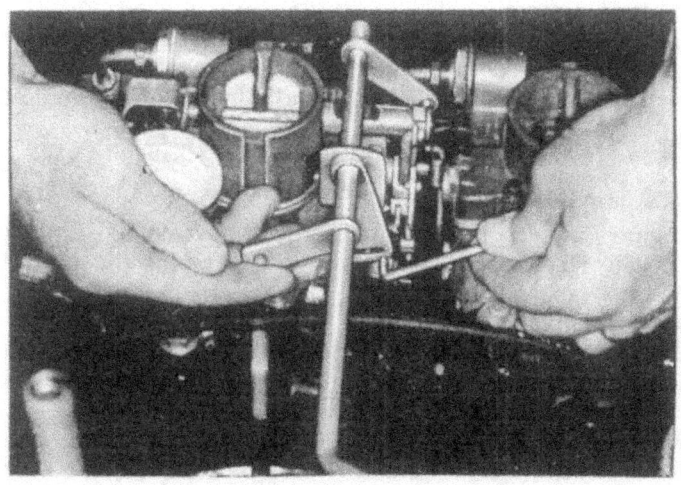

Synchronization of Secondary Carburetor

CORVAIR WITH TURBOCHARGER

The optional turbocharged engine for the 10700 series Corvair has external changes to provide for mounting the Turbocharger and internal changes for the increased power. THE TURBOCHARGER UNIT SHOULD NEVER BE REMOVED FROM THIS SPECIAL ENGINE TO BE INSTALLED ON ANOTHER CORVAIR ENGINE.

Internal changes include the following:
Piston rings and crankshaft.
Cylinder heads.
  a. L.H. includes sending unit (Thermister), for head temperature gauge
  b. R.H. includes Turbocharger oil drain.
  c. 8:1 compression ratio.

External changes include the following:
12 plate oil cooler.
Single side draft Carter YH carburetor.
Fuel lines and routing.
Distributor assembly and timing tab.
Front and right side seal shield revised to bring exhaust pipes to Turbocharger.
R.H. heater duct revised for exhaust pipe clearance.
Exhaust pipes and muffler.
Front shield material (heat resistant) on right side and heat insulator material around exhaust pipes.
Wiring harness changed to include heat indicator and warning buzzer system.
Engine rear housing gasket and oil filter adapter changed to provide oil feed to the Turbocharger.
Air recirculation—same as air conditioned Corvair vehicles.

SERVICE OPERATIONS

ENGINE TUNE-UP

Engine Tune-up remains basically the same as outlined for the Corvair 10100 and 10500 series except for the procedures outlined.

Accelerator Linkage Adjustment

This adjustment must be performed with the engine at operating temperature or with air cleaner off to block choke valve open (engine stopped).
1. Disconnect accelerator rod swivel (3) from crossshaft lever (4).
2. Check throttle lever to see that it is against idle speed screw, then check to see that linkage angle "X" is approximately 126° as shown. Adjust this angle by lengthening or shortening rod (1).
3. Pull accelerator rod (5) rearward against bellcrank stop on transmission and rotate lever (4) to full throttle position (throttle lever on carburetor will rest against stop boss on flange).

Turbocharged Engine (Installed)

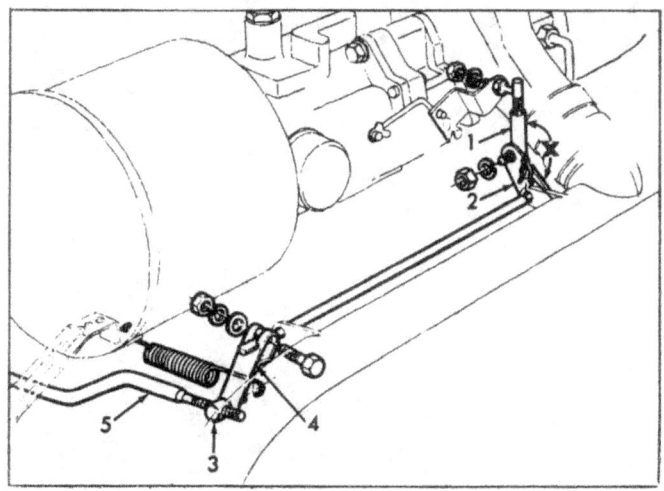

Accelerator Linkage

4. Adjust swivel (3) to just enter the hole in lever (4), then connect swivel to lever and install retaining clips.
   NOTE: It is better for swivel pin to be just short of lever hole than just past, or linkage may be bent.
5. Move accelerator rod from idle to full throttle and check to see that the throttle lever on carburetor goes to full throttle and back to idle with no bind.

Idle Speed and Mixture Adjustment

1. Start engine and bring to operating temperature.
2. Stop the engine and perform following preliminary adjustments:
    a. Back idle speed screw away from throttle lever, then adjust in until the throttle valve is slightly open.
    b. Turn idle mixture screw lightly to its seat and back out 3/4 turn.
    c. Attach tachometer at coil and vacuum gauge at manifold connection for distributor.
3. Make sure the fast idle linkage is off fast idle. This can be determined by removing air cleaner and looking at choke valve. It should be wide open.
4. Start engine and adjust idle speed screw to obtain speed of 850 rpm, then adjust mixture screw and speed screw (alternately as needed) to obtain the highest steady vacuum at 850 rpm.
5. Stop engine, disconnect instruments and reconnect distributor pressure retard hose.

Ignition Timing

Automatic Choke Adjustment

The automatic choke setting is index and accomplished by loosening three choke coil housing retaining screws and rotating (by hand) the housing; then hold in position and tighten the screws.

Adjust Ignition Timing
1. Connect tachometer and timing light to engine.
2. Start engine and adjust idle (if necessary) to 850 rpm (with engine at operating temperature).
3. Aim timing light at timing tab above crankshaft pulley and adjust timing to 24° advance by turning distributor the same manner as on regular Corvair engine.

> **CAUTION:** Under no conditions should the timing be set more than 24° advance.

> **NOTE:** It is necessary to disconnect the spark advance hose and block the vacuum port on this engine.

4. Stop engine and disconnect test instruments.

UPPER SHROUD
Upper shroud removal requires removal of Turbocharger, turbine inlet and exhaust piping, turbocharger oil lines, and diffuser tube as outlined. Shroud may then be removed in the same manner as outlined for 10100 and 10500 series.

LEFT SHIELD
Left shield is removed as outlined for 10100 and 10500 series, after removal of fuel filter and disconnection of manifold pressure line.

RIGHT SHIELD
Right shield is removed as outlined for 10100 and 10500 series after removing exhaust insulator plate screws and sliding the plate upward ½" to 1" clearance.

FRONT SHIELD
Front shield is removed as outlined for 10100 and 10500 series, after removal of Turbocharger assembly, (including carburetor and air cleaner) and removal of the fuel filter.

AIR CIRCULATING PLATES
Air circulating plate (left side only); removed in winter—installed in summer.

ROCHESTER HV CARBURETORS

This section covers the two identical Rochester HV Carburetors used on Corvair 10100 and 10500 series and also used as primary carburetors on the Corvair 10700 series (4x1 Carburetors). For Carburetor Synchronization, Idle Speed and Mixture Adjustment and Choke Adjustment refer to Engine Tune-Up.

Additional Checks and Adjustments

The following checks and adjustments may be made without removing the carburetor from the vehicle. Refer to Repair Procedures, Assembly and Adjustments.

Float Adjustments.
Pump Rod Adjustment
Vacuum Break Adjustment
Choke Unloader Adjustment

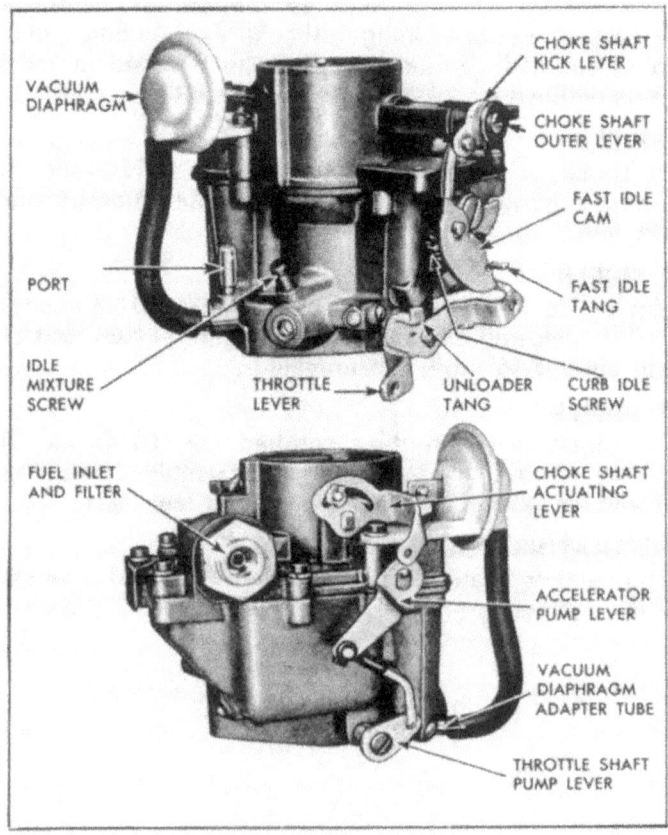

Rochester HV Carburetor

Fast Idle Cam Adjustment
Vapor Vent Adjustment

Choke Coil Replacement

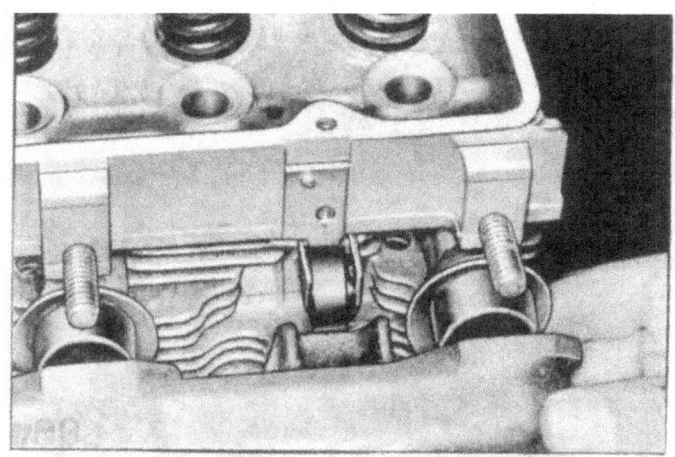

Choke Coil Mounting

1. Disconnect and remove upper choke control rod.
2. Remove engine lower shroud as outlined in Section 6.
3. Using a sharp chisel and hammer, with light blows, (hard blows will snap head off rivet), tap head of twist rivet in a counter-clockwise direction until rivet starts out.
4. Grip head of twist rivet with vise-grip pliers and remove by turning counter-clockwise.
5. Remove choke coil and control rod assembly from cylinder head.
6. Remove control rod from choke coil and install in new choke coil.
7. Position choke coil and control rod assembly in cylinder head and tap twist rivet in place with a hammer.
8. Install lower shroud as outlined.
9. Install, adjust and connect upper choke control rod as outlined in Engine Tune-Up.

Removal

1. Remove air cleaner assembly.
2. Disconnect choke control rod at each carburetor choke shaft lever.
3. Disconnect accelerator return spring and accelerator rod. Disconnect carburetor rods at carburetor throttle levers.
4. Remove all cross-shaft retainer screws and remove cross-shaft assembly.
5. Disconnect gas inlet line from carburetors.
6. Remove two nuts and washers attaching carburetor to intake manifold studs.
7. Remove vacuum advance hose from right carburetor.
8. Remove carburetor from the mounting studs.

Disassembly

　　CAUTION: A power enrichment circuit has been added to the

1965 Rochester HV carburetor and care should be taken not to loose the power enrichment needle valve (located under venturi cluster) during carburetor disassembly.

1. Detach clip attaching pump rod to pump lever, remove clip and detach rod from pump lever.
2. Remove fuel inlet nut and gasket and remove filter element and spring.
3. Remove choke trip lever attaching screw and levers from choke shaft.

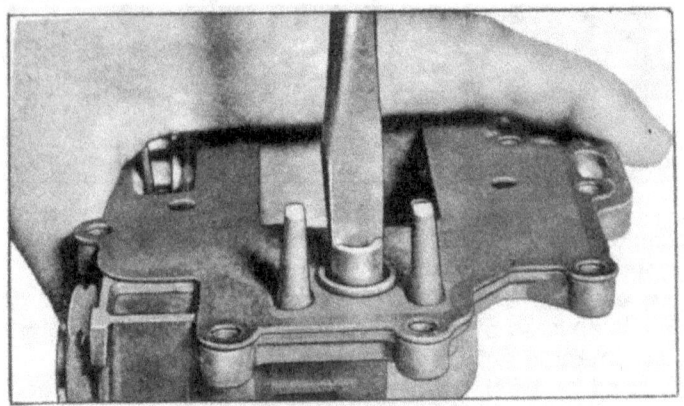

Removing Needle Seat

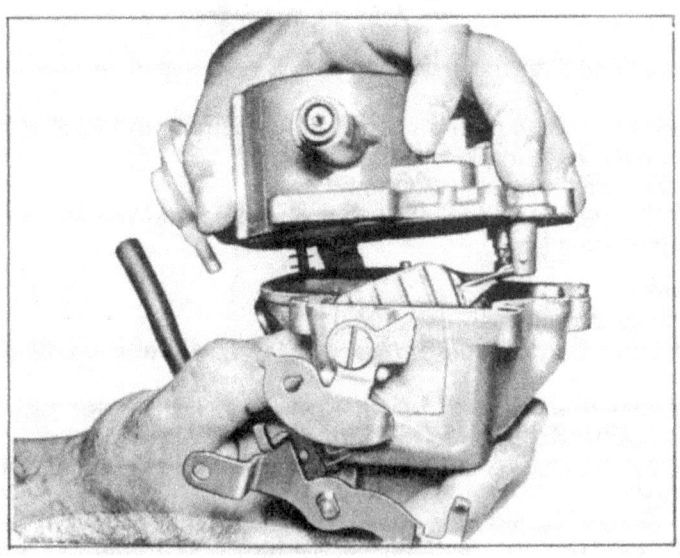

Removing Bowl Cover

4. Remove bowl cover attaching screws then remove cover assembly.
5. Remove vacuum diaphragm assembly by rotating assembly to align notch and free it from link.

6. Remove pin attaching floats to bowl cover assembly and check floats for damage.
7. Lift out float needle. Check seat for dirt or corrosion.
8. If necessary, needle seat and gasket may be removed by using a large size screw driver. It may then be cleaned or replaced as needed.
9. Accelerator pump may be removed if necessary. Remove clip and pump. Remove shaft and lever, if desired, by removing clip, shaft and lever.

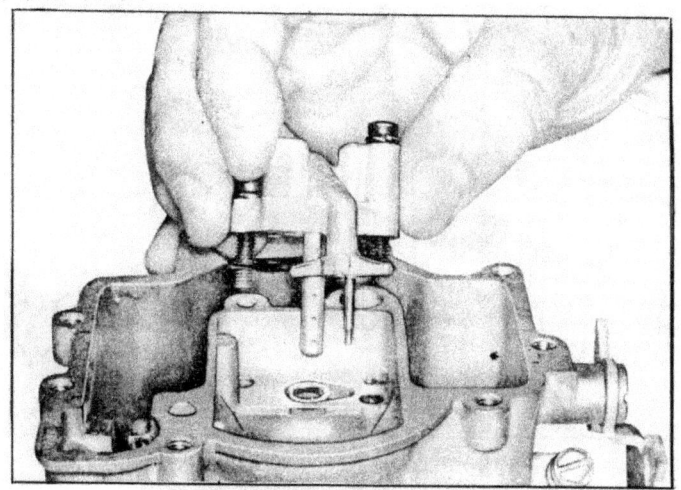

Removing Venturi Cluster

10. Remove the two screws and lock washers attaching venturi cluster to the bowl assembly and lift out the cluster, gasket and main well insert.
11. Remove the pump discharge needle valve and power enrichment needle valve.
12. Remove the idle mixture adjusting needle and spring. Remove main metering jet.
13. Remove vapor vent assembly.
14. If necessary, remove two choke valve retaining screws and slide choke valve out of choke shaft. Remove choke shaft from carburetor bowl cover.
15. Remove fast idle cam.
16. If necessary, invert carburetor bowl and remove throttle valve retaining screws and remove throttle valve and shaft assembly.

Cleaning and Inspection

Dirt, gum, water or carbon contamination in the carburetor or on the exterior moving parts are often responsible for unsatisfactory performance. For this reason, efficient carburetion depends upon careful cleaning and inspection while servicing.
1. Thoroughly clean carburetor castings and metal parts in clean

cleaning solvent.

CAUTION: Pump plunger and gaskets should never be immersed in carburetor cleaner.

2. Blow out all passages in castings, dry with compressed air and blow out all parts until they are dry.

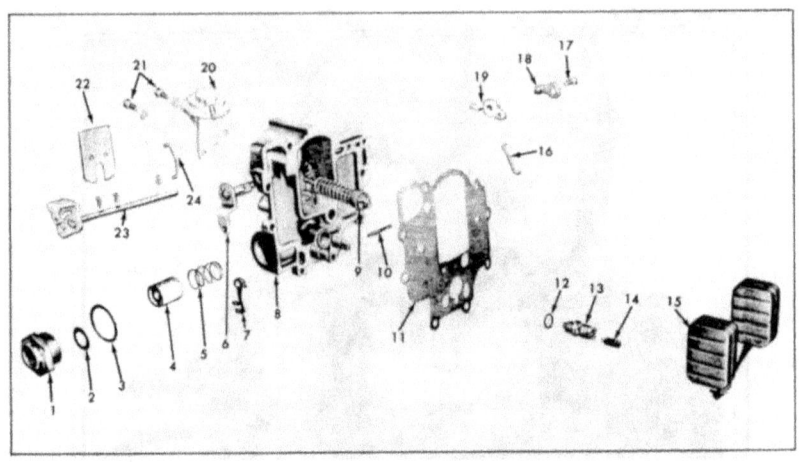

Bowl Cover—Exploded View

1. Inlet Nut
2. Fuel Filter Gasket
3. Inlet Nut Gasket
4. Fuel Filter Element
5. Fuel Filter Spring
6. Accelerator Pump Lever and Shaft
7. Clip
8. Bowl Cover
9. Accelerator Pump
10. Float Pin
11. Bowl Cover Gasket
12. Needle Seat Gasket
13. Needle Seat
14. Needle
15. Float Assembly
16. Fast Idle Rod
17. Choke Shaft Lever Screw
18. Choke Shaft Outer Lever
19. Choke Shaft Kick Lever
20. Vacuum Diaphragm
21. Retainer Screws
22. Choke Valve
23. Choke Shaft and Lever Assembly
24. Diaphragm Link

Make sure all jets and passages are clean. Do not use wires or drills for cleaning fuel passages or air bleeds.

3. Check all parts for wear. If wear is noted, defective parts must be replaced.

NOTE ESPECIALLY THE FOLLOWING:

A. Check float needle and seat for wear. If wear is noted the assembly must be replaced.

B. Check float hinge pin for wear and float for dents or distortion. Check floats for fuel leaks by shaking.

C. Check throttle shaft for water and out-of-round in the throttle body section of the bowl casting.

D. Inspect idle adjusting needles for burrs or grooves and misalignment. Such a condition requires replacement.

E. Inspect pump plunger rubber; replace pump if damaged

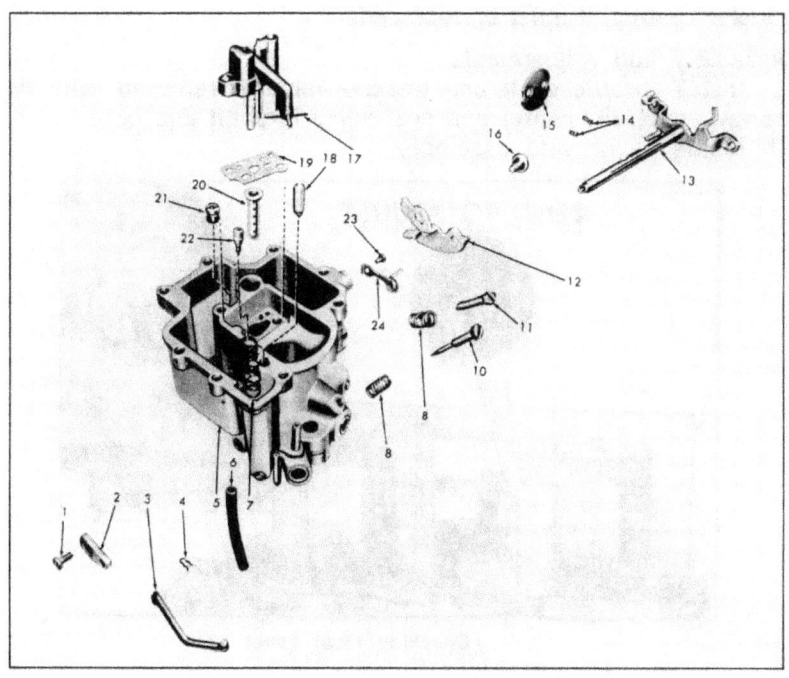

Carburetor Body—Exploded View

or worn.
F. Inspect pump well in fuel bowl for wear or being scored.
G. Check that main well nozzle and idle tube is not bent. Should be exactly 90° from cluster.
H. Check choke shaft for wear and choke valve for nicks.
I. Inspect pump discharge needle and power enrichment needle for wear, burrs or grooves.

4. Inspect gaskets to see if they appear hard or brittle or if the edges are torn or distorted. If any such condition is noted they must be replaced.
5. Check filter element for dirt or lint. Clean and if it is distorted or remains plugged, replace.
6. If for any reason parts have become loose or damaged in the cluster casting, it must be replaced.

Assembly and Adjustments
1. Install throttle shaft and throttle valve, if removed, with two screws, carefully center and seat valve in shaft and bore.
2. Install vapor vent assembly.

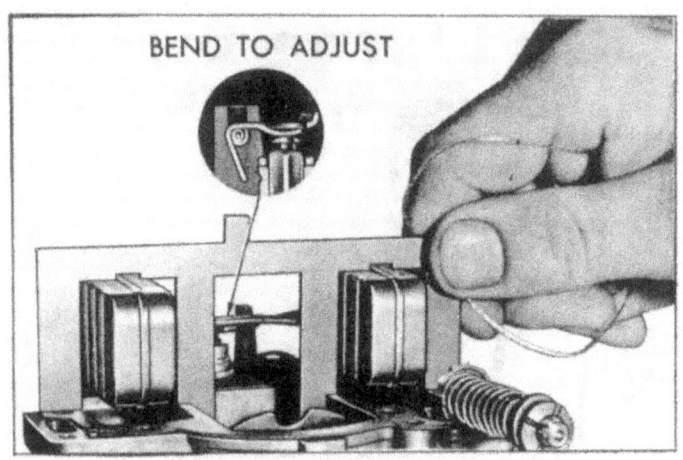

Checking Float Level

3. Install power valve and main well insert, then install venturi cluster and gasket bowl assembly, and install the two screws and lock washers.
4. If accelerator pump has been removed, replace pump assembly and install clip.

   NOTE: Be sure that the pump return spring is in place in bowl assembly.
5. Install pump discharge needle.
6. Install choke valve, choke kick lever and outer lever cam. Retain choke valve with two screws. (Choke shaft assembly should rotate freely without binds).
7. Install float needle seat if previously removed from bowl cover.
8. Carefully replace float needle.
9. Install a new gasket and replace float and pin. Check float level and float drop with Tool J-21614 as follows:
10. **Check float level and float drop with Tool J-21614 as follows:**
    Invert the cover on a flat surface. Place float level tool in Chain Gauge Set J-21614 over float.
    Bend tang located just above the float needle until each float

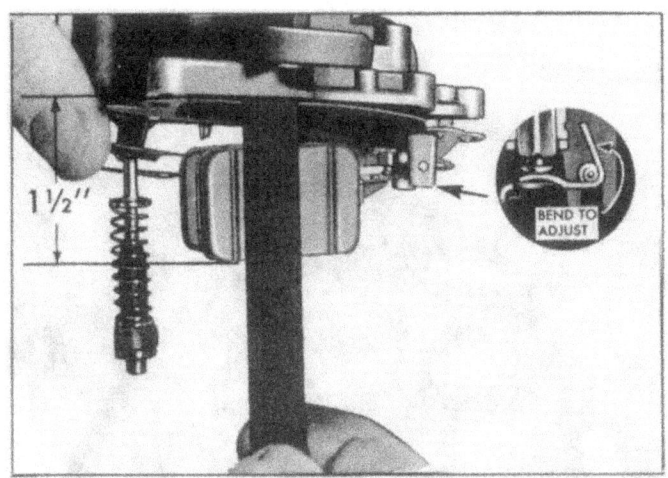

Measuring Float Drop

just touches the top of the gauge. Move gauge fore and aft to check that the floats are parallel within 1/32 to the bowl cover. Carefully bend float arms horizontally until floats are centered between the gauge legs. Tilt the assembly each way to check that the floats do not touch or rub gauge legs. Recheck float level if alignment is necessary. The float level dimension (top of float to gasket) should be 1-13/64 if measured without the gauge.

Hold bowl cover in an upright position and measure the distance from the gasket to the bottom of the float. This dimension should be 1½". Bend the tang at the end of the float hinge arm to obtain the correct drop, recheck setting after this adjustment.

NOTE: Float gauge can be indexed at the 1½" point as a permanent gauge.

11. Carefully place bowl cover assembly and new gasket on bowl assembly and install the six screws and lock washers.
12. Replace filter spring, filter gasket, gasket and inlet nut.
13. Install pump rod in pump lever and retain with clip.
14. **Adjust Pump Rod as follows:**
    Back off curb and fast idle screws until throttle valve is completely closed.
    Holding throttle valves closed, check to see that the scribe mark on the accelerator pump lever is aligned with the raised cast tang (front edge) on the bowl cover.
    The accelerator pump rod may be carefully bent, using a carburetor rod bending, such as Tool J-4552, to obtain the correct adjustment.
15. **Adjust Vacuum Break as follows:**
    Hold vacuum break arm in against diaphragm.
    Measure clearance between lower edge of choke valve and wall

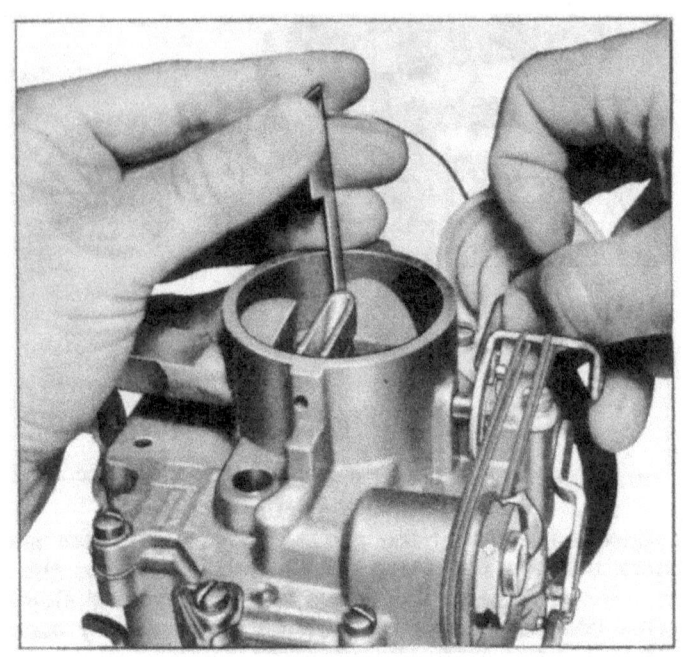

Vacuum Diaphragm Adjustment

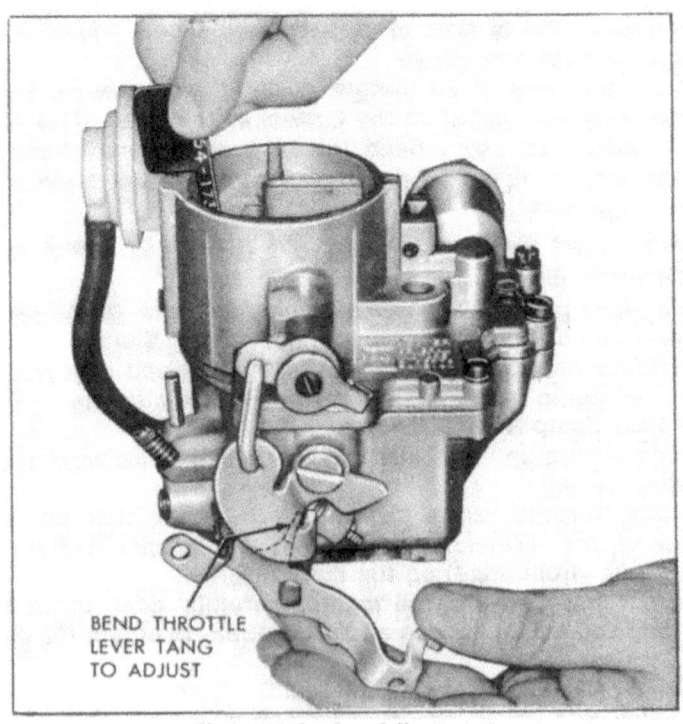

Choke Unloader Adjustment

of bowl cover. Clearance should be .180"-.195".

If necessary to adjust, bend diaphragm link.

At this setting, throttle lever fast idle tang should rest on second highest step of fast idle cam. If not, adjust by bending other choke shaft lever tang.

16. **Adjust Choke Unloader as follows:**

    Check unloader adjustment by holding throttle valve in wide open position and insert a .312" wire gauge between choke valve lower edge and wall of bowl cover.

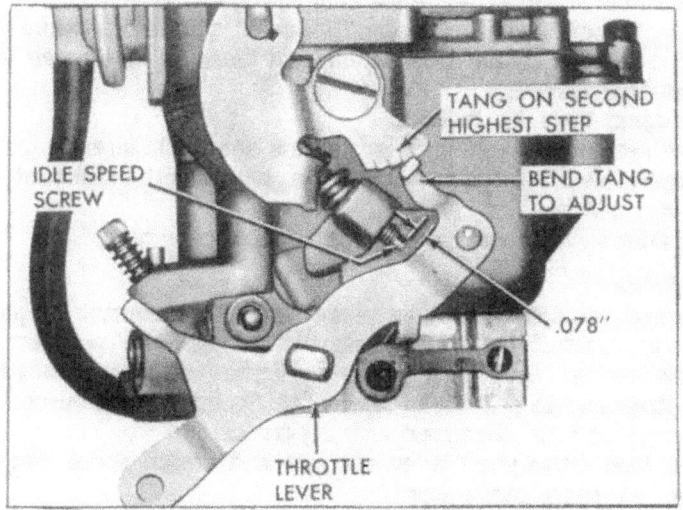

Fast Idle Adjustment

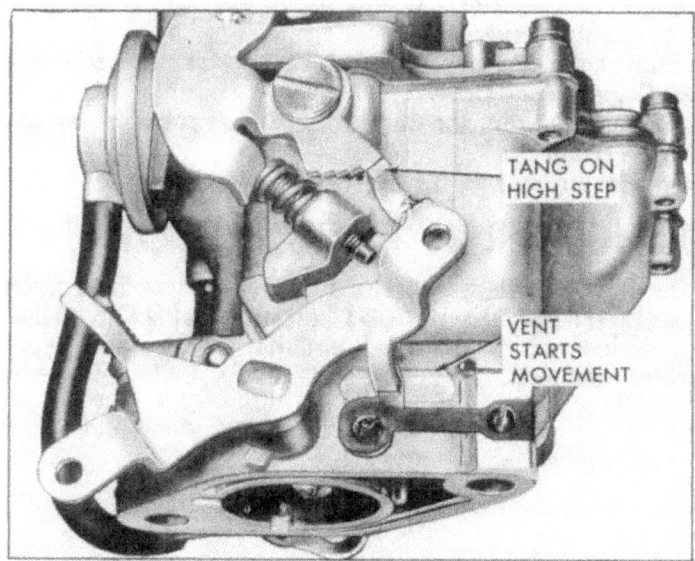

Vapor Vent Adjustment

To adjust, if necessary, bend tang on throttle lever.

NOTE: Unloader adjustment should be checked especially if it has been necessary to adjust the choke shaft outer lever tang during choke diaphragm link check.

17. **Adjust Fast Idle Cam as follows:**
Insert a strip of paper between idle screw and throttle lever, then holding throttle lever in the closed position with a rubber band, turn idle screw in until a firm drag is felt on the strip of paper.
Turn idle screw in 1½ additional turns.
With throttle lever on second highest step of fast idle cam, bend tang to obtain .078" clearance between idle speed screw and throttle lever.

18. **Adjust Vent as follows:**
The vent should just start movement when idle screw is on high step of fast idle cam. The valve will then be open at curb idling setting.
If necessary, adjust by bending throttle lever tang.

Installation
1. Install insulator block in place, install carburetor on intake manifold studs. Install two attaching nuts and washers and tighten evenly. On right carburetor, install vacuum advance line with other end to distributor advance. On the left carburetor, the vacuum port tube is capped with a plastic cap.
2. Replace cross-shaft lever support and install three attaching screws at each carburetor.
3. Connect gas inlet lines.
4. Connect accelerator rod and return spring. Connect throttle rods to throttle levers.
5. Install choke control rod to each carburetor. Adjust as outlined under Engine Tune-Up.
6. Check carburetors for Carburetor Synchronization as outlined in Engine Tune-Up.
7. Replace air cleaner assembly.

ROCHESTER H CARBURETOR

The Rochester H Carburetor used as a secondary carburetor on the Corvair 10700 series (4x1 carburetors) has no choke, idle, power enrichment or low speed circuits. Service and Repair are otherwise identical.

CARTER YH CARBURETOR

This section covers the Carter YH Carburetor, used in conjunction with the Turbocharger, as optional equipment. For Accelerator Linkage Adjustment, Idle Speed and Mixture Adjustment and Choke Adjustment refer to Engine Tune-Up (Turbocharger Option).

Additional Checks and Adjustments

The following checks and adjustments may be made without removing the carburetor from the vehicle. Refer to Repair Procedures, Assembly and Adjustments.

Metering Rod Adjustment
Float Adjustments
Fast Idle Adjustment
Choke Unloader Adjustment
Choke Adjustment

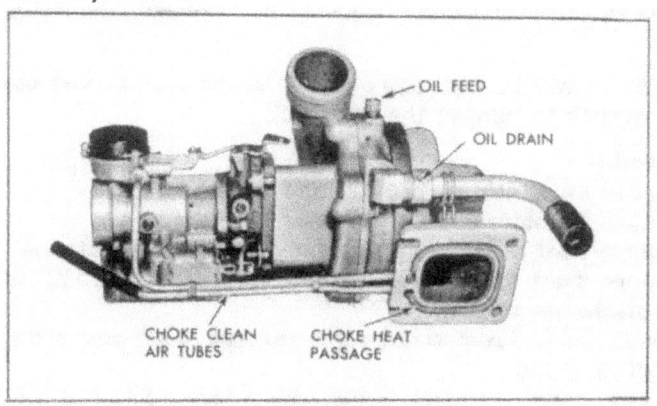

Carter YH Carburetor

Fuel Filter Replacement

The fuel filter is a separate unit mounted on the air cleaner support bracket at the left of the air cleaner.

Replacement consists of disconnecting the inlet, outlet and bypass fuel lines, loosening clamp screw and removing filter unit. Reverse to install new unit. (Arrows show flow direction.)

Removal

With Turbocharger as an Assembly

This method is outlined under Turbocharger—Removal. When this method is used, caution is necessary to prevent damage to turbine wheel, during disassembly of carburetor from Turbocharger

Separately from Turbocharger

1. Remove air cleaner.
2. Disconnect choke heat tube, fuel line and accelerator linkage

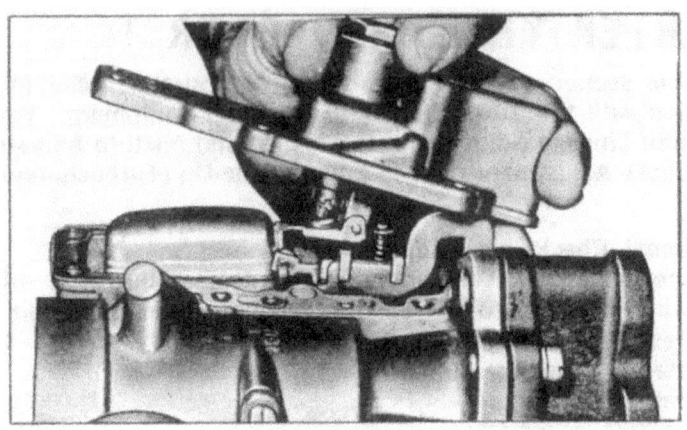

Removing Bowl Cover

at carburetor.
3. Remove carburetor mounting nuts and remove carburetor from vehicle.

NOTE: It will be necessary to use a short or curved open-end wrench to remove the front nut.

Disassembly

1. Remove inlet filter screen nut and screen.
2. Remove six screws and float bowl cover.
3. Remove float hinge pin, float and float needle and seat.
4. Remove float bowl cover gasket, tip carburetor and remove pump discharge needle.
5. Loosen pump lever screw from throttle shaft and slide lever off shaft and link.
6. Depress small spring on pump with a screw driver and remove spring seat and spring.
7. Lift metering rod arm and metering rod from pump rod and metering jet.
8. Raise pump arm enough to remove the link, then remove pump arm.
9. Remove 4 screws and remove diaphragm pump assembly.
10. Remove fuel splash deflector plate and metering jet.
11. Remove choke link clip and choke link.
12. Remove choke housing cover screws, cover, gasket and baffle plate, then slide choke lever out of housing.
13. Remove three throttle flange-to-carburetor body screws and remove flange and gasket from body section.
14. Remove idle speed screw and spring from flange. For normal cleaning and inspection, the carburetor is disassembled as far as is necessary. The choke valve, choke piston or throttle valve should be removed only if valve is damaged or shaft and piston are binding. If either condition exists, complete the disassembly as follows:

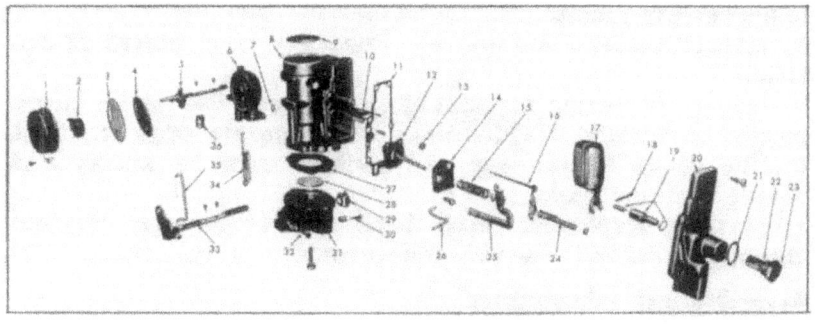

Carburetor—Exploded View

1. Choke Coil Housing
2. Choke Coil
3. Gasket
4. Baffle Plate
5. Choke Shaft
6. Choke Housing
7. Vacuum Passage "O" Ring Seal
8. Carburetor Body
9. Choke Plate
10. Bowl Splash Baffle
11. Bowl Cover Gasket
12. Diaphragm Pump Assembly
13. Main Jet
14. Pump Housing
15. Pump Lower Spring
16. Metering Rod and Arm Assembly
17. Float
18. Hinge Pin
19. Needle and Seat Assembly
20. Bowl Cover
21. Gasket
22. Inlet Screen
23. Screen Nut
24. Upper Pump Spring
25. Pump Actuating Link
26. Connector Link
27. Gasket
28. Throttle Plate
29. Throttle Lever Pump Arm
30. Idle Mixture Screw
31. Throttle Body
32. Idle Speed (Air) Screw
33. Throttle Shaft
34. Fast Idle Link
35. Fast Idle Connector Link
36. Choke Piston

15. File staked ends of throttle plate screws, level with throttle shaft (to avoid damaging throttle shaft threads), then remove the screws and throttle valve and slide shaft from flange.
16. File staked ends of choke valve screws, level with choke shaft, then remove screws and choke plate.
17. Remove choke shaft and choke piston by rotating the shaft until the piston comes out of the bore, then slide shaft assembly from carburetor.
18. Remove three choke housing screws, remove housing and discard vacuum passage "O" ring seal.

Cleaning and Inspection

The most frequent causes of carburetor malfunction are gum, dirt, carbon and water. Carefully clean and inspect all parts and castings during carburetor overhaul.
1. Wash all parts, except choke coil housing and pump, in carburetor cleaning solution.
2. Choke coil housing should be cleaned in gasoline.
3. Inspect links and operating lever holes for wear.
4. Inspect throttle and choke plates for gouges or other damage and their shafts for binding or excessive wear.
5. Inspect float for dents or leaks.
6. Inspect choke piston for free operation in its cylinder. Remove welch plug from cylinder only if piston sticks and it is necessary to clean the cylinder. Clean the cylinder with fine sandpaper if necessary.
7. Inspect float needle and seat for burrs or ridges. If present, replace both the needle and seat; never replace separately or try

to file burrs or ridges.

8. Inspect metering rod and jet. Replace if bent, burred or distorted.

9. Inspect all mating surfaces of castings and flanges for burrs, gouges or surface irregularities. Use a square edge to check throttle flange for warpage. All surfaces must be smooth and square to prevent leaks.

10. Inspect accelerator pump diaphragm for damage. Replace diaphragm and rod assembly if necessary.

Assembly and Adjustments

1. If throttle shaft was removed:
   a. Slide shaft in throttle flange.
   b. Position throttle plate on flat of shaft with numbered side to shaft, then install new screws loosely.
   c. Center throttle plate on shaft and in the bore and tighten the screws. Peen the screws securely.
2. Choke shaft was removed:
   a. Use a new vacuum passage "O" ring seal, position the choke housing on air horn and install three attaching screws just snug.
   b. Slide choke shaft into air horn part way, then install piston to shaft and position the shaft by rotating while installing piston into its cylinder.
   c. Tighten choke housing attaching screws.
   d. Position choke plate on flat of shaft with identification numbers on air cleaner side.
   e. Install new choke plate attaching screws loosely, center the plate on shaft and in bore and tighten the screws. Peen the screws securely (using pliers).
3. Install throttle flange gasket and flange onto carburetor body with three retaining screws.
4. Install pump diaphragm assembly in diaphragm housing, then install diaphragm spring (lower) and spring retainer.
5. Install metering rod jet (no gasket with this jet).
6. Install diaphragm housing screws in housing and thread them 2 or 3 threads into diaphragm (to hold diaphragm in alginment), then install the assembly in carburetor bowl and tighten screws.
7. Install splash shield between metering rod jet and pump housing.
8. Install metering rod onto the metering rod arm, hook the spring and install retainer clip.
9. Install pump and metering rod linkage as follows:
   a. Pump lifter in guide opening, insert throttle lever connector link onto pump lifter link (connector must be installed before lifter link is completely in position) then place lifter arm down over pump rod.
   b. Metering rod in jet and arm over pump rod and lifter arm.

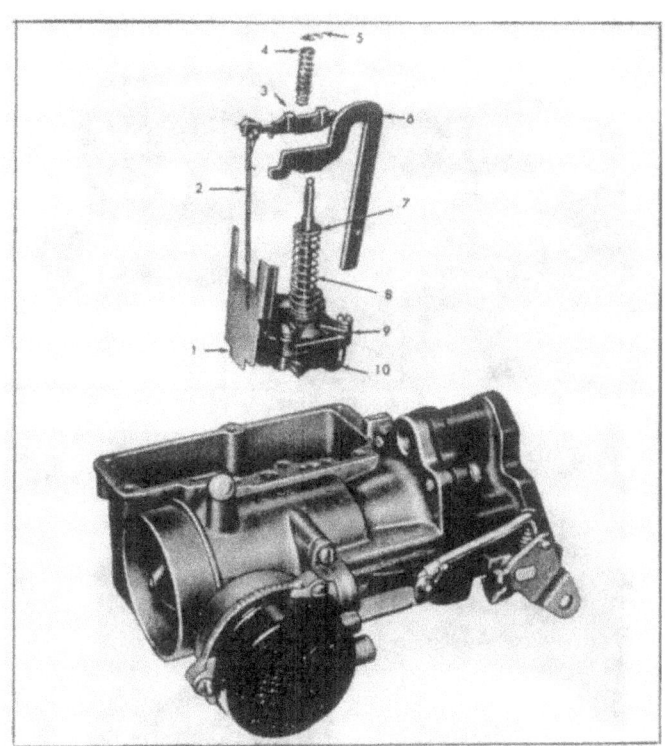

Pump and Metering Rod Assembly

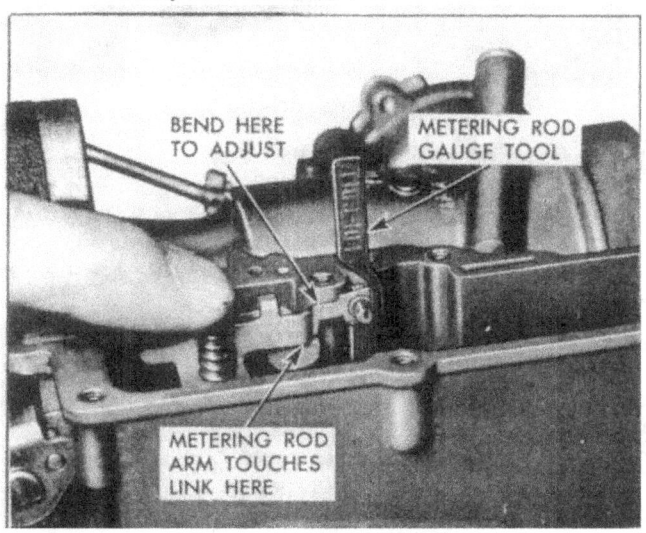

Adjust Metering Rod Arm

   c. Upper spring over pump rod, compress with screw driver and install retainer.

   d. Install throttle shaft pump lever over throttle shaft and pump link, then tighten retaining screw.

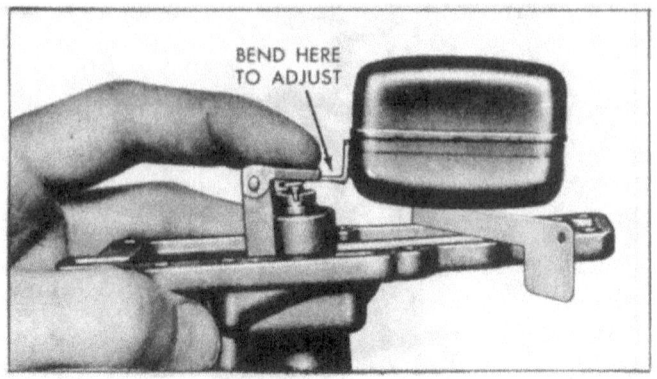

Adjusting Float Level

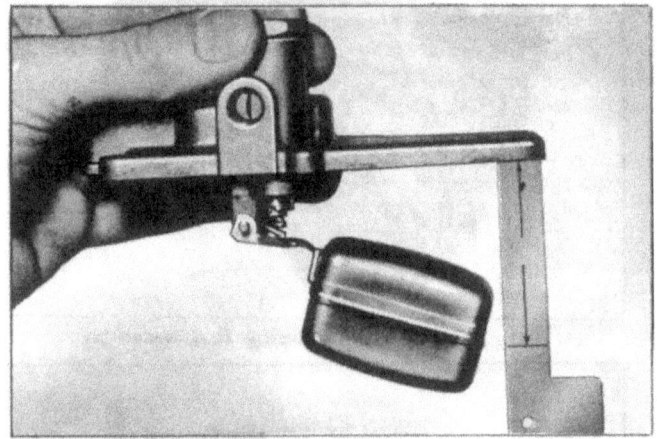

Measuring Float Drop

10. **Adjust metering rod as follows:**
    a. Hold throttle valve tightly closed.
    b. Remove metering rod from carburetor and place Gauge Tool J-21056 in metering jet.
    c. Push down on pump diaphragm rod until the metering rod arm just touches the lifter link.
    d. With the gauge (Tool J-21056) in the jet, the metering rod arm pin should just contact the top surface of gauge tool.

    e. If necessary, adjust by bending metering rod arm at point shown.
11. Install new float needle valve seat and needle valve in bowl cover, then install float and float hinge pin with the hinge pin shoulder to outboard side of carburetor bowl.
12. **Adjust Float as follows:**
    Invert cover and measure the distance between cover gasket and surface and float at center of float. This FLOAT LEVEL dimension should be 5/8" or use Tool J-21056.

Adjust, if necessary, by bending float arm.

Invert cover to upright position allowing float to hang down.

Measure the distance between cover gasket surface and seam of float at free end. This FLOAT DROP dimension should be $2\frac{3}{8}'' \pm \frac{1}{16}''$.

Adjust by bending the tang at hinge end.

13. Install pump discharge-needle, then install a new cover gasket on bowl and install bowl cover and six screws.

14. Install fast idle link into choke housing and hook unloader projection over tang on fast idle cam assembly.

15. Install choke link connector link to throttle lever keyed hole then to choke link with clip.

16. **Adjust fast idle as follows:**

    a. Hold choke valve tightly closed and close throttle valve as far as it will go. (This places fast idle link on high step of cam.)

    b. Hold the throttle valve in this position, a .030" gauge (Tool J-21056) should just go between throttle valve and bore at side opposite idle port.

    c. If necessary, adjust by bending fast idle connector link at curvature.

    NOTE: Always perform fast idle adjustment before unloader adjustment.

17. **Check unloader adjustment as follows:**

    a. Open throttle to wide open position while holding tension in opposite direction on choke valve.

    b. Measure the distance between choke valve edge and bore opposite the vent tube side. This unloader measurement should be 7/16".

    c. If necessary, adjust by bending unloader tang on fast idle cam.

18. Install choke baffle plate, gasket, choke coil housing, housing retainer clips and screws onto choke housing with screws just snug.

19. **Adjust coil housing to specifications, then tighten housing retainer screws.**

Installation

1. Install carburetor over mounting studs on Turbocharger; install lower front nut and washer first, then install the other two nuts and washers and tighten.
2. Connect choke heat tube and fuel line at carburetor.
3. Install air cleaner and connect clean air tube at air cleaner (be sure air cleaner to carburetor "O" ring seal is in place).
4. Connect accelerator linkage at carburetor.
5. Start the engine and adjust idle speed and mixture and throttle return check valve clearance as outlined under Engine Tune-Up (Turbocharger Option).

TURBOCHARGER

The Turbocharger for the Corvair engine is a device to improve engine breathing, thereby increasing horsepower output. The Turbocharger consists of a precision balanced rotating group, enclosed in a contoured housing, with a turbine wheel at one end and a centrifugal impeller at the other. The name Turbocharger is used because the impeller is turbine driven, rather than mechanical as in a supercharger.

Hot exhaust gases are directed against the turbine blades, spinning the turbine, shaft and impeller at a high rate of speed. The impeller, in the Turbocharger housing, draws air-fuel mixture from the carburetor and passes it to the intake manifold at a higher-than-atmospheric pressure. This increases the amount of air-fuel mixture available to the cylinders and results in a greater horsepower output.

As a result of the increase in volume and temperature of the exhaust gases when the engine is under heavy load, the Turbocharger speed automatically increases. This provides more air-fuel mixture, to meet the engine demand.

The Turbocharger turbine and impeller shaft rotates on a semi-floating sleeve bearing. The bearing is lubricated with engine oil, under pressure, from the oil filter adapter. The oil is drained through a large tube into the rocker arm area of the right cylinder head.

Periodic Inspection

Whenever routine service of the engine is performed, inspect the Turbocharger as follows:
1. Inspect the hoses and connections of the air intake system between the carburetor and the Turbocharger and from Turbocharger to intake manifold for leakage due to cracks, damaged gaskets, loose clamps or connections and for restriction due to collapsed hoses or dented tubing.
2. Inspect for exhaust leakage due to cracked exhaust manifold, loose Turbocharger mountings or damaged gaskets.
3. Inspect oil lines and fittings for kinks, damage or leakage.
4. Observe engine exhaust. Excessive smoke may indicate a restricted air cleaner, over rich mixtures or faulty Turbocharger (seal) operation.
5. Note unusual noises or vibration that would warrant further inspection of Turbocharger.

Major Inspection

Every 50,000 miles, or if trouble is suspected in Turbocharger, it should be inspected and serviced as follows:
1. Disconnect oil drain line at Turbocharger elbow. Connect a hose from the elbow to a container placed at side of engine, then start engine and run at idle speed for one minute to determine

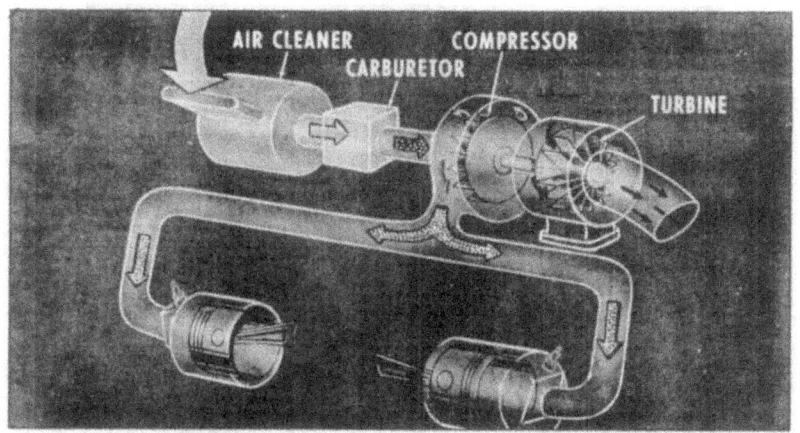

Turbocharger Operational Schematic

oil flow (should be approximately 1 quart per minute at idle).

2. Remove Turbocharger and carburetor assembly from the engine.
3. Remove carburetor from Turbocharger assembly.
4. Inspect the turbine wheel for:
   a. Cracks, erosion: chipped, nicked, missing or bent blades.
   b. Carbon build-up on blades.
   c. Carbon accumulation on back face of turbine wheel.
   d. Free rotation by depressing the shield against the spring ring, then rotating the wheel. If the turbine wheel does not rotate freely, disassemble the unit and inspect for damaged parts or foreign material causing the interference.
5. Remove six retaining bolts and remove compressor housing and gasket.
6. Inspect compressor housing for scoring, wiping, erosion or pit marks on the inner contour.
7. Inspect impeller wheel for damaged blades or evidence of rubbing in the housing.
8. Note any oil accumulations in housing or on impeller indicating a defective oil seal.
9. If the impeller requires cleaning, use a nylon bristle brush and a solvent such as Diesel fuel or kerosene to remove accumulated dirt. Thoroughly clean the impeller and compressor housing.

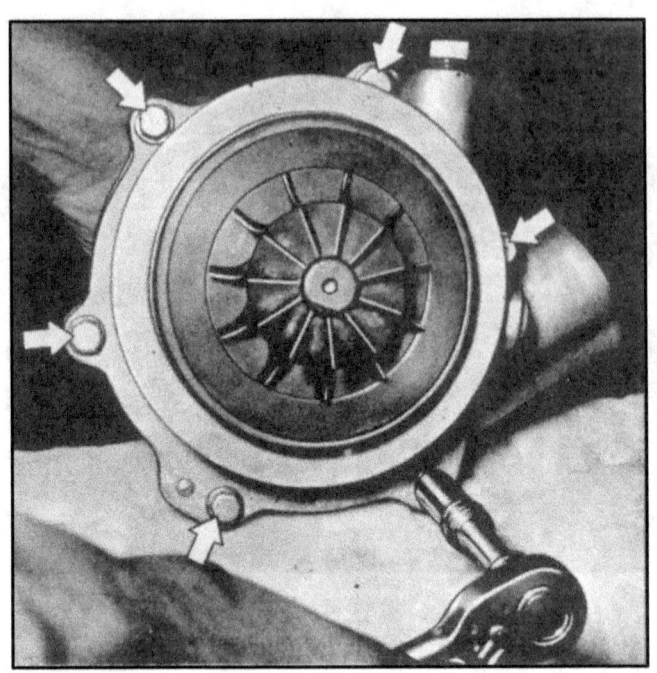

Compressor Housing Retaining Bolts

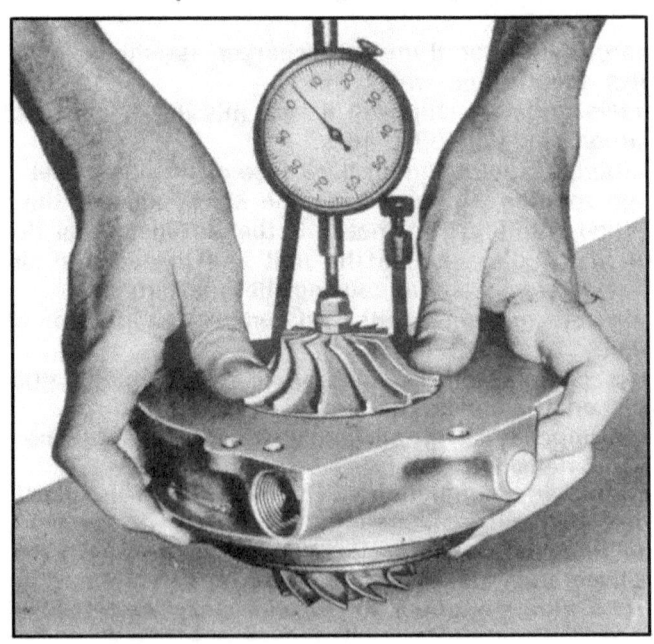

Gauging Turbine Shaft End Play

NOTE: Failure to remove all dirt may result in a more severe unbalance than existed prior to cleaning.

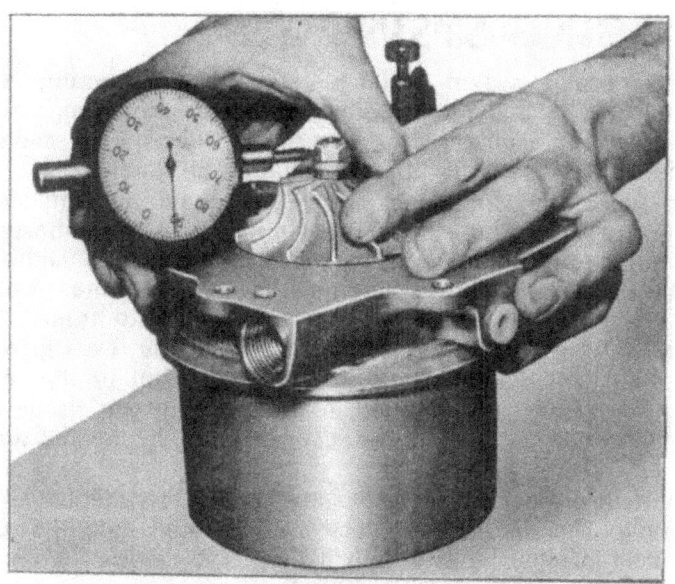
Gauging Turbine Shaft Radial Play

10. Measure turbine shaft end play as follows:
   a. Attach a dial indicator to the bearing housing so that indicator point is resting on the impeller nut.
   b. Rest assembly squarely on hub of turbine wheel, then push down on housing and record the indicator reading. Release pressure on the housing and then repeat the operation at least once to check measurement. (The shield spring ring acts to return the wheel and shaft opposite the pressure on housing; it is not necessary to hold the shield away from the turbine wheel.)
   c. Allowable end play is .005" to .008". If end play is excessive, the Turbocharger should be rebuilt.
11. Measure turbine shaft radial play as follows:
   a. With the assembly on the support ring (Tool J-21004), position the dial indicator so its point is resting on a flat of the impeller nut and needle set at zero.
   b. Push the impeller from side to side against indicator point and record readings, then repeat at least once to check your reading.
   c. Recheck at 90° position to give cross reading.
   d. The maximum allowable radial play is .022". If radial play is excessive, rebuild the Turbocharger.
   e. Remove dial indicator.
12. If the unit is in satisfactory condition, install compressor housing (using a new gasket and torque the six bolts to 80 inch lbs.
13. Install carburetor to Turbocharger, then install the assembly onto the vehicle.

CHARGING SYSTEM

The charging system includes the battery, generator, regulator, tell tale light, ignition switch and necessary wiring to connect these components. The Delcotron is offered as a standard equipment, with two capacities available on all models.

The Delcotron continuous output A.C. generator consists of two major parts, a stator and a rotor. The stator is composed of a large number of windings assembled on the inside of a laminated core that is attached to the generator frame. The rotor revolves within the stator on bearings located in each end frame. Two brushes are required to carry current through the two slip rings to the field coils wound concentric with the shaft of the rotor. Six rectifier diodes are mounted in the slip ring end frame and are joined to the stator windings at three internally located terminals.

Diodes are mounted in heat sinks to provide adequate heat dissipation. The six diodes replace the separately mounted rectifier as used in other types of application. The diodes change the Delcotron A.C. current to D.C. current.

The function of the regulator in the charging system is to limit the generator voltage to a pre-set value by controlling the generator field current. The double-contact regulator assembly consists of a double contact voltage regulator unit and a field relay unit. This unit uses two sets of contact points on the voltage regulator

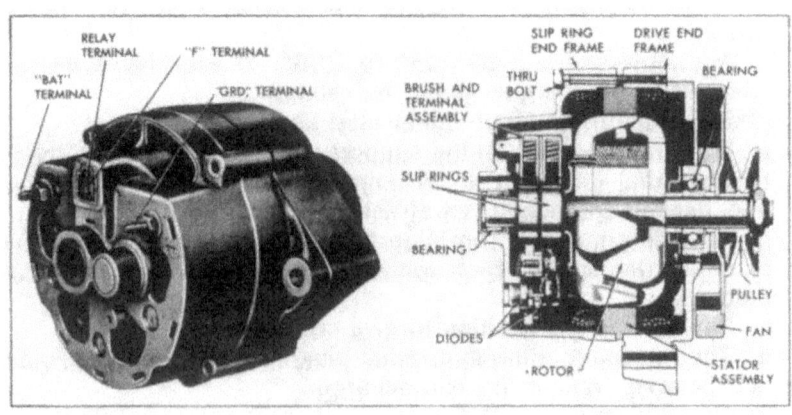

5.5" Delcotron

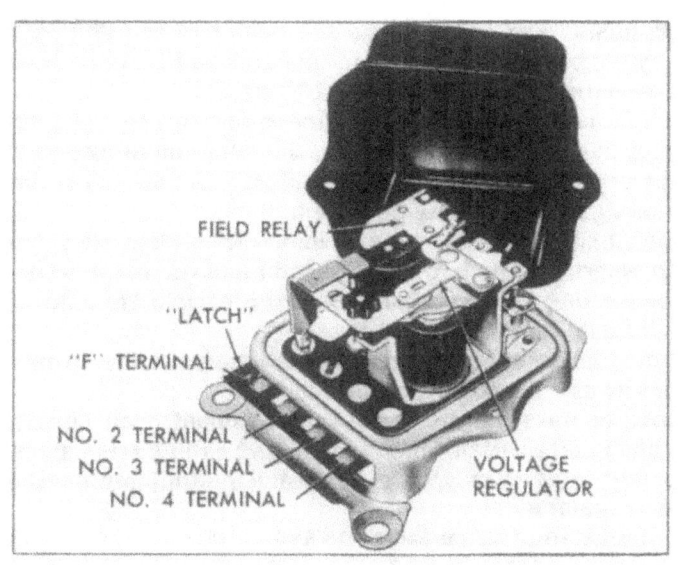

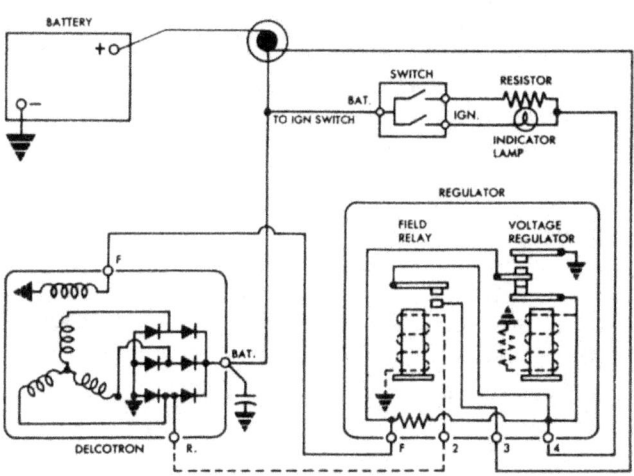

Two Unit Voltage Regulator

unit to obtain desired field excitation under variable conditions. When the higher output Delcotron unit is used, the regulator incorporates an external field discharge diode in the field circuit. A wiring diagram of the regulator internal circuits is illustrated.

The field relay unit allows the lamp to light (as a bulb check) with the ignition key on and engine not running. When the engine is started and the generator begins to charge, the indicator light goes out indicating that the system is operating normally.

At regular intervals, inspect the terminals for corrosion and loose connections, and the wiring for frayed insulation. Check mounting bolts for tightness. Check the drive belt for alignment, proper tension and wear. Because of the higher inertia and load capacity of the rotor used in A.C. generators, PROPER BELT TENSION is more critical than on D.C. generators.

Since the Delcotron and its companion regulator are designed for use on negative polarity systems only, the following precautions must be observed. Failure to observe these precautions may result in serious damage to the charging system.

1. **When installing a battery, always make absolutely sure the ground polarity of the battery, generator and regulator is the same.**
2. **When connecting a booster battery, make certain to connect the correct battery terminals together.**
3. **When connecting a charger to the battery, connect the correct charger leads to the battery terminals.**
4. **Never operate the generator on an uncontrolled open circuit. Make absolutely certain all connections in the circuit are secure.**
5. **Do not short across or ground any of the terminals on the generator or regulator.**
6. **Do not attempt to polarize the generator.**
7. **Do not disconnect lead at generator without first disconnecting battery ground cable.**

Trouble in the A.C. charging system will usually be indicated by one or more of the following conditions:
1. Faulty indicator lamp operation.
2. An undercharged battery (usually evidenced by slow cranking speeds).
3. An overcharged battery (usually evidenced by excessive battery water usage).
4. Excessive generator noise or vibration.

Described in this section are a series of on-the-vehicle quick checks which are designed to assist in locating troubles within the various components of the engine electrical system.

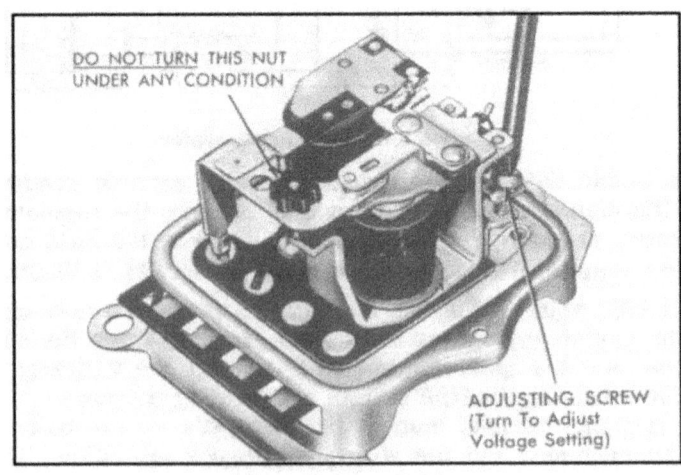

Adjust Voltage Setting

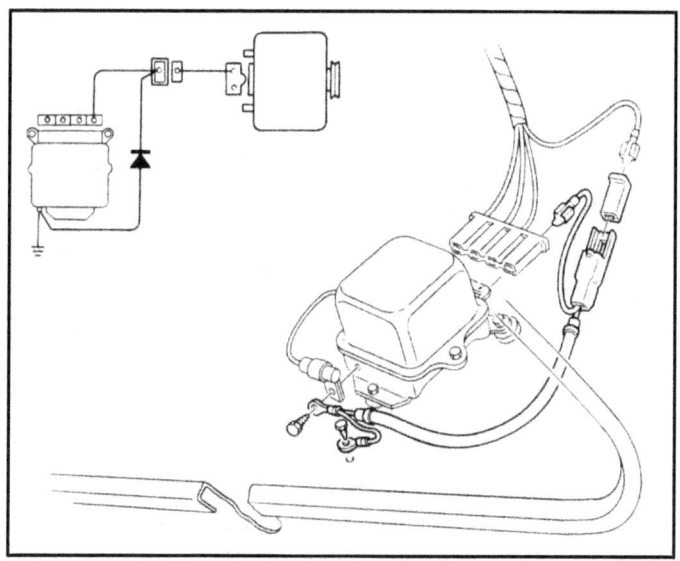

External Field Discharge Diode

STATIC CHECKS

Before making any electrical checks, perform the following static checks:
1. Check for loose or broken blower belt.
2. Check for defective battery.
3. Inspect all connections, including the slip-on connectors at the regulator and Delcotron.

NOTE: Do not short field to ground to check if generator is charging since this will seriously damage the charging system.

SYSTEM CONDITION TEST

This test is used in indicate the overall condition of the charging system (both good and defective) and to isolate the malfunctioning unit if the system is defective.
1. With ignition off, perform the prescribed Static Checks. Then set hand brake and shift transmission into neutral.
2. Connect a voltmeter from junction block on horn relay to ground at regulator base.

CAUTION: Be sure meter clip does not touch a resistor or terminal extension under regulator.

3. Connect a tachometer on engine.
4. Turn ignition switch to "ON" and check indicator lamp. If lamp fails to glow, perform appropriate tests and corrections (see Indicator Lamp Circuit tests) before continuing test.
5. If lamp glows, start the engine and run it at 1500 rpm or above. Check indicator lamp. If lamp fails to go out, perform

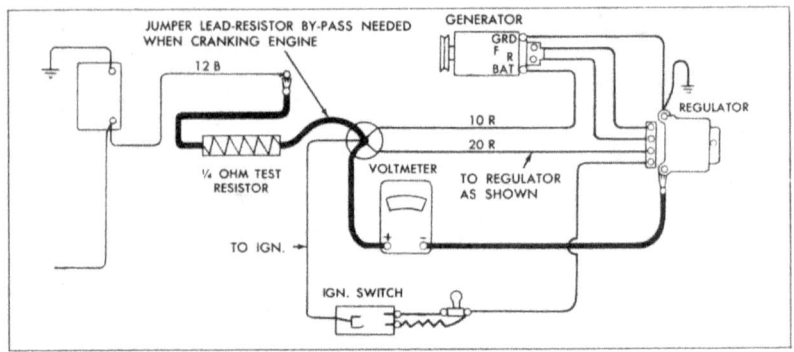

Voltage Setting Test Connections

appropriate test and corrections (see Indicator Lamp Circuit tests) before continuing test.

NOTE: At this point a field circuit has been established and any other problem will lie in generator or regulator.

6. Turn on high-beam headlights and heater blower motor to high speed, run engine at or above 1500 rpm (for a few minutes, if necessary) and read the voltage on meter.

NOTE: Voltage will not greatly exceed 12½ volts until battery develops a surface charge, a few minutes generally, unless the battery is severely discharged or is hot.

If reading is:
a. 12½ volts or more, turn off electrical loads, stop engine and proceed to Step 7.
b. Less than 12½ volts, perform "Delcotron Output Test— Voltmeter Method".
  1. Delcotron tests bad—repair or replace Delcotron, then repeat Step 6.
  2. Delcotron tests good—disconnect regulator connector, remove regulator cover and reconnect the connector. Then repeat Step 6 and turn voltage screw to raise setting to 12½ volts. Turn off loads, stop engine and proceed to Step 7. If 12½ volts cannot be obtained, install a new regulator and repeat Step 6.

7. Connect a ¼ ohm-25 watt fixed resistor (purchased commercially) into the charging circuit at junction block as shown. Test

Connection Diagram.

NOTE: Between both leads and the terminal.

ADJUSTING REGULATOR VOLTAGE

8. Run engine at 1500 rpm or above for at least 15 minutes of warm-up, then cycle regulator voltage control (by disconnecting and re-connecting regulator connector) and read voltage.

If voltage is 13.5 t o 15.2, the regulator is okay.

If voltage is not within 13.5 to 15.2 volts, leave engine running at 1500 rpm or above and:

a. Disconnect four terminal connector and remove regulator cover. Then re-connect four terminal connector and adjust voltage to 14.2 to 14.6.

b. Disconnect four terminal connector and reinstall regulator cover, then reinstall connector.

c. Continue running engine at 1500 rpm for 5-10 minutes to re-establish regulator internal temperature.

d. Cycle regulator voltage by disconnecting and reconnecting regulator connector. Read voltage. A reading between 13.5 and 15.2 indicates a good regulator.

CAUTION: Be sure four terminal regulator connector is discontinued when removing or installing cover. This is to prevent regulator damage by short circuits.

DELCOTRON OUTPUT TEST

Voltmeter Method

1. Disconnect the four-terminal connector from the regulator.
2. Disconnect the two-terminal connector from the Delcotron F and R terminals.

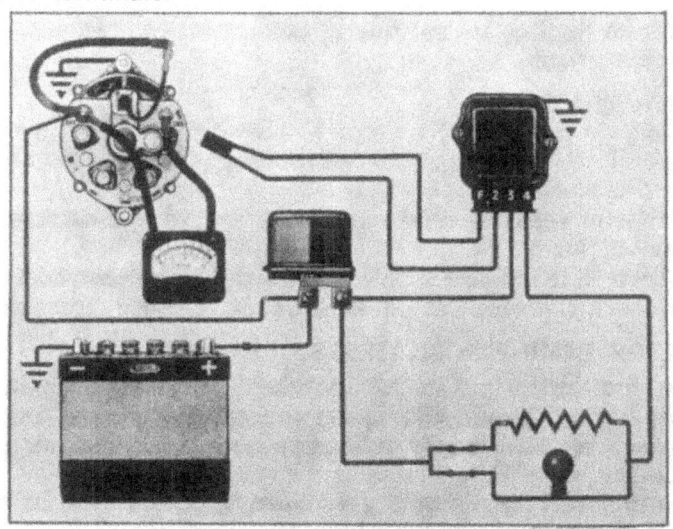

Output Test Connections (Typical)

3. Connect a jumper wire from the Delcotron BAT terminal to the Delcotron F terminal. This provides full field excitation.
4. Connect a voltmeter from the Delcotron BAT terminal to the Delcotron GRD terminal.
5. Start engine and turn on high beam headlights and either high speed heater blower motor or medium speed on the air conditioner blower motor. Run engine 1500 rpm or above and note whether voltage exceeds 12.5 volts. If voltage exceeds 12.5 volts within a few minutes, Delcotron output is O.K. Stop engine, turn off all electrical loads, and reconnect wiring.

> **CAUTION:** If battery is in a normal state of charge, voltage will exceed 12.5 volts as soon as engine speed is increased. Engine speed should be increased slowly to prevent voltage from exceeding 16 volts during test.

6. If voltage is less than 12.5 volts, perform other Delcotron tests and repairs outlined.

DELCONTRON DIODE AND FIELD TEST

> **NOTE:** These tests will indicate good, shorted or open field or shorted diode but will not indicate a failed open diode.

1. Disconnect battery ground cable at battery.
2. Positive diodes (Test A) connect an ohmmeter between "R" terminal and "BATT" terminal and note reading, then reverse the leads at same terminals and note this reading. Meter should read high resistance in one direction and low in the other.
3. Negative diodes (Test B) connect ohmmeter between "R" terminal and "GRD" and note reading, then reverse the leads and note this reading. Meter should read high in one direction and low in the other.

> **NOTE:** A high or low reading in both directions indicates a defective diode.

4. Open Field Check:
   a. Connect an ohmmeter from "F" terminal to "GRD" terminal stud and note reading on the lowest range scale. Meter should read 7 to 20 ohms.
   b. If meter reads zero or excessively high resistance, the Delcotron is faulty.
5. If above tests indicate a defective Delcotron, remove and completely check Delcotron as outlined under "Service Operations."

INDICATOR LAMP CIRCUIT TESTS

The indicator lamp circuit provides initial field excitation (causing lamp to glow). The light is cancelled by closing the field relay which applies battery voltage to both sides of bulb (bulb goes out).

The indicator light should glow when ignition switch is "ON" and go out almost immediately when engine starts.

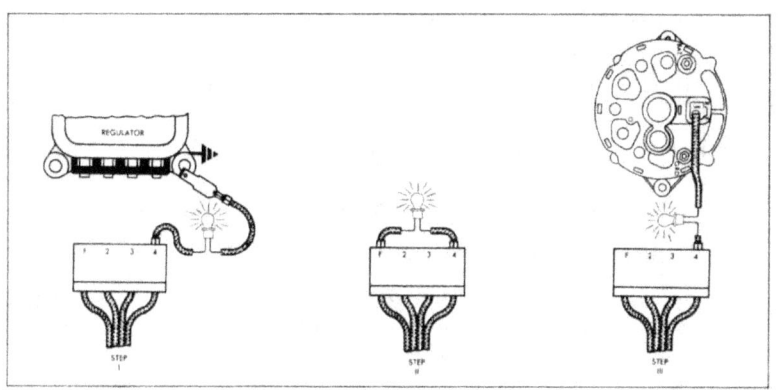

Indicator Lamp Circuit Tests

If Lamp Fails to Glow the Possible Causes Are:
1. Faulty bulb.
2. Faulty bulb socket.
3. An open circuit in wiring, regulator, or field.
4. A shorted positive diode—(may also cause glow with ignition switch "OFF").

Test as Follows:
1. Disconnect connector from regulator and connect a jumper lead from connector terminal "4" to ground (Step 1). Turn ignition switch to "ON" momentarily and note indicator lamp:
    a. Lamp fails to glow—check for faulty bulb, socket or open circuit between switch and regulator connector. Repair as needed.
    b. Light goes on—failure is in regulator, Delcotron or wire between "F" terminals on regulator and Delcotron. Go to Step 2.
2. Disconnect jumper lead at ground end and connect between connect "F" and "4" terminals (Step 2), then turn switch to "ON" momentarily and note lamp:
    a. Lamp glows—problem is in regulator. An open circuit in regulator or relay is stuck closed.
    b. Fails to glow—problem is in wire between "F" terminals on generator and regulator or in field windings. Go to Step 3.
3. Disconnect jumper at connector "F" terminal and connect "F" terminal on Delcotron (Step 3), then turn switch on momentarily

and note lamp:
- a. Lamp glows—an open circuit in wire between "F" terminals —correct as needed.
- b. Fails to glow—Delcotron field has open circuit.

If Lamp Fails to Go Out the Possible Causes Are:
1. Loose drive belt—adjust as necessary.
2. Faulty field relay—(see relay test and adjustment).
3. Defective Delcotron—(see Delcotron output test).
4. At normal idle—parallel resistance wire open (see Resistance test).
5. Switch off—positive diode shorted (see Diode test).

FIELD CIRCUIT RESISTANCE WIRE TESTS

The resistance wire is an integral part of the ignition harness. However, the resistance wire is not solderable; it must be spliced with a crimp-type connector. It is rated at 10 ohms, 6.25 watts minimum.

The check for an open resistor (connected to the ignition switch "ACC" terminal) is as follows:
1. Connect a test lamp from the wiring harness connector terminal to ground as shown in Step 1.
2. Turn the ignition switch to the "ON" position and note test bulb.
3. If the test lamp does not glow, the resistor is open.

NOTE: The telltale lamp does not glow during this test because series resistance of the 2 bulbs causes amperage to be low.

OTHER HARNESS CHECKS

Other wires in the charging system harness need be checked for continuity by use of an ohmmeter or a test light (12 Volt). Connect the test so the wire in question is in series in the test circuit.

FIELD RELAY CHECKS AND ADJUSTMENT

To check for a faulty relay proceed as follows:
1. Connect a voltmeter into the system at the regulator No. 2 terminal to ground.
2. Operate the engine at fast idle (1500 to 2000 rpm) and observe voltmeter reading.
3. If voltmeter shows zero voltage at regulator, check circuit between No. 2 terminal on regulator to "R" terminal on Delcotron.
4. If voltage at regulator exceeds closing voltage specification and light remains on, regulator field relay is faulty. (Refer to specifications at the end of this section.) Check and adjust regulator as outlined under "Closing Voltage Adjustment."

CLOSING VOLTAGE ADJUSTMENT

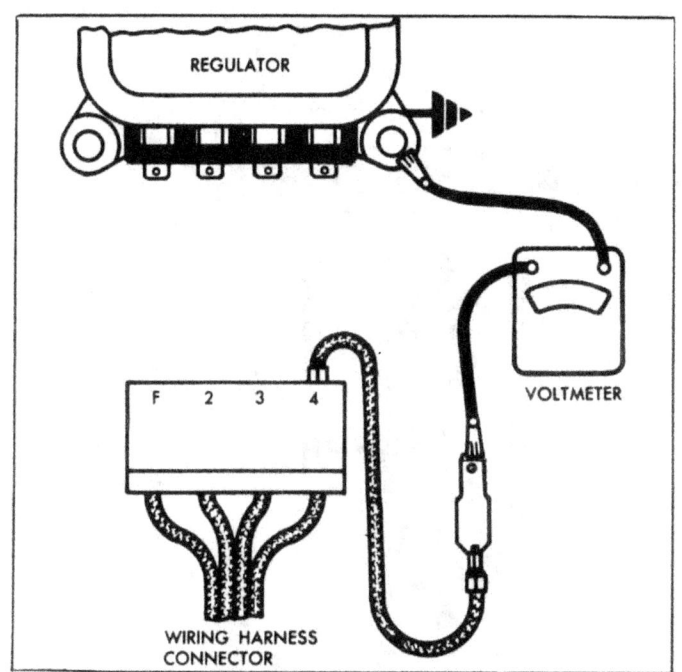

Circuit Resistance Wire Test

Checking Field Relay Closing Voltage

1. Make connections as shown using a 50 ohm variable resistor.
NOTE: This provides a variable resistance from a hot lead to the relay coil.
2. Turn resistor to "open" position.
3. Turn ignition switch off.
4. Slowly decrease resistance and note closing voltage of the

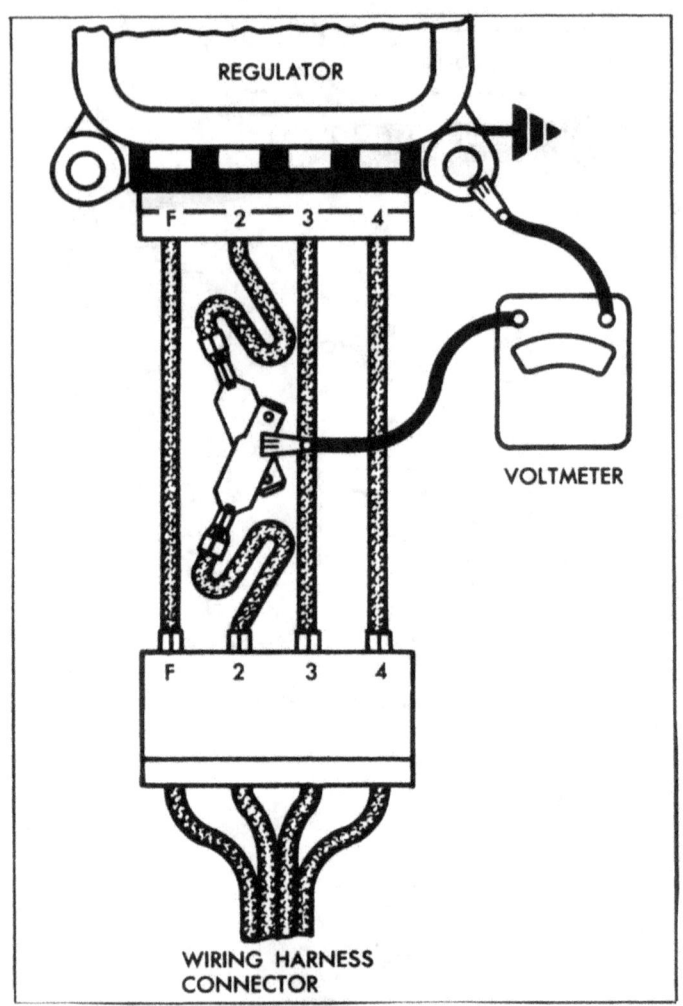

Checking Field Relay

relay. Adjust by bending heel iron in the manner illustrated.

SERVICE OPERATIONS

GENERATOR

REMOVAL AND INSTALLATION

1. Disconnect battery ground cable at battery.
2. Disconnect wiring leads at Delcotron.
3. Remove blower belt from Delcotron pulley
4. Remove three attaching bolts and remove Delcotron from vehicle.
5. To install Delcotron, position unit to mounting bracket and

Adjusting Field Relay Closing Voltage

brace and install attaching bolts.
6. Install and adjust blower belt as outlined in Section 6, Tune-up.
7. Connect wiring harness to rear of Delcotron.
8. Connect battery ground cable at battery and check operation of unit.

PULLEY REPLACEMENT

Single Groove Pulley
1. Place 15/16" box wrench on retaining nut and insert a 15/16" allen wrench into shaft to hold shaft while removing nut.
2. Remove washer and slide pulley from shaft.
3. To install, slide washer and pulley onto shaft and tighten self locking retaining nut.
4. Using a torque wrench with a crow-foot adapter (instead of a box wrench), torque the nut 50 to 60 ft. lbs.

CLUTCH

GENERAL DESCRIPTION

A bent finger diaphragm spring clutch mounted on a step face flywheel is used with the manual transmission. The clutch consists of two basic assemblies, the clutch cover and pressure plate assembly, and the clutch disc assembly. The clutch is attached at the front of the engine to the flywheel and is completely enclosed by the clutch housing. The driven disc is assembled between the flywheel and pressure plate.

A shorter throwout bearing and fork ball stud are used with the bent finger clutch. Only the short ball stud is available in service with a spacer to be used when extra length is needed. Use of the longer throwout bearing (flat finger type) will cause inability to obtain free pedal travel, resulting in slippage and rapid clutch wear if incorrectly used on bent finger clutch assemblies.

The input shaft from the transmission to the clutch is flexible torsionally; thus eliminating the need for damper springs in the clutch disc.

The clutch is operated with a conventional clutch fork, except that it is shorter and operates by pulling instead of pushing. The clutch fork engages the throwout bearing which is piloted on the axle housing.

The clutch fork pull rod assembly is a two piece design and provides for clutch lash at the swivel end which attaches to the cross shaft.

At the other end of the cross shaft assembly, the control cable is attached by means of a threaded swivel which is also adjustable to retain proper tension on the control cable. The clutch lever control cable assembly is made up of 3/32 inch diameter plastic coated cable crimped into the end of a 1/4 inch diameter steel rod. The cable assembly has an overall length of approximately 93 inches and is serviced as a complete assembly.

At the clutch pedal end, the pedal is attached to the clutch pedal shaft assembly which in turn also retains the brake pedal assembly. The clutch pedal shaft assembly is provided with a lever at one end with provisions for the attachment of the clutch lever control cable assembly. The shaft assembly is supported at the center by the dash brace and retained at the lever end by a bearing plate.

Turbo-Super Charged Engine Clutch

This clutch has a pearlitic malleable or nodular iron pressure plate identified by 6 large cast lugs on the outer diameter and must be used on this engine. The complete assembly may be used with the super-turbo-air engine.

3. Torque (5) Nut to Swivel (6) using indicated torque of 8-12 ft. lbs.
4. Install (9) Spring (7) Washer and (8) Pin.
5. Manually pull (4) Clutch Pull Rod until shock is taken up at clutch fork. With (4) Clutch Pull Rod in this position align (3) Adjusting Rod with hole in outboard to Shaft Assembly Lever. Back off (3) Adjusting Rod **three** turns and assemble to lever with (2) Clip.

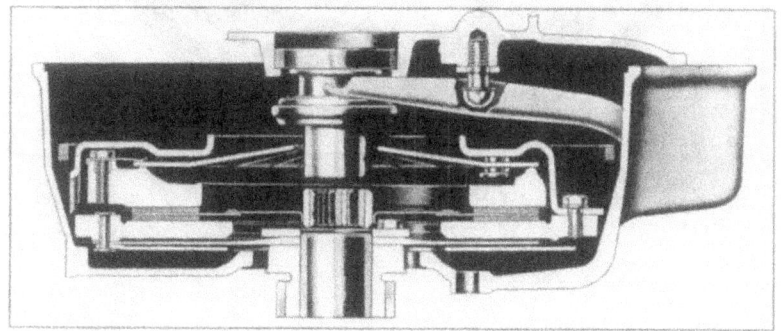

Clutch Cross-Section

CLUTCH LINKAGE ADJUSTMENT

1. Drive (5) Nut to within $\frac{1}{8}$" of end of threads on Clutch Cable Rod Assembly.
2. Tension Clutch Cable Rod Assembly to 15 lbs. and thread (6) Swivel to line up with hole in (1) Shaft Assembly inboard Lever with lever located $\frac{7}{8}$" from the transmission crossmember. (View B)

Hi-Performance Clutch

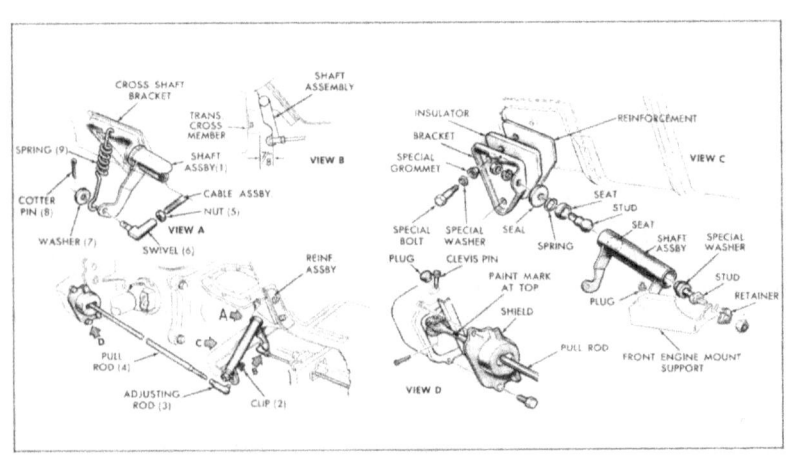

Clutch Linkage Exploded

SPECIAL TOOLS

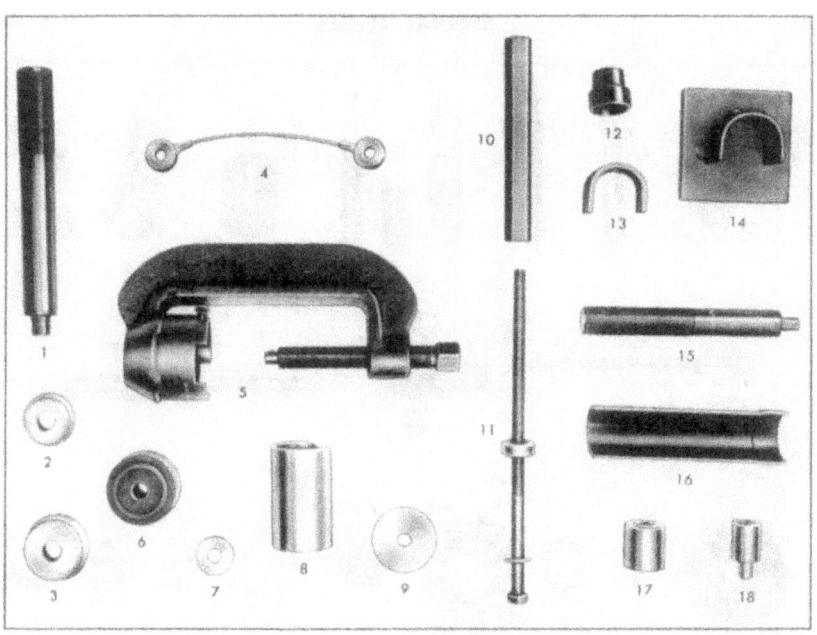

1. J-8092   Driver Handle
2. J-8849   Outer Race Installer
3. J-8850   Inner Race Installer
4. J-4988   Cable
5. J-9519-10   Ball Joint Remover
6. J-9519-16   Ball Joint Installer
7. J-21058-5   Bridge for J-21876-1
8. J-21058-6   Receiver
9. J-21058-7   Bridge for J-21058-6
10. J-21058-8   Puller Screw Nut
11. J-21058-15   Puller Screw
12. J-21876-1   Lower Control Arm Bushing Remover and Installer
13. J-21876-2   Lower Control Arm Spacer
14. J-5888-3   Support
15. J-7079-2   Driver Handle
16. J-8345-1   Upper Control Arm Spacer
17. J-8345-2   Upper Control Arm Bushing Installer
18. J-8345-3   Upper Control Arm Bushing Remover

SPECIAL TOOLS

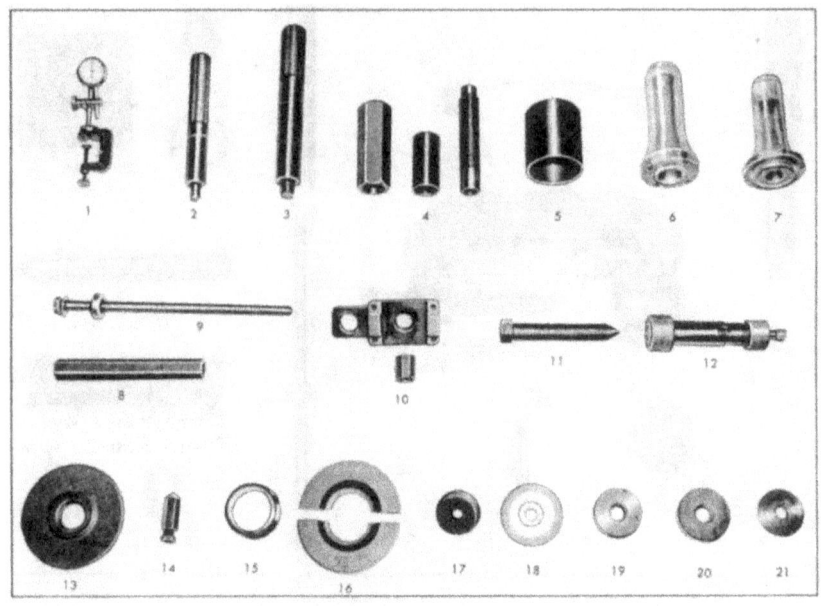

(Rear Suspension)

1. J-8001 — Dial Indicator Set (Use with J-8364 Stand—not Illustrated)
2. J-7079-2 — Driver Handle (insert type)
3. J-8092 — Driver Handle (threaded type)
4. J-21843 — Wheel Drive Spindle Flange and Bearing Installer—Consists of 21843-1 Bolt, 21843-2 Sleeve and 21843-3 Nut
5. J-21830-4 — Torque Arm Bushing Remover Sleeve
6. J-21837 — Drive Spindle Inner Seal Installer
7. J-21842 — Drive Spindle Outer Seal Installer
8. J-21058-8 — Torque Arm Bushing Remover Nut
9. J-21058-15 — Torque Arm Bushing Remover Bolt
10. J-21859 — Drive Spindle Flange Remover—Consists of J-21859-1 Nut, J-21859-2 Plate and J-21859-3 Bolt. Used with J-8614-3.
11. J-8614-3 — Drive Spindle Flange Remover Power Screw
12. J-21836 — Drive Spindle Spacer Selector Gauge
13. J-9436 — Drive Spindle Outer Bearing Installer Plate
14. J-21831 — Drive Spindle Remover—Consists of J-21831-1 Bolt, and J-21831-2 Nut
15. J-21844 — Torque Arm Bushing Installer
16. J-8331 — Drive Spindle Outer Bearing Remover Plates
17. J-21474-2 — Torque Arm Bushing Adapter
18. J-21830-7 — Torque Arm Bushing Bridge
19. J-8850 — Drive Spindle Outer Bearing Installer
20. J-7817 — Drive Spindle Inner Bearing Cup Installer
21. J-21058-7 — Torque Arm Bushing Adapter

SPECIAL TOOLS

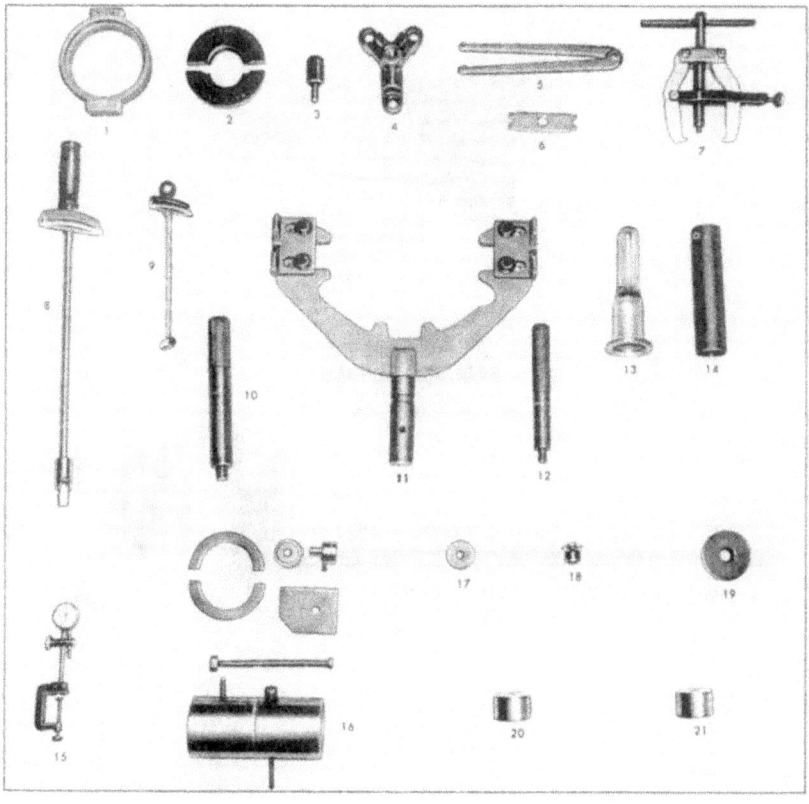

(Rear Axle)

1. J-0358-1 Pinion Bearing Remover Press Plate Holder
2. J-8331 Pinion Bearing Remover Plates—Used with J-0358-1 Holder
3. J-2619-4 Positraction Axle Torque Adapter
4. J-5748 Positraction Axle Torque Adapter Plate—Used with J-2619-4 Adapter
5. J-972 Pinion Adjusting Sleeve Wrench
6. J-8342 Differential Side Bearing Adjusting Sleeve Wrench
7. J-7112 Differential Side Bearing Puller
8. J-1313 0-150 ft. lbs. torque wrench
9. J-5853 0-50 in. lbs. torque wrench
10. J-8092 Driver Handle (threaded type)
11. J-3289 Differential Carrier Holding Fixture
12. J-7079-2 Driver Handle (insert type)
13. J-8340 Pinion Shaft Front Oil Seal Installer
14. J-5590 Pinion Shaft Bearing Installer
15. J-8001 Dial Indicator Set
16. J-6266 Pinion Setting Depth Gauge—Consists of J-6266-18 Adapters, J-6266-25 Plug, J-6266-19 Gauge, J-6266-5 Plate and J-6266-1 Cylinder
17. J-8107-2 Differential Side Bearing Puller Pilot Adapter
18. J-8362 Pinion Turning Adapter
19. J-7137 Pinion Rear Bearing Race—Installer Used with J-7079-2 Handle
20. J-8359 Differential Side Bearing Installer—Used with J-7079-2 Hdl.
21. J-8448-1 Pinion Shaft Rear Oil Seal Installer

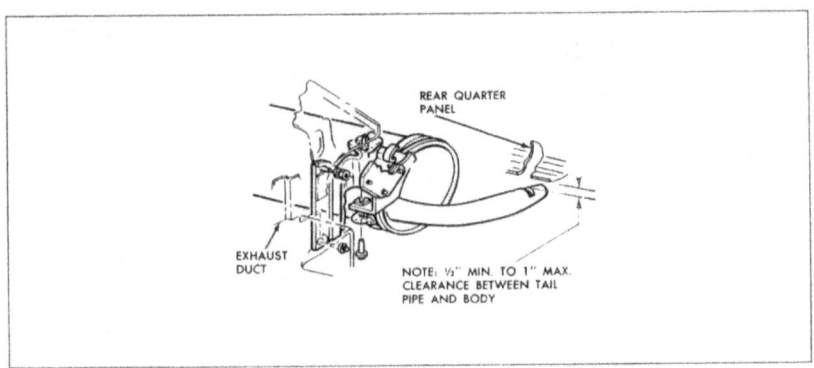

Muffler and Bracket Attachment

SPECIAL TOOLS

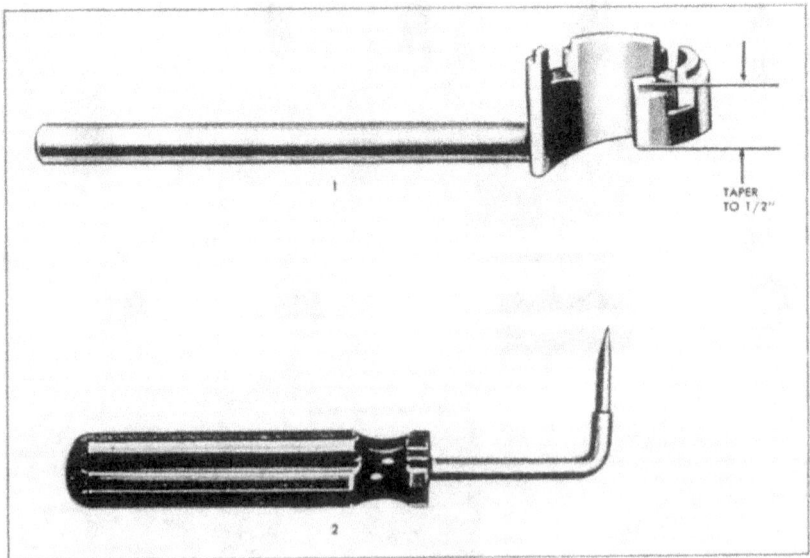

1. J-8950 Fuel Tank Gauge Unit Spanner
2. J-7777 Fuel Line Clip Installer

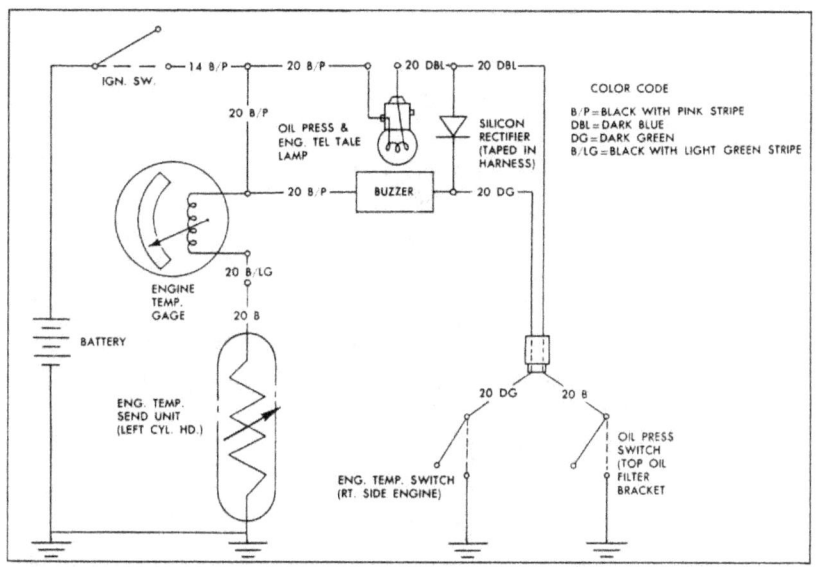

Oil Pressure and Engine Temperature Tell-tale Lamp, Temperature Gauge and Warning Buzzer Wiring

WIRING CIRCUIT COLOR CODE

DIAGRAM KEY	WIRE COLOR
B	Black
B/LG	Black with Light Green Stripe
B/LBL	Black with Light Blue Stripe
B/P	Black with Pink Stripe
B/OR	Black with Orange Stripe
B/W	Black with White Stripe
B/Y	Black with Yellow Stripe
BRN	Brown
DBL	Dark Blue
DG	Dark Green
PPL	Purple
R	Red
T	Tan
GY	Gray
W/OR/P	White with Orange and Pink Stripes

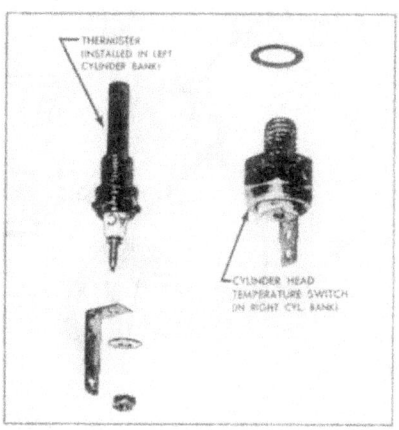

Cylinder Head Temperature Sensing Units

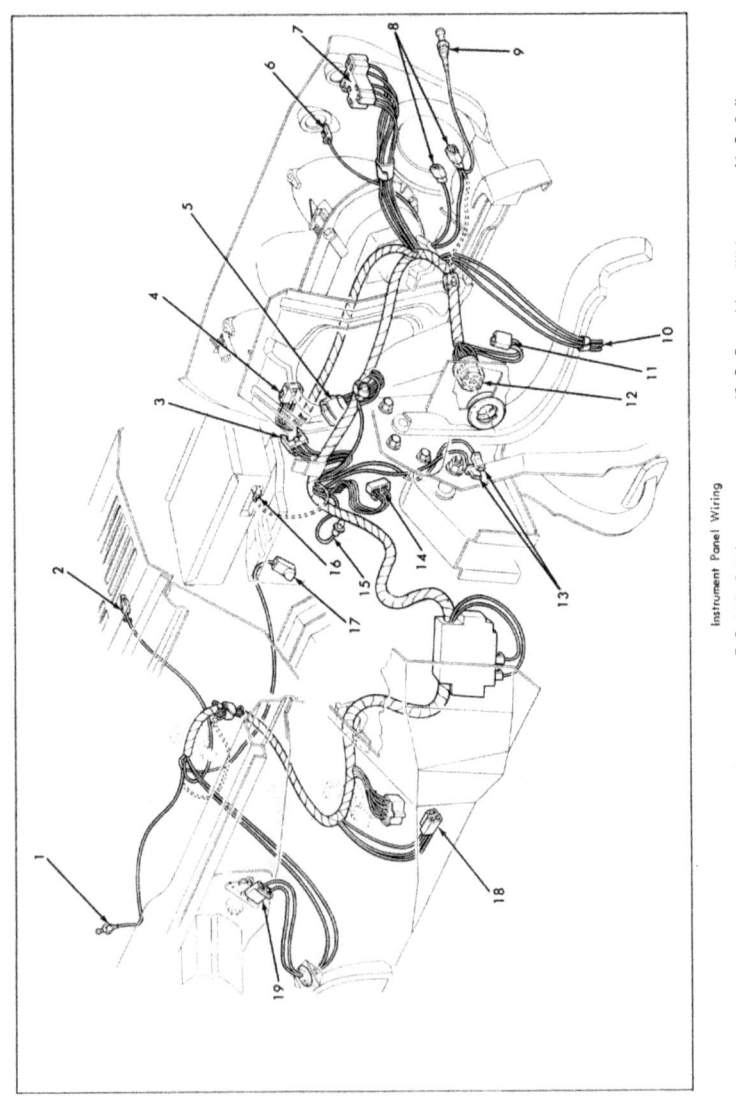

Instrument Panel Wiring

1. R.H. Door Jamb Switch (10500-700)
2. To Instrument Panel Compartment Light (10500-700)
3. To Ignition Switch
4. To Instrument Cluster Wiring Harness
5. To Directional Signal Harness
6. To Wiper Switch
7. To Light Switch
8. To Dome Lamp
9. L.H. Door Jamb Switch
10. To Dimmer Switch
11. To Warning Buzzer (10700 only)
12. To Forward Lamp Wiring Harness
13. To Stop Lamp Switch
14. To Heater Blower Switch
15. Heater Control Lamp
16. To Radio
17. To Cigarette Lighter
18. To Heater Resistor
19. To Wiper

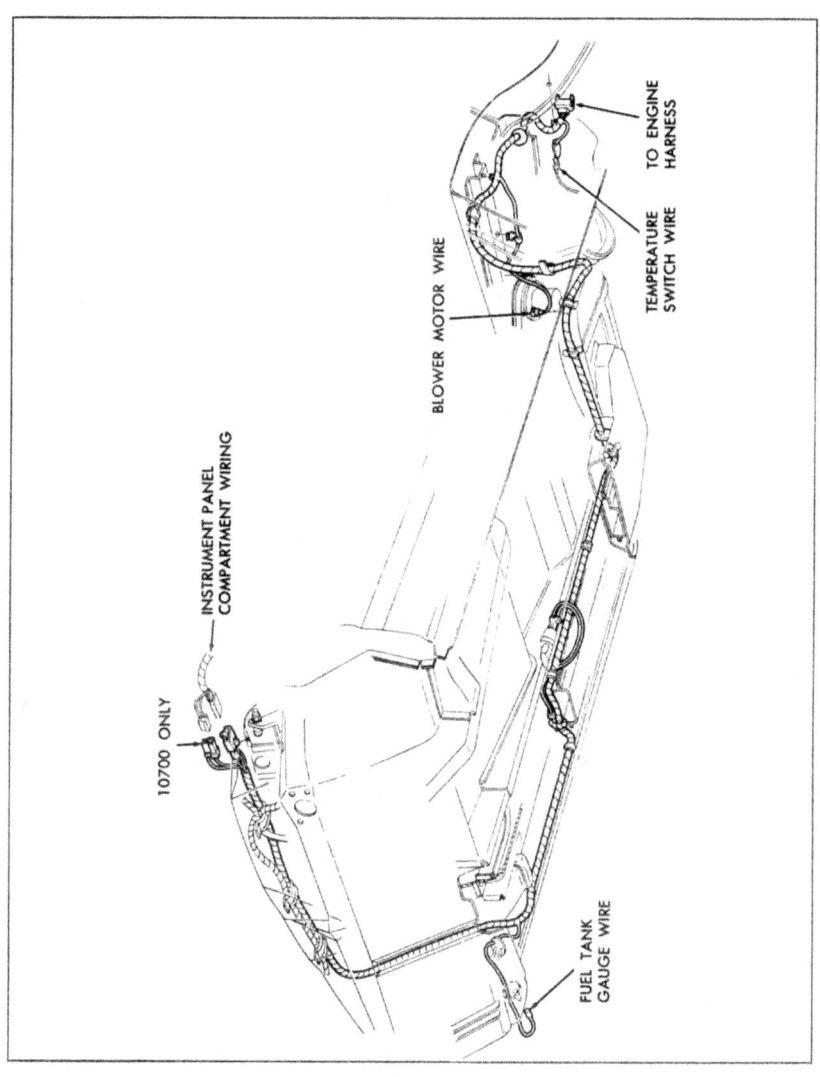

Body Wiring Harness

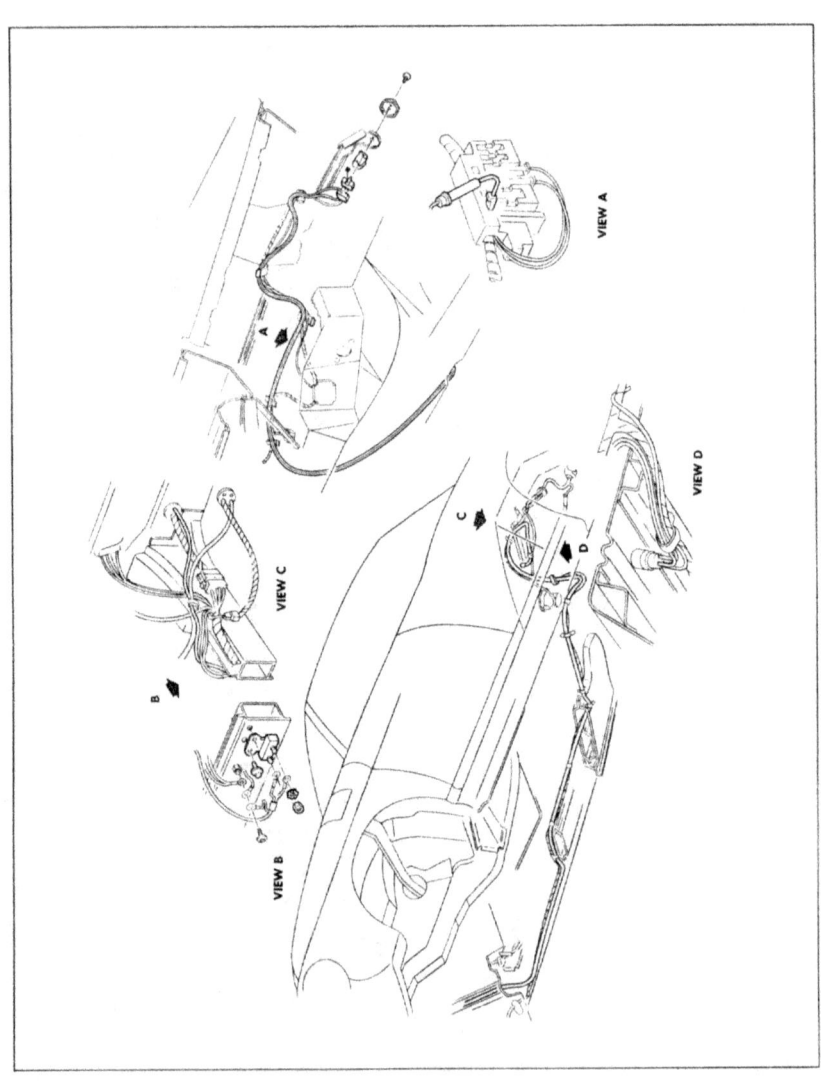

Power Feed Wiring

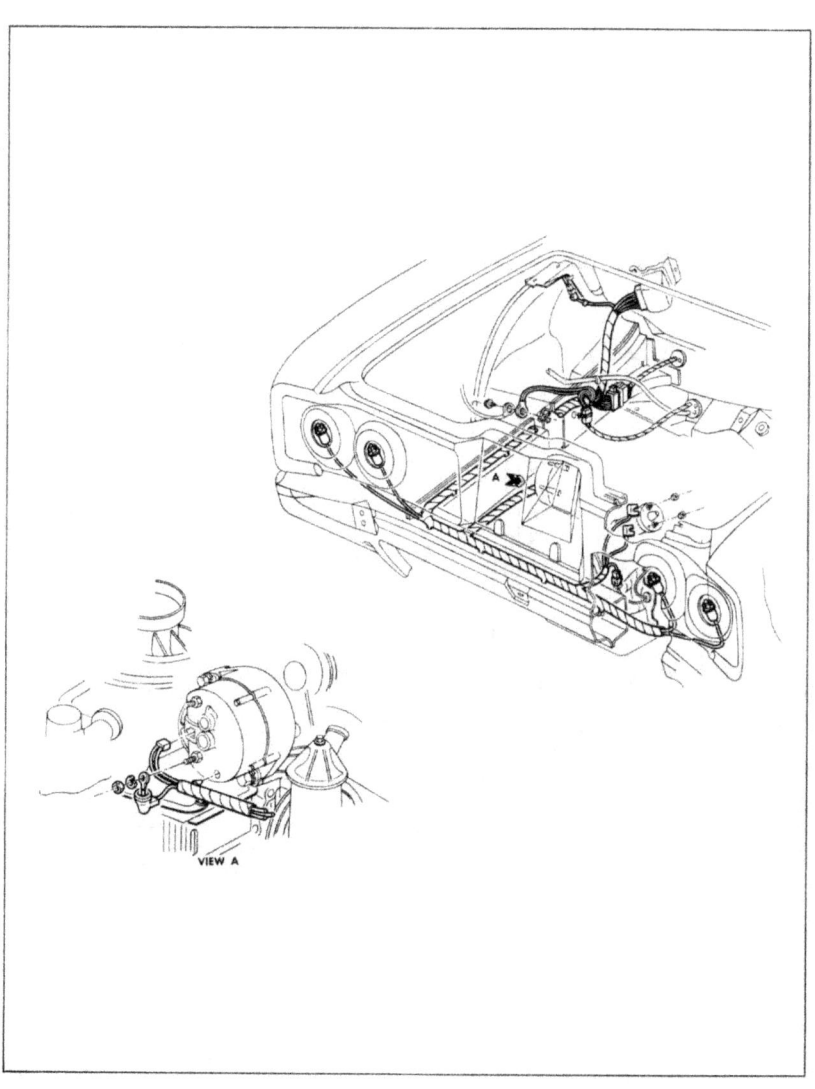

Engine Compartment Wiring

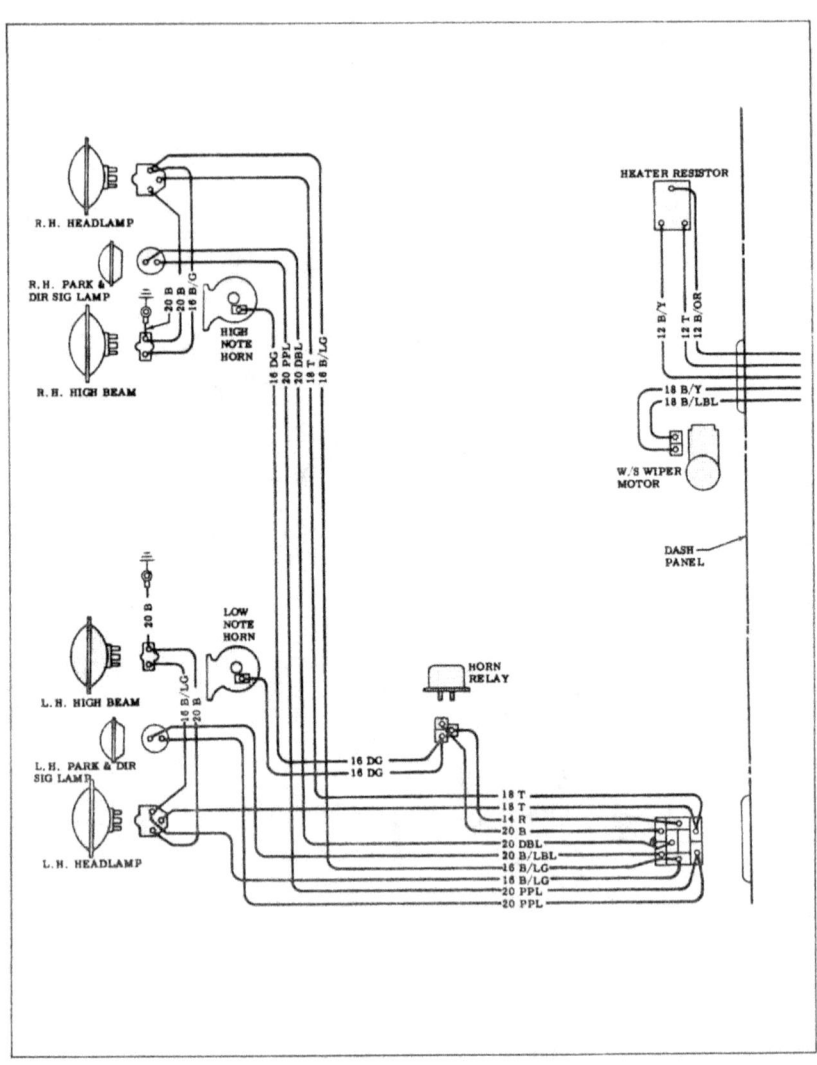

Front End

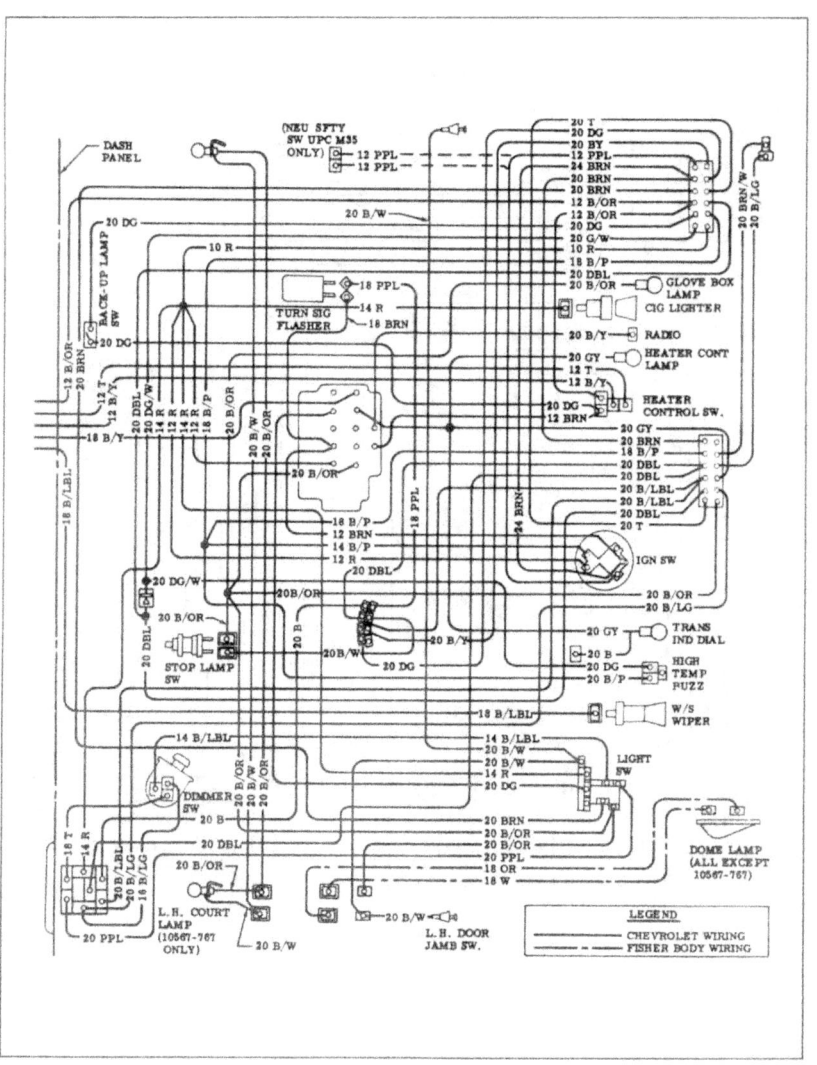

Engine and Tail Lamps

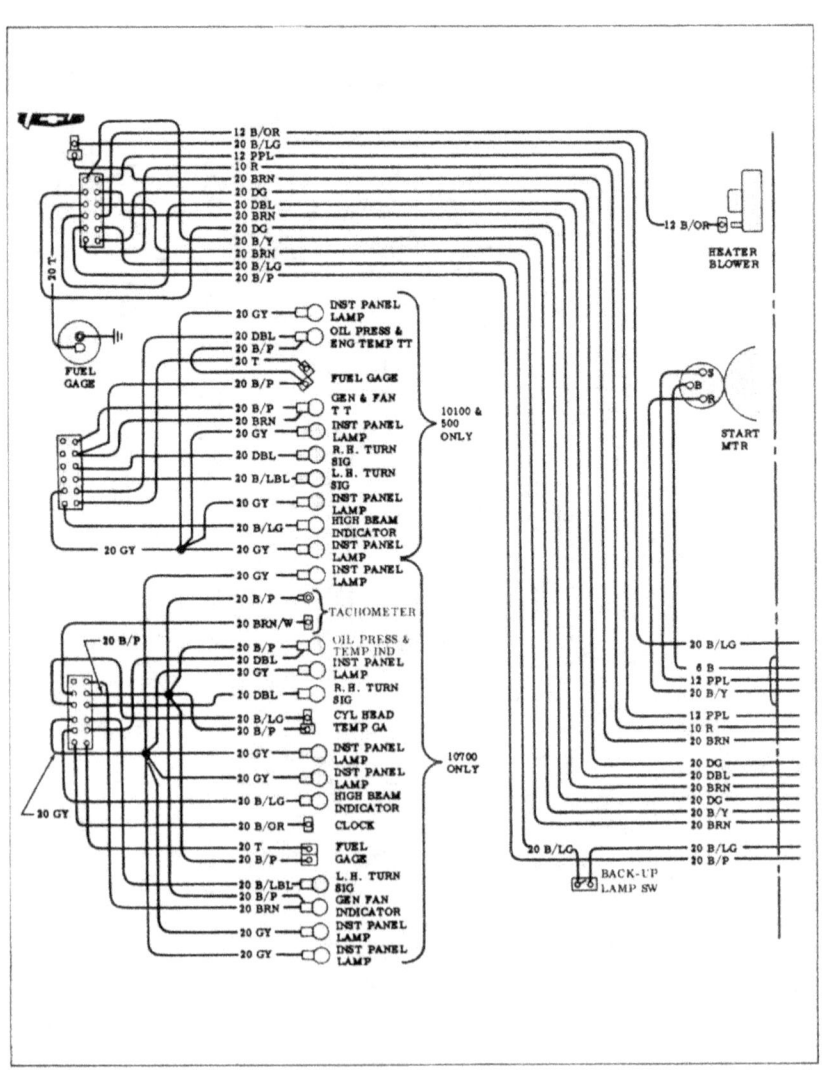

Instrument Cluster and Body Harness

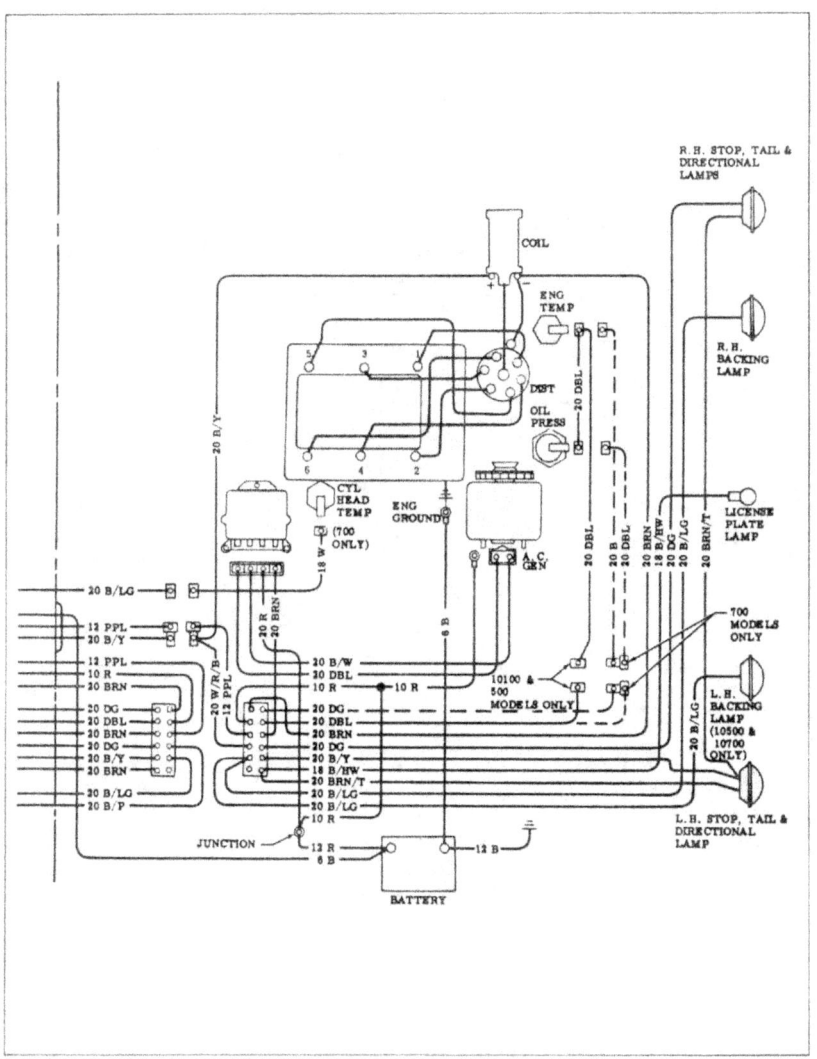

Fuse Panel and Instrument Panel

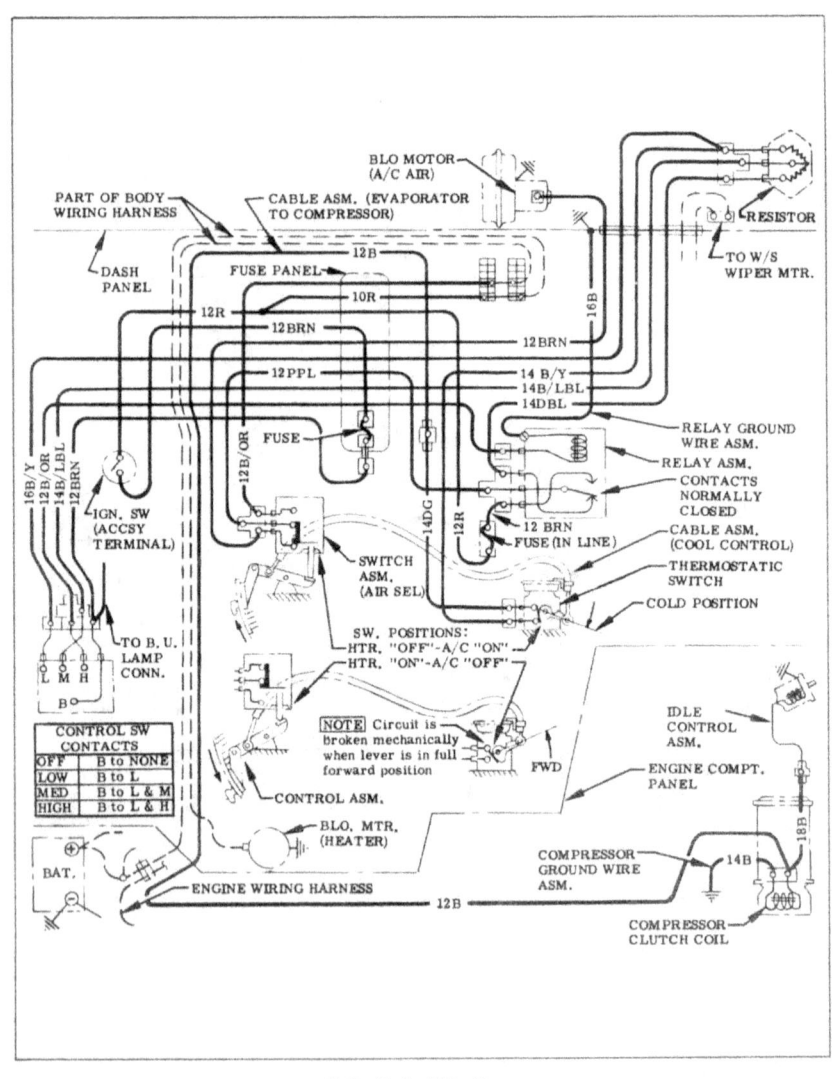

Air Conditioning Wiring Diagram

SPECIFICATIONS

FRONT SUSPENSION

Caster .... Positive 2° ± 1/2°*
Camber .... Positive 1° ± 1/2°*
Steering Axis Inclination .... 6 1/2° ± 1/2°
Toe-in (Total)
  Front .... 1/4" to 3/8"
Wheel Nut Torque .... 55 to 65 lbs. ft.
Wheel Bearing Endplay .... .001" to .008"

*Within 1/2° of opposite side.

Riding Height:

MODEL	DIMENSION "A" (See page 3-9)
All Models	26.2" ± 1/2"**

**Measurements between sides should be within 1/2" of each other.

REAR AXLE AND SUSPENSION

REAR AXLE

Type .... Differential integral with engine and transmission, driving rear wheels independently through universal joints.
Lubricant Capacity (Pints) 4 1/2
Type Recommended . SAE 80, Multi-Purpose, meeting requirements of U.S. Ordnance Spec. MIL-L-2105B
Ratio (to 1) 3.27, 3.55
Gear Backlash .... .003-.010" (.005-.008" desired)

Pinion Bearing Preload (in. lbs.) New 5-10
Pinion Adjustment .... Shim
Differential Bearing Adjustment .... Sleeves
Bolt Torques
  Ring Gear .... 40-60 ft. lbs.
  Drive Spindle Flange .... 100-150 ft. lbs.
  Drive Spindle Yoke Nut .... 100 ft. lbs.
  Pinion Adjusting Sleeve Lock ..... 20-25 ft. lbs.
  Differential Cover .... 130-230 in. lbs.
  Differential Carrier to Transmission . 35-50 ft. lbs.

REAR SUSPENSION

Type .... Stamped steel torque control arms with adjustable brackets for toe-in setting. Rubber mounted front and rear lateral strut rods with eccentric cam bolt at rear strut rod outer pivot for camber adjustment.

Shock Absorbers
  Make .... Delco
  Type .... Direct, double-acting; hydraulic

Toe-in (Total) Rear .... 1/8" to 3/8"
Camber (Rear) .... Neg. 1° to 0

Bolt Torques
  Rear Wheel Spindle Support
    to Torque Control Arm .... 25-35 ft. lbs.
  Torque Control Arm Bracket
    to Underbody .... 20-30 ft. lbs.
  Front Strut Rod Outer Nuts ...... 11-15 ft. lbs.
  Front Strut Rod Bracket to
    Transmission Support .... 20-30 ft. lbs.
  Torque Arm Bushing Pivot Nut ... 90-130 ft. lbs.
  Rear Strut Rod Pivot Nut .... 75-90 ft. lbs.
  Rear Strut Rod Bracket to
    Differential Carrier .... 20-30 ft. lbs.
  Rear Shock Absorber Lower
    Attaching Nut .... 35-55 ft. lbs.
  Rear Shock Absorber Upper Nut ... 75-100 in. lbs.

BRAKES

Main Cylinder Diameter
  Organic .... 1.0"
Wheel Cylinder Diameter
  Front .... .875"
  Rear .... .9375"
Brake Lining (Bonded)
  Width
    Front .... 2.5"
    Rear .... 2.0"

Thickness
  Primary .... .17"
  Secondary .... .20"
  Minimum Serviceable .... .030"
Length (Front and Rear)
  Primary .... 9.01"
  Secondary .... 9.75"

ENGINE

ENGINE MECHANICAL

ENGINE		Base	Hi-Perf.	4 x 1	Turbo-Charged
GENERAL DATA:					
Horsepower @ rpm		95 @ 3600	110 @ 4400	140 @ 5200	180 @ 4000
Torque @ rpm		154 @ 2400	160 @ 2800	160 @ 3600	265 @ 3200
Type		Flat Opposed			
Number of Cylinders		6			
Bore		3-7/16"			
Stroke		2-15/16"			
No. System	Left Bank	2-4-6			
(Rear to Front)	Right Bank	1-3-5			
Firing Order		1-4-5-2-3-6			
Compression Ratio		8.25:1	9:1	9:1	8:1
CYLINDER BORE:					
Out of Round (max.)		.002"			
Taper (max.)		.005"			
Diameter (base)		3.4370"			
PISTONS:					
Clearance Limits	Top Land	.022"-.031"			
to Cylinder	Skirt	.0011"-.0017"			
Ring Groove	Compression	.1785"-.1865"			
Depth	Oil	.1717"-.1750"			
PISTON RINGS:					
	Width	.064"-.065"			
Compression	Clearance in Groove	.0017"-.004"			
	Gap	.013"-.025"			
	Width	.126"±.0005"			
Oil Ring	Clearance in Groove	.0012"-.005"			
	Gap	.015"-.055"			
PISTON PINS:					
Length		2.630"-2.650"			
Diameter		.7999"-.8002"			
	In Piston	New	.00015"-.00025"		
Clearance		Wear Limit	.001"		
	In Rod		Press Fit		

CONT'D.

ENGINE			Base	Hi-Perf.	4 x 1	Turbo-Charged
CONNECTING RODS:						
Bearing	Clearance	New		.0007"-.0027"		
		Max.		.003"		
	End Play	New		.005"-.010"		
CRANKSHAFT:						
End Play				.002"-.006"		
End Thrust Taken By				(#1) Rear Main Bearing		
Main Bearing Journal	Diameter			#1 & 2 (2.0978"-2.0988")		
				#3 & 4 (2.0983"-2.0993")		
	Clearance			#1 & 2 (.0012"-.0027")		
				#3 & 4 (.0007"-.0022")		
	L. Runout (max.)			.001"		
	Taper (max.)			.001"		
Crankpin Journal	Diameter			1.799"-1.800"		
	Taper			.001"		
	Runout			.001"		
CAMSHAFT:						
Lobe Lift Measured at Push Rod	Intake		.257"		.260"	
	Exhaust		.257"		.260"	
Journal Diameter	Front			1.440"		
	All Others			1.200"		
Journal Runout (max.)				.0015"		
VALVE SYSTEMS:						
Lifters Type				Hydraulic		
Rocker Arm Ratio				1.5:1		
Valve Lash Intake & Exhaust				1 Turn down from "NO LASH"		
Intake	Face Angle			45°		
	Seat Runout (max.)			.002"		
	Seat Angle			45°		
	Recommended Seat Width			1/32"-1/16"		
	Stem to Guide Clearance			New .001"-.0027" Used .001"-.004"		
	Lift at Valve Stem		.385"		.390"	
Exhaust	Face Angle			44°		45°
	Seat Runout (max.)			.002"		
	Seat Angle			45°		
	Recommended Seat Width			1/16"-3/32"		
	Stem to Guide Clearance			New .0014"-.0029" Used .002"-.005"		
	Lift at Valve Stem		.385"		.390"	
Valve Springs	Outer Spring Press. and Length	Free Length		2.08"		
		Pressure lb. @ in.		78 to 86 @ 1.660"		
		Pressure lb. @ in.		170 to 180 @ 1.260"		
	Inner Spring Damper	Size		.045" x .250"		
		Type		Flat Wound		
		No. Coils		Approx. 4		
	Installed Height			1-21/32" ± 1/32"		

ENGINE COMPONENT TORQUES

Size	Usage	Torque
1/4-20	Oil Pan	85-105 in. lbs.
	Oil Pump Cover	60-80 in. lbs.
	Oil Cooler to Cylinder Head	40-60 in. lbs.
	Shroud Attachment	60-80 in. lbs.
	Valve Rocker Cover	40-60 in. lbs.
	Oil Suction Screen Pipe Clamp	30-50 in. lbs.
5/16-18	Crankcase L.H. to R.H. (One in Oil Sump)	7-13 ft. lbs.
	Crankcase Cover	7-13 ft. lbs.
	Oil Cooler Adapter to Crankcase	7-13 ft. lbs.
	Oil Filter and Delcotron Adapter	7-13 ft. lbs.
	Rear Housing	7-13 ft. lbs.
	Clutch Cover and Pressure Plate	15-20 ft. lbs.
11/32-24	Flywheel (Syn. Transmission)	40-50 ft. lbs.
	Flex Plate (P/G Transmission)	20-30 ft. lbs.
3/8-16	Oil Cooler to Adapter	8-12 ft. lbs.
	Shroud Attachment	10-20 ft. lbs.
	Skid Plate	15-20 ft. lbs.
	Flywheel or Clutch Housing	20-30 ft. lbs.
	Crankshaft Pulley to Balancer	25-35 ft. lbs.
7/16-20	Crankcase L.H. to R.H.	50-55 ft. lbs.
	Oil Filter	15-20 ft. lbs.
1/2-20	Crankshaft Pulley or Balancer	40-50 ft. lbs.
5/16-24	Connecting Rod	20-26 ft. lbs.
3/8-16	Exhaust Manifold Clamp	22-27 ft. lbs.
	Rear Mounting Bracket	40-50 ft. lbs.
3/8-16	Stud - Cylinder Head to Crankcase	10-30 ft. lbs.
	Switch - Cylinder Head Temperature	10-15 ft. lbs.
3/8-24	Cylinder Head Nut	32-38 ft. lbs.
	Valve Rocker Arm Stud	32-38 ft. lbs.
	Adjusting Nut - Valve Rocker Arm	55-125 in. lbs.
	Distributor Clamp Nut	8-12 ft. lbs.
	Sending Unit - Cylinder Head Temperature	5-10 ft. lbs.
	Switch Cylinder Head Temperature	10-15 ft. lbs.
1/2-20	Oil Pan Drain Plug	30-35 ft. lbs.
1/8-27	Oil Pressure Switch	45-65 in. lbs.
9/16-18	Oil Pressure Regulator Valve Plug	10-20 ft. lbs.
14 mm.	Spark Plug	15-20 ft. lbs.

ENGINE MOUNT TORQUES

Attaching Part	Torque
Front Mount Nuts	60-80 ft. lb.
Bracket-to-Transmission	20-30 ft. lb.
Front Mount-to-Crossmember	20-30 ft. lb.
Rear Mount Nuts	50-60 ft. lb.
Rear Mount-to-Frame	14-22 ft. lb.

CARBURETORS

APPLICATION	CARBURETOR
95 H.P. Engine Syn. or P/G	7025023*
110 H.P. Engine Syn.	7025023*
110 H.P. Engine P/G	7025024*
140 H.P. Engine Primary	7025023
140 H.P. Engine Secondary	7025226
All With Air Conditioning	7025025
180 H.P. Engine Turbocharged	3856713

*Not Used with Air Conditioning

Carburetor	Rochester HV			Rochester H	Carter YH
	7025023	7025024	7025025	7025026	3856713
Float Level	1-1/16"				5/8"
Float Drop	1-1/2"				2-3/8"
Pump Rod	Index Line				
Choke	2 Turns Up from Free Entry to Lever				Index
Unloader	.312"				7/16"
Fast Idle	.078"				
Vacuum Break	.180"-.195"				
Main Jet	.051"	.050"	.051"	.050"	.098"
Idle Tube	.024"				.031"
Bowl Vents	2 Internal	1 External Idle		2 Internal	1 Internal
Metering Rods					.057" / .048"
Pump Discharge Jets	Two @ .022"				One @ .028"
Throttle Bore	1-1/4"				1-1/2"
Main Venturi	1"				1-3/8"

ENGINE ELECTRICAL

BATTERY		1980007
Ground		Neg
Plates		54
Ampere Hour		44
GENERATOR	1100639	1100698
Application	Base	Optional
Cold Output amps	35	45
Cold Output Volts	14	14
Field Current Draw @ 12 V. 80°F	2.2-2.6	2.8-3.2
VOLTAGE REGULATOR		1119515
Application		All*
Voltage Regulator		
Air Gap		.067
Setting @ 85°F		13.8-14.8
Point Opening		.014
Field Relay		
Air Gap		.015
Point Opening		.030
Closing Voltage		1.5-3.2
STARTING MOTOR	1108306	1108307
Application	Std. Trans.	Auto. Trans.
Brush Spring Tension (oz.)	35	35
Free Speed		
Volts	10.6	10.6
Amperes	58	58
rpm	6750-10,500	6750-10,500
Resistance Test		
(Armature Locked)		
Volts	4.0	4.0
Amperes	280	280
Torque-Mounting Pad Bolts (ft.-lbs.)	20-30	20-30
Solenoid		
Hold-in Windings	10.5-12.5 Amperes @ 10V	
Both Windings	42-49 Amperes @ 10V	
IGNITION COIL		
Application		All
Primary Resistance, ohms		1.28-1.42
Secondary Resistance, ohms		7200-9500
IGNITION RESISTOR		
Type		Special Wire—Part of Harness
Resistance		1.8 ohms
SPARK PLUGS	AC-44FF	AC-46FF
Application	110, 140 and 180 hp	95 hp
Size	14 mm.	14 mm.
Plug Gap	.030"	.035"
Torque	15-20 lb. ft.	

*External Field Discharge Diode Circuit with Generator 1100698.

DISTRIBUTOR	1110310	1110311	1110319	1110329	1110330
Application	95 HP Std. Trans.	95 HP Powerglide	110 HP (All)	180 HP Turbo-Charged	140 HP 4 x 1 BBL
Rotation-View from Drive End	CCW	CCW	CCW	CCW	CCW
Breaker Point Gap	.019" New—.016" Used				
Breaker Arm Tension	19-23 oz. (Measured just behind points)				
Condenser Capacity	.18-23 Micro Farads				
Firing Order	1-4-5-2-3-6				
Ignition Timing @ Idle	6° BTDC	14° BTDC	14° BTDC	24° BTDC	18° BTC
Cam Angle (Dwell)	31°-34°				
Centrifugal Advance Start	0° @ 700 rpm	0 @ 1700 rpm	0° @ 800 rpm	0° @ 4000 rpm	0° @ 800 rpm
Intermediate	4° @ 1200 rpm				
Maximum	28° @ 4200 rpm	24° @ 4200 rpm	20° @ 4800 rpm	18° @ 4900 rpm	18° @ 2800 rpm
Vacuum Advance Start	0° @ 6" Hg	0° @ 7" Hg	0° @ 7" Hg	0° @ 2 psi*	0° @ 6" Hg
Full Advance (+ Engine)	24° @ 14" Hg	24° @ 15" Hg	24° @ 15" Hg	12° @ 4.5 psi*	22° @ 14" Hg

*Retard

CLUTCH

ENGINE	Name		Turbo-Air 164		Turbocharged 164
	Horsepower		95	110	150
	Displacement, cu. inches		164		
TRANSMISSION			3-Speed 4-Speed		
CLUTCH ASSEMBLY					
Type			Single Dry Disc, Centrifugal		
Clutch Cover and Pressure Plate Assembly	Effective Plate Load, lb.		1250-1450		1275-1475
	Type of Drive		Steel Straps		
	Pressure Plate	Material	Cast Iron		Nodular or Perlitic Malleable Iron
		OD	9.28		
	Clutch Spring	Type	Diaphragm, Bent Finger Design		
		Material	HR Spring Steel		
	Ring Gear	Material	HR Steel		
		No. of Teeth	147		
		Face Width	.363-.387		
		PD	12.25		
		Attachment	Welded to Clutch Cover		
	Attachment to Flywheel		6 Bolts, 5/16-18, .82 Long; Bolt Circle Dia. 10.625		
Drive Plate Assembly	Type		Single Disc with Two Friction Surfaces		
	Cushions		Flat Spring Steel between Rings		
	Friction Ring	Material	Woven Asbestos		
		OD	8.00		9.12
		ID	6.00		6.12
		Total Area (sq. inches)	44.00		71.8
		Width (ea.)	.135		
Flywheel	Material		Cast Iron		
	OD		11.6		
Bearings	Release	Type	Single Row Ball		
		Lubrication	Packed with Temperature High Viscosity Grease		
	Pilot	Type	Sintered Powdered Bronze Bushing		
		Lubrication	Oil Impregnated		
Controls	Clutch Fork		Drop Forged Steel, Pivot Mounted on Ball		
	Pedal Mounting		Pendent, from Brace on Dash		
Clutch Housing	Material		Aluminum Alloy		
	Attachment to Engine		9 Bolts, 3/8-16 UNC 2A: 7 Short, 1-3/8 Shank; 2 Long, 1-5/8 Shank		

TRANSMISSIONS

MANUAL TRANSMISSIONS

GENERAL DATA
Make . . . . . . Chevrolet synchromesh, manual shift
Type 3-Speed, 4-Speed
Location . . . . In rear compartment-integral with engine and differential.
Transmission Case Material. . . . Cast aluminum alloy

GEAR SHIFT
Control . . . . Remote
Type. . . . . Lever
Location . . . . Floor mounted

GEARS
Type . . . . Helical
Material . . . . Forged steel, hardened

	3-SPEED	4-SPEED
Synchronization	2nd and 3rd	1st, 2nd, 3rd, 4th
Constant Mesh Gears	2nd and 3rd	1st, 2nd, 3rd, 4th
Sliding Gears	1st and reverse	Reverse

10,100, 10,500, 10,700 SERIES

RATIOS	3-Speed	4-Speed
First	3.22:1	3.20:1
Second	1.84:1	2.19:1
Third	1.00:1	1.44:1
Fourth		1.00:1
Reverse	3.22:1	3.66:1

LUBRICANT
Type Recommended . . . . Multipurpose Gear Lubricant SAE 80.
Capacity (pt.) 2.2   3.6

AUTOMATIC TRANSMISSIONS

GENERAL DATA
Make and Type . . . . Chevrolet, hydraulic torque converter with automatic planetary gear system for reverse and low.
Transmission Case Material. . . . Cast aluminum alloy
Converter Maximum Torque Ratio (at stall) 2.6:1
Total Transmission Torque Multiplication (converter planetary gear ratio)
   Maximum overall transmission ratio 4.73:1
   Low gear drive or low range . . . 4.73:1 to 1.82:1
   Reverse range . . . . 4.73:1 to 1.82:1
Oil Type . . . . "A", suffix "A"
Oil Capacity (pt.)
   Dry . . . . Approx. 13
   Refill . . . . Approx. 6
Oil Cooled By . . . . Air
Selector Lever
   Location . . . . At right of steering column on instrument panel.
   Operation . . . . Actuates manual valve in hydraulic control system.
   Positions (indicated on quadrant on instrument panel). Four (bottom to top)—L-Low, D-Drive, N-Neutral, R-Reverse.

HYDRAULIC TORQUE CONVERTER
Type . . . . Three element
Driving Member (pump) . . . . Sheet metal, multi-vane type, spot welded to torque converter housing. Housing cover is bolted to flywheel.
Driven Member (turbine) . . . . Sheet metal, multi-vane type, supported by torque converter housing cover. Turns independently of housing. Splined to input shaft.

Reaction Member (stator) . . . . . . Aluminum air foil type supported on stationary sleeve by an over-running clutch of cam and roller design.

CLUTCHES
Type . . . . Multiple disc
High
   Discs, Driving
      Number and type . . . . . . Two, non-metallic faced
   Discs, Driven
      Number and type . . . . Three, steel
Reverse
   Discs, Driving
      Number and type . . . Three, non-metallic faced
   Discs, Driven
      Number and type . . . . Three, steel plates and one cast iron pressure plate.

PLANETARY GEAR UNIT
Type . . . . Compound planetary
Gear Ratios
   Cruising range . . . . 1:1 (direct drive)
   Low range 1.82:1
   Reverse 1.82:1
   Low brake band . . . . Double-wrap design
   Low band servo
      Type . . . . Piston, one release spring

HYDRAULIC CONTROLS
Manual Valve
   Type . . . . Spool
Pressure Regulator Valve
   Type . . . . Spool
Governor
   Type . . . . Centrifugal
   Drive . . . . From transmission output shaft

STEERING

STEERING GEAR

Type . . . . Recirculating Ball
Steering Ratio
  Gear 18:1
  Overall 23.5:1

LINKAGE

Type . . . . Parallel Relay
Location. . . . . Front of Wheels
Tie Rods 2

TORQUE CHART

Worm Bearing Preload . . . . 3-1/2 to 4-1/2 in. lbs.
Sector Lash Adjustment . . . . 8 to 10 in. lbs.
                                  in excess of above
Max. Steering Gear Preload . . . . 14 in. lbs.
Steering Gear Mounting Bolts . . . . . 25-35 ft. lbs.
Pitman Shaft Nut . . . . 80-105 ft. lbs.
Steering Wheel Nut . . . . 25-35 ft. lbs.
Tie Rod End Nut . . . . 29-43 ft. lbs.
Tie Rod Clamp Bolts . . . . 12-16 ft. lbs.
Idler Arm Mounting Bolts . . . . 14-20 ft. lbs.

CHASSIS ELECTRICAL

Bulb Application	Candle Power	Number
Headlamp Unit—Outer: High Beam	37-1/2 Watt	4002
Low Beam	55 Watt	Sealed Beam
Inner: High Beam	37-1/2 Watt	4001
Parking Lamp, Tail, Stop and Directional Lamps	4-32	1157
Back-up Lamps	32	1156
Instrument Lamps	3	1816
Directional Signal Indicator, Headlamp High Beam Indicator and Heater Control Panel Lamps	1	1445
Temperature-Pressure (Oil) Indicator, Generator-Fan Indicator, Glove Compartment Lamps	2	1895
Dome Lamp (Cartridge Type)	12	211
Courtesy Lamp	6	631
License Plate Lamp	4	67
Radio Dial Lamp	2	1893

FUSES AND CIRCUIT BREAKER

A 15 ampere circuit breaker in the light control switch protects the headlamp circuit, thus eliminating one fuse.

Fuses located in the junction block beneath the dash are:

- Heater Blower
  Glove Compartment Lamp—3AG/AGC-10 amp
- Tail and Stop Lamps, Dome Lamp
  Cigarette Lighter—3AG/AGC-10 amp
- Heater (Total)
  Back-Up Lamp—3AG/AGC-20 amp
- Radio—3AG/AGC-2.5 amp
- Instrument Panel Lamp
  Radio Panel Lamp
  Heater Control Panel Lamp—3AG/AGC-3 amp
- Windshield Wiper—3AG/AGC-20 amp

Air Conditioner Fuses . . . . 3AG/AGC-15 amp.
(Located in 14 GA and 12 GA gray wires in area of ignition switch.)

WIPER MOTOR

Single Speed

Type . . . . Electric
Crank Arm Rotation
  (looking at the crank arm) . . . . CCW
Crank Arm Speed (No Load) . . . . 43 rpm
Operating Voltage . . . . 12 VDC
Current Draw (Free Speed) . . . . . . 3.0 amp Max.
             (Dry Windshield) . . . . 3.5 amp Max.
Stall Current . . . . 11 amp

Two Speed

Operating Volts	12 VDC
Gear Ratio	36:1
Crank Arm Rotation (looking at Crank Arm)	CCW
Crank Arm Speed (rpm's) (No Load):	
Lo	34 Min.
Hi	65 Min.
Current Draw: amps	
No Load (Lo Speed)	3.6
Installed in Car—(Dry Glass)	4.5
Stall	12
Shunt Field Resistance	24

WASHER PUMP

Number of "squirts" at full pressure	12
Pressure (psi)	11-15
Coil Resistance (ohms)	20

WIRING CIRCUIT COLOR CODE

DIAGRAM KEY	WIRE COLOR
B	Black
B/LG	Black with Light Green Stripe
B/LBL	Black with Light Blue Stripe
B/P	Black with Pink Stripe
B/OR	Black with Orange Stripe
B/W	Black with White Stripe
B/Y	Black with Yellow Stripe
BRN	Brown
DBL	Dark Blue
DG	Dark Green
PPL	Purple
R	Red
T	Tan
GY	Gray
W/OR/P	White with Orange and Pink Stripes

ACCESSORIES

AIR CONDITIONING

Compressor

Make	Frigidaire
Type	6 Cylinder AXIAL
Displacement	10.8 Cu. In.
Rotation	Counter-Clockwise

Blower Motor

Volts	14
Amps (Cold)	9.4 (Max.)
RPM (Cold)	3100

Compressor Clutch Coil

Ohms (at 80°F)	3.85
Amps (at 80°F)	3.2 @ 12 Volts

System Capacities

Refrigerant	R-12
Compressor Oil	Frigidaire 525 Viscosity
R-12	5 lbs.
Compressor Oil	10 oz.
Fuse	2 fuses: 1 in-line and 1 in fuse block (both 15 amp).

AUTOBOOKS WORKSHOP MANUALS

ALFA ROMEO GIULIA 1300, 1600, 1750, 2000 1962-1978 WSM
BMW 1600 1966-1973 WSM
BMW 2000 & 2002 1966-1976 WSM
BMW 2500, 2800, 3.0 & 3.3 1968-1977 WSM
BMW 316, 320, 320i 1975-1977 WSM
BMW 518, 520, 520i 1973-1981 WSM
FIAT 1100, 1100D, 1100R & 1200 1957-1969 WSM
FIAT 124 1966-1974 WSM
FIAT 124 SPORT 1966-1975 WSM
FIAT 125 & 125 SPECIAL 1967-1973 WSM
FIAT 126, 126L, 126 DV, 126/650 & 126/650 DV 1972-1982 WSM
FIAT 127 SALOON, SPECIAL & SPORT, 900, 1050 1971-1981 WSM
FIAT 128 1969-1982 WSM
FIAT 1300, 1500 1961-1967 WSM
FIAT 131 MIRAFIORI 1975-1982 WSM
FIAT 132 1972-1982 WSM
FIAT 500 1957-1973 WSM
FIAT 600, 600D & MULTIPLA 1955-1969 WSM
FIAT 850 1964-1972 WSM
JAGUAR E-TYPE 1961-1972 WSM
JAGUAR MK 1, 2 1955-1969 WSM
JAGUAR S TYPE, 420 1963-1968 WSM
JAGUAR XK 120, 140, 150 MK 7, 8, 9 1948-1961 WSM
LAND ROVER 1, 2 1948-1961 WSM
MERCEDES-BENZ 190 1959-1968 WSM
MERCEDES-BENZ 220/8 1968-1972 WSM
MERCEDES-BENZ 220B 1959-1965 WSM
MERCEDES-BENZ 230 1963-1968 WSM
MERCEDES-BENZ 250 1968-1972 WSM
MERCEDES-BENZ 280 1968-1972 WSM
MG MIDGET TA-TF 1936-1955 WSM
MINI 1959-1980 WSM
MORRIS MINOR 1952-1971 WSM
PEUGEOT 404 1960-1975 WSM
PORSCHE 911 1964-1973 WSM
PORSCHE 911 1970-1977 WSM
RENAULT 16 1965-1979 WSM
RENAULT 8, 10, 1100 1962-1971 WSM
ROVER 3500, 3500S 1968-1976 WSM
SUNBEAM RAPIER, ALPINE 1955-1965 WSM
TRIUMPH SPITFIRE, GT6, VITESSE 1962-1968 WSM
TRIUMPH TR2, TR3, TR3A 1952-1962 WSM
TRIUMPH TR4, TR4A 1961-1967 WSM
VOLKSWAGEN BEETLE 1968-1977 WSM

VELOCEPRESS AUTOMOBILE BOOKS & MANUALS

ABARTH BUYERS GUIDE
AUSTIN-HEALEY 6-CYLINDER WSM
AUSTIN-HEALEY SPRITE & MG MIDGET 1958-1971 WSM
BMW 600 LIMOUSINE FACTORY WSM
BMW 600 LIMOUSINE OWNERS HAND BOOK & SERVICE MANUAL
BMW ISETTA FACTORY WSM
BOOK OF THE CARRERA PANAMERICANA - MEXICAN ROAD RACE
COMPLETE CATALOG OF JAPANESE MOTOR VEHICLES
CORVAIR 1960-1969 OWNERS WORKSHOP MANUAL
CORVETTE V8 1955-1962 OWNERS WORKSHOP MANUAL
DIALED IN - THE JAN OPPERMAN STORY
FERRARI 250/GT SERVICE AND MAINTENANCE
FERRARI 308 SERIES BUYER'S AND OWNER'S GUIDE
FERRARI BERLINETTA LUSSO
FERRARI BROCHURES AND SALES LITERATURE 1946-1967
FERRARI BROCHURES AND SALES LITERATURE 1968-1989
FERRARI GUIDE TO PERFORMANCE
FERRARI OPP, MAINTENANCE & SERVICE H/BOOKS 1948-1963
FERRARI OWNER'S HANDBOOK
FERRARI SERIAL NUMBERS PART I - ODD NUMBERS TO 21399
FERRARI SERIAL NUMBERS PART II - EVEN NUMBERS TO 1050
FERRARI SPYDER CALIFORNIA
FERRARI TUNING TIPS & MAINTENANCE TECHNIQUES
HENRY'S FABULOUS MODEL "A" FORD
HOW TO BUILD A FIBERGLASS CAR
HOW TO BUILD A RACING CAR
HOW TO RESTORE THE MODEL 'A' FORD
IF HEMINGWAY HAD WRITTEN A RACING NOVEL
JAGUAR E-TYPE 3.8 & 4.2 WSM
LE MANS 24 (THE BOOK THAT THE FILM WAS BASED ON)
MASERATI BROCHURES AND SALES LITERATURE
MASERATI OWNER'S HANDBOOK
METROPOLITAN FACTORY WSM
MGA & MGB OWNERS HANDBOOK & WSM
OBERT'S FIAT GUIDE
PERFORMANCE TUNING THE SUNBEAM TIGER
PORSCHE 356 1948-1965 WSM
PORSCHE 912 WSM
SOUPING THE VOLKSWAGEN
TRIUMPH TR2, TR3, TR4 1953-1965 WSM
TUNING FOR SPEED (P.E. IRVING)
VEDA ORR'S NEW REVISED HOT ROD PICTORIAL
VOLKSWAGEN TRANSPORTER, TRUCKS, STATION WAGONS WSM
VOLVO 1944-1968 ALL MODELS WSM
WEBER CARBURETORS (EMPHASIS ON ALFA & FIAT)

BROOKLANDS BOOKS & ROAD TEST PORTFOLIOS (RTP)

AC CARS 1904-2009
ALFA ROMEO 1920-1933 ROAD TEST PORTFOLIO
ALFA ROMEO 1934-1940 ROAD TEST PORTFOLIO
BRABHAM RALT HONDA THE RON TAURANAC STORY
BUGATTI TYPE 10 TO TYPE 40 ROAD TEST PORTFOLIO
BUGATTI TYPE 10 TO TYPE 251 ROAD TEST PORTFOLIO
BUGATTI TYPE 41 TO TYPE 55 ROAD TEST PORTFOLIO
BUGATTI TYPE 57 TO TYPE 251 ROAD TEST PORTFOLIO
DELAHAYE ROAD TEST PORTFOLIO
FERRARI RACE CARS 1946-1956 ROAD TEST PORTFOLIO
FIAT 500 1936-1972 ROAD TEST PORTFOLIO
FIAT DINO ROAD TEST PORTFOLIO
HISPANO SUIZA ROAD TEST PORTFOLIO
HONDA ST1100/ST1300 PAN EUROPEAN 1990-2002 RTP
JAGUAR MK1 & MK2 ROAD TEST PORTFOLIO
LOTUS CORTINA ROAD TEST PORTFOLIO
MV AGUSTA F4 750 & 1000 1997-2007 ROAD TEST PORTFOLIO
TATRA CARS ROAD TEST PORTFOLIO

VELOCEPRESS MOTORCYCLE BOOKS & MANUALS

AJS SINGLES & TWINS 250cc THRU 1000cc 1932-1948 (BOOK OF)
AJS SINGLES 1955-65 350cc & 500cc (BOOK OF)
AJS SINGLES 1945-60 350cc & 500cc MODELS 16 & 18 (BOOK OF)
ARIEL 1939-1960 4 STROKE SINGLES (BOOK OF)
ARIEL LEADER & ARROW 1958-1964 (BOOK OF)
ARIEL MOTORCYCLES 1933-1951 WSM
ARIEL PREWAR MODELS 1932-1939 (BOOK OF)
BMW M/CYCLES R26 R27 (1956-1967) FACTORY WSM
BMW M/CYCLES R50 R50S R60 R69S (1955-1969) FACTORY WSM
BSA BANTAM (BOOK OF)
BSA ALL FOUR-STROKE SINGLES & V-TWINS 1936-1952 (BOOK OF)
BSA OHV & SV SINGLES - 250cc 1954-1970 (BOOK OF)
BSA OHV & SV SINGLES 1945-54 250-600cc (BOOK OF)
BSA OHV SINGLES 350 & 500cc 1955-1967 (BOOK OF)
BSA PRE-WAR MODELS TO 1939 (BOOK OF)
BSA TWINS 1948-1962 (BOOK OF)
BSA TWINS 1962-1969 (SECOND BOOK OF)
CATALOG OF BRITISH MOTORCYCLES (1951 MODELS)
DOUGLAS PRE-WAR ALL MODELS 1929-1939 (BOOK OF)
DOUGLAS POST-WAR ALL MODELS 1948-1957 FACTORY WSM
DUCATI 160cc, 250cc & 350cc OHC MODELS FACTORY WSM
HONDA 50 ALL MODELS UP TO 1970 INC MONKEY & TRAIL (BOOK OF)
HONDA 90 ALL MODELS UP TO 1966 (BOOK OF)
HONDA MOTORCYCLES 125-150 TWINS C/CS/CB/CA WSM
HONDA MOTORCYCLES 250-305 TWINS C/CS/CB WSM
HONDA MOTORCYCLES C100 SUPER CUB WSM
HONDA MOTORCYCLES C110 SPORT CUB 1962-1969 WSM
HONDA TWINS & SINGLES 50cc THRU 305cc 1960-1966 (BOOK OF)
HONDA TWINS ALL MODELS 125cc THRU 450cc UP TO 1968 (BOOK OF)
INDIAN PONYBIKE, BOY RACER & PAPOOSE ILL PARTS LIST & SALES LIT
LAMBRETTA ALL 125 & 150cc MODELS 1947-1957 (BOOK OF)
LAMBRETTA LI & TV MODELS 1957-1970 (SECOND BOOK OF)
MATCHLESS 350 & 500cc SINGLES 1945-1956 (BOOK OF)
MATCHLESS 350 & 500cc SINGLES 1955-1966 (BOOK OF)
NORTON 1932-1947 (BOOK OF)
NORTON 1938-1956 (BOOK OF)
NORTON DOMINATOR TWINS 1955-1965 (BOOK OF)
NORTON MODELS 19, 50 & ES2 1955-1963 (BOOK OF)
NORTON MOTORCYCLES 1957-1970 FACTORY WSM
NORTON PREWAR MODELS 1932-1939 (BOOK OF)
NSU QUICKLY ALL MODELS 1953-1963 (BOOK OF)
ROYAL ENFIELD SINGLES & V TWINS 1937-1953 (BOOK OF)
ROYAL ENFIELD SINGLES 1946-1962 (BOOK OF)
ROYAL ENFIELD 736cc INTERCEPTOR FACTORY WSM
ROYAL ENFIELD 250cc & 350cc SINGLES 1958-1966 (SECOND BOOK OF)
SUZUKI 50cc & 80cc UP TO 1966 (BOOK OF)
SUZUKI T10 1963-1967 FACTORY WSM
SUZUKI T20 & T200 1965-1969 FACTORY WSM
TRIUMPH PRE-WAR MOTORCYCLE 1935-1939 (BOOK OF)
TRIUMPH MOTORCYCLES 1937-1951 WSM
TRIUMPH MOTORCYCLES 1945-1955 FACTORY WSM
TRIUMPH TWINS 1956-1969 (BOOK OF)
VELOCETTE ALL SINGLES & TWINS 1925-1970 (BOOK OF)
VESPA 1951-1961 (BOOK OF)
VESPA 125 & 150cc 1955-1963 (SECOND BOOK OF)
VESPA 90, 125 & 150cc 1963-1972 (THIRD BOOK OF)
VESPA GS & SS 1955-1968 (BOOK OF)
VINCENT MOTORCYCLES 1935-1955 WSM

PLEASE VISIT OUR WEBSITE
www.VelocePress.com
FOR A DETAILED DESCRIPTION
OF ANY OF THESE TITLES